ORIGINAL
BLESSING

Also by Matthew Fox

BREATHTHROUGH
Meister Eckhart's Creation Spirituality in New Translation

THE COMING OF THE COSMIC CHRIST

CREATION SPIRITUALITY
Liberating Gifts for the Peoples of the Earth

HILDEGARD OF BINGEN'S BOOK OF DIVINE WORKS
with Letters and Songs (editor)

ILLUMINATIONS OF HILDEGARD

MANIFESTO FOR A GLOBAL CIVILIZATION
(with Brian Swimme)

MEDITATIONS WITH MEISTER ECKHART

ON BECOMING A MUSICAL, MYSTICAL BEAR
Spirituality American Style

THE REINVENTION OF WORK

SHEER JOY
Conversations with Thomas Aquinas on Creation Spirituality

A SPIRITUALITY NAMED COMPASSION
and the Healing of the Global Village, Humpty Dumpty and Us

WESTERN SPIRITUALITY
Historical Roots, Ecumenical Routes (editor)

WHEE! WE, WEE ALL THE WAY HOME
A Guide to Sensual, Prophetic Spirituality

ORIGINAL BLESSING

MATTHEW FOX

A Primer in Creation Spirituality
Presented in Four Paths,
Twenty-Six Themes,
and Two Questions

BEAR & COMPANY
PUBLISHING
SANTA FE, NEW MEXICO

Bear & Company, Inc.
PO Box 2860
Santa Fe, NM 87504-2860

Cover Design: Melinda Belter

Cover Illustration: "The Human as Microcosm of the Macrocosm"
from Hildegard of Bingen (1098-1179), courtesy of Otto Muller Verlag,
Salzburg, through arrangement with Friends of Creation Spirituality,
Box 19216, Oakland, CA 94619; all rights reserved, Otto Muller Verlag.

Editor, Interior Design: Gerald Clow

Index: Richard Weber, OCSO

Printed in the United States of America by BookCrafters

30 29 28 27 26 25

TABLE OF CONTENTS

PATH IV BEFRIENDING NEW CREATION: COMPASSION, CELEBRATION, EROTIC JUSTICE, THE VIA TRANSFORMATIVA

INTRODUCTION: TWO QUESTION APROPOS OF WISDOM AND HUMAN/ EARTH SURVIVAL

In the introduction to this book—which I hope is more a journey for the readers than a book—I wish to pose two questions:

1. In our quest for wisdom and survival, does the human race require a new religious paradigm?

2. Does the creation-centered spiritual tradition offer such a paradigm?

As the reader may guess, my answer to both these questions is: *yes*. When I use the word "wisdom," I think of the definition that the Native American tradition gives us: that the people may live. I am very at home with this understanding of wisdom. I believe it encompasses the breadth and depth of cosmic and human living and I believe it names what God the Creator wants for all of her children: that the people of this precious earth, all global peoples, may live. Bangladesh people, old people, hungry children people, robust adolescent people, people in socialist countries, people in capitalist countries—that the people may live. But wisdom wants the people *to live*. What does that mean? Obviously, that they not die before their time. But what else does it mean? To live is not merely to survive. Living implies beauty, freedom of choice, giving birth, discipline, celebration. Living is not the same as going shopping or buying, nor is it the same as making a nest in which to escape the sufferings of one another. Living has something to do with Eros, love of life, and with the love of others' lives, others' right to Eros and dignity. Here lies wisdom: that the people may live. But where do we find it?

The late E. F. Schumacher believed that there are two places to find wisdom: in nature and in religious traditions. To seek wisdom in nature we should obviously go to those who have loved nature enough to study it. Because science explores nature it can be a powerful source of wisdom. It often has been. For in just about

9

every culture imaginable, religion and science were teammates who offered to the people a cosmic myth that allowed them to understand their universe, to find meaning in it, and to live out their lives with meaning. In the West, however, religion and science have been at odds ever since the seventeenth century. This split has been disastrous for the people: religion has become privatized and science a violent employee of technology, with the result that the people have become alternately bored, violent, lonely, sad, and pessimistic. Above all, the people have become victims—victims of world wars, massive military taxes, needless unemployment, dire conflict between haves and have-nots.

The seventeenth century, that era of such great scientific genius and discovery, actually began with the burning of Giordano Bruno at the stake in 1600 by Church authorities. Bruno, in spite of whatever errors he may have made in his lifetime, was a religious person (he had been a Dominican friar) who sought to discover the cosmos anew according to the scientific work of his contemporaries. His murder by religious and political authorities did not go unnoticed by scientists, who at that time held little power in the political establishment.

In our century the tide has turned so that scientists, now sharing power with the military, corporate, and political chiefs of our nation-states, are not without sin: they are implicated in the innocent lives sacrificed in a Hiroshima or Nagasaki, or at Love Canal or in the rain forests of Brazil or the ovens of Auschwitz. Clearly, there has been enough sin on both the religious and the scientific fronts in Western cultural history. We seek now a truce—and more than a truce, a common exploration for wisdom among scientists and spiritual seekers alike: the wisdom that nature can teach us and the wisdom that religious traditions can teach us. It is evident that the Einsteinian and post-Einsteinian models of the universe are opening up such avenues of wisdom from nature to the scientist, and to the rest of the culture via the scientists.

But how about religion? Is it in touch with its sources of wisdom? Is it willing to let go of outdated, dualistic paradigms with the courage with which science lets go? Alfred North Whitehead writes, "Religion is tending to degenerate into a decent formula wherewith to embellish a comfortable life. . . . Religion will not regain its old power until it can face change in the same spirit as does science."[1] To recover the wisdom that is lurking in religious traditions we have to let go of more recent religious traditions—"Only those who dare to let go can dare to reenter," advises Meister Eckhart. Specifically, what religion must let go of in the West is an exclusively fall/redemption model of spirituality—a model that has dominated theology, Bible studies, seminary and novitiate training, hagiography, psychology for centuries. It is a dualistic model and a patriarchal one; it begins its theology with sin and original sin, and it generally ends with redemption. Fall/redemption spirituality does not teach believers about the New Creation or creativity, about justice-making and social transformation, or about Eros, play, pleasure, and the God of delight. It fails to teach love of the earth or care for the cosmos, and it is so frightened of passion that it fails to listen to the impassioned pleas of the *anawim*, the little ones, of human history. This same fear of passion prevents it from helping lovers to celebrate their experiences as spiritual and mystical. This tradition has not proven friendly to artists or prophets or Native American peoples or women.

The fall/redemption spiritual tradition is not nearly as ancient as is the creation-centered one. The former goes back principally to St. Augustine (354-430 A.D.); to Thomas à Kempis, who said, "Every time I go into creation, I withdraw from God"; to Cardinal Bossuet; Cotton Mather; and Father Tanquerry. The creation-centered tradition traces its roots to the ninth century B.C., with the very first author of the Bible, the Yahwist or J source, to the psalms, to wisdom books of the Bible, to much of the prophets, to Jesus and much of the New Testament, and to the very first Christian theologian in the West, St. Irenaeus (c. 130-200 A.D.). Other members of this tradition are included in this book and can be seen readily in Appendix A, "Toward a Family Tree of Creation-Centered Spirituality." To see the differences between the two traditions briefly, consult Appendix B, "Fall/Redemption and Creation-Centered Spirituality Compared at a Glance."

To consider this ancient tradition as a paradigm for religion would prove a whole new starting point not only for religion in the West and in the world but for the relationship of religion and science. Because the fall/redemption tradition considers all nature "fallen" and does not seek God in nature but inside the individual soul, it is not only silent toward science but hostile to it. Professor Michael Polanyi has written that Augustine "destroyed interest in science all over Europe for a thousand years" because for him science "contributed nothing to the pursuit of salvation."[2] To recover a spiritual tradition in which creation and the study of creation matters would be to inaugurate new possibilities between spirituality and science that would shape the paradigms for culture, its institutions, and its people. These paradigms would be powerful in their capacity to transform. For if wisdom comes from nature and religious traditions, as Schumacher teaches, then what might happen if science and religious traditions agreed to birth together instead of ignoring, fighting, or rejecting one another? Is not recovering a creation-centered spirituality recovering two sources of wisdom at once, that of nature via science and that of nature via religious traditions? The creation-centered tradition seems to combine the best of both worlds in our search for wisdom today.

When I use the word "new," as in "new paradigm," I do not mean we are to birth a religious vision off of the tops of our heads, brand new in the 1980's. By "new" I mean that in the past three centuries of Western culture and religion, the creation tradition has been forgotten almost entirely as religion. It has been kept alive by artists, poets, scientists, feminists, and political prophets, but not by theologians. Creation spirituality is a tradition: it has a past; it has historical and biblical roots; it boasts a communion of saints. But it is for the most part new to religious believers of our time. And it is utterly new to our culture, which, if it has been touched by religion at all, has been touched by fall/redemption and not creation-centered spirituality. When I talk of tradition I do not mean that all we have to do is to study the past, much less that all we need do is to imitate it. There is indeed a newness to what our generation will do with this tradition, to what forms and expressions we will create along with current scientists, mystics, artists, peace and justice workers, feminists, and Third World peoples. But in the great task of recreating a culture, which in our times means creating the first global culture, one needs all the help one can get. And it comes as very good news indeed that wisdom comes from this tradition, from the past, and, for Westerners, even from our religious traditions. Following are ten reasons why I believe the creation-centered tradition offers a new and needed paradigm for wisdom and human survival today.

1. **The Crises.** Two crises loom over all the earth today. They affect all persons equally, whether Christian, Buddhist, or agnostic; whether capitalist or communist; whether black, white, yellow, brown, or red; whether old or young, whether rich or poor; First World or Third World. The first of these crises is *the ecological crisis,* of which nuclear war is one example. Geologian Thomas Berry believes that "the bomb has already gone off" even without a nuclear war. He is referring to the chemicals that humans have

already dumped into waters, shot into the air, pumped into the earth. This attitude of arrogance toward the earth cannot continue. Nuclear war would be just the last and most conspicuous sin of ecological devastation. Einstein wrote, "The unleashed power of the atom has changed everything except our way of thinking. Thus we are drifting toward a catastrophe beyond comparison. We shall require a substantially new manner of thinking if mankind is to survive." I believe that the creation-centered spiritual tradition can so energize the wisdom from artists and scientists and world religions that it offers "a substantially new manner of thinking."

The fall/redemption attitudes toward creation are not even neutral; they are, as Thomas Berry points out, antagonistic.

> Human society is not an abstraction. The only real society is the complete society of the natural world. We are awkward at this manner of thinking because our religious as well as our humanist traditions carry a certain antagonism toward the natural world. But now the refusal of human beings to become intimate members of the community of the earth is leading to their own destruction.[3]

The nuclear age means, as Jonathan Schell puts it, that with the splitting of the atom "a basic energy of the cosmos" has been unleashed on the earth for the first time in a major way. I ask, how can humans deal with cosmic energy and their responsibility for it without a cosmic spirituality? Schell comments on what a nuclear holocaust would mean: it would spell "not merely a human but a planetary end—the death of the earth." And he feels sadness at this prospect. "We not only live on the earth but also are of the earth, and the thought of its death, or even of its mutilation, touches a deep chord in our nature." The ecosphere itself may well be damaged beyond repair by a nuclear blast if we cannot discipline the "instruments of cosmic power" that we hold.[4] The human chauvinism that has so narrowed our vision that we can talk of "nuclear survival" and spend a million dollars per minute on weapons of cosmic destruction must cease. It is religion's task to reintroduce a cosmic vision, a less arrogant and less humanly chauvinist way of seeing our world. It is also religion's task to motivate for discipline and sacrifice, for the deep letting go of which humans are capable. Today it is more and more evident that the time has come for humanity to let go of war, to admit that it has outgrown war, and to move beyond war as a way of settling differences. Just as humanity one hundred years ago outlawed slavery, so it is capable today of outlawing war. The creation-centered spiritual vision can contribute greatly to this important vision.

Part of the ecological crisis is the issue of famine versus food. The creation-centered spiritual tradition, by putting us in touch with a love of our bodies and of Mother Earth, raises the prophetic questions of what foods are healthy and whether the processes of attaining them and distributing them are just and harmonious. It urges us to let go of eating habits that are luxurious and of farming practices that are injurious to generations to come. As Hildegarde of Bingen puts it, "The earth which sustains humanity must not be injured! It must not be destroyed!"

The second universal crisis of our time is *unemployment*. In the First World today there are over forty-five million unemployed adults, many of them young adults. And in the Third World there are another four hundred fifty million unemployed persons. Does unemployment not have everything to do with wars and rumors of wars? With dissatisfaction with self and society? With crime and drugs and dropping out on a mass scale? This crisis is intimately related to the ecological crisis mentioned above, first because money spent on weapons is not a good investment in putting people to work. In fact, a study done this past fall found that for every billion dollars spent on military, 18,000 jobs were lost.[5] It has been estimated that "the money required to provide adequate food, water, education, health and housing for everyone in the world" would be seventeen billion dollars per year. This is the amount that the world spends on arms every two weeks.[6] When the human race wakes up to see that it has outgrown war, it will realize that to put our energies of people, knowledge, talent, and capital to work to feed, educate, heal, and house the human community would provide work and more than enough work for everyone. Indeed, I do not believe that we have unemployment in the world at all. What we have is *misemployment*. If we considered artists as workers, we would put 15 percent of the population to work today making our lives more erotic for us by music, by clowning, by storytelling, by tumbling and juggling in our midst. How can there be unemployment in a world where so much work needs to be done? How many people are invited to go to work at building the New Creation—yet no one has invited them yet? The creation-centered tradition, by emphasizing human creativity and our capacity for letting go, can move humanity to a consciousness of full employment. For it cares deeply about the New Creation. And how will there be new creation without new creators?

When using the word "crisis," I find it helpful to consider that in Chinese thought the word "crisis" also means "opportunity." And in Greek, from which we derive our word "crisis," the word means "judgment." The ecological/nuclear crisis and the unemployment crisis are both opportunities and occasions for the human race to begin judging and choosing consciously, to grow up, to let go, to redefine how it will settle conflicts and to redefine what is meant by work. Breakdown is very often the surest starting point for a genuine breakthrough.

2.   **The Scientific Awakening.**   Science has itself broken down in our century and is going through a profound breakthrough, a fashioning of a new paradigm by which to model the universe. This new paradigm is sure to affect all elements of society—from education to medicine, from religion to economics, from politics to psychology —just as the previous Newtonian model has done for three centuries. Recently a physicist wrote me a letter in which he stated, "A new era of scientific understanding is unfolding, and one where the best scientists in all fields are discovering the organicist paradigm that holds value and fact together." He also comments that "the central sickness of our world is precisely the split between religious wisdom and scientific knowledge and power." The creation-centered spiritual tradition can not only dialog with science, it can also create with science. I know this from experience, for we have been doing this at our Institute in Culture and Creation Spirituality (ICCS), in writings[7] and in workshops with theologians and scientists for several years now. While physicist Fritjof Capra has gone east for his religious wisdom, the rediscovery of the creation-centered spiritual tradition of the West would make this movement of holistic science and holistic religion occur much faster, since our roots are Western and even science's roots are Western. The doctrine of the Incarnation is itself an invitation to all believers to love the earth, cherish it, find the divine in it.

3.   **Global Ecumenism.** The creation-centered spiritual tradition is truly ecumenical. All persons and all religions share creation in common. A global awakening can only happen from a spiritual awakening that is of global dimensions. As we move from an *egological* to an *ecological* consciousness,[8] this basic understanding of our true interdependence will overcome our tendencies to make battle with each other. Teilhard de Chardin felt this way when he wrote that "our consciousness, rising above the growing (but still much too limited) circles of family, country and race, shall finally discover

15

that the only truly natural and real human unity is the spirit of the earth."[9] All humans are born from the earth, are nurtured from it, and are destined to return to it. What is more universal than that? All religions, when they are true to themselves, celebrate this truth.

In ten years of lecturing and writing on creation spirituality I have seen how excited and amazed listeners get over how deeply this tradition cuts through religious differences and touches spiritual points of convergence. An Eastern Orthodox Christian who heard me lecture once told me that if what I spoke about was truly Roman Catholicism, there would be no need for the Roman/Orthodox split. A Taoist called my lecture "pure Taoism." The Buddhist Dr. D. T. Suzuki calls Meister Eckhart the most important single spokesperson for the creation spirituality in the West, a Zen master. This week I received a letter from a Sufi on his love of Meister Eckhart. Dr. Jung Young Lee's book on Eastern religion and Christianity is a book on creation theology.[10] Native American spirituality is a creation-centered tradition, as are the other prepatriarchal religions of the world such as African religions, Celtic religions, and the matrifocal and Wikke traditions that scholars and practitioners like Starhawk are recovering.[11] The contemporary mystical movement known as "new age" can also dialog and create with the creation spiritual tradition. It is important that religious ecumenism not be limited to dialog among patriarchal religions of the past 5000 years at best. Included must be the more ancient traditions, such as Native American and feminist or matrifocal, and the more recent New Age movements. Creation spirituality can not only dialog with these traditions but move to co-creating with them as well. Even in the scriptures, the creation tradition invariably represented the universalist dimension of religion. After all, the Creator God is the God of all that is.

4. **Justice and Liberation Movements.** We are told by Schumacher that wisdom can be found in religious traditions, but in the prophetic tradition of Judaism and Christianity we learn that within religious traditions themselves wisdom is to be gained especially from the *anawim*, the forgotten and oppressed ones. The creation spiritual tradition, so much that of the prophets, has itself suffered the fate of an *anawim* theology in the West. It has been at times repressed, forgotten, condemned. Consider, for example, how many Benedictines know Augustine but do not know their own Hildegarde of Bingen. Consider how many Dominicans either do not know their own Meister Eckhart or have succumbed to the false philosophical thesis that Eckhart is a Neoplatonist, when in fact he is a biblical

theologian who is steeped in the Jewish spirituality of the royal person, of compassion, of prophecy, of earthiness.[12] Consider how many Carmelites have misinterpreted John of the Cross, telling us that he was, in Thomas Merton's words, "a life-denying and world-hating ascetic when in reality his mysticism superabounds in love, vitality and joy."[13] Consider how we English-speaking people have not only ignored Julian of Norwich, but persist to this day in mistranslating her through dualistic, fall/redemption ideologies. I speak of a recent translation of Julian which (as just one example of fall/redemption projections) translates her phrase "noughting for love," a phrase about letting go and letting be and trusting nothingness, as "despise as nothing all created things."[14] Julian's phrase is perfectly understandable and gentle in light of Path II in creation spirituality (see Theme Thirteen below) and, of course, in light of Path I, wherein we learn that all creatures are divine. But to introduce the will power that is implied in the word "despise" as representative of Julian simply shows an utter unfamiliarity with the spiritual tradition from which she springs, that of creation spirituality. How many of our other mystics have been mishandled and mistranslated through ignorance of the creation tradition? And how much of scripture too has been mistranslated and misunderstood through the ignoring of this tradition?

Creation spirituality is a justice spirituality—Meister Eckhart, its greatest spokesperson, says, "The person who understands what I have to say about justice understands everything I have to say." It is also a "street spirituality" that the oppressed can recognize as their own. While the fall/redemption tradition has served the needs of what Johannes Metz calls "the history of the successful and the established" during the marriage of empire and religion since the fourth century in the West, the creation tradition has a different historical tale to tell. Metz writes:

> It is of decisive importance that a kind of anti-history should develop out of the memory of suffering—an understanding of history in which the vanquished and destroyed alternatives would also be taken into account: an understanding of history *ex memoria passionis* as a history of the vanquished.[15]

This book and the tradition it presents represent such an alternative history. Ironically, however, too few liberation theologians have realized that the memory of suffering is only complete when it embraces memories of beauty, of pleasure, of original blessing.

Why? Because suffering is proportionate to what is lost—the Via Negativa follows on the Via Positiva—you can only truly lose what you love. The pathos of the crushing of individuals' dignity happens because individuals have dignity; the pathos of crushing creativity happens because individuals are creative; that of divinity, because people are divine with the image of God alive in them.

5. **Feminist Movements.** Patriarchal religions and patriarchal paradigms for religion have ruled the world's civilizations for at least 3500 years. The creation-centered tradition is feminist. Wisdom and Eros count more than knowledge or control in such a spirituality. Together, feminist women and men are invited to rebirth a religious vision that is more creation-centered. And they can have fun doing it, because play is a grace in such ritual-making and rebirthing. Feminist Susan Griffin names the ecological crisis of our time when she says, "Man's notion of nature is again threatened."[16] A patriarchal religious vision such as that fall/redemption spirituality offers cannot deal with this deep "threat." Creation spirituality welcomes a new stage in nature awareness. Author Carol Christ raises the tension that exists among feminists who are energized by nature and those who are energized by political movements.[17] But the creation spiritual tradition sees this as an unnecessary dualism comparable to the religious dualism of salvation versus creation. Political movements for justice are part of the fuller development of the cosmos, and nature is the matrix in which humans come to their self-awareness and their awareness of their power to transform. Liberation movements are a fuller development of the cosmos's sense of harmony, balance, justice, and celebration. This is why true spiritual liberation demands rituals of cosmic celebrating and healing, which will in turn culminate in personal transformation and liberation of peoples. Not only was the prepatriarchal period feminist, but the postpatriarchal period will be as well—provided patriarchy, in its deep pessimism, leaves us a world to play on and work on and celebrate.

6. **Hope versus Pessimism, Cynicism, and Sadism.** The late Erich Fromm once wrote, "Those whose hope is weak settle for comfort or for violence." The comfort of consumerism and the violence of militarism which dominate our times would suggest that we are a people with little or no hope. Have we lost or are we rapidly losing hope? One reason for this pessimism that leads to cynicism and lack of caring is a fall/redemption religious paradigm that begins its theology with original sin. With this doctrine as a starting point, one is old before one comes into the world. To teach original sin and never

to teach original blessing creates pessimism and cynicism. Psychologist Otto Rank insists that all sadism is pessimistic, that the Marquis de Sade "was as full of hate for the whole world as Catherine of Siena was full of love for God."[18] The creation-centered tradition is not optimistic; it is too much in touch with the pain and tragedy of existence for that. But it is hopeful, and it is cosmically passionate about the blessing that life is. Julian of Norwich calls those who dwell on sinfulness "foolish." This creation-centered mystic actually invented the word "enjoy" in the English language. Joy beyond measure is part of everyone's potential experience. It is part of recovering an erotic God who plays, takes pleasure, births, celebrates, and feels passion. Eros and hope are part of the blessings of existence.

7. **Religious Transformation.** How is religion to be an agent of transformation if religion itself is not transformed? A recovery of creation-centered spirituality will bring an excitement back to the adventure that faith is meant to be. It will invigorate lives of people and their institutions, awakening them to their spiritual potential. But it will not do this until and unless religion confesses its sins in having followed too one-sidedly and too dutifully the fall/redemption paradigm. Frederick Turner, writing from the perspective of the Native American experience with Christians, observes: "With a few bright exceptions Christian mystics are characterized more by their denial of large aspects of creation than by any joyful acceptance of the same; by negative desires instead of positive; by the imagery and love of death rather than commitment to life." This is "especially" the case, he continues, regarding attitudes toward the body.[19] We are victims of a cosmic loneliness and an anthropocentric isolation from creation that we bring upon ourselves.

Fall/redemption theology concentrates on sin—yet sin, after all, is part of the anthropomorphizing of our existence. For if the universe is twenty billion years old, human sin is only as old as humanity or at most four million years old. This means that fall/redemption theology leaves out nineteen billion, nine hundred ninety-six million years of divine/earthly history! One result of this rather substantial lacuna is, ironically, the very trivializing of sin, the inability to grasp sins like geocide and ecocide and biocide of which the human race is fully capable. Another consequence is the trivializing of the gospel message itself. Gandhi complained of "Christianity without Christ," a far-too-common situation in his opinion. Father Edward Schillebeeckx comments that "without creation, spirituality becomes pure projection."[20] How much pure projection wanders about the church pieties of today? How much of the piety of "Jesus is my best friend" or "Jesus saves" comes perilously close to pure projection—when in fact Jesus, like all the prophets, taught people to heal themselves and others, to be instruments of New Creation, and to do works greater than he did? How much of the gospel, how much of the person and message and spirit of Jesus Christ has been lost by overconcentration on fall/redemption religion in the West? That creation spirituality has been ignored is clear from all my experiences in teaching persons about it. For example, following a recent lecture I received a letter that said, "I ran into the creation-centered tradition during my wanderings away from the church three years ago. To discover that it is a part of my own tradition is a true gift and shockingly exciting." A man who discovered the creation tradition told me he had two deep reactions: first, an ecstasy and profound joy; and secondly, a deep anger that all his life his religious instruction had deprived him of knowing that the creation tradition in fact existed in his own Christian faith.

Earlier in this introduction I called for a return to the creation-centered sources for Catholic religious orders like the Benedictines, Carmelites, and Dominicans. It is just as necessary that Protestantism be renewed, and I believe that this religious transformation will come about by an awakening to the best sort of prophetic mysticism, such as one finds in Eckhart and the Rhineland mystics. This, after all, is what drew the deep praise of Martin Luther in his very first writing, his preface to the *Theologica Germanica*, which he calls "the best theology." Only this reawakening to the mystical/prophetic creation spirituality will heal the sad breach between the so-called "radical reformers" and mainline Protestantism—a division that neither Christianity nor society can afford any longer. As I travel and lecture around this continent, I find more and more Protestants, especially students in seminaries, coming out of the closet and admitting they are mystics. But, sad to tell, there are so few ministers and theology professors who know the creation spiritual tradition and who can greet them and encourage them in their deep spiritual journeying. In fact, for Protestantism to recover creation spirituality would be for it to recover its charisma of protest and prophecy (see Path IV below). Protestant skepticism about mysticism that flees from protest and social justice is well taken vis-à-vis the fall/redemption spiritual tradition. But as applied to the creation-centered tradition, it makes absolutely no sense. The sooner Protestant theologians and seminary directors welcome this tradition with its deep spiritual/political roots, the better for all who seek a thorough renewal of Christianity.

Why do I emphasize so much how creation spirituality is a *tradition*? Because what distinguishes a spirituality from a cult is precisely tradition. The Moonies have a cult and a personality figure leading them—but not tradition. So too with the Jim Jones movement. I emphasize how truly we are dealing with a tradition in this book by the use of quotes from various sources to introduce each theme and by Appendix A, wherein I name some of the principal spokespeople for creation spirituality in the West.

The more I meditate on the twenty-six themes that I present in this book as central to creation spirituality, the more struck I am by their absence in 99 percent of religious and even theological training in the West of late. The departmentalizing of theology that took place in the eighteenth century à la Newton by Christian Wolff and others no longer speaks any sense. When I listen to theological or seminary students tell me, in the 1980's, that they are majoring in "systematics" or "biblical" or "dogmatic," I have to wonder if they have yet heard of Einstein and of relativity and of the whole. All theological studies have to return to a whole and let go of their Newtonian, specialized parts-mentalities. This is why the term "spirituality" is not even found in solid theological thinkers of the Middle Ages, as for example Thomas Aquinas: the whole theological enterprise was one of finding one's place in the universe. The four paths and twenty-six themes of the creation tradition can, I believe, form a working structure for rethinking and rerelating theology to its own inner disciplines and to other disciplines as well. The term "creation-centered" is to distinguish this tradition from those dominant spiritualities of the past few centuries, such as Jesuit exercises, which are in fact psychologically centered and not creation-centered. Recently the wife of a Jesuit wrote a rather acerbic public letter to me in which, among other things, she said Ignatius was creation-centered because he mentions creation a few times in his *Exercises*. This is to trivialize the creation tradition. Even Augustine alludes to creation, but his theology is fall- and redemption-centered, not creation-centered; and Ignatius' spirituality is psychologically centered, with a sixteenth-century psychology, that is its strength and that is its weakness. Krister Stendahl understands the introspective and therefore non-creation-centered influence that Augustine, the great exponent of fall/redemption theology, has had on the West.

> With Augustine, Western Christianity with its stress on introspective achievements started.... Man turned in on himself, infatuated and absorbed by the question not of when God will send deliverance in the history of salvation, but how God is working in the innermost individual soul.... The introspective conscience is a Western development and a Western plague.... It reached its theological climax and explosion in the Reformation, and its secular climax and explosion in Sigmund Freud. But Paul himself was never involved in this pursuit.[21]

Leo Scheffczyk, in his study on *Creation and Providence*, comments on how Augustine began a "duality of thought about creation" that has persisted for centuries and how his "ontological thought was achieved at the expense of the scriptural concept of Creation as part of the economy of salvation."[22] When one begins to develop a theology around the creation themes presented in this book, one is more and more struck by how new this sounds to Christians. Topics like cosmos, earthiness, divinization, original blessing, sensuality, prophecy, creativity, new creation, royal personhood, panentheism, letting go, nothingness, beauty, celebration, compassion—these are not even words, much less categories, in the books and minds of most theologians or more seminaries or most theology schools.

The abysmal, theologically one-sided dominance of Augustine over Jesus and the prophets must cease. And the hegemony of salvation as deliverance over salvation as blessing (to use Claus Westermann's distinction)[23] must be let go of. When this happens, then theology will join practice. Many livers of spirituality within and without the churches have already moved into the living of the twenty-six theological themes discussed in this book. I realize now why so many persons, on hearing me lecture on creation spirituality over the years, have said to me, "Now you have articulated what I live and have experienced."

All theology ought to be endeavoring to articulate the work of the Spirit in people's experience and ought to resist using a tired ideology as a procrustean bed to tell people what they ought to experience. I recall a sixty-year-old woman approaching me this year at a workshop and saying, "I always wondered what I was being redeemed from, but I was afraid to ask."

More people's lives begin with original blessing that many theologians have ever dreamed of. It is time more and more theologians and their theological structures started allowing their hearts and right brains as much attention as they have given their left brains.

I realized when I finished this book that it calls for a complete restructuring of theological education. Every priest and every minister ought to get recycled in creation-centered spirituality, and fast. Instead of cutting up theology into the Newtonian fragments of biblical, systematic, historical, ascetic, we need the Four Paths that guarantee an organic understanding of our spiritual journey and of our theological heritage from scripture, from the mystics, from the prophets, and from the artists of our tradition.

These paths are spiral, not ladderlike. Like the movements of a symphony, each of the paths spirals in and out of the others until the spiritual journey expands and expands. And within the paths, each of the twenty-six themes also spirals in and out of the others. This interweaving, interconnecting, interdependent spiraling can easily carry us beyond Augustine and beyond Newton. The meditative reader of this book will realize how thoroughly interconnected all the themes and paths are. Path I, the Via Positiva of Befriending Creation, cannot be fully experienced without Path II, the Via Negativa of Befriending Darkness and Letting Go, Letting Be. This path in turn finds its fulfillment in Path III, the Via Creativa of Befriending Creativity, since all creativity—as distinct from reshuffling—is *ex nihilo*, from nothingness and darkness. Path IV, the Via Transformativa and the Befriending of New Creation, fulfills Path III, for the direction of increased compassion as celebration and justice is the direction our creativity needs to take us. Yet Path IV reconnects with Path I, just as new creation is related to creation itself. Around each of these paths we can ask what art, politics, and science have to teach us, as well as theology. I look forward to the day when I will run into theology students who tell me they are majoring, for example, in "blessing theology," that they are bringing to bear on this theme all they can from scripture, prophetic history, art, science, and that they are relating it to Path IV, social transformation.

8. **Educational Transformation: Welcoming the Right Brain in Each Person.** How can education be an instrument of transformation without itself being transformed? The creation-centered spiritual tradition cannot be taught within the confines of Cartesian, left-brained, academic structures alone. Spirituality demands not only solid theory but solid practice. This means that cosmic and creative mysticism demands the experience of art as meditation and the experience of the oppressed that gives rise to passion and imagination for social change. I am amused and of late a bit exasperated by comfortable academics with tenure who tell us, strictly from

their left brain of course, how radical and Marxist they are. If they were radical they would criticize their own privileges in academia and ask why the right brain has been so excluded from the intellectual life of late and what they can do about this banishment. In the five years of our Institute in Creation-Centered Spirituality, I have learned what a round peg creation spirituality must be for the square holes of academia. There is simply no way to teach creation-centered spirituality in the context of a definition of academia that derives from Newtonian and Cartesian parts-mentalities. Educational forms must themselves be altered to make room for the spiritual renewal that a creation spirituality can begin—and in all candor I do not know why, for a change, seminaries and theology schools could not *lead* in this reformation instead of waiting around for someone else to do it. Couldn't. Catholic school systems, for example, take the lead in reconnecting science, mysticism, art, and social transformation? This book is a challenge as much to let go of Newton's and Descartes's influence on education as it is to let go of Augustine's influence on religion. Left-brain-itis is a lethal disease that today has quite literally the power to destroy all the earth. The right brain's contribution of feeling and connection-making, of mysticism and cosmic delight, of darkness and sensuousness needs to be taught and appreciated. Education needs to include the disciplining and motivating of the right as well as the left brain. For wisdom does not proceed from either right or left brain, but from the happy marriage of the two, functioning well as equal partners in pursuit of truth.

With good reason does Whitehead talk about "a celibacy of the intellect" found in specialized and professional education that "produces minds in a groove." Educational methods, he believes, "are far too much occupied with intellectual analysis." The result is loss of wisdom, for "wisdom is the fruit of a balanced development." What is his solution to left-brain-itis in education? *Art,* what he calls "aesthetic education," what I name in Path III as the Via Creativa. Only art as meditation can make us green again, to use Hildegarde's term. Or, as Whitehead puts it, the "fertilization of the soul is the reason for the necessity of art." (45.283–290).

9. **An Argument From Default.** Creation-centered spirituality was not in the driver's seat when Christianity married the empire in the fourth century and began an alliance that lasted at least until the French Revolution. Creation spirituality was a spirituality of the oppressed and representative of the oppressed. It did not dictate the dualisms of saved/unsaved, fallen/redeemed that gave so much

impetus to the Crusades, the Inquisitions, genocide toward Native Americans, the burnings of Jews, witches, homosexuals, scientists, of Protestants by Catholics and Catholics by Protestants.

Given the unbalanced hegemony of fall/redemption spirituality in Christianity, it is evident that this is a book about Christian liberation, i.e., liberating Christianity from its patriarchal self—which is not its better self. From its overly introspective and fearful self. From its dualistic self. From its violent self. From its marrying-with-empires self. From its fear of passion, of prophecy, and of Eros. As mystics among scientists, educators, artists, justice-makers, and Protestant seminarians emerge more and more out of their closets into the light of day, they need and deserve a hearty embrace from a solidly prophetic spiritual tradition. The creation-centered spirituality is that tradition, and if it were well-known and well-heralded, fundamentalism of religion and politics would not carry the weight they carry today the world over.

10. **Vision, Adventure, Community.** After years of devoting his life to healing efforts, Carl Jung made a striking observation about how people are and are not healed. He wrote:

> All the greatest and most important problems of life are fundamentally insoluble. . . . They can never be solved, but only outgrown. This "outgrowing" proved on further investigation to require a new level of consciousness. Some higher or wider interest appeared on the patient's horizon, and through this broadening of his or her outlook the insoluble problem lost its urgency. It was not solved logically in its own terms but faded when confronted with a new and stronger life urge.[24]

I am convinced from practice as much as from theory that the creation-centered spiritual tradition will bring with it a "new and stronger life urge." It has the power to birth people anew, and with that birthing to rebirth structures and ways of living. The "patient" today is not an individual seeking a psychologist's support; the patient is nothing less than Western civilization and indeed humankind itself. We need a new and stronger life urge. We need a religious vision for wisdom. As Whitehead put it, "The fact of the religious vision, and its history of persistent expansion, is our one ground for optimism." (45.275) If religion can expand to recover its oldest and deepest tradition in the West, that of creation-centered spirituality, then truly there is room for hope. And for high adventure and for much new employment towards New Creation. For too long Christians seeking comfort have been defining community as a noun. In fact, community is people building something together, working on a common project (*cum-munio*). To throw ourselves into a common project of retrieving wisdom for an ecological era—this is no small task, no mean adventure. Whitehead warns that "the death of religion comes with the repression of the high hope of adventure." The prophetic mystics of the creation-centered tradition did not kill religion or repress adventure. They and this book invite people to make wisdom together.

For the ten reasons given above, I believe that the creation-centered spiritual tradition represents the appropriate spiritual paradigm for our time. I also believe that this tradition and the living of it represents a Copernican revolution in religion. Copernicus moved people from believing that Earth was the center around which the universe revolved to believing that Earth moved about the sun. In religion we have been operating under the model that humanity, and especially sinful humanity, was the center of the spiritual universe. This is not so. The universe itself, blessed and graced, is the proper starting point for spirituality. Original blessing is prior to any sin, original or less than original. I do not consider this book to be a polemic against Augustine or the fall/redemption model for religion. Maybe it was necessary that humanity concentrate during a certain period on its fallenness. But the time has come to let anthropocentrism go, and with it to let the preoccupation with human sinfulness give way to attention to divine grace. In the process sin itself will be more fully understood and more successfully dealt with.

A few words about the reading of this book appear in order. This is less a book than a program between the covers of a book. Spirituality is a journey, an in-depth journey, one that in Rabbi Heschel's words touches our "recesses," both personal and social. Therefore this book/program names the four *paths* on that journey. These four paths supplant the three paths—purgation, illumination, and union—that Neoplatonic mysticism has based itself on. The research behind this book has been from practice feeding theory and theory feeding practice. This has happened in our ICCS program for five years and in the lives of the four hundred-plus students who have experienced that program and have been living it out in life and ministry.

The subtitle for this book is *A Primer in Creation-Centered Spirituality*. A primer, according to my dictionary, is a small introductory book usually for children. It is my experience as a student of theology for over twenty years and in three countries, and as a teacher and lecturer in spirituality in literally hundreds of colleges, universities, retreat centers, and spirituality and religious conferences on several continents over the past twelve years, that in the West *we are all children when it comes to creation-centered spirituality*. And I mean *all*—theologians and biblical scholars as much as wandering troubadours or seminary students or parish activists. Many people—mostly laypersons who are artists, scientists, peasants, lovers, or other kinds of mystics—have been living creation spirituality, but without the theological articulation and encouragement they have a right to from the churches.

Fall/redemption ideologies have so prevailed in theological scholarship that the very questions that are asked and not asked, the very translations of scriptures and of the mystics, the very meaning of holiness and the list of saints, have been dictated by this one stream of Christian tradition. Luther says, drawing on ancient tradition, that there are three articles of faith: 1. Creation; 2. Redemption; 3. Sanctification.[25] Yet if we skip over creation—which Protestant and Catholic theology has been doing for four centuries—then is not redemption distorted? And sanctification as well? This is why in this book I work on retrieving some overly familiar religious language; concepts like sin, salvation, even the person of Christ and the meaning of faith take on new vigor when creation spirituality is allowed to breathe life into them. For example, would there have been a three-century debate on the term "justification by faith" if the term were translated as "justice by trust?" Trust—which is the primary biblical and creation-centered meaning for faith—finds a special meaning in each of the four paths, as the reader will notice. I can envision no better follow-up to this book than for the reader to supplement the text with a time investment in the great creation-centered mystics of the West, in particular Hildegarde of Bingen, Mechtild of Magdeburg, Meister Eckhart, and Julian of Norwich. I draw heavily on these giants of the creation-centered tradition in this book. The sources for all their sayings can be found in the *Meditations With*™ series of books from Bear and Company,[26] and for this reason, unless otherwise indicated, I have not bothered to footnote them in the usual manner. Reading these mystics in the light of the four paths and twenty-six themes of this book will make them—and ourselves—live again.

Since this is a primer, an introductory book, each theme is an unfinished meditation that is only briefly sketched out. I trust the reader to make connections and applications and to carry on the theological revisioning that must follow from this new (but ancient) vision. I believe that the various quotes I have chosen to introduce each theme will assist the reader in this connection-making. In fact, I recommend that on finishing each theme the reader return to the page or two of opening quotes for that theme and reread the various comments in a deeper and fresher light. I have included what I call a "Family Tree in Creation-Centered Spirituality" as Appendix A to provide more areas of deeper research, to acknowledge my own debt to tradition, and to awaken one and all to the richness and wonder of the creation tradition. I wish to stress that this is a representative but highly unfinished list, and I invite readers to add their own creation-centered persons to this communion of saints—and not to exclude themselves!

I have had it said to my face by persons with Ph.D.'s in religion, the Bible, etc., that "There is no such thing as a creation tradition in the West." This family tree, plus the quotes with each theme, plus this whole book, puts an end to such shameful ignorance. And it raises the following disturbing question: If Christianity has two spiritual streams, fall/redemption and creation-centered, and if Christians only know the first, then has even the first stream been properly understood?

Appendix B, "Fall/Redemption and Creation-Centered Spiritualities Compared at a Glance," allows the reader to recognize some differences between the two spiritual traditions. Some people will object that to contrast fall/redemption and creation spirituality is to create a dualism of either/or instead of living out a dialectic of both/and. But when it comes to human concepts, there are either/or choices that we must make—a psychology that says, "The soul makes war with the body," (fall/redemption, Augustine) and one that says, "The soul loves the body," (creation spirituality, Eckhart) are not saying the same thing. Only a mushy and basically sentimental mind would say they are of equal value. We must choose. A spirituality is a way, a path. We do not come to two paths in a road and say, out of timidity and fear to make a decision, "I will go down both roads at once." The West has been traveling the fall/redemption path for centuries. We all know it; we all have it ingrained in our souls; we have given it 95 percent of our energies in churches both Catholic and Protestant. And look where it has gotten us. Into sexism, militarism, racism, genocide against native peoples, biocide, consumerist capitalism, and violent communism. I believe it is time we chose another path. The path that is the most ancient, the most healing, the most feminist of the paths, even in the biblical tradition itself. If we throw ourselves into this path, who can predict what the happy results might be? After all, since the fourth century the followers of Jesus have rarely as a body explored this path.

Appendix C, "An Annotated Bibliography in Creation-Centered Spirituality," will allow the serious student to pursue this tradition in greater depth. It also allows me to acknowledge my indebtedness and to simplify my footnoting procedures. References to any of the books in this selected bibliography are incorporated into the text according to the number in my list and the page. For example, the reference (15.3) indicates Matthew Fox, *A Spirituality Named Compassion,* page 3.

I wish the readers and livers of this primer much wisdom, much spiral journeying, and much making of erotic justice. And may we meet someday in our ever deeper and deeper journeys.

Institute in Culture and Creation Spirituality
Holy Names College
Oakland, California
Easter, 1983

PATH I
BEFRIENDING CREATION:
THE VIA POSITIVA

cosmos blessing earthy cosmic trust panentheistic royal personhood realized eschatology hospitality thanks sin salvation christ-incarnation creation

O n his deathbed the great psychologist and lover of the human race Erich Fromm turned to his friend Robert Fox and asked, "Why is it, Bob, that the human race prefers necrophilia to biophilia?" A significant question, this. Why *do* we prefer love of death to love of life? Missiles to celebration? Power-over to power-with? Greed to letting go?

I am sure that a question as poignant as this one can yield many rich answers, but I would like to offer just one answer from my own perspective as a theologian. It is this: Western civilization has preferred love of death to love of life to the very extent that its religious traditions have preferred redemption to creation, sin to ecstasy, and individual introspection to cosmic awareness and appreciation. Religion has failed people in the West as often as it has been silent about pleasure or about the cosmic creation, about the ongoing power of the flowing energy of the Creator, about original blessing.

If the failure of religion in the West is one very basic reason for our culture's love of death—and I have no doubt that it is—then the recovery of a creation-grounded spirituality promises much newness and renewal to society, provided this recovery is not too late and is not thwarted by a lot of backward-leaning battles with tired fall/redemption theological preoccupations.

Let there be no question about it: what has been most lacking in society and religion in the West for the past six centuries has been a Via Positiva, a way or path of affirmation, thanksgiving, ecstasy. In this chapter we will take up each of nine themes that pertain to the Via Positiva. These are more than conceptual themes, however. They are journeys, deeply entered into, deeply felt, and deeply

33

shareable. They are journeys of life, not death; of awareness, not numbness; of Eros, not control. And therefore they are journeys of salvation, i.e. healing power. The Via Positiva represents a new power, in the sense that it has been forgotten; the power that pleasure is and that wisdom is. It is no coincidence that in both the Latin language and the Hebrew language the words for "wisdom" are related to "tasting." "Taste and see how good the Lord is" shouts the psalmist. The Via Positiva is a way of tasting the beauties and cosmic depths of creation, which means us and everything else. Without this solid grounding in creation's powers we become bored, violent people. We become necrophiliacs in love with death and the powers and principalities of death. With the Via Positiva, all creation breaks out anew.

The ten themes or stopping places along the path of the Via Positiva are as follows:

1. Dabhar: The Creative Energy (Word) of God.

2. Creation as Blessing and the Recovery of the Art of Savoring Pleasure.

3. Humility as Earthiness: Our Earthiness as a Blessing along with Passion and Simplicity.

4. Cosmic, Universalist: Harmony, Beauty, Justice as Cosmic Energies.

5. Trust: A Psychology of Trust and Expansion.

6. Panentheism: Experiencing the Diaphanous and Transparent God.

7. Our Royal Personhood: Our Dignity and Responsibility for Building the Kingdom/Queendom of God. Creation Theology as a Kingdom/Queendom Theology.

8. Realized Eschatology: A New Sense of Time.

9. Holiness as Cosmic Hospitality: Creation Ecstasies Shared Constitute the Holy Prayer of Thanksgiving and Praise.

10. Sin, Salvation, Christ from the Perspective of the Via Positiva: A Theology of Creation and Incarnation.

1 DABHAR: THE CREATIVE ENERGY (WORD) OF GOD

You have made all your works in wisdom.
—*Ps. 104:24*

The Word is living, being, spirit, all verdant greening, all creativity. This Word manifests itself in every creature.
—*Hildegarde of Bingen*

Every grain of dust has a wonderful soul.
—*Joan Miró*

Every creature is a word of God and is a book about God.
—*Meister Eckhart*

The whole world and all creatures will be to you nothing else than an open book and a living Bible, in which you may study, without any previous instruction, the science of God and from which you may learn his will.
—*Sebastian Franck*[1]

The force that through the green fuse drives the flower
Drives my green age; . . .
The force that drives the water through the rocks
Drives my red blood.
—*Dylan Thomas*[2]

Our children need to learn not only how to read books composed by human genius but also how to read the Great Book of the World. Reading this Great Book is natural to children.
—*Thomas Berry*[3]

Creation not only exists, it also discharges truth. . . . Wisdom requires a surrender, verging on the mystical, of a person to the glory of existence.
—*Gerhard Von Rad (43.165)*

When we try to pick out anything by itself, we find it hitched
to everything else in the Universe.... No particle is ever
wasted or worn out, but eternally flowing from use to use.
  —John Muir[4]

The universe is the primary revelation of the divine, the primary scripture, the primary locus of divine-human communion.
  — Thomas Berry[5]

The word that goes forth from my mouth does not return to
me empty.
  —Isa. 55:11

By the word of the Lord his works come into being.
As the shining sun looks on all things,
 so the work of the Lord is full of his glory.
  —Sir. 42:15,16

Humanity participates by nature in all cosmic events, and is
inwardly as well as outwardly interwoven with them.
  *—Richard Wilhelm on the Chinese concept of
  Tao*[6]

In the beginning was the word
The word was with God
and the word was God.
And the word became flesh
and dwelt among us.
  —John 1:1,14

In the West, a theology of the word of God has practically killed the
word of God. This very paradoxical statement is true to the extent
that theologians have been translating the Hebrew word "Dabhar"
as "word" practically without regard to what the words "word" and
"words" have come to mean in our culture. The word "Dabhar"
simply does not mean what we now mean by "word" or "words".
The Protestant Reformation, coming as it did at the time of the
invention of the printing press and at a time when two-thirds of the
people in Western Europe were completely illiterate, wisely recaptured
a theology of preaching the word of God. But today's situation is
different. Left-brain hegemony since the Enlightenment has produced a culture that inundates us in the verbal. Advertisers,

newspapers, presidential speeches, paperback books, voluminous libraries, and now word processors are all busy changing the meaning of the word "word" and in a sense cheapening it by the very overuse of words. If we are to regain our own lives, our spiritual roots that nourish us into growth, we must return to the pre-word times of original creation. To the time before the printed word, the radio word, the word processor, the printing press; to a time when there was so much silence about that words still meant something significant. The spoken word, the storied word, the word that gave birth. Therefore, the word that is the divine creative energy.

In the biblical tradition this time-before-time and time-before-words is associated with wisdom. It involves play.[7]

> Yahweh created me when his purpose first unfolded,
>> before the oldest of his works.
> From ever-lasting I was firmly.set,
>> from the beginning, before earth came into being. . . .
>
> I was by his side, a master craftsman,
>> delighting him day after day,
>> ever at play in his presence,
> at play everywhere in his world,
>> delighting to be with the sons of men. (Prov. 8:22,23,30,31)

Gerhard Von Rad, the scholar of wisdom in the Hebrew scriptures, defines wisdom or the word behind creation as "the primeval world order, as the mystery behind creation of the world." Wisdom extends to all of being, all of creation. It "rules in a similar fashion in the non-human creation as well as in the spheres of human society. . . . It is oriented toward man, offering him help." (43,161,162) Thus all of creation contains the living wisdom and word of God, and all of it is for all of us. The human word is only one among billions of words that God has spoken and that therefore emanate from the divine splendor. To make contact with wisdom is to go beyond human words, which have, after all, existed for only about four million years—and have appeared on paper for only a few thousand years and in print for only five hundred. We are invited to return to the many billions of years of ongoing creation that also constitute God's talking.

What happens when we let go of a chauvinistic control of words, which means exclusively the human word, and return to Dabhar as the creative energy of God? According to Von Rad, truth happens; and affection happens; and God happens. For "creation not only exists, it also discharges truth." Imagine that—creation itself, and

37

not just books, is a source of truth and of revelation. A book about God, as Meister Eckhart put it, a Bible therefore. Nature itself is "the primary scripture," according to "geologian" Thomas Berry. But Von Rad goes even further. What most astonishes us, he points out, is that "this mysterious order in the world not only addresses man; it also loves him." (43.166) Thus the true Dabhar of God is as much right brain (affection, play, and love) as it is left brain (verbal, truth-oriented, cognitive). This is one more reason why to translate Dabhar as "word of God" today is destructive of the rich meanings behind God's creative energy. One is reminded, when hearing of how nature loves us, of a stanza from Baudelaire:

> We walk through forests of physical things
>   that are also spiritual things
>   that look on us with affectionate looks. (7.44)

Notice how abundant the creative energy of God is—we do not walk just through *a* forest but all our lives long through *forests* of physical things that love us and pour out truth to us. But are we listening? Are we awake? Do we have our heads out of our manmade word books, even the holiest of them, enough to feel and be vulnerable to the ongoing creative energy of God? Von Rad surprises us and the many left-brained Christian theologians who have tried to tell us that the God of Israel is interested in salvation and not in nature when he goes on to say, "The idea of a testimony emanating from creation is attested to only in Israel." (43.175) Of course, Von Rad ought not to have left out Native American traditions or the Wikke and other pre-patriarchal religious traditions. But what he is saying is very powerful: that in fact Israel, through its wisdom tradition, offers a very lively appreciation of the communion between Creator and creation; indeed, a unique trust in creation as a source of divine revelation, unique at least among the religions of the ancient Middle East in the time of Israel. It follows also that wisdom is sensual, for all of creation is; in fact it is "almost voluptuous" in Von Rad's words. And the mysteries of the world, mysteries which modern science is only now coming close to unveiling as mysteries for us, are "all mysteries of God" for the writers of wisdom literature (43.307).

What follows from all this? What is our human response along our spiritual journey? First, an awareness that there is one flow, one divine energy, one divine word in the sense of one creative energy flowing through all things, all time, all space. We are part of that flow and we need to listen to it rather than to assume arrogantly that our puny words are the only words of God. Von Rad calls for a falling in love with what is, with existence, when he says that what is required is "a surrender, verging on the mystical, of man to the glory of existence." Wherever existence is loved for its own sake and its own beauty, that is, as "the glory of existence," there you have creation-centered spirituality happening. Meister Eckhart puts it this way: "Isness is God." A certain divinity exists (scripture calls it "glory," or beauty) in all that is, all that flows, from a divine source.

When we recover Dabhar, the creative energy of God, we recover the true meaning of the first chapter of Genesis, where we are told that God spoke and then the powerful beings of creation—light and darkness, sun and moon—came into existence. In Hebrew the word "Dabhar," which we translate as "word," implies deeds and actions not just words. Accomplishments, not talk. Creation, not verbalizing Thus in Genesis we read, "God said 'Let there be light' and there was light." "God said, 'Let the earth produce vegetation . . . and so it was." (1:3, 11) This kind of word is truly creative energy and not cheap or impotent. Here too is a link with the prophetic word, the creative energy of the prophets who call for new creation and the letting go of death-filled ways of living. The prophetic word too is a part of the flow of the one creative energy—it breaks out when this flow is dammed up by greed, corruption, boredom, or injustice. For Dabhar will not be kept down; God's energy will not be aborted; creation will take place. Meister Eckhart puts it this way: "God is a great underground river that no one can dam up and no one can stop." Leonard Bernstein captures this sense of the ongoing flow of the word of God in his *Mass*. His song follows the reading of a letter from a young man who is in prison because he refused to go to war.

> You can lock up the bold men,
> Go and lock up your bold men
> And hold men in tow.
> You can stifle all adventure
> For a century or so.
> Smother hope before it's risen,
> Watch it wizen like a gourd.
> But you cannot imprison
> The Word of the Lord.
> No, you cannot imprison
> The Word of the Lord.[8]

The truly energetic creative word of God, Dabhar, will not be imprisoned, will not be locked up for long. Our spiritual task is to get out of its way enough that we might be filled with it and go about our task of healing, celebrating, and co-creating. For Dabhar wishes to be incarnate in us.

And this, of course, is what Christians say they believe, namely that the primeval wisdom, the word-before-words, the creative energy of God has become one of us. If we begin to translate the New Testament too along lines that are more Hebraic and less arrogantly anthropomorphic, a new power emerges from the Christ story. For example, let us listen anew to the first chapter of John's Gospel.

> In the beginning was the Creative Energy:
> The Creative Energy was with God
> and the Creative Energy was God.
> It was with God in the beginning.
> Through it all things came to be,
> not one thing had its being but through it.
> All that came to be had life in it
> and that life was the light of persons,
> a light that shines in the dark,
> a light that darkness could not overpower. . . .
> The Creative Energy was the true light
> that enlightens all people;
> and it was coming into the world.
> It was in the world
> that had its being through it,
> and the world did not know it. . . .
> But to all who did accept it
> it gave power to become children of God. . . .
> The Creative Energy was made flesh,
> it pitched its tent among us,
> and we saw its glory,
> the glory that is its as the only Child of the Creator,
> full of grace and full of truth. (John 1:1-5,9,10,12,14.)

Truly Dabhar is active, imaginative, and playful. A creation-centered spiritual person is sensitive and aware, alive and awake to the ever-flowing, ever-green, unfolding of the divine Dabhar. For such a person, creation itself constitutes the primary sacrament. Creation is by no means in the past, as fundamentalists propose in a kind of unconsciously perverse attempt to lock God (and therefore God's creation) up: Creation is as ongoing as we are; as vast as our experience of it. It is in us and we in it; it is us and far beyond us. Humanity constitutes a uniquely sacramental receptacle for God's holy Dabhar, as Meister Eckhart testifies.

Everything which God created millions of years ago
and everything which will be created by God after millions
    of years—
if the world lasts that long—
God is creating all that in the innermost and deepest
    realms of the human soul.
Everything of the past
and everything of the present
and everything of the future
God creates
in the innermost realms of the soul.

2 CREATION AS BLESSING AND THE RECOVERY OF THE ART OF SAVORING PLEASURE

God is the good
and all things which proceed from him
are good.
—Hildegarde of Bingen

Glory be to God for dappled things—
For skies as couple-colour as brindled cows;
For rose-moles all in stipple upon trout that swim.
—Gerard Manley Hopkins [1]

Just to be is a blessing.
Just to live is holy.
—Abraham Heschel

The doctrine of original sin is not found in any of the writings of the Old Testament. It is certainly not in chapters one to three of Genesis.
—Herbert Haag (21.19)

It would be a perversion of the biblical data to reduce God's dealings with his people to the one concept "salvation."
—Claus Westermann (44.28)

The concept of original sin is alien to Jewish tradition.
—Elie Wiesel [2]

Blessing included that which we call material as well as the spiritual. But first and foremost, blessing is life, health, and fertility for the people, their cattle, their fields. . . . Blessing is the basic power of life itself.
—Sigmund Mowinckel (44.20)

The extravagant gesture is the very stuff of creation. After the one extravagant gesture of creation in the first place, the universe has continued to deal exclusively in extravagances, flinging intricacies and colossi down aeons of emptiness, heaping profusions on profligacies with ever fresh vigor. The whole show has been on fire from the word go!
—Annie Dillard [3]

Beauty is all about us, but how many are blind to it! People take little pleasure in the natural and quiet and simple things of life.
—*Pablo Casals*[4]

Should one faint by the way who gains the blessings of one mountain day/Whatever his fate, long life, short life, stormy or calm, he is rich forever.
—*John Muir*[5]

I know well that heaven and earth and all creation are great, generous and beautiful and good.... God's goodness fills all his creatures and all his blessed works full, and endlessly overflows in them.... God is everything which is good, as I see it, and the goodness which everything has is God.
—*Julian of Norwich*

The manifold delight I learn to take in earthly things
can never drive me from my Love.
For in the nobility of creatures,
in their beauty and in their usefulness,
I will love God—
and not myself!
—*Mechtild of Magdeburg*

To those who followed Columbus and Cortez, the New World truly seemed incredible because of the natural endowments. The land often announced itself with a heavy scent miles out into the ocean. Giovanni di Verrazano in 1524 smelled the cedars of the East Coast a hundred leagues out. The men of Henry Hudson's *Half Moon* were temporarily disarmed by the fragrance of the New Jersey shore, while ships running farther up the coast occasionally swam through large beds of floating flowers. Wherever they came inland they found a rich riot of color and sound, of game and luxuriant vegetation. Had they been other than they were, they might have written a new mythology here. As it was, they took inventory.
—*Frederick Turner (41.256)*

As a rule, it was the pleasure-haters who became unjust.
—*W. H. Auden*

It is clear, I am sure, from the first theme, Dabhar, that the "great event" in the creation-centered spiritual tradition is not the Fall (always with a capital *F*) but the creative energy or word of God. This creative energy is still active today—it is constantly creating and inviting others to participate in creating. Creation is continuous and never stops. And neither do blessing and blessings. Blessing is the word behind the word, the desire behind the creation. For God the Creator, like any artist, is not indifferent or neutral to his/her work of art. Like any parent, God loves her creation and that love which is an unconditional sending forth into existence is blessing. God's creation is desirable; that means it is a blessing. As the Book of Sirach puts it, "How desirable are all his works, how dazzling to the eye! Who could ever be sated with gazing at his glory?" (Sir. 42:22,23,26)

Blessing involves relationship: one does not bless without investing something of oneself into the receiver of one's blessing. And one does not receive blessing oblivious of its gracious giver. A blessing spirituality is a relating spirituality. And if it is true that all of creation flows from a single, loving source, then all of creation is blessed and is a blessing, atom to atom, molecule to molecule, organism to organism, land to plants, plants to animals, animals to other animals, people to people, and back to atoms, molecules, plants, fishes. On and on Dabhar flows, on and on blessing flows. For where there is Dabhar, there is blessing.

Biblical theologian Claus Westermann, in his excellent study *Blessing in the Bible and the Life of the Church*, points out that there are two basic ways by which the God of the Bible deals with humankind: by deliverance and by blessing. (44.1-15) The hegemony of fall/redemption theology, however, has left believers bereft of the rich tradition of life as blessing and of the God of blessing in the Bible. Indeed, most believers I know, if asked what blessing means, would give a hurried sign of the cross or simply shrug their shoulders. Blessing—much less original blessing—has not been preached or taught in Christian spirituality for centuries. Indeed, there has hardly been any Via Positiva in Christian spirituality for centuries, and the main theological reason for this is that there has been no theology of blessing.

But more has been lost to believers than even the loss of a theology of blessing and therefore a Via Positiva as a spiritual experience. Ironically, the fall/redemption tradition, in its overemphasis on sin, guilt, and introspection, has actually managed to deaden the meaning of salvation itself. As Westermann points out, "it is assumed that everyone knows" what salvation means—but in fact we do not. By leaving creation out, the myriad theologians preoccupied with "salvation history" have succumbed to distorting the scriptures, as Westermann indicates. "No concept of history that excludes or ignores God's activity in the world of nature can adequately reflect what occurs in the Old Testament between God and his people." (44.6)

The God of the Covenant is the God of blessing. The promises made to Israel are promises of good things, of fruitful lands, of healthy children and wholesome living. And Israel is to bless Yahweh in return for this lavish gift.

> For Yahweh your God is bringing you to a good land, a land of streams of water, of fountains and springs flowing forth in valleys and hills, a land of wheat and barley, and of vines and fig trees and pomegranates, a land of olive trees and honey in which you will not eat bread in poverty, in which you will not lack anything . . . you shall eat and be satisfied, and you shall bless Yahweh your God in the good land which he has given you. (Deut. 8:7-10)

Blessing is not an abstraction to the people who knew Yahweh the Creator God. Blessing is about survival and about enjoying life's basic gifts. When it came time for the aging Isaac to bless his son, these were his words: "May God give to you of the dew of heaven and of the fatness of the earth and much grain and wine." (Gen. 27:28) As Walter Brueggemann points out, neither blessing nor cursing in the Bible is spiritualized or "religious"; rather, both "were concerned with the socioeconomic, political, and material welfare of the community."[6] Indeed, Abraham, called the father of faith, has his entire vocation carved out for him in terms of blessing.

> Go forth from the land of your kinsfolk and from your
>   father's house to a land that I will show you.
> I will make of you a great nation,
> and I will bless you;
> I will make your name great,
> so that you will be a blessing.
> I will bless those who bless you
> and curse those who curse you.
> All the communities of the earth shall find blessing in you.
> Abram went as the Lord directed him (Gen. 12:1-4a)

45

Path I

Not only does blessing permeate the story of Israel, it also permeates all Dabhar and all creation from the very beginning. We can say blessing preceded creation too, for blessing was its purpose. Thus there is no doubt that original blessing is the basis of all trust and of all faith. Original blessing underlies all being, all creation, all time, all space, all unfolding and evolving of what is. As Rabbi Heschel puts it, "Just to be is a blessing; just to live is holy." It is telling that the Hebrew word for blessing, *berakah,* is closely related to the word for create, *bara* (in its noun form, *beriyah*). This suggests that a creation is necessarily a blessing, is wrapped up as a blessing. There is no distrust of creation here. Furthermore, the very word for blessing in Hebrew also means "pool," and with the change of one vowel, to *berekah,* the word means a reservoir where camels kneel as a resting place. The images of a pool and a reservoir created by a desert people tell us all we need to know about the desirability behind a theology of blessing. The word for covenant, *beriyth,* is also directly related to the words for "create" and for "blessing." A covenant is a blessing agreement, a promise to bless and to return blessing for blessing.

If this be the case, namely that original blessing is behind all that is, what about the famous doctrine of original sin? There is no question whatsoever in my mind that among those who call themselves Christians, whether practicing or not, ninety-nine percent know about original sin; and barely one percent have ever in their lives heard about original blessing. This is the great price we have paid in the West for following a one-sided, fall/redemption theology. There is a genuine scandal involved in this dangerous distortion of life and of biblical data. The scandal is one of ignoring—and then despising—creation and those who love creation, such as Native American peoples or matriarchal religions. Even if original sin is to be taken literally, still the facts are as follows: that, if we take the universe to be about twenty billion years old, as scientists are advising us to do, then sin of the human variety is about four million years old, since that is how long humans have been around. But creation is 19,996,000,000 years older! Fall/redemption theology has ignored the blessing that creation is because of its anthropomorphic preoccupation with sin! The result has been, among other things, the loss of pleasure from spirituality, and with this loss the increase of pain, of injustice, of sado-masochism, and of distrust. Nineteen billion years before there was any sin on earth, there was blessing.

But let us take a closer look at this pivotal doctrine of original sin.

The concept is not a Jewish one. Even though the Jewish people knew Genesis for a thousand years before Christians, they do not read original sin into it. As the twentieth-century Jewish prophet Elie Wiesel points out, "The concept of original sin is alien to Jewish tradition." This is strong language—to call a doctrine "alien" that Christians believe they found in Jewish scriptures! But today biblical scholars who are themselves Christian agree that original sin is not found in the Bible. Herbert Haag, former president of the Catholic Bible Association of Germany and author of *Is Original Sin in Scripture?*, writes:

> The doctrine of original sin is not found in any of the writings of the Old Testament. It is certainly not in chapters one to three of Genesis. This ought to be recognized today, not only by Old Testament scholars, but also by dogmatic theologians. (21.19)

And, I insist, by spiritual theologians as well! For until we understand the very shakey biblical grounds on which original sin doctrine is based, we will never let go of it as our starting point for belief enough to let the true biblical starting point—that of Dabhar and original blessing—into our lives. Professor Haag goes on:

> The idea that Adam's descendants are automatically sinners because of the sin of their ancestor, and that they are already sinners when they enter the world, is foreign to Holy Scripture. (21.106)

We enter a broken and torn and sinful world—that is for sure. But we do not enter as blotches on existence, as sinful creatures, we burst into the world as "original blessings." And anyone who has joyfully brought children into the world knows this. As one person wrote me recently, describing the birth of her first grandchild, a natural childbirth she was privileged to witness, "Being present in the delivery room for the birth of my first grandchild and being the first person to hold him stands unrivaled for being the most awesome, numinous moment of my life. Time certainly stood still. Babies certainly are original blessings, but I never knew it as poignantly with my own four children."

According to Professor Haag,

> No man enters the world a sinner. As the creature and image of God he is from his first hour surrounded by God's fatherly love. Consequently, he is not at birth, as is often maintained, an enemy of God and a child of God's wrath. A man becomes a sinner only through his own individual and responsible action. (21.107)

47

Creation-centered mystics have always begun their theology with original blessing and not original sin. Julian of Norwich, for example, writes that "God never began to love us. We have been known and loved from without beginning." And Mechtild of Magdeburg shares the same conviction. "From the very beginning God loved us. The Holy Trinity gave itself in the creation of all things and made us, body and soul, in infinite love. We were fashioned most nobly." Meister Eckhart declares that when he was born "all creatures stood up and shouted: 'Behold! Here is God!' " It is not only for Jews that the doctrine of original sin is unfamiliar: Orthodox Christianity, which did not build its theology on Augustine, is very suspicious of Western Christianity's sliding into what can be called a doctrine of "original guilt." As Timothy Ware puts it,

> Most Orthodox theologians reject the idea of "original guilt," put forward by Augustine and still accepted (albeit in a mitigated form) by the Roman Catholic Church. Men automatically inherit Adam's corruption and mortality, but not his guilt: they are only guilty in so far as by their own free choice they imitate Adam.[7]

The distinction that Ware makes between sin and guilt is a very important one. And, as he points out, in a real sense original sin is not sin. A Western theologian who came from the East is St. Irenaeus, who is truly creation-centered and who claims that "God became human in order that humans might become God"—not so that original sin might be wiped away. The Fall is not basic to his theology. "Irenaeus did not therefore believe in Original Sin in the proper sense of the word. The inherited defect of the human race is represented as a grievous disability, but not as involving man in guilt or constituting him the object of God's wrath."[8]

One reason that Irenaeus, like the Jews, did not believe in original sin is that Irenaeus preceded Augustine by two hundred fifty years and no one believed in original sin until Augustine. Original sin is an idea that Augustine developed late in his life and, to his credit, it was not all that significant in his theology either. Sad to say, however, original sin grew to become the starting point for Western religion's flight from nature, creation, and the God of creation. Augustine's effort to find original sin in the scriptures was hopelessly flawed—he actually mistranslated the Bible in his zeal to prove his hypothesis—yet the doctrine still constitutes a starting point for fall/redemption spiritualities and fundamentalist theologies. In Paul's *Letter to the Romans* he says, "Therefore, as sin came into the world through one man and death through sin, and so death spread to all men *because all men sinned.*" Augustine translated this last phrase: "in whom all men sinned." And using a faulty Latin translation which left out the word "death" he translates as follows: "Through one man sin entered into the world and through sin, death, and thus spread to all men, in whom all have sinned." (*Contra Julianum*) Haag comments that Augustine's "interpretation, together with the whole weight of this personal confession of faith, entered into the history of Latin theology, and it lies at the basis of the Council of Trent's decree on original sin."[9]

It is well known that the Council of Trent insisted on the doctrine of original sin. To understand the relativity of what is cultural and what is clearly theological in a counciliar decision of the sixteenth century is not my purpose here, but I can say the following for certain:

1) Original blessing is far more ancient and more biblical a doctrine and ought to be the starting point for spirituality. The council did not deny this, nor could it, given today's Bible scholarship.

2) The Council of Trent never said what original sin means, and this leaves discussion wide open among theologians. The creation-centered tradition, while it does not begin its spirituality with original sin but with original blessing, does indeed have an understanding of original sin or the sin behind sin. From Meister Eckhart to Mary Daly, the sin behind all sin is seen as dualism. Separation. Subject/object relationships. Fractures and fissures in our relationships. Take any sin: war, burglary, rape, thievery. Every such action is treating another as an object outside oneself. This is dualism. This is behind all sin. Interestingly enough, this understanding of the sin behind sin is found in Eastern spiritualities as well, for example in Mahatma Gandhi.

> Gandhi held to the Buddhist and Jain view that all sins are modifications of *himsa*, that the basic sin, the only sin in the ultimate analysis, is the sin of separateness, or *attavada*. According to a Jain maxim, he who conquers this sin conquers all others.[10]

3) Augustine mixed his doctrine of original sin up with his peculiar notions about sexuality. Thus for him all begetting of children and all lovemaking were at least venially sinful because one "lost control." Gnosticism also defined original sin as human sensuality. Biblical spirituality cannot tolerate this put-down of the blessing that sexual-

49

ity and lovemaking are by veiled references to original sin. The sooner the churches put distance between themselves and Augustine's bad scriptural exegesis and translation and Augustine's put-down of women and of sexuality, the sooner original sin will find its proper and very minor role in theology.

4) Whatever is said of original sin, it is far less hallowed and original than are love and desire, the Creator's for creation and our parents' for one another. Our origin in the love of our parents and in their love-making, and the celebration of creation at our birth, are far, far more primeval and original in every sense of that word than is any doctrine of "original sin."

5) A word about doctrine. Doctrine is not the basis of faith or its starting point. Creation is the basis of trust, which is the biblical meaning of faith. Doctrine serves as a parameter, much like the sidelines in a soccer game, within which believers play out their faith. An experiential living out of faith births insight which later generations sometimes summarize as doctrine. When doctrine becomes a starting point for faith, I fear faith is already dead. Faith concerns action and trust and the best that right and left brain can bring together. Doctrine, which is left-brained, has a limited but useful role to play. Much as a painter needs a frame within which to paint the best picture she can, so doctrine allows persons to concentrate on in-depth play. One does not study the sidelines and call this knowing soccer; so one does not study doctrine and call this theologizing, much less living a spiritual life.

6) And, most importantly, since doctrine is for people, not people for doctrine, it is important to raise this question: How much pain and how much sin have come about because of an exaggerated emphasis on the doctrine of original sin? What trust is lost in oneself, in one's body, in the cosmos, when children are instructed that they came into the world as blotches on God's creation? As William Eckhardt has demonstrated in his substantial study on the psychology of compassion, he never found a compassionate adult who did not have a radical trust in human nature.[11] Does this help explain why compassion has played so puny a part in Christian theology and spirituality of late—because original sin has played so dramatic a part?

The doctrine of original sin plays special havoc on the *anawim*, on those whose self-trust and self-image are not supported by society at large. It is a veritable weapon in the hands of those bent on controlling others. I recently met a woman in her sixties at a conference who came up to me at the end of the day and said, "I have always wondered what I was being redeemed from. But I was afraid to ask." The haunting insecurity we can all feel from time to time in the face of existence is not put to rest, is not overcome by faith/trust, when there is this mysterious sin from our past that haunts us but about which "we are afraid to ask." The homosexual can quite easily understand his or her homosexuality as an original sin; the woman is encouraged to look at her sex as an original sin; to the black in a white society, his or her blackness is an original sin. And so it goes, on and on. The doctrine of original sin can itself contribute to sin.

Ashley Montagu believes that the evidence is now in that societies can indeed be unaggressive and cooperative if they choose to be. "Traditional ideas concerning human nature, especially the doctrine of 'original sin,' have led us into all sorts of disastrous activities," he comments, citing Professor Herbert J. Muller on the price we have paid in the West for beginning our cultural education with the doctrine of original sin.

> Throughout Christian history the conviction that man's birthright is sin has encouraged an unrealistic acceptance of remediable social evils, or even a callousness about human suffering. It helps to explain the easy acceptance of slavery and serfdom, and a record of religious atrocity unmatched by any other religion.[12]

Paul Ricoeur expresses similar misgivings about the cultural effects of original sin doctrines.

> The harm that has been done to souls, during the centuries of Christianity, first by the literal interpretation of the story of Adam, and then by the confusion of this myth, treated as history, with later speculations, principally Augustinian, about original sin, will never be adequately told.[13]

The churches are moving subtly away from Augustine's original sin hypothesis as is evident, for example, in the renewed theology of baptism which orients the sacrament properly so that it becomes a celebration of new life in Christ and in a voluntarily Christian community instead of being an occasion for removing original sin. For adults, of course, baptism becomes a sacrament for the removal of sin. The sooner the churches embrace the more primitive doctrine of original blessing, however, the more compassionate our living will be.

If creation is a blessing and a constantly original one, then our proper response would be to enjoy it. Pleasure is one of the deepest spiritual experiences of our lives. Ecstasy is the experience of God, as I tried to make clear in my *Whee! We, wee* book. (14.73-78) But pleasure does not come easily to a society inundated by consumer consciousness on the one hand and by original sin mentalities on the other. Ashley Montagu defines pleasure as "what we are pleased to do." Pleasure truly pleases and does not merely titillate. Today the true contemplative will teach us what it means to con-temple once again, i.e., to become so thoroughly one with what we love and enjoy that we make a holy tabernacle of the event. The true contemplative will teach us the art of savoring. For creation needs savoring more than it needs inventory-making, as Frederick Turner points out in his statement cited at the beginning of this section. If we savored more, we would buy less. We would be less compulsive, less unsatisfied. We would also work less and play more, and thus open up work opportunities to the many unemployed and underemployed in our culture. If we savored more we would communicate more deeply, relate more fully, compete less regularly, and celebrate more authentically. We would be relating more deeply to ourselves, to creation in all its blessedness, to history past and future, to the Now and to God. We would be more in touch with our moral outrage because our love of life would increase so dramatically that we would become less and less tolerant of death forces. The art of savoring is our prayer along the Via Positiva route: we befriend and pray creation by entering into it all in search of tasting its "honey-sweetness," to use Meister Eckhart's words. And, as Eckhart points out, "all honey-sweetness comes from God." The source of all authentic pleasure is God. Anyone who has taken time to savor the blessings of life knows that they are profoundly, deliciously, deeply sweet. And naturally so.

Pleasure has not always been advocated as an essential and indeed radical dimension to our spiritual lives. The fall/redemption tradition does not countenance a pleasure-oriented spirituality or indeed a consciousness of Via Positiva and blessing at all. Many Catholics, for example, will remember the all-too-familiar test of whether an action was a sin or not in that tradition. The question was, "Did you take pleasure in it?" The lesson learned, that the taking of pleasure is the sign of sin, plays havoc with any temptations one might have to entertain a biblical, blessing theology. That constantly-used word in wisdom literature, "delight," is replaced in one's unconscious by that word so often cheaply invoked by non-creation-centered spiritualists, "sin." The fall/redemption spiritual theologian Tanquerry begrudgingly talks in a rare instance about pleasure, and says: "The moderate enjoyment of pleasure if referred to its end—moral and supernatural—is not an evil."[14] It strikes me, however, that this sense of puny-minded pleasure is not pleasure at all! Why must pleasure be limited to being "moderate"? It is my experience that ecstasy is quite grand. And I prefer a biblical approach to pleasure, such as that of the psalmist who sings as he celebrates the pleasure we give God by our own pleasure.

> Glory for ever to Yahweh!
> May Yahweh find joy in what he creates,
> at whose glance the earth trembles,
> at whose touch the mountains smoke!
>
> I mean to sing to Yahweh all my life,
> I mean to play for my God as long as I live.
> May these reflections of mine give him pleasure,
> as much as Yahweh gives me! (Ps. 104:31-34)

How indeed can the psalmist know "how much pleasure Yahweh gives him" if he has not tasted the pleasure? Our calling requires us to return pleasure for pleasure.

A theology of blessing is a theology about a different kind of power. Not the power of control or the power of being over or being under, but the power of fertility. Blessing is fertility to the people of Israel and to the Native American and other pre-patriarchal religions. This ongoing and fructifying dimension to the Dabhar or creative energy of God is captured by the prophet Isaiah: "Yes, as the rain and the snow come down from the heavens and do not return without watering the earth, making it yield and giving growth to provide seed for the sower and bread for the eating, so the word that goes from my mouth does not return to me empty, without carrying out my will and succeeding in what it was sent to do." (Isa. 55:10,11) Just how fertile is creation and the Creator's imagination in making it so? Annie Dillard marvels at the "extravagance" of nature's ways. An example she gives is as follows: A single rye plant in four months can grow 378 miles of root and 14 billion root hairs. In one cubic inch of soil the length of these root hairs would total 6000 miles. Now that is fertility!

The New Testament too praises this new power that blessing/fertility is. In Luke's Gospel Mary the mother of Jesus is praised for her fertility. "Of all women you are the most blessed, and blessed is the fruit of your womb." Mary is blessed because she believed in the promise or covenant of blessing. "Blessed is she who believed that the promise made by the Lord would be fulfilled." (1:43,45) Moreover, the Beatitudes that Jesus recites for all to enter into are a litany of blessings. "Blessed are those who hunger and thirst after justice, for they will be satisfied." (Matt. 5,6) The prophetic tradition is deeply a tradition of blessing in the midst of pain, of hope in the face of injustice. Jeremiah writes, for example:

> They will come and shout for joy on Mount Sion,
> they will stream to the blessings of the Lord,
> to the flocks of sheep and the herbs.
> Their life will be like a watered garden.
> They will never be weary again. (Jer. 31:12)

I believe that one reason why blessing is so integral a motif to the prophets is that blessing is itself a kind of deliverance. (Biblical scholars can make far too much of the distinction between blessing and deliverance just as many have of the distinction between nature and history). Blessing delivers because it builds trust and pride and hope—and these are absolutely essential ingredients by which a people can *deliver themselves* and thus be responsible instruments of a blessing/saving God.

Given this overwhelming evidence that our scriptures are concerned with original blessing much more than with original sin, a worthwhile question to ask—for it may help prevent such theological distortion in the future—is the following: Why has original sin played so important a role for sixteen centuries of Western Christian theology, an even more important role than it did for its originator, St. Augustine? I believe that the basic reason is political. I believe that an exaggerated doctrine of original sin, one that is employed as a starting point for spirituality, plays kindly into the hands of empire-builders, slavemasters, and patriarchal society in general. It divides and thereby conquers, pitting one's thoughts against one's feelings, one's body against one's spirit, one's political vocation against one's personal needs, people against earth, animals, and nature in general. By doing this it so convolutes people, so confuses and preoccupies them, that deeper questions about community, justice, and celebration never come to the fore. Blessing is politically dangerous; the art of savoring is politically suspect; pleasure is too often a route to sharing the pleasure—which is justice-making. And

54

justice-making conjures up passionate criticism of what is. As W. H. Auden put it, "As a rule it was the pleasure-haters who became unjust." The prophets and others who disturbed the status quo did not seek only justice. They sought blessing, blessing for the many, not just for the few. It paid and paid well and is still paying well (witness, for example, the financial success of fundamentalist preachers on television) to keep guilt going and self-doubt going and distrust going, all in the name of an avenging God. To drown out the God of blessing is a powerful political act. But such silencing cannot go on forever. The God of Dabhar and of blessing does not tolerate being dammed up for long. She has too much Eros, too much love of life, too much desire to share the blessing and delight in our response to it. God's ecstasy will not forever be forgotten. Is that what Jesus the Christ came to remind us about?

Another reason why the prophets preach a blessing theology is that pleasure, not will power and coercion, is how you most deeply transform people. When the human race learns—if it learns soon enough—that it is to our pleasure to outlaw war, then war will be outlawed. As Gestalt psychologist Fritz Perls put it, "The organism does not move by will, but by preference." A blessing theology names our deepest preferences and encourages us to name them and celebrate them. Thomas Aquinas also taught that people are changed more by pleasure than by anything else. I have often found this to be the case. Take my spiritual director, who is my dog, for example. If he wants to chase a squirrel in the backyard and I don't want him to, what are my options? Well, there is, because I live in America, the military option: I can shoot him, or the squirrel, or both. I could lock him in a closet; I could reason with him, though I would be sure to lose. My best option is to know him well enough to know a pleasure (blessing) greater to him than chasing a squirrel in the backyard. It happens that I do. To be invited out the front door for a walk is a greater pleasure. The result? He forgets the squirrel in the backyard. Yes, pleasure and blessing will indeed change people and structures. I believe that one price the West has paid for ignoring blessing theology is that Christianity has very few tactics for social change. This is because we have not contempled with pleasure, have not entered fully into it, have not savored deeply enough. When we do, we will learn what simple living means. And we will resist strongly the efforts of secular *or* religious hucksters to define for us what our greatest pleasures are. We will make connections again—i.e., be healed and therefore saved—to creation itself and to our proper but not arrogantly superior place in it. We will marvel at the gift and mystery that creation is, as Jacques Cousteau does from his con-templing, for example, with the whale.

> The cycle of life and death is especially impressive when embodied in these giants of the deep. These creatures, with their fifty-foot bodies and their forty or fifty tons of flesh, are not built to a human scale; and yet, they breathe, they love, and they suffer as we do. Our lives and theirs, though different, are not finally distinct.[15]

Like Jesus, we will draw divine lessons from such divine parables.

3 HUMILITY AS EARTHINESS: OUR EARTHINESS AS A BLESSING ALONG WITH PASSION AND SIMPLICITY

Wine flowing straight to my Beloved,
as it runs on the lips of those who sleep.
I am my Beloved's,
and his desire is for me.
Come, my Beloved,
let us go to the fields.
We will spend the night in the villages,
and in the morning we will go to the vineyards.
— *Song of Songs* 7:9-12

The primary intention of the Canticle of Canticles deals with human sexual love—the experience of it, its delights, and its power.
— *Roland E. Murphy*[1]

Holy persons draw to themselves all that is earthly....
The earth is at the same time mother,
She is mother of all that is natural,
mother of all that is human.
She is the mother of all,
for contained in her
are the seeds of all.
— *Hildegarde of Bingen*

All praise be yours, my Lord, through Sister Earth, our mother,
Who feeds us in her sovereignty and produces various fruits
and colored flowers and herbs.
— *Francis of Assisi*

Path I

Our sensuality is grounded in Nature,
in Compassion and in Grace.
In our sensuality, God is.
God is the means
whereby our Substance
and our Sensuality
are kept together
so as never to be apart.
                    —Julian of Norwich

Do not disdain your body.
For the soul is just as safe in its body
as in the Kingdom of Heaven.
                    —Mechtild of Magdeburg

You cannot devalue the body and value the soul—or value
anything else. The isolation of the body sets it into direct
conflict with everything else in Creation.
Nothing could be more absurd than to despise the body and
yet yearn for its resurrection.
                    —Wendell Berry (3.107f)

Sex is the manifestation of the driving life force energy of the
universe. Sexuality is an expression of the moving force that
underlies everything and gives it life.
                    —Starhawk[2]

The nuclear peril is usually seen in isolation from the threats
to other forms of life and their ecosystems, but in fact it should
be seen as the very center of the ecological crisis.
                    —Jonathan Schell (33.111)

The earth does not belong to people; people belong to the
earth. . . . This earth is precious to the Creator and to harm the
earth is to heap contempt upon its Creator. . . . Our dead never
forget this beautiful earth, for it is the mother of the red
people. We are part of the earth and it is part of us.
                    —Chief Seattle[3]

The sensual is a reality in itself.
                    —Susan Griffin (20.751)

The soul loves the body.
　　　　　—Meister Eckhart

Our faith imposes on us a right and duty to throw ourselves
into the things of the earth.
　　　　　—Teilhard de Chardin[4]

God with honour hang your head,
Groom, and grace you, bride, your bed
With lissome scions, sweet scions,
Out of hallowed bodies bred.
　　　　　—Gerard Manley Hopkins[5]

Do you have a body? Don't sit on the porch!
Go out and walk in the rain!
　　　　　—Kabir (6.32)

The fall/redemption spiritual tradition has taught us all what it
means by humility. The fall/redemption spiritual theologian Tanquerry advises the following prayer of humility: "May I know Thee,
O Lord, that I may love Thee; May I know myself, that I may
despise myself."[6] Indeed, this definition of humility from that tradition has made its way into the English language, where, for example,
Webster's Dictionary defines humility as "not assertive," being "in a
spirit of deference or submission," or "ranking low in a hierarchy or
scale." The first synonym it offers is "insignificant."

The creation-centered spiritual tradition does not define humility
in that fashion. Meister Eckhart, who repeats this message dozens
of times in his writings, points out that the word "humility" comes
from the word *humus* or earth. In the creation tradition, then, to be
humble means to be in touch with the earth, in touch with one's own
earthiness, and to celebrate the blessing that our earthiness, our
sensuality, and our passions are. To deny our earthiness is to bottle
up deep and divine energies of creativity and imagination, as
Berdyaev points out. "Decadent humility keeps humanity in a condition of repression and oppression, chaining its creative power."
(16.22) It therefore leads to violence, a subject/object relationship
with our own passions that finds its fulfillment in a perverse power-
over or power-under relationship, that is, in sado-masochism. (14.1-28)
A decadent humility, one that is out of touch with earthiness,
represses the child in one and around one. To repress the child is to
repress the divine. Edna Hong puts it this way:

The senses you created in us are on the side of spirit.
Lord, creation-callousness
is not separate from Kingdom-callousness!
Blunting, dulling, and deadening
the senses of Child,
killing the sentient Child,
is not only a sin against nature—
It is a sin against the Kingdom![7]

The theme of blessing and fertility which we celebrate as so integral to Dabhar and to the Via Positiva cannot be experienced without earthiness and sensuousness. An arrogant type of humanity has told us that knowledge is of the head or soul (Descartes located the soul in the pineal gland in the brain!) and that our passions and feelings are inferior and always needing to be controlled. Indeed, Thomas à Kempis, in his widely distributed *Imitation of Christ*, uses the word "passion" fourteen times but *always* pejoratively. He counsels people to "fight against your passions," to "get rid of passion and desire," pray to be "set free from evil passions." He feels "weighed down by passions," "oppressed by many an evil passion," and complains that his readers' passions are "so unsubdued," and "ill-regulated." Clearly this writer and the tradition he represents believed that our passions are not a blessing but a curse.

Instead of controlling passions such as desire and moral outrage, which is anger, Eckhart and the creation tradition counsel us to "put on them the bridle of love." What does this mean? A bridle is a steering device one puts on a presumably energetic horse. While the ascetic tradition would control the stallion in each of us by cutting off a leg or by putting a hundred-pound sack of potatoes on its back, Eckhart advises a bridle of love. Don't cut back on the passion, we are urged; rather learn to make it work for you, to take you and the community into arenas where it needs to go. The bridle is itself a loving bridle, not an instrument of torture or of punishment. Good advice, this. It is time we practiced it. Eckhart explains why he believes that "asceticism is of no great importance." It sets up dualisms that interfere with the attitude of blessing we ought to have toward our passions and feelings. It creates "more instead of less self-consciousness." Gandhi and Martin Luther King, Jr., also believed that "truth-force" demanded bodily contact. It would

include the body and the meeting of bodies: the facing of the opponent "eye to eye," the linking of arms in defensive and advancing phalanxes, the body "on the line:" all these confrontations symbolize the conviction that the solidarity of unarmed bodies remains a leverage and a measure even against the cold and mechanized gadgetry of the modern state.[8]

Barry Lopez, who like Gandhi disciplined his body but did not seek to control it, lived among wolves and laments what the human race loses by going to great lengths to eliminate the animal in us.

> We who have largely lost contact with wild animals, have indeed gone to lengths to distinguish ourselves from them, can easily miss the significance of such a view of the human world in which the natural world is so deeply reflected. The view is fully integrated. It produces, often, an utter calm, a sense of belonging. It is this need, I think, that people most wish to articulate when they speak of "a return to the earth." (24.113)

Can we believe that our earthiness and sensuality and passions are a blessing? Or are we condemned forever to a hostile relationship with our very nature and therefore with all of nature? Here, in the topic of humility healthily understood, lies just one very practical application of the doctrine of original blessing that we explored in the previous section.

The opposite of arrogance is indeed humility—but not the decadent humility of denying one's gifts and uniqueness. Rather, the healthy humility of remaining true and close to the earth and the things of the earth. Simple living. Simplicity is today's very accurate synonym for humility. For the earth and its simple creatures—the vine and the water, the dogs and the flowers, the birds and the fishes—do not tolerate arrogance for long. I recall that, when the Three Mile Island disaster first happened and the country sat on edge waiting for the news to break concerning the future of the state of Pennsylvania, a local resident was interviewed. He had tears in his eyes and said, "The birds have all gone." Those arrogant people (some of whom are still authoring science textbooks) who tell us that the notion of wisdom in nature is "sentimental"[9] ought to reflect on the facts of life, the truly bottom line, that nature has to teach us all. Humility, true humility, recognizes this.

Psychologist Carl Gustav Jung has made explicit the connection between the repression of our earthiness—our fear of mud—and the killing of creativity. He writes:

> Life itself flows from springs both clear and muddy. Hence all excessive "purity" lacks vitality. A constant striving for clarity and differen-

tiation means a proportionate loss of vital intensity precisely because the muddy elements are excluded. Every renewal of life needs the muddy as well as the clear. This was evidently perceived by the great relativist Meister Eckhart.[10]

Jung very appropriately relates this movement to creativity and Eros, a life of "vital intensity," to the Mother Earth of feminist spiritualities. Eckhart, who talks about God as "a great underground river"—and an underground river passes through mud to rise to where humanity dwells—was steeped in this Mother Earth spirituality.

The faith of Israel too has been extolled by biblical theologians such as Von Rad for its "wonderful earthiness."[11] So undualistic is Jewish spirituality—the spirituality from which Jesus sprang—that in Hebrew there does not even exist a word for body or for soul. The living person versus the deadening or disspirited person is what is at stake in Hebrew phrases that we often mistranslate as "flesh versus spirit" or "body versus soul." For the Jews, the carnal is not opposed to the spiritual. "Because he is not a dualist and because he lacks the concept 'body,' the Hebrew has a sense and a love of the carnal because he has a sense of the spiritual and perceives the presence of the spiritual *within* the carnal."[12]

The celebration of vine and wine, of vineyard and fertility, of kisses and lovemaking in wisdom literature, as for example in the *Song of Songs*, is no superficial praise of our authentic humility. Efforts by dualistic theologians through the ages to sublimate the eroticism of Israel's sacred books by saying that the writers are actually extolling the relationship of the soul to Christ or of God to the Church is as bad psychology as it is bad exegesis. Indeed, it is exegesis at its worst, reading into the Jewish tradition a dualism between soul and body and an alien original sin mentality that are not there. In the *Song of Songs* the phrase "to drink wine" means "to make love" (5:1; 8:2). The kisses of the beloved are celebrated as being like the finest wine (7:10), the woman's breasts are like "clusters of the vine" (7:9), and the reference to vineyards in blossom can refer not only literally to the time of year but also to the arousal of love and its quest for satiation (2:15). Very likely the woman speaking of "my very own vineyard" is in fact speaking of her sexual parts.[13] After steeping himself in the wisdom tradition, Von Rad emerges to call wisdom itself "almost voluptuous." (43.168) True humility—especially in today's violent and superficially sexual atmosphere—would return to an erotic and truly sensual way of living and of savoring the gifts of our earthy lives.

For Christians, the mystery of the Incarnation consists in the revelation that God became totally enfleshed, as thoroughly animalized as ourselves. The heresy of Docetism, which is often though subtly taught in the name of fall/redemption Christolotries, would deny Jesus his humanity, his earthiness, his sensuality and sexuality; in short, his true humility: his relation to the earth and to earth's simple folk. Yet if we know anything for certain about Jesus, it is that he was in love with the birds of the air, the lilies of the field, the fishes, sheep, and goats, the sun and the rain falling, the mustard seeds and the fig trees. That is to say, he was in love with them enough to pray to them, which means to enter into them, to be transformed by them. This is why his parable teachings are so steeped in relationship with his creaturely brothers and sisters.

Augustine was fond of saying that "God is never disturbed by any passions." This tells us a lot more about Augustine, it seems to me, than about God. Indeed, in his autobiography, *Confessions*, Augustine tells us how, as an adolescent at the public baths with his father, he was mortified by his first sexual arousal. Being disturbed by his passions haunted Augustine all his life and, unfortunately, it has also haunted much of the Western church that took his fall/ redemption theology as gospel. The creation-centered tradition does not think so suspiciously about passion—indeed, Thomas Aquinas taught that human virtues are actually contained in the passions[14], and Eckhart taught that "no deed is accomplished without passion."[15] Julian of Norwich, too, holds a different view of God's relationship to our earthiness than does Augustine. Body and soul, she declares, form a "glorious union," and our holy sensuality begins at the very moment of our original blessing. "It is when our soul is breathed into our body that we are made sensual." When it comes to imaging the relationship of body and soul, she says simply, "Let each of them take help from the other." Mutuality is the key, not control and not up-manship. Indeed, in quite Jewish fashion, Julian questions the very use of the word "soul" as distinct from body and person. "As regards our sensuality, it can rightly be called our soul because of the union it has with God." God, far from being put off by our sensuality, "is in our sensuality." We are to treat our sensuality and earthiness kindly and harmoniously, for they are "founded in nature, in compassion and in grace." God does not stand on the sidelines of our struggle with being whole; God for Julian actually constitutes the "glue" or the salvific and whole-making power of our wholeness. "God is the mean which keeps the sub-

stance and the sensuality together, so that they will never separate."
One senses in reading Julian that she has taken seriously the biblical
injunction, "What God has joined together let no person tear asunder."
In this case, it is the marvelous joining or "knitting" (Julian's phrase)
of humanity and creation, body and soul, God and sensuality.

Julian is not abstract or abstracted in her naming of the holiness
that is our earthiness. She goes so far as to relay how "the simplest
natural functions of our body" such as going to the bathroom are
acts of co-creation with God. Interestingly enough, this section in
Julian's writings has been edited out in many modern versions of
her works, but it is very much present in the critical edition of her
manuscript. She writes:

> A person walks upright, and the food in her body is shut in as if in
> a well-made purse. When the time of her.need arrives, the purse is
> opened and then shut again in most fitting fashion. *And it is God who
> does this,* as it is shown when he says that he comes to us in our
> humblest needs. For God does not despise what he has made, nor
> does he disdain to serve us in the simplest natural functions of our
> body, for love of the soul which he created in his own likeness. For as
> the body is clad in the cloth, and the flesh is clad in the skin, and the
> bones in the flesh, and the heart in the chest, so are we, soul and
> body, clad and enclosed in the goodness of God. (Italics mine.)

The moving image with which she ends this powerful reminder of
what healthy humility can mean confirms Jung's observation about
the material nature of a creation-centered theology. The image is
obviously one of maternal embracing. Not only does our God embrace us in this fashion, but also all the levels of our being do so one
to another. True humility will celebrate the most basic of life's
blessings (a healthy bowel movement is among these) and will thus
root up the arrogance of the chauvinism whereby humanity tries to
cut itself off from the rest of creation. For the letting go of waste
products is a divine act that all creatures share in common. Clearly,
Julian belongs in the same spiritual line as Hildegarde, who declared two centuries earlier, "The truly holy person welcomes all
that is earthly." And between them, nourished on the same beautiful energy, was Mechtild of Magdeburg, who wrote:

> Do not disdain your body. For the soul is just as safe in its body as in
> the Kingdom of Heaven—though not so certain. It is just as daring—
> but not so strong; just as powerful—but not so constant; just as
> loving, but not so joyful; just as gentle, but not so rich; just as holy,
> but not yet so sinless; just as content, but not so complete.

Hildegarde draws out the interconnectedness that one comes to when one learns to reverence human earthiness and thus the earthiness of the rest of creation. "Humankind needs a body that at all times honors and praises God. This body is supported in every way through the earth. Thus the earth glorifies the power of God." Hildegarde also makes the link explicit between earthiness and fertility, earthiness and blessing. And the ultimate blessing is the coming to earth of the Blessed One.

> The earth is at the same time mother, she is mother of all that is natural, mother of all that is human. She is the mother of all, for contained in her are the seeds of all. The earth of humankind contains all moistness, all verdancy, all germinating power. It is in so many ways fruitful. All creation comes from it. Yet it forms not only the basic raw material for humankind, but also the substance of the incarnation of God's son.

Surely a return to a spiritual tradition that understands humility as earthiness promises a blessed and creative New Creation! Here there is hope that we might come to our senses and let life on earth and in the good earth go on. Poet and farmer Wendell Berry puts the issue of what I have been calling humility in the following manner.

> I have been groping for connections—that I think are indissoluble, though obscured by modern ambitions—between the spirit and the body, the body and other bodies, the body and earth. . . . It is impossible to care for each other more or differently than we care for the earth. . . . There is an uncanny *resemblance* [sic] between our behaviour toward each other and our behaviour toward the earth. Between our relation to our own sexuality and our relation to the reproductivity of the earth, for instance. (31.123f)

Thomas Berry reports that in America today four billion tons of topsoil are lost every year. We assault the land just as we assault our bodies. We deeply require an earthy spirituality.

4 COSMIC, UNIVERSALIST: HARMONY, BEAUTY, JUSTICE AS COSMIC ENERGIES

From coast to coast, desert to woodland, the Native peoples perceive themselves to be an integral part of the Creation. Native languages talk of the Creation in family terms such as "Mother Earth," "Grandmother Moon," "The Grandfather winds."[1]

Every added protection against the natural world contributes its bit to the steadily building illusion of independence from nature, so that in time that greatest of illusions is erected: the omnipotence of man.
    —*Frederick Turner (41.25)*

When religion lost the cosmos, society became neurotic. And we needed to invent psychology to deal with the neurosis.
    —*Otto Rank (7.30)*

Free thinker, do you think you are the only thinker on this earth in which life blazes inside all things? Your liberty does what it wishes with the powers it controls, but when you gather to plan, the universe is not there.
    —*Gérard de Nerval*

It is almost a commonplace today to find people who, quite naturally and unaffectedly, live in the explicit consciousness of being an atom or a citizen of the universe. This collective awakening must inevitably have a profound religious reaction on the mass of mankind—either to cast down or to exalt.
    —*Teilhard de Chardin*[2]

The most important function of art and science is to awaken the cosmic religious feeling and keep it alive.
    —*Albert Einstein*

One should identify with the universe itself.
    —*Simone Weil*

Mystical experience is the mirror image of negative paranoia. It sees "the universe is a conspiracy organized for my benefit."
  —*Andrew Weil, M.D.*[3]

I'm not into isms and asms. There isn't a Catholic moon and a Baptist sun. I know the universal God is universal.... I feel that the same God-force that is the mother and father of the pope is also the mother and father of the loneliest wino on the planet.
  —*Dick Gregory*

a touch is enough to let us know
we're not alone in the universe, even in sleep
  —*Adrienne Rich (30.30)*

If, in a nuclear holocaust, anyone hid himself deep enough under the earth and stayed there long enough to survive, he would emerge into a dying natural enviornment. The vulnerability of the environment is the last word in the argument against the usefulness of shelters: there is no hole big enough to hide all of nature in.
  —*Jonathan Schell (33.61)*

The exhilarating quest for discovery, the search to find what magic lies beyond the stars and inside the atom, is at once wonderfully insatiable and wonderfully satisfying. We cannot find happiness in contemplating ourselves; but we can find it in contemplating infinity. Reaching out, with our imaginations, toward its majesty, it will in turn embrace us and inspire us.
  —*Jacques Cousteau*[4]

For Gandhi, to become divine is to become attuned in thought, feeling and act to the whole of creation.... *Dharma* or morality cannot be ultimately divorced from *rta* or cosmic order.
  —*Raghavan Iyer (22.91,100)*

The creative Wisdom of all things has established marvelous and ineffable harmonies by which all things come together in a concord or friendship or peace or love or however else the union of all things can be designated.
  —*John the Scot*[5]

All praise be yours, my Lord, through Sister Moon and Stars;
All praise be yours, my Lord, through Brothers Wind and Air;
All praise be yours, my Lord, through Sister Water.
                —Francis of Assisi

The scope, the casual irresponsibility, and the cruelty of wolf killing is something else. I do not think it comes from some base, atavistic urge, though that may be a part of it. I think it is that we simply do not understand our place in the universe and have not the courage to admit it.
                —Barry Lopez (24.196)

Humanity has reached the biological point where it must either lose all belief in the universe or quite resolutely worship it. This is where we must look for the origin of the present crisis in morality. . . . Henceforth the world·will only kneel before the organic centre of its evolution.
                —Teilhard de Chardin (40.110)

The New Prosperity requires a new language. This new language is primarily the language of the earth, a language of living relationships that extend throughout the universe.
                —Thomas Berry[6]

I have often said that God is creating the entire universe fully and totally in this present now. Everything God created six thousand years ago—and even previous to that—as he made the world, God creates now all at once.
                —Meister Eckhart

Earth and heaven are in us.
                —Mahatma Gandhi (22.176)

Glance at the sun. See the moon and the stars.
Gaze at the beauty of earth's greenings.
Now, think.
What delight God gives to humankind
with all these things. . . .
All nature is at the disposal of humankind.
We are to work with it. For
without we cannot survive.
                —Hildegarde of Bingen

The truly wise person
kneels at the feet of all creatures
and is not afraid to endure
the mockery of others.
                    —*Mechtild of Magdeburg*

A creation-centered spirituality is cosmic. It is open, seeking, and explorative of the cosmos within the human person and all creatures and of the cosmos without, the spaces between creatures that unite us all. The more and more deeply one sinks into our cosmic existence the more fully one realizes the truth that there does not exist an inside and an outside cosmos but rather one cosmos: we are in the cosmos and the cosmos is in us. As John Muir put it, "When we try to pick out anything by itself, we find it hitched to everything else in the Universe. . . . The whole wilderness is unity and interrelation is alive and familiar."[7] All things are interrelated because all things are microcosms of a macrocosm. And it is all in motion, it is all en route, it is all moving, vibrant, dancing, and full of surprises. It is all a blessing, an ongoing and fertile blessing with a holy, salvic history of about twenty billion years.

This consciousness of a cosmic spirituality is alive and vibrant wherever creation-centered spirituality is allowed to play its tune. This is evident from the testimonies of such diverse poets and thinkers as I have presented in the prelude to this theme. Hildegarde of Bingen, so steeped in the psychology of a microcosm/macrocosm focus, sings as follows:

> The fire has its flame and praises God.
> The wind blows the flame and praises God.
> In the voice we hear the word which praises God.
> And the word, when heard, praises God.
> So all of creation is a song of praise to God.

The Celtic theologian John the Scot (who in fact was an Irishman) writes, "By universe I mean God and creation." For the medieval tradition of microcosm/macrocosm, the cosmos is not an abstraction, nor is it an enemy, an object to run from. Rather, the cosmos is a gift, a maternal womb wherein we all play, as it was for the biblical writers of wisdom literature, for example. M. D. Chenu comments on what the cosmos meant to our medieval ancestors. "The whole penetrates each of its parts; it is one universe; God conceived it as a

69

unique, living being, and its intelligible Model is itself a whole.... The universitas is a cosmos; its contemplation is a source of delight."[8] Imagine—the cosmos is alive, a "unique, living being," and it is a pleasure—"a source of delight"! The universe itself is sacramental, "filled with God." Dabhar is effective in its creativity and utters the cosmos as its ongoing work of art. To explore the cosmos is to explore God. Thus Honorius of Autun wrote in about 1125:

> All in God's creation gives great delight to anyone looking upon it, for in some things there is beauty, as in flowers; in others healing, as in herbs; in others food, as in produce; in others meaning, as in snakes and birds.... The supreme Artisan made the universe like a great zither upon which he placed strings to yield a variety of sounds.... A harmonious chord is sounded by spirit and body, angel and devil, heaven and hell, fire and water, air and earth, sweet and bitter, soft and hard, and so are all other things harmonized.[9]

Again, we feel the assurance of pleasure and delight that a cosmically aware spirituality teaches; we see the image of the Creator as a craftsperson who has made the universe like one great zither, and as a refreshingly nonjudgmental kind of God. And the result of all this cosmic music? Harmony and harmonizing, of course.

There is in the sense of cosmos a sense of balance, of harmony, and therefore of justice. For the word "cosmos" is in fact the Greek word for "order." A cosmic spirituality is a justice spirituality, for it cares with a heartfelt caring for harmony, balance, and justice. Indeed, injustice is precisely a rupture in the order of the cosmos, a rupture in creation itself. The Hebrew people believed that the entire cosmos stood on two pillars: a pillar of justice and a pillar of righteousness, which was justice internalized. "Justice and right are the pillars of your throne." (Ps. 89:14) If a crack or rupture appears in either of these two pillars, then the entire cosmos becomes off center, off balance. Injustice then is a cosmic issue. Many of the laments of the psalmist and the prophets voice the fear that human injustice will in fact jeopardize the cosmos itself. "All the foundations of the earth are shaken," the psalmist shudders, "when the weak and the orphaned are deprived of justice. (Ps.82:3-5)

Yahweh is praised for making creation a balanced or ordered cosmos. "He has imposed an order on the magnificent works of his wisdom, he is from everlasting." (Sirach 42:21) While we in our culture are used to imagining justice as a scale, I believe a more useful image of the cosmos as justice would be a mobile such as one hangs from a

ceiling fixture. The variety and interdependence, the motion and
wonder-filledness of a mobile is a fine metaphor of how the cosmos
does indeed harmonize and hold together. "All things hold together
by means of his word." (Sirach 43:28) Architect Louis I. Kahn
expresses his deep experience of the cosmic order which just is.

> I tried to find what Order is. I was excited about it, and I wrote many,
> many words of what Order is. Every time I wrote something, I felt it
> wasn't quite enough. If I had covered, say, two thousand pages with
> just words of what Order is, I would not be satisfied with this
> statement. And then I stopped by not saying what it is, just saying,
> "Order is." And somehow I wasn't sure it was complete until I asked
> somebody, and the person I asked said, "You must stop right there.
> It's marvelous; just stop right there, saying, 'Order is.' "[10]

Hildegarde describes what happens when portions of the cosmic
mobile are badly treated out of human injustice. "The elements
themselves cry out to their creator in a scream of agony, for they
have been perverted by the sins of humankind." She speaks out
forcefully on behalf of the land around Three Mile Island, for
example, or the waters and earth of Michigan poisoned by the
dumping of PCBs and dioxins: "As often as the elements are stained
through the mishandling of humans, God nevertheless cleanses
them through the sufferings and pains of those same human creatures."
The cosmos keeps a ledger—not God; and the cosmic order will not
in the long run tolerate human greed, human indifference to its
beauties and its laws of balance and harmony, or human injustice.

To speak of the cosmos is not to speak of something very big "out
there." It is to awaken a way of seeing, a way of living and of consciousness that in fact every human person is capable of. It is a
psychology in itself, the micro/macrocosmic vision of the world. Paul
Ricoeur speaks to this truth when he writes, "To manifest the 'sacred'
on the 'cosmos' and to manifest it *in* the 'psych' are the same thing. . . .
Cosmos and Psyche are the two poles of the same 'expressivity'; I express myself in expressing the world; I explore my own sacrality in
deciphering that of the world."[11] Here dualisms of us and cosmos, of
inside and outside, of receiving and giving are broken through. Here
unity is celebrated. Here we see a connection between the cosmic
order implied in Dabhar understood from the Jewish tradition and
the sense of Tao in the Chinese tradition. Richard Wilhelm tells us
that all of Chinese philosophy is built

> on the premise that the cosmos and man, in the last analysis, obey the
> same law; that man is a microcosm and is not separated from the

macrocosm by any fixed barriers. The very same laws rule for the one as for the other. The psyche and the cosmos are to each other like the inner world and the outer world. Therefore man participates by nature in all cosmic events, and is inwardly as well as outwardly interwoven with them.[12]

Does this sense of a microcosmic/macrocosmic psychology explain why the word "Dabhar," which as we have seen applies to the cosmic creative energy of God, also means for the Hebrew the law, the commandments, the keeping of law? Is this not also what the medievals mean by "natural law"? Geologian Thomas Berry believes this is so and that the consequences for today's spiritual living are significant. "Any particular activity upon the earth must take its norm from the principles governing the total community. This is the new expression in our times of the natural law vision of the medieval world."[13]

Thomas Aquinas writes that every human person is *capax universi*, capable of the universe. He is inviting every human person to a cosmic awakening, a cosmic relationship. But the obverse of this statement needs to be meditated on as well: If every person is capable of the universe but if most people are not encouraged to find their relationship to the universe and to celebrate it, then what happens to persons and their institutions? They become sick and violent. For we were made for something cosmic and will not fit peacefully into anything much smaller. And when we try to build our lives around anything smaller than cosmos we become grotesque, and our institutions, be they religious or familial or educational or governmental, are asked to do too much. They become misshapen and malformed and turn into instruments of cosmic and personal destruction. The erotic love-of-being that Aquinas possessed, getting high on being, which is to say creation wherever it is, drove G. K. Chesterton to ask whether a recovery of Aquinas' love of being would "give the twentieth century back a cosmos."[14] Aquinas believed the entire cosmos was graced—he never spoke of a parochial kind of "Christian grace," for example. And he believed that ecstasy was everywhere in the cosmos—*"amor facit ecstasim,"* he said. This means "love," any kind of love—love of a tree or a violin or a person or the earth or ideas—produces ecstasy.

The French philosopher Gabriel Marcel finds a necessary connection between cosmos and wisdom when he explores both Eastern and Western sages. It has to do with the kind of order—the size of the order and harmony—that a society seeks. He writes:

The true function of the sage is surely the function of linking together, of bringing into harmony. I am not thinking only or even chiefly of the Greeks, but of classical China, of the China of Lao Tse, and what here strikes me in a really marvellous light is that the sage is truly linked with the universe. The texts are unmistakable and revealing: the order to be established in life—whether of the individual or of the city or of the empire—is in no way separable from the cosmic order.

Humankind cannot live wisely, sanely, or gently without the cosmos. Without the cosmos humanity becomes arrogant and manipulative in its idolatry of itself and its ways.

The important thing—and I think it is hardly possible to insist on it too much—is that in this outlook the true aim of knowledge and of life is to be integrated in the universal order, and not at all to transform the world by bringing it into subjection to the human will, to man's needs or his desires.[15]

Not only the Eastern religions Marcel refers to but also the pre-patriarchal religions of the West, including the Wikke and Native American, were steeped in cosmic awareness, cosmic celebration, and cosmic healing. Indeed, all ritual is meant to be a cosmic healing and celebration in these traditions. In the matrifocal religions, for example, the power of the microcosm is celebrated as a Goddess who "encircles the universe."

In the Craft, we do not *believe* in the Goddess—we connect with Her; through the moon, the stars, the ocean, the earth, through trees, animals, though other human being, through ourselves. She is here. She is within us all. She is the full circle: earth, air, fire, water, and essence—body, mind, spirit, emotions, change.[16]

Thus ritual in the Wikke tradition takes place invariably in circles and spirals to mirror the cosmos, which is also curved. When Native Americans gather to worship they too gather in circles and believe that each time ritual is celebrated in this way the center of the cosmos is found in the center point of the worshipping circle. Native Americans could not imagine worshipping without a cosmos.

The early Christians too celebrated the cosmic Christ, of whom Paul writes in Colossians, Ephesians, and Philippians, some of the oldest texts we possess of early Christian practice. The words recorded therein are hymns from the earliest Christian rituals. And they are cosmic hymns about cosmic healing and cosmic rejoicing. In Ephesians 1:3-23, Paul sings of how with Christ "everything in

73

the heavens and everything on earth" comes together (verse 10) and how Christ "fills the whole creation" (verse 23). A cosmic rebirth is celebrated in Christ. And in Colossians the hymn calls Christ "the first-born of all creation in whom were created all things in heaven and on earth." And through him Christians celebrate the reconciliation of "all things, . . . everything in heaven and everything on earth." (Col. 1:15, 20) The ancient Christian hymn from Philippians celebrates the rejoicing of the entire cosmos: "All beings in the heavens, on earth and in the underworld," reverence the name of Jesus and "every tongue acclaims" him. (Phil. 2:10,11) In his letter to the Romans, which surely represents Paul's most mature theology and which still antedates any of the gospels, the cosmic meaning of Christ's life and death are celebrated. "From the beginning till now the entire creation, as we know, has been groaning in one great act of giving birth; and not only creation but all of us who possess the first-fruits of the Spirit." (Rom. 8:22,23) Clearly, a cosmic spirituality and a cosmic awareness were not lacking in the earliest rituals of the Christians.

Not only in Paul do we celebrate a cosmic Christ, but in the gospels themselves. The prologues to the gospels, we are told by New Testament scholar Eugene La Verdiere, "constitute a synthesis of the entire work which follows."[17] But the cosmos is a critical category in the prologue to John's Gospel, as we saw in dealing with Dabhar or the universal creative energy of God. It is also very much present in chapters 1 through 3 of Luke, where it is stressed that Jesus represents a new creation birthed by the Holy Spirit of God the Creator. (Luke 1:35) All the beings of the cosmos join in the Good News:

> And suddenly with the angel there was a great throng of the heavenly host, praising God and singing: "Glory to God in the highest heaven, and peace to persons who enjoy his blessing." (Luke 2:13,14)

If the blessed fruit of Mary's womb represents a new creation, then Mary's womb represents the new cosmos over which the fruitful Spirit hovered and brought forth fruit.

We have seen cosmic wakefulness as integral to the wisdom of Eastern religions; of Native American and Wikke religions; of Israel. The Hebrew scriptures celebrate the cosmos wherein the Creator "sees to the ends of the earth, and observes all that lies under heaven." (Job 28:24) The whole universe sings the Creator's praises.

The spirit of the Lord indeed fills the whole world, and that which holds all things together knows every sound that is uttered to be—for this God created all. (Wisdom 1:7, 14)

When the Jews worshipped in the temple of Jerusalem they believed that the temple represented the center of the universe. In the New Testament and the earliest hymns of the Christian community and in medieval, creation-centered spirituality, the cosmos is present. But is it present today in Western religions? Is it present in Western worship? In the dominant rituals of the Protestant or Catholic churches? In our culture as a whole?

The sad answer to these questions is no. The cosmos has been lost in the West, and especially in religion and in its rituals. This is the truth of Otto Rank's observation that "when religion lost the cosmos society became neurotic and had to invent psychology to deal with the neurosis." There are many reasons for this sad and death-dealing loss of cosmos. One reason has been the Newtonian parts mentality of the scientific era of the past few centuries, which does not allow one to feel the mystery and the interconnectedness of microcosm and macrocosm. Another reason is patriarchal politics: the condemnation of Meister Eckhart's creation-centered spirituality was one example of a threatened ecclesial establishment trying to control those who suggest that life is bigger than controls, that life is cosmic for everyone. This repressive ecclesial attitude becomes blatantly political a few centuries later when a papal document tells us that "the pope is ruler of the universe."[18] Today the Pentagon and the White House and the Politburo are telling us the same thing: that they are rulers of the universe. The patriarchal play goes on, only the players change. And the play is a political play about who rules creation, who controls the cosmos.

But another reason why the West lost the cosmos is theological. The fall/redemption tradition does not trust the cosmos and does not celebrate it. Augustine has no cosmic Christ. Leo Scheffczyk writes:

The stress which Augustine lays on the immanent Trinity and its metaphysical and psychological interpretation helps to explain why he fails to develop the notion of Christ's cosmic role or arrive at a vision of the world in the framework of the economy of salvation.[19]

Philosopher R. A. Markus comments on Augustine's attitude toward nature, "The world of nature was not in itself an object of particular interest in Augustine. In Cosmological thinking of the kind to be found in Aristotle's *Physics*, for instance, he had little interest."[20] It is for this reason, because the cosmos is excluded from Augustine's thought, that the great historian of science Michael Polanyi writes:

> Scientific stringency, inflexibility ... may yet issue in a sweeping reaction against science as a perversion of truth. This happened before, with much less justification, in the fourth century, when St. Augustine denied the value of a natural science which contributed nothing to the pursuit of salvation. His ban destroyed interest in science all over Europe for a thousand years.[21]

The fall/redemption tradition is profoundly introspective, and introspection does not lead to cosmic relating or cosmic caring or cosmic celebration. Augustine's genius was in writing what is probably the first autobiography in the West. But here too lies his weakness. Too much guilt, too much introspection, too much preoccupation with law, sin, and grace rendered Augustine, and the theology that was to prevail in his name for sixteen centuries in the West, oblivious of what the Eastern Christian church celebrates as *theosis*, the divinization of the cosmos. The fall/redemption preoccupations with personal salvation destroy justice and cosmic connection-making. Eastern theologian Nicolas Berdyaev saw this clearly. "The central idea of the Eastern fathers was that of *theosis*, the divinization of all creatures, the transfiguration of the world, the idea of the cosmos, and not the idea of personal salvation." (16.123) And Lutheran theologian Krister Stendahl has written a classic article on how Augustine's "introspective conscience" has actually distorted the entire reading of the Bible by Western believers since Augustine's time. (39.78f) We have surely misunderstood Paul. "We look in vain for a statement in which Paul would speak about himself as an actual sinner," Stendahl writes. There are no such passages in all of Paul. He writes about his weaknesses, but not his personal sins. (39.91) For Augustine and the introspective tradition he launched in the West, ecstasy itself is interior only and is cut off from the cosmos. God becomes excessively interiorized. We will recall that for Aquinas, ecstasy is any experience of love. Not so for the Augustinian, Bonaventure. "Here we touch on the ultimate difference between ecstasy in Bonaventure and in Thomas: for the latter, ecstasy finds a universal application, but for the former ecstasy is limited to relations of the soul with God."[22] The fall/redemption tradition considers the soul to be an interior dimension to our bodies, held in check by the cage that our bodies are. This is not the case in a cosmic spirituality, where one knows from experience that the soul grows as large as we want it to grow. It expands. Thus Meister Eckhart can turn things around and declare that "the soul is not in the body so much as the body is in the soul." Once the concept of "soul" is released from the puny-mindedness that a fall/redemption distrust of body dictates, then cosmos can happen once again both as a psychic and cultural reality.

When humans cannot welcome the cosmos and reverence it as the blessing it is, then we will fight it. Along with everything else. An ad on television in our time boasts a man in suit and tie talking tranquilly of our need to buy an Atari game for adults and children alike in which we can "destroy entire planets." This kind of cosmic violence, being sold in the intimacy of our living rooms and bed-rooms by persons in suit and tie, could only happen in a civilization that is arrogant beyond imagining. But in the long run we are our own worst victims, victims of what Frederick Turner calls an "introspective civilization." (41.14) We are without cosmos, without myth, without ritual worthy of the name. No wonder we are cosmically sad, cosmically lonely, cosmically destructive in our military plans to rain death on the rest of the creation we know. It is time that religious believers of all creation-centered traditions unite forces to wake themselves, other believers, and the culture up. Before it is too late. For the creator God of the cosmos deserves such a thank you. So do our children, and theirs. The earth can no longer tolerate the sin of introspective religion.

I believe it is important, in order to understand both the appeal and the tragedy of a too-introspective spirituality, to grasp the critical distinction between an *inner* journey and an *inward* one. An inner journey is altogether healthy and necessary—we take *inner* journeys into ourselves, into our loved ones, into trees, into Mozart's music, into death, into pain and suffering and injustice, ideally all the time. To pray is to enter in, thus to make an inner journey. But a person who takes an *inward* journey looks only into himself or herself for God or for spiritual refreshment. It is introspection. There lies the death of cosmic spirituality, the death of cosmos, and the excessive quest for personal salvation. The world does not need more inward journeys; but there are no limits to the inner journeys we can make.

A cosmic spirituality is necessarily an ecumenical spirituality. As Dick Gregory remarked, there is no Catholic moon and Baptist sun.

When the cosmos is celebrated, barriers and manmade borders are seen for the relative truths they represent. Jacques Cousteau, commenting on what humanity has learned from satellite photographs of our earth, puts it this way.

> We are struck by the important difference between the way cartographers make our planet and the way it can be seen, given the perspective of the universe. There are no boundaries on the real planet Earth. No United States, no Soviet Union, no China, Taiwan, East Germany or West. Rivers flow unimpeded across the swaths of continents. The persistent tides—the pulse of the sea—do not discriminate; they push against all the varied shores on earth.[23]

The cosmos teaches us acceptance of diversity and awareness of the relativity of all human efforts to encapsulize, whether for nationalistic or for religious causes. Thus Nicholas of Cusa, the fifteenth-century cardinal and creation-centered mystic who worked tirelessly for union of Eastern and Western churches, wrote, "In the multiplicity of rites, there is only one religion." And he prayed,

> What do the living ask, but to live? What does he who is asked, but to be? You, therefore, who are the giver of life and of being, are also the One who seems to be sought in the various rites and in various fashions, who is called by various names, and who yet remains unknown and ineffable. ... Reveal your face and all peoples shall be saved.[24]

The universe teaches universality. Without cosmic consciousness all universality is torn asunder and only parochialisms, ego trips, and with them institutionalized violence reign. Approaching the cosmos with reverence and eagerness assures the approaching of others—especially those different from ourselves—with equal reverence. "Native thought has always held that all of the elements of the Creation are available for everyone. That everything was placed here for the benefit of everyone."[25]

When we recover the cosmos in our spirituality and let go of too much introspection, we recover the awesome nature of sin and cease trivializing sin as so often has happened in Western theology. We learn all over again that *the fate of the earth* is literally in our hands and not just the fate of an individualized and atomized and quite puny (because it has ignored the cosmos) soul. Injustice represents the ultimate cosmic rupture, the ultimate human tragedy, the ultimate in dualism. Wisdom literature was keen on this lesson, no less than were the prophets of Israel. Wisdom scholar Roland Murphy summarizes the "central concept" behind the greatest influence on Israeli wisdom literature, that of Egypt, in this way.

> The central concept is *ma'at*, translated as "justice," "order," etc. This is the divinely established harmony between nature and society, an order that must be preserved or restored, and hence the goal of human activity.[26]

What is the alternative to a wisdom that includes the cosmos and therefore justice? Chaos. Disorder. Extinction. Gestalt therapist Fritz Perls puts it this way:

> Cultures come—and go. And when a society is in clash with the universe, once a society transgresses the laws of nature, it loses its survival value. So, as soon as we leave the *basis of nature*—the universe and its laws— . . . we lose the possibility of existence.[27]

It is clear that our passion for life rightfully includes our passion for cosmos, for that divine harmony, balance, and ongoing order that Dabhar brings about and that for Christians is signified in the unity in Christ. Passion for cosmos is itself an aesthetic act, a commitment to beauty. For all our deep experiences, and certainly those of beauty and of pain, touch our cosmic depths. Every true artist also touches us in our cosmic depths and has first in one way or other been touched in a cosmic way. Artist Robert Henri testifies to this:

> Everything that is beautiful is orderly, and there can be no order unless things are in their right relation to each other. Of this right relation throughout the world beauty is born. . . . Art is the noting of the existence of order throughout the world, and so, order stirs imagination and inspires one to reproduce this beautiful relationship existing in the universe, as best one can. Everywhere I find that the moment order in nature is understood and freely shown, the result is nobility—the Irish peasant has nobility of language and facial expression; the North American Indian has nobility of poise, of gesture; nearly all children have nobility of impulse. This orderliness must exist or the world could not hold together.[28]

Here we have a powerful testimony to what a return to microcosm/ macrocosm will do for us, for welcoming the artist back to our midst and from our midst. Einstein's statement reverberates: "The most important function of art and science is to awaken the cosmic religious feeling and keep it alive." But can our religions of the West themselves become receptive to and big enough for a cosmic spirituality? If they cannot, then we are clearly doomed. As Henri warns, "It is disorder in the mind of man that produces chaos of the kind that brings about war.... Any right understanding of the proper relation of man to man and man to the universe would make war impossible."[28] If Otto Rank is correct that society became neurotic when religion lost the cosmos, does this mean that as religion substitutes creation theology for fall/redemption theology society will become sane? Were this to happen, we would put a lot of psychologists out of work and a lot of artists and celebrators of life and of ritual and of blessed earthiness to very good work indeed.

5 TRUST: A PSYCHOLOGY OF TRUST AND EXPANSION

[The world of wisdom literature in the Bible] is a world that is
thoroughly worthy of trust.
> —*Gerhard Von Rad (43.306)*

There is nothing in all the world more beautiful or significant
of the laws of the universe than the nude human body. In fact
it is not only among the artists but among all people that a
greater appreciation and respect for the human body should
develop.
> —*Robert Henri*[1]

Trust shows the way.
> —*Hildegarde of Bingen*

Trust in the Lord with all your heart. . . .
Happy is she who trusts in the Lord. . . .
He who trusts in the Lord will be enriched.
> —*Pss. 3:5; 16:20; 28:25*

Go your way. Your trust has healed you.
> —*Jesus Christ*

You can never trust God too much.
Why is it that some people do not bear fruit?
It is because they have no trust
either in God or in themselves.
> —*Meister Eckhart*

What God does first and best and most is to trust his people
with their moment in history. He trusts them to do what must
be done for the sake of his whole community.
> —*Walter Brueggemann*[2]

The immanence of God gives reason for the belief that pure
chaos is intrinsically impossible.
> —*Alfred North Whitehead*[3]

Often our trust is not full.
We are not certain that God hears us
Because we consider ourselves worthless and as nothing.
This is ridiculous
and the very cause of our weakness.
I have felt this way myself.
                    —*Julian of Norwich*

Where there is fear, there is no religion.
                    —*Mahatma Gandhi (22.138)*

Fear is driven out by perfect love.
                    —*1 John 4:18*

A devastating psychological corollary of the fall/redemption tradition is that religion with original sin as its starting point and religion built exclusively around sin and redemption does not teach trust. Such religion does not teach trust of existence or of body or of society or of creativity or of cosmos. It teaches both consciously and unconsciously, verbally and non-verbally, *fear*. Fear of damnation; fear of nature—beginning with one's own; fear of others; fear of the cosmos. In fact, it teaches distrust beginning with distrusting of one's own existence, one's own originality, and one's own glorious entrance into this world of glory and of pain. Mahatma Gandhi understood the weakness in such a distrusting religious faith when he said, "What is gained through fear lasts only while the fear lasts." (22.232) This means that religion built on fear must keep preaching its own fears in order to keep the religion going—such a religion will flee further and further from society, from the cosmos, from anything that is non-introspective. This keen observation from Gandhi also helps to explain why many people leave religion in the West: because they are growing up and growing out of fear and into trust, and very often they do not find Western religion adequate to their adult spiritual needs. What if, however, religion was not meant to be built on psychologies of fear but on their opposite—on psychologies of trust and of ever-growing expansion of the human person?

This is in fact the psychology that undergirds *all* of creation-centered spirituality. Each of the four paths is a journey into trust and a journey of deepening trust. In the Via Positiva we have already experienced the sense of trust in Dabhar, in life as blessing, in our earthiness, and in the cosmos by which we launch our spiritual journey. There is a necessary connection between trust learned regarding our own body and our own existence—original blessing and the blessing that earthiness is—and trust of cosmos. Artist Robert Henri testifies to this when he says that "there is nothing in all the world more beautiful or significant of the laws of the universe than the nude human body." We begin to trust at the earliest stages of our lives and if, by bad parenting, we have been so deprived as to have missed this lesson of trust, then we must be healed elsewhere along the line many times to regain trust. This kind of healing ought to be what religion provides by its bodily and cosmic rituals, by its sacraments of reconciliation, and by its explicit care for the cosmos and our relating to the cosmos within and without. The world that the Creator has made "is a world that is thoroughly worthy of trust," according to wisdom scholar Gerhard Von Rad. (43.306) (See Sirach 42:21-25.) The Catholic scholar of wisdom literature Roland Murphy supports this same theme when he says that the two most important factors in learning wisdom according to the scriptures are "an openness to experience and nature and a basic trust." He elaborates even further that "the reason for this openness is trust."[4] Furthermore, the New Testament word most often used by Jesus for "faith" and which Augustine understood as "intellectual assent" in fact means "trust" (*pisteuein*) in the original Greek. Jesus time and again assures people that "your trust has healed you." He recognizes the salvific power of trust. And he also laments how little trust he finds among people, "O you of little trust."

More and more we learn that trust is not just a psychological issue—it is in fact a faith issue, indeed *the* faith issue, because in fact trust is the most basic meaning of faith. Biblical scholar Walter Brueggemann, in his remarkable essay "The Trusted Creature," traces the growth of King David's life of faith as a growth in trust. The "new David," Brueggemann points out, "has to break the categories" of the pieties of his ancestors in order "that his actual person and work can be discerned."[5] The result of David's gradual learning to trust his own uniqueness and the uniqueness of the times in which he lived is that his monarchy will come to represent "a radical innovation which will not be subsumed under the already existing structures." David in fact brings about "a new perspective toward human history, human responsibility, human caring, human deciding and the human use of power." Like Jesus, David will "overturn conventional notions of what is sacred."[6]

But the biggest struggle David has with trust (faith) is coming to the realization—and the trusting action that flows from that realization—that he is trusted by God. He and humanity are *entrusted* by the Creator with creation. "What God does first and best and most is to trust his people with their moment in history. He trusts his people to do what must be done for the sake of his whole community." The Yahwist account of creation in Genesis 2 is also about God entrusting humankind with the garden (2:15). Calling this Gospel of David "radical" and a "theological revolution," Brueggeman says that Yahweh

> has trusted David and turned him loose to make what he can of the great trust vested in him, without reservation. . . . The picture which emerges is a man who knew himself a fully free man, fully responsible, fully involved but fully his own. . . . David thus embodies the best of wisdom theology.[7]

Since David becomes a type for all humanity as Adam is in Genesis 2, we are all called to the kind of trust that makes divine entrusting possible.

Goethe understood the implications of self-trust and other-trust when he wrote, "If you treat a person as she appears to be, you make her worse than she is. But if you treat a person as if she already were what she potentially could be, you make her what she should be." A trust psychology is necessarily a growth psychology, one that encourages the ever-expanding possibilities of ourselves and the universe. The psychology behind creation-centered spirituality is not a psychology of preservation, whether of innocence or money or reputation or status quo or personality or institutions. It is the psychology of Jesus in the parable of the talents—that we are here to expand our gifts and not, *"out of fear,"* to bury them. The psycho-spiritual expansion is so great that Meister Eckhart can say that a person—even a saint—who lived a thousand years would know more about love in the last hour of the thousandth year than at any previous time. Our expansion has no limit—God is the limit! We are as big as we allow ourselves to be. Julian of Norwich experienced this same sense of our bigness, indeed of our divinity. "We are of God. That is what we are. I saw no difference between God and our Substance but as if it were all God." A blessing theology is necessarily a spirituality of maturation, of growth, of expansion, for this is the manner in which nature's processes operate. We grow from seed and egg to flowers to fruits, and then we are transformed by our many deaths into new life of many kinds. This reverence for growth and the cycles it leads us into mirrors the psychology of the Jewish people. As Claude Tresmontant puts it, "The Hebrews showed a passionate attention to the process of fecundity, the maturing process."[8] We ought to invest our passion not in keeping things the way they are but into our growing and expanding. Thus Meister Eckhart calls us to our ultimate growth, our growth into divinity. "A seed of God is in us. Now a seed of a pear tree grows into a pear tree; a hazel seed into a hazel tree. A seed of God grows into God."

When you build your basic understanding of the universe on nature's cycles (as the creation-centered tradition does) rather than on a mythical past state of perfection (as the fall/redemption tradition does), you learn to reverence change and process. Eckhart underlines this sense of respect for process and growth when he says, "Now God creates all things but does not stop creating. God forever creates and forever begins to create, and creatures are always being created and in the process of beginning to be created." Here lies an ultimate sense of our humility and simplicity—that each of us is only "beginning to be created"! But here too lies a cosmic-sized invitation to grow and grow and grow.

For St. Irenaeus, too, the key to spirituality is a psychology of growth. For him the Fall is not a fall from perfection but a frustration of growth. In his view of the myth of Garden of Eden, Adam and Eve were children and we are to develop beyond them. A person "ripens for the sight and comprehension of God," he declares, comparing our "ripening" to the maturation of the fetus and the ripening of wheat on a stalk.[9] The Irenaean theology, which is a creation theology, does not attribute to Adam before the fall a state of perfection, but rather sees the perfection of creation in its potential for growth and for allowing humans to grow by joy and by pain as well as by sin and by forgiveness. "If, then, you are God's workmanship, wait the hand of your Maker who creates everything in due time; in due time as far as you are concerned, whose creation is still being carried out."[10] Indeed, as we shall see below, what salvation means for Irenaeus is the human person's "renewed growth."

The expansion we undergo culminates in that final, explosive expansion we call "death." The fall/redemption tradition tends to identify death with sin, as if death came into the world as a result of sin. But a reasonable meditation on creation would not come to this conclusion at all. In fact, what we learn by examining nature is that all things have their cycles of life, death, and transformation. As brilliant as a New England autumn can be, the very brilliance of the stunning golds and reds that cover the mountains derives from the fact that the leaves are saying goodbye—and probably thank you—as they prepare to exit this life for another. They will become food for another generation of leaves. The creation-centered spiritual tradition does not teach fear about death. In fact, the trust one learns about love, life, and ecstasy and the pain that accompanies every layer of ecstatic living carry through in the death experience as well. Death too can be trusted. And in a real sense we are entrusted with death so that we ought to be reverencing that aspect of living as much as any other aspect. The hospice movement in our time is a movement of persons who are dealing with the truth of death in just such a wholesome way. The very awesomeness of death experiences unveils for us—and for some people for the very first time—the cosmic depth of our lives, the cosmic connections of our lives.

The great student of Gandhi Raghavan Iyer offers an important insight as to the connection between a spirituality founded on trust and one that also promotes growth and expansion. He points out that for Gandhi (as for Irenaeus, Eckhart, and Julian) spirituality cannot begin with a doctrine of original sin. Gandhi in fact found it important "to combat the doctrine of original sin." But Gandhi was unable to support "his castigation of the doctrine of original sin without advancing also a theory of human perfectibility, divine grace and the upward tendency of cosmic and human evolution. *Dharma* or morality cannot be ultimately divorced from *rta* or cosmic order." (22.97, 99f.)

Every spirituality needs to be questioned as to its psychological presuppositions. In this theme of Trust and of Expansion I have laid out the explicit psychology behind creation-centered spirituality. In each of the paths that follow we will see trust grow into different levels of expansion and need. Each path requires the recovery of faith as trust and a willingness to grow and expand. Trust constitutes the psychology of wisdom literature, of the royal persons as personified by David, of the Yahwist author of the Hebrew Bible, and of Jesus. It is also the psychology that alone leads to compassion, for as William Eckhardt demonstrates in his formidable study on the psychology of compassion, "compassion is a function of faith [read trust] in human nature, while compulsion is a function of lack of faith in human nature."[11] The compulsions that have accompanied the fall/redemption era in religion and spirituality have not prepared the way for compassion. Compassion is not an important spiritual category in that tradition, even though it represented the fulfillment of Jewish and of Jesus' spiritual teaching and living. One reason why compulsion rather than compassion has so characterized the patriarchal era of religion is that trust has been so much less important than fear. And spiritual expansion has been so much less important than guilt. But a new era dawns. For you cannot long imprison the word of the Lord.

6 PANENTHEISM: EXPERIENCING THE DIAPHANOUS AND TRANSPARENT GOD

In music, in the sea, in a flower, in a leaf, in an act of kindness.
... I see what people call God in all these things.
> —*Pablo Casals*[1]

My Beloved is the mountains,
And lonely wooded valleys,
Strange islands,
And resounding rivers,
The whistling of love-stirring breezes,
The tranquil night
At the time of rising dawn,
Silent music,
Sounding solitude,
The supper that refreshes and deepens love.
> —*John of the Cross*[2]

God is love
and anyone who lives in love lives in God
And God in her.
> —*1 John 4:16*

It is in God that we live, and move, and have our being.
> —*Paul in Acts 17:28*

God created all things in such a way that they are not
outside himself, as ignorant people falsely imagine.
Rather, all creatures flow outward, but nonetheless
remain within God.
> —*Meister Eckhart*

The day of my spiritual awakening was the day I saw
—and knew I saw—all things in God
and God in all things.
> —*Mechtild of Magdeburg*

We are in God
and God, whome we do not see,
is in us.
                    —*Julian of Norwich*

God hugs you.
You are encircled by the arms
of the mystery of God.
                    —*Hildegarde of Bingen*

Make your home in me, as I make mine in you,
I am the vine, you are the branches.
Whoever remains in me, with me in him,
bears plentiful fruit.
                    —*John 15: 4,5*

Father, may they be one in us,
as you are in me and I am in you;
I have given them the glory you gave to me,
that they may be one as we are one.
With me in them and you in me.
                    —*John 17: 21,22*

Matter is transparent and malleable in relation to spirit.
                    —*Teilhard de Chardin (40.130)*

I laugh when I hear the fish in the water is thirsty.
                    —*Kabir (6.9)*

What sort of a God would it be, who only pushed from
without?
                    —*Goethe*

C. G. Jung has written that there are two ways to lose your soul. One
of these is to worship a god outside you. If he is correct, then a lot of
churchgoers in the West have been losing their souls for generations
to the extent that they have attended religious events where prayer
is addressed to a god outside. The idea that God is "out there" is
probably the ultimate dualism, divorcing as it does God and humanity and reducing religion to a childish state of pleasing or pleading
with a God "out there." All theism sets up a model or paradigm of
people here and God out there. All theisms are about subject/object
relationships to God. The Newtonian theism that posited a clockmaker

God who wound the universe up and sat back found its logical conclusion in Laplace's statement that he had no need in his scientific system for such a God. But this agnosticism and eventual atheism finds its logical antecedents in religious theism itself, which kills God and the soul alike by preaching a God "out there."

What is the solution to the killing of God and the loss of human soul? It is our moving from theism to panentheism. Now panentheism is not pantheism. Pantheism, which is a declared heresy because it robs God of transcendence, states that "everything is God and God is everything." Panentheism, on the other hand, is altogether orthodox and very fit for orthopraxis as well, for it slips in the little Greek word *en* and thus means, "God is in everything and everything is in God." This experience of the presence of God in our depth and of Dabhar in all the blessings and the sufferings of life is a mystical understanding of God. Panentheism is desperately needed by individuals and religious institutions today. It is the way the creation-centered tradition of spirituality experiences God. It is not theistic because it does not relate to God as subject or object, but neither is it pantheistic. Panentheism is a way of seeing the world sacramentally. Indeed, as we have seen previously, in the creation-centered tradition, the primary sacrament is creation itself—which includes every person and being who lives. Other sacraments derive their fruitful and creative power from this primary sacrament. This is one thing that distinguishes pantheism from panentheism—pantheism has no need of sacraments, but panentheism does. For while everything is truly in God and God is truly in everything, this is not always evident to our experience. The sacrament who is Christ, the Dabhar of God incarnated, and the sacraments of bringing new life into the community, of reconciliation, of Eucharist, of marriage, of spiritual leadership, of confirmation and of healing of the sick make the power of God's presence more emphatic, more recognizable, more fruitful.

The sacramental consciousness of panentheism develops into a transparent and diaphanous consciousness wherein we can see events and beings as divine. The Good News and the Bad News bear divine grace. As Eckhart says, "We must learn to penetrate things and find God there." Prayer, the entering into reality, is always the entering into God, for that is where God is. And suffering is as much a revelation of God's presence as joy is. As Eckhart puts it, "Everything praises God. Darkness, privations, defects, evil too praise God and bless God." As one grows more and more deeply into a panentheistic awareness, one's need to invoke the actual name of God becomes less compelling. This is why the Hebrew tradition boasts two sacred books—the *Song of Songs* and the *Book of Esther*—which never mention the name God once. Francis of Assisi's *Canticle of the Sun* does not mention Jesus Christ. Yet none of these works is less sacred for its silence. Rather, they are the more transparent themselves, allowing as they do the divine presence to spread its own light through their essentially empty, transparent imagery. Like glass, they provide windows between the human psyche and the Creator. This may be the fullest vocation of the artist, to become transparent. Surely the artists of the spirit are to become themselves transparent conduits through which God's Dabhar may flow unimpeded by human words.

A panentheistic spirituality expresses itself in maternal images of God. Julian of Norwich, that champion of the motherhood of God, defines motherhood in one place as our "being enclosed." For her, the maternal side of God is enveloping, embracing, welcoming, inclusive, cosmic, and expansive.[3] Using similar panentheistic and maternal imagery, Eckhart talks of how everything that exists "is bathed in God, is enveloped by God, who is round-about us all, enveloping us." This same image of the maternal and enveloping God is found in Jesus' favorite theme—the kingdom of God theme. "The kingdom/queendom of God is among you," he says (Luke 17:21). The sense of "amongness" is a panentheistic image, of our being in God and God in us. But it requires our waking up to transparent consciousness to realize its full implications. In many respects the entire four-fold journey of creation spirituality is an explication, an unfolding, of a panentheistic God. Beginning with the omnipresent blessing that Dabhar is (Path I), we move through darkness where God is felt as an enveloping absence more than as presence (Path II); through creativity, where omnipresent Dabhar truly births forth (Path III), and to compassion, where we celebrate our group immersion in God on the one hand and struggle for justice among God's creatures on the other (Path IV). Path IV brings panentheism to its rightful conclusion, just as Jesus did in Matthew's Gospel when he said that to relieve another's pain is to relieve his own. For a transparent consciousness culminates in service to one another, in celebration with one another, and in relieving one another's pain. This is why Teilhard de Chardin is correct in calling transparency "mutual penetration" which can be called "the miracle of our liberation." (40.130)

Panentheism is a mature doctrine about the presence of God,

about the deep with-ness of God. Jewish scholar Ronald Miller says that for the Hebrew people, "God is the ultimate with." Yahweh as named in Exodus 3:14 is "the one who will be there." We will know Yahweh in his with-ness. The with-ness of God is especially significant because, while Greeks focus on nouns in their literature, Jews focus on prepositions such as with, against, from, etc. The Covenant is a sign of God's with-ness. To be without covenant would be unbearable for the Jewish believer. God, then, is a preposition for the Jew. And the preposition is basically one of presence, of with-ness.[4] The title of Jesus as Emmanuel, God-with-us, is spelled out in the infancy story of Matthew's Gospel, "They will call him 'Emmanuel,' a name which means 'God-is-with-us.'" (Matt. 1:23. Cf. Isa. 7:4) Christ, says Paul, "is everything and he is in everything." (Col. 3:11) There is then a kind of Christo-panentheism, the presence of Jesus among us as a human being and the spirit of Jesus that comes after his departure from this earth.

If God is so omnipresent as a panentheistic theology suggests, then Kabir is right to laugh when the fish says he is thirsty. I too am often tempted to laugh when persons tell me they don't pray anymore, which ninety-nine percent of the time means "I don't pray like I used to," or "I don't pray like they are praying in my church's worship services." If we used to pray theistically, if Christian liturgies are still theistic in their prayer forms, then it is a blessing indeed to hear people who are growing up enough spiritually so that they are becoming less and less comfortable with dualistic worship. Worship that, if not altered, will kill the soul, as Jung suggests. It is time to rejoice and to laugh when we hear that God's spirit is moving persons to a more adult and more authentically mystical prayer life, one where we truly enter into the deep with-ness of God, a God who is in all and the All that is in God. (Cf. 1 Cor. 15:28) This movement means that we are indeed growing, indeed maturing and ripening, and that we are moving from fall/redemption religion to creation-centered spirituality.

7 OUR ROYAL PERSONHOOD: OUR DIGNITY AND RESPONSIBILITY FOR BUILDING THE KINGDOM/QUEENDOM OF GOD. CREATION THEOLOGY AS A KINGDOM/QUEENDOM THEOLOGY.

Yahweh is king, robed in majesty
Yahweh is robed in power,
he wears it like a belt.
You have made the world firm, unshakeable;
Your throne has stood since then,
You existed from the first.
                    —*Ps. 93:1,2*

You have made humans a little less than God,
    and you have crowned them with glory and honor.
You have given them dominion over the works of your hands,
    putting all things under their feet.
                    —*Ps. 8:6,7*

Royal dignity was yours from the day you were born,
    on the holy mountains,
royal from the womb, from the dawn of your earliest days.
                    —*Ps. 110:3*

In a very real sense every Christian is called to be a *royal person*. Like the kings, every person is created to have dominion in the world, i.e., to be stewards of the world and builders of community within society. In the Hebrew scriptures human beings are described as God's creatures with a royal status and kingly responsibilities.
                    —*Helen Kenik (16.47)*

The kingdom and queendom of God is among you.
                    —*Luke 17:21*

Blessed are the poor, for yours is the kingdom of God.
                    —*Luke 6:20*

There is no need to be afraid, little flock, for it has pleased your Creator to give you the kingdom.
                    —*Luke 12:32*

Every human person is an aristocrat. Every human person is noble and of royal blood, born from the intimate depths of the divine nature and the divine wilderness.
                    —*Meister Eckhart*

To come to Jesus or to follow him is to accompany him into the kingdom. Becoming a disciple is an alternative way of speaking about entering into the kingdom.
                    —*Albert Nolan (27.145)*

Good People,
most royal greening verdancy,
rooted in the sun,
you shine with radiant light.
                    —*Hildegarde of Bingen*

Human nature has ineffable dignity.
                    —*John the Scot*

To the Negro, going to jail was no longer a disgrace but a badge of honor. The Revolution of the Negro not only attacked the external cause of his misery, but revealed him to himself. He was somebody. He had a sense of somebodiness.
                    —*Martin Luther King, Jr.*[1]

When will we teach our children in school what they are? We should say to each of them: Do you know what you are? You are a marvel. You are unique. In all of the world there is no other child exactly like you. In the millions of years that have passed there has never been another child like you. And look at your body—what a wonder it is! your legs, your arms, your cunning fingers, the way you move! You may become a Shakespeare, a Michelangelo, a Beethoven. You have the capacity for anything. Yes, you are a marvel. And when you grow up, can you then harm another who is, like you, a marvel?
                    —*Pablo Casals*[2]

The kingdom of God is no small thing.
                    —*Meister Eckhart*

As Americans we are not altogether at home with talk of kings or queens, kingdoms, queendoms, or royal persons. After all, our ancestors did fight a revolutionary war to rid themselves of such notions. However, Israel was not eighteenth-century England and King David was not George VI. Israel had a unique understanding of kingship, and it is essential if we care to understand biblical spirituality that we let go of our biases about royalty long enough to hear Jewish theology out on the subject. Since the core of the preaching of Jesus Christ was his announcement of the nearness of the kingdom/queendom of God, Christians can hardly ignore the invitation to explore the meaning of the reign of God in ancient Israel. One can discern three stages in the delineation of a theology of royal person in Israel.

1) The first meaning of "king" for Israel is that God is King. This means three things: First, it means that God journeys and is with his people, leading them. Here we have the recurrent theme in creation theology of *Emmanuel*, God-with-us. The authentic king journeys with his people. Secondly, what it means for Israel to say that God is King is that God is Creator. King and Creator are parallel terms in this theology. As the psalmist sings,

> Let Israel be glad in their *maker*,
> Let children of Zion rejoice in their *king*. (Ps. 149:2)

Given the parallelism that characterizes Jewish poetry, this psalm explicitly identifies Maker with King. The enthronement psalms celebrate the fact that when Yahweh is King the entire cosmos is in order. "Is Yahweh with us?" is the question that the people ask in times of chaos. And the reassuring reply is: Yes, Yahweh is King and the whole world—not just the temple—is God's throne, and order and creation are thriving. Following are some examples of the cosmic celebration—as distinct from mere cultic usage—that the psalmist makes of God as King of the cosmos.

> For Yahweh is a great God,
> a greater King than all other gods;
> from depths of earth to mountain top
> everything comes under his rule; the sea belongs to him, he made it,
> so does the land, he shaped this too. (Ps. 95:3-5)

> Clap your hands, all you peoples,
> acclaim God with shouts of joy;
> for Yahweh, the Most High, is to be dreaded,

95

the Great King of the whole world....
God is king of the whole world:
play your best in his honor!
God is king of the nations,
He reigns on his holy throne. (Ps. 47:1,2,7,8)

Yahweh is king, robed in majesty,
Yahweh is robed in power,
he wears it like a belt.
You have made the world firm, unshakeable;
Your throne has stood since then,
You existed from the beginning, Yahweh. (Ps. 93:1,2)

The third dimension to Yahweh's being King is that as King Yahweh preserves creation and sustains it by being a just king. Justice preserves creation and makes it thrive and blossom in ever-fertile ways. The psalmist praises this aspect of God as King/Creator as well.

Say among the nations, "Yahweh is king!"
Firm has he made the world, and unshakeable;
he will judge each nation with strict justice.
Let the heavens be glad, let earth rejoice,
Let the sea thunder and all that it holds,
let the fields exult and all that is in them,
let all the woodland trees cry out for joy
at the presence of Yahweh, for he comes,
he comes to judge the earth,
to judge the world with justice
and the nations with his truth. (Ps. 96:10-13)

Yahweh is king! Let the earth rejoice,
the many isles be glad!
Cloud and darkness surround him,
Righteousness and Justice support his throne. (Ps. 97:1,2)

Let all the rivers clap their hands
      and the mountains shout for joy,
at the presence of Yahweh, for he comes
      to judge the earth,
to judge the world with righteousness
      and the nations with strict justice. (Ps. 98:8,9)

You are a king who loves justice,
insisting on honesty, justice, virtue,
      as you have done for Jacob. (Ps. 99:4)

96

The prophets as well as the psalmist make connections between Yahweh as King, as Creator, and as Justice-maker. Isaiah, for example, says,

> I am Yahweh, your Holy One,
> the Creator of Israel, your king. (Isa. 43:15)

It was common among all the religions of the Orient in the time of ancient Israel to recognize that kingship began with the creation of the world.

2) The second stage in Israel's understanding of kingship and spirituality is its reflection on the king in Israel, the human king that is. The human king is meant to be imbued with the spirit of the divine king to be with and lead the people, and above all to lead with the spirit of justice. The last words ascribed to David in 2 Samuel are as follows:

> The spirit of Yahweh speaks through me,
> his word is on my tongue;
> The God of Jacob has spoken,
> the Rock of Israel has said to me:
> He who rules men with justice,
> who rules in the fear of God,
> is like morning light at sunrise
> on a cloudless morning
> making the grass of the earth sparkle after rain. (2 Sam. 23:2-4)

God, Creator and King, has entrusted to humans the needs of the creation and its preservation. As B. Anderson puts it, "God has given man responsibility for the world. In a limited sense, he is intended to be a king who, in the ceaseless conflict of history, helps to sustain the creation in the face of the menacing powers of chaos."[3] It was the work of the prophets to constantly confront the kings when they failed—as they so often did—at carrying on creation by way of preservation and justice-making. After the time of the prophets this important task of reminding and confronting was to be undertaken by the sages of the wisdom tradition of Israel. As wisdom scholar Roland Murphy puts it, commenting on Proverbs 8, wisdom "assumes the role of royalty (verse 15) and even of divinity, to speak with the prerogative of Yahweh (verse 17), the relation of Yahweh to the king is taken over by wisdom."[4]

Just as justice insures order and balance in the whole of creation, so does injustice bring about chaos; it undoes all of creation. With injustice, "all the foundations of the earth are shaken." (Ps. 82:5b)

It is no wonder, given the stakes at hand and given the amazing act of entrusting the divinely royal responsibilities to human beings, that Israel prayed hard for its kings to be worthy kings. The true king is a compassionate doer of justice who pays special attention to the *anawim*, the afflicted ones.

> God, give your own justice to the king,
>   your own righteousness to the royal son,
> so that he may rule your people rightly
>   and your poor with justice.
>
>   He will defend the poorest,
> he will save the children of those in need,
>   and crush their oppressors.
> He will free the poor man who calls to him,
>   and those who need help,
> he will have pity on the poor and feeble,
>   and save the lives of those in need;
> he will redeem their lives from exploitation and outrage,
>   their lives will be precious in his sight. (Ps. 72:1,2,4,12-14)[5]

3) The third stage of kingship for Israel is found in the messianic tradition, wherein the messiah would be a king of the sort who truly embodies the divine reign of justice and care for creation. This king will possess the "spirit of Yahweh" which births all creation. And this king, springing from the line of David, will possess the prophetic spirit of justice and of wisdom. Isaiah writes:

> A shoot springs from the stock of Jesse,
> a scion thrusts from his roots:
> on him the spirit of Yahweh rests,
> a spirit of wisdom and insight,
> a spirit of counsel and power, ...
> He judges the poor with integrity,
> and with fairness gives a verdict for the poor of the land. ...
> Justice will be around his waist like a loincloth
> and faithfulness a belt around his hips. (Isa. 11:1-5)

The messiah will be a son of God, that is of royal blood, who will rule "to the ends of the earth" with an "iron sceptre." (Ps. 2:8,9) "Let me proclaim Yahweh's decrees: He tells me: 'You are my son, today I have begotten you.'" (Ps. 2:8,9;7) Psalm 110 also celebrates this passing on of the divine, royal kingship.

Yahweh's decrees to you, my Lord, "Sit at my right hand
and I will make your enemies a footstool for you."

Yahweh will force all your enemies
under the sway of your sceptre in Zion.
Royal dignity was yours from the day you were born, on
      the holy mountains,
royal from the womb, from the dawn of your earliest days.
(Ps. 110:1-3)

Christians believe that such a royal person occurred in the person
of Jesus Christ. Christ is with the people; he judges, he calls for love
and justice, he even sits at God's right hand. But above all, he calls
people to the kingdom/queendom of God; that is, he invites all
peoples to be royal persons. He calls them to their dignity as images
of God—the theology of human dignity and royal personhood that
the Yahwish author of Genesis 2-3 writes about and that the psalmist praises:

You have made humans a little less than God,
    and you have crowned them with glory and honor.
You have given them dominion over the works of your hands
    putting all things under their feet. (Ps. 8:6,7)

What the Yahwist author and Jesus call people to in reminding them
of their royal personhood is two things: first, their dignity. Next,
their responsibility. A royal person has dignity, the dignity of the
divine king. Jesus chose especially the poor and the sinners of
society to give them a sense of their own dignity, their own royal
personhood, that would in turn be a starting point to their being
released from captivity. By reclining with them at table he made
them feel "clean and acceptable," and since Jesus was considered a
man of God, they were now approved by him, acceptable to God. As
Albert Nolan observes, Jesus offers the poor "the full recognition of
their dignity as human beings," and it is by this power from Jesus
that the poor are empowered. "He gave them a sense of dignity and
released them from their captivity." (27.57, 39) The Good News
that Jesus brings is News that all are considered royal persons by
God, all have rights, all have divine dignity. He is sensitive to the
pain that the oppressed undergo but insists that no one can rob them
of their divine and royal dignity.

Blessed are the poor because yours is the kingdom of God.
Blessed are you who are hungry now because you shall be satisfied.

99

> Blessed are you who weep now because you shall laugh. (Luke 6:20,21)

All of Jesus' teaching on the kingdom represents a crescendo in the Jewish teaching of royal personhood. This teaching included the assurance that Yahweh would make the *anawim* a royal people.

> Who is like Yahweh our God?—
> Enthroned so high, he needs to stoop
> to see the sky and earth!
>
> He raises the poor from the dust;
> he lifts the needy from the dunghill
> to give them a place with princes,
> with the princes of his people.
> He enthrones the barren woman in her house
> by making her the happy mother of sons. (Ps. 113:5-9)

But with the dignity of all persons—who are all royal persons—goes the responsibility. The responsibility for justice-making and preserving creation. On the part of the poor, this means being actively involved in asserting one's dignity, which means one's rights, and of letting go of oppressive self-images that others have handed on to one. On the part of those who are comfortable, this means letting go and siding with the afflicted. This challenge of Jesus is put forth in many parts of the gospels, especially that of Luke, but is expressed in a special way in the following parable.

> You are the salt of the earth. But if salt becomes tasteless, what can make it salty again? It is good for nothing, and can only be thrown out to be trampled underfoot by men.
> You are the light of the world. A city built on a hilltop cannot be hidden. No one lights a lamp to put it under a tub; they put it on the lamp-stand where it shines for everyone in the house. In the same way your light must shine in the sight of men, so that, seeing your good works, they may give praise to your Father in heaven. (Matt. 5:13-16)

It is significant that in Matthew's Gospel this passage follows immediately Jesus' Sermon on the Mount and his telling his followers that they are the successors of the prophets. (Matt. 5:11,12) Clearly Jesus is calling persons to their dignity in this passage where he parallels the assertive exposure of a lighted lamp with the need to let shine before people one's goodness, one's being a blessing, one's royal deeds. But the powerful connection of this parable with the theme of royal personhood has often been missed by commentators on the phrase "you are the salt of the earth." In the Hebrew tongue, the word for salt, *melach*, sounds almost identical to the word for king, *melek*, and the word meaning "to ascend the throne and reign," *malak*. Jesus, who spoke his stories and did not write them, was very attuned to plays on words, as all Jews are. In this parable, therefore, Jesus is calling all of us to our royal personhood with its consequent dignity and responsibility.

When Jesus declares that the kingdom of God is "not here or there" but "among you," he is emphasizing the cosmic and indeed panentheistic nature of true royal personhood. God's kingdom is not a parochial or nationalistic thing; it concerns creation itself, as one scholar points out. "The only way we could speak of the 'Kingdom of God' in a territorial sense [in the New Testament] would be in regard to the whole universe." Indeed, "the establishment of the eschatalogical Kingdom can be nothing else than the perfect joy of the whole world,"[6] and this is what the psalmist is celebrating in the royal psalms 96, 97, and 98, which we have considered above. Theologian Krister Stendahl emphasizes that when Jesus uses the word "kingdom" he means "creation." Jesus' sense of kingdom does not signify a "rule in the heart" but a concrete effort to make right, to make just, to mend creation when it becomes broken by injustices and human violence.[7] Our responsibility is a cosmic one. We are part of the universe.

Humanity is not separate from the royal kingdom/queendom that the universe is. As science has made clear, humanity represents the most laborious and lengthy effort of the cosmos and therefore of Dabhar to grow ever more beautiful. In humanity for the first time in twenty billion years, the cosmos can reflect on itself. Here the awesome doctrine of our being royal persons finds a beautiful expression, one that moved Teilhard de Chardin to exclaim, "Being in the forefront of the cosmic wave of advance, the energy of humanity assumes an importance disproportionate to its apparently small size." (40.121)

The fall/redemption tradition tends to lose sight of the important theme of royal personhood because it confuses the kingdom of God with the church. This provoked theologian Alfred Loisy to complain: "Jesus came preaching the kingdom and what we got was the churches—what a letdown!" Of course the churches exist to build up God's kingdom/queendom, and a kingdom theology does not exclude the contributions that the churches can and must make. But a royal person theology is vaster than the churches. It is cosmic, universal, it announces the Good News that Dabhar and blessing permeate all things. It is a spirituality of cosmic justice that builds and preserves creation itself. Nothing less. As Meister Eckhart says, "The kingdom of God is no small thing." As the churches let go of their preoccupation with being churches and enter more fully into a kingdom/queendom spirituality, they will more fully become what they most want to be: eschatological signs of the kingdom come, of God-with-us. On that day all will hear and grasp the prayer of Jesus: "Your kingdom come, your will be done on earth as it is in heaven."

8 REALIZED ESCHATOLOGY: A NEW SENSE OF TIME

The time has come.
The kingdom/queendom of God is near.
　　　—Mark 1:15

I have a feeling that my boat
has struck, down there in the depths,
against a great thing.
　　　　　　　And nothing
happens! Nothing ... Silence ... Waves ...

　—Nothing happens? Or has everything happened,
and are we standing now, quietly, in the new life?"
　　　—Juan Ramón Jiménez (7.105)

We are more truly in heaven than on earth.
　　　—Julian of Norwich

In this life we are to become heaven so that God might find a
home here.
　　　—Meister Eckhart

Friend, hope for the Guest while you are alive.
Jump into experience while you are alive!
Think ... and think ... while you are alive.
What you call "salvation" belongs to the time before death.

If you don't break your ropes while you are alive,
do you think
ghosts will do it after?

The idea that the soul will join with the ecstatic
just because the body is rotten—
that is all fantasy.
What is found now is found then.
If you find nothing now,
you will simply end up with an apartment in the City of Death.
If you make love with the divine now, in the next life
　　you will have the face of satisfied desire.
　　　—Kabir (6.24)

103

All good deeds that are prompted by hope of happiness in the next world cease to be moral.
  —*Mahatma Gandhi (22.64)*

Time . . . can be used either destructively or constructively. More and more I feel that the people of ill will have used time much more effectively than have the people of good will. We must use time creatively, in the knowledge that the time is always ripe to do right. Now is the time to make real the promise of democracy and transform our pending national elegy into a creative psalm of brotherhood. Now is the time to lift our national policy from the quicksand of racial injustice to the solid rock of human dignity.
  —*Martin Luther King, Jr.*[1]

The flux of time is society's most natural ally in maintaining law and order, conformity, and the institutions that relegate freedom to a perpetual utopia; it makes people oblivious to the better past and the better future.
  —*Herbert Marcuse*[2]

A spiritual awakening is not only about a new and charged experience of sacred space—the experience of the kingdom/queendom of God *among us*, of the panentheistic divine energy and grace bathing us everywhere. Such an awakening is also about a newly charged experience of time. What is most evident when we look at time or the times is how absent divine beauty and divine justice seem to be. How the innocent still suffer, how the wicked prosper still and get very light jail sentences if any, and how little seems to have changed since Job lamented this unjust state of affairs. This temporal pessimism, this depression any one of us could feel when we consider the times, theologians call "unrealized eschatology," i.e., the experience that God's time, the fullness of time, "when justice will flow like a river" and the lion will lie down with the lamb, seems very far off indeed.

Much of time consciousness in the fall/redemption tradition deal with this evident pessimism in two ways: First, by assuring believers that "eternal life" is something that happens for the most part after death. This life is a proving ground, a testing time, but the real union of God and humanity happens after death or in the future with a glorious second coming of Jesus. The more extreme fall/

redemption persons, those fundamentalists who dwell quite con-spicuously in our midst these days, actually talk about "the rapture" with glee—meaning the second coming of Jesus would be hastened by a calamity like a nuclear war. The fall/redemption tradition inserts a stark dualism into theological time-talk. The dualism be-tween this life and the next becomes a dualism between a time in heaven and a time on earth.

Another characteristic of time consciousness in the fall/redemption tradition is that when it is not oriented forward it puts most of the divine action in the past. Creation is less an ongoing thing than a six-day event *in the past*—whether this past is 6000 years ago (as some still believe) or 20 billion years ago is not the point here. The point is the looking backward for divine action. Salvation too is put in the past in the nativity at Bethlehem and in the crucifixion of Jesus at Golgotha. And even human sin, the "original sin," basically took place in the past.

The creation-centered spiritual tradition experiences sacred time very differently. It rejects the dualism of heaven/earth, and works and prays, as Jesus did, that the divine "kingdom/queendom of God come on earth as it is in heaven." While not denying unrealized eschatology, while not covering its eyes to the poignancy of injustice and sin and sadness in this life, its response is not to flee the present for either a more heavenly future or a more miraculous past. Rather, its response is to trust (i.e., believe) so deeply in the depths of the present that realized eschatology becomes a reality. Realized escha-tology is the experience that Now is the time; Now is the place; Now is the occasion; Now is the bringing together of the best of the past and of the future; Now is the moment of divine breakthrough and Dabhar. We have already died—that is what Paul teaches baptism is about in his letter to the Romans. Therefore heaven has already burst forth into human and cosmic times; it has burst forth—believe it or not—in the person of ourselves. And in the times during which we live and in which we make our choices of lifestyle and work, of worship and struggle. Creation spirituality recognizes the potential for divine despair in one's own time. By not being preoccupied with an original sin in the past, it makes evident the truth that we humans today hold the capacity for what could be the most basic and most original of sins—a nuclear holocaust that would wipe out life and beauty on God's planet Earth. Yet, because the creation-centered tradition emphasizes that Dabhar and the divine creative energy are always being born and that we are all to be sons and daughters of God as Jesus Christ taught us, it offers hope. Only hope can give us the courage to face the future and to stand deeply in the present without running from it. We escape the present, as Ernest Becker put it, "by drugs, by alcohol or by going shopping, which amounts to the same thing." Or, I might add, by heeding fundamentalist religions' preoccupation with a second coming when Jesus' first coming has barely begun to be appropriated by the human race.

Christ too is not in the past nor exclusively in the future, but is as present as we are to the cosmos, to the divine blessing and the divine Dabhar, to the salvation that compassion always brings about. This is why Eckhart could say in his sermon on Christmas night, "What good is it to me if Mary gave birth to the Son of God 1,400 years ago and I don't give birth to God's Son in my person and my culture and my times?" The creation-centered spiritual tradition talks about redemption as reminding. For the Hebrew, salvation comes from remembering—"Do this in memory of me," Jesus said at the Last Supper. The paschal meal is about making the past present. It is not a nostalgic return to a past event but a reliving in the sense of a making alive again of past events of breakthrough and liberation. This is why Eckhart calls Jesus "the Great Reminder." In the reminding comes the healing of past and present, future and present, past and future in the present. The energy of the divine present moment combined with the energy of the divine presence (sacred time and sacred space commingling) finds an explosion in the words, "This *is* my body; This *is* my blood"; "The kingdom/queendom of God *is* among you"; "This *is* eternal life: to know God the Father, Creator." There is no lack of realized eschatology in Jesus' preaching, in Paul, or in John's Gospel. But where there is a lack of it in our spiritualities, we ought to be aware and alert, for there a basic mistrust has crept in, a mistrust in this case of the present now, of the divine right and desire to break through our lives at any time—and especially at the present time. A spirituality built on trust trusts even time to be an appropriate occasion for the divine breakthrough, for hope to emerge. If Mary and Jesus did anything for humanity, they did this for us: they woke us up to the nearness of divine time to our times. They awakened our hope that, in the midst of bad times and tough times and sad times and violent times, realized eschatology—the best times God has to offer—is also present.

The invitation to explore the depths of the Now time is also an invitation to let go of all time. For an entry into the divine power of the present constitutes an entry into that divine space where all time stands still, where timeless play is operative, where time is at last suspended, forgotten, shed, so that God may be "all in all." (1 Cor. 15:28) A healthy meditation of letting go of images and not one of adding to images will help many persons to experience the reality of time suspended, which also becomes time resurrected and reborn. We shall see more of this in Path II.

9 HOLINESS AS COSMIC HOSPITALITY: CREATION ECSTASIES SHARED CONSTITUTE THE HOLY PRAYER OF THANKSGIVING AND PRAISE

Be holy. For I, Yahweh your God, am holy.
—*Lev. 19:2*

What we are all more or less lacking at this moment is a new definition of holiness.
—*Teilhard de Chardin (40.110)*

Today it is not nearly enough to be a saint, but we must have the saintliness demanded by the present moment, a new saintliness, itself is without precedent.
—*Simone Weil*[1]

We have abandoned our role as shepherds of Being.
—*Louis Kahn*[2]

How should one live? Live welcoming to all.
—*Mechtild of Magdeburg*

I welcome all the creatures of the world with grace.
—*Hildegarde of Bingen*

What is the test that you have indeed undergone this holy birth? Listen carefully. If this birth has truly taken place within you, then every single creature points you toward God.
—*Meister Eckhart*

Grace spreads widely and shows the greatly abundant and generous hospitality of the royal Lordship in God's astonishing courtesy towards us.
—*Julian of Norwich*

Oh, come to the water all you who are thirsty;
though you have no money, come!
Buy corn without money, and eat,
and, at no cost, wine and milk.
—*Isa. 55:1*

Wisdom has built herself a house,
she has slaughtered her beasts, prepared her wine,
   she has set her table.
To the fool she says,
"Come and eat my bread,
drink the wine I have prepared!
Leave your folly and you will live,
   walk in the ways of perception."
         —*Prov. 9:1,2,4-6*

There is one thing in the world that satisfies,
and that is a meeting with the Guest.
         —*Kabir (6.1)*

Let all guests who arrive be received like Christ, for he is going to say, "I came as a guest, and you received me." And to all let due honor be shown. . . . Let both Abbot and community wash the feet of all guests. In the reception of the poor and of pilgrims the greatest care and solicitude should be shown, because it is especially in them that Christ is received. For as far as the rich are concerned, the very fear which they inspire wins respect for them.
         —*Rule of St. Benedict*

The true saints are those who transfer the state of house-holdership to the house of God, becoming father and mother, brother and sister, son and daughter, to all creation, rather than to their own issue.
         —*Erik Erikson*[3]

People often ask me how Buddhists answer the question: 'Does God exist?' The other day I was walking along the river. . . . I was suddenly aware of the sun, shining through the bare trees. Its warmth, its brightness, and all this completely free, completely gratuitous. Simply there for us to enjoy. And without my knowing it, completely spontaneously, my two hands came together, and I realized that I was making *gassho*. And it occurred to me that this is all that matters: that we can bow, take a deep bow. Just that. Just that.
         —*Rev. Eido Tai Shimano*[4]

If the only prayer you say in your whole life is "thank you," that would suffice.
         —*Meister Eckhart*

> Let the sea thunder and all that it holds,
>   and the world, with all who live in it;
> let all the rivers clap their hands
>   and the mountains shout for joy.
>   —*Ps. 98:7,8*

> Let thanksgiving be your sacrifice to God,
> fulfill the vows you make to the Most High;
> Whoever makes thanksgiving his sacrifice honors me;
> to the upright person I will show how God can save.
>   —*Ps. 50:14, 23*

"Holiness" is a word worth retrieving. One of the most telling questions that can be asked about a period's spirituality is, what is its understanding of holiness? A people's grasp of what constitutes holiness will affect its entire way of living, of question, of celebrating. The dominant definition of holiness in the fall/redemption tradition is perfection. Holiness is the quest for perfection. Thus, in a typical statement on holiness buttressed by a typical biblical text, the very influential fall/redemption spiritual writer Father Tanquerry says, "Our Lord proposes to us as the idea of holiness the very perfection of Our Heavenly Father: 'Be ye therefore perfect, as also your heavenly Father is perfect.' "[5]

There are several problems with this definition of holiness, psychological difficulties which culminate in social difficulties. More and more psychological thinkers are pointing out how superficial and indeed destructive the quest for perfection is. Otto Rank talks about "the *disease* of perfection" (29.199f.) and how a perfection quest is an ego quest and not a deeply spiritual quest of the human person. Alfred Adler speaks of "the courage of *im*perfection."[6] And the feminist and Jewish poet Adrienne Rich also writes

> Let us return to imperfection's school
> No longer wandering after Plato's ghost.[7]

The fact is that for people who have truly learned to trust creation one of the first lessons is how beauty and *im*perfection go together. Every tree is beautiful; but if you approach it closely enough you will see that every tree is imperfect. The same is true of the human body: every human body is beautiful, but every human body is imperfect. In nature, in creation, imperfection is not a sign of the absence of God. It is a sign that the ongoing creation is no easy thing. We all bear scars from this rugged process. We can—and must—celebrate the scars. The alternative is to opt out of the ongoing work of Dabhar.

This is where the ego quest for perfection does so damaging a thing to the individual, to society, and to whatever unique gifts the individual may be able to give society. By dwelling on imperfection, such a spirituality misses the whole point of what our communal and cosmic spiritual journey is all about. It is in fact our imperfections that most unite us and make of us a social organism whose parts are busy assisting one another. For it is shared weakness and need that draws from a group its gifts and powers of healing. A perfection-oriented spirituality of holiness is intrinsically privatizing and does not lead to a spirituality for the people. If my tongue did not admit that it could not hear, would I need ears? If my ears did not lack the perfection of seeing, would I need eyes? The same holds for any body politic as well: our imperfections unite us, not our perfections.

One has to ask how much of the quest for perfection is a look back, a nostalgic quest for a time that never was. Certain myths about creation teach that humanity was created in a "state of perfection" and that original sin disrupted that "perfect" state. Fall/redemption theologians like Augustine teach this. Thus the quest for holiness as perfection is a quest for a past event. Once again we are face to face with a world view that ignores what we know of evolutionary history, that flees from nature, and that makes too big a thing of the past. The fullness we seek and the ripening into fuller, compassionate people that we desire draws us into the future much more than into a past that most probably never existed.

There are also deeply serious biblical problems with the understanding of holiness as "perfection." The text invariably invoked for this definition, the one cited on the previous page from Matthew's Gospel (5:48), simply "does not refer to moral perfection" and "does not have here the later Greek meaning of being totally free of imperfection."[8] The Greek word that has been misleadingly translated as "be you perfect" is *teleioi*, which means, "be full-grown, be adult, be complete and whole." The text has a parallel in Luke's Gospel which could hardly be more straightforward: "Be you compassionate as your Creator in heaven is compassionate." (Luke 6:36) In a static cosmos, perfection takes on static connotations, and so does holiness. In an ongoing cosmos, imbued with Dabhar, the ever-creative spirit of God, our goal is to expand, to "ripen," as St.

Irenaeus would say, to grow into fullness. This, as we saw when we discussed the psychology of trust and of growth that is Theme Five, constitutes the psychological energy behind the creation tradition. If it is true that holiness in the scriptures is compassion—and this is a fact, for the Israelites believed compassion to be the most divine of all energies[9]—then our deepest ripening and growing happens in our growth into compassion. In terms of the paths enunciated in this book, we ripen from Via Positiva through Via Negativa through Via Creativa to Via Transformativa, that is into compassion. Then we journey all over again at ever deeper levels through these four paths.

Still a fourth objection to defining holiness as perfection comes from what our culture has done with this definition. Consumer society has, I believe, built its entire advertising edifice on the fall/redemption theology of holiness as perfection. Consider the female models who are labeled "10," whom the camera presents to us only as perfect; the same unreality is portrayed in male models attempting to sell us some goods. Consumerism, like fall/redemption religion, plays on our inferiority complexes, on the fears or guilt or inhibitions we possess from not being perfect. It offers us wares with the implicit and often explicit promise that "Here Lies Perfection." Interestingly enough, the idea that perfection is the meaning for salvation is very much an idea of the gnostics, as Hans Jonas testifies.[10] The best way to undercut such potent appeals to our weakest sides is to let go of the quest for perfection and to sink more deeply into a spiritual value system that cherishes what is and considers isness holy.

Having criticized the dominant definition of holiness as perfection, what does the creation-centered tradition have to offer as a substitute? In this tradition I believe it can be said that holiness consists in *hospitality. Cosmic* hospitality.

Hospitality comes from the word for host or hostess. If there is any conclusion that can be reached about the journey of the Via Positiva that we have taken in eight themes up to now, it is this: that the Creator God is a gracious, an abundant, and a generous host/ hostess. She has spread out for our delight a banquet that was twenty billion years in the making. A banquet of rivers and lakes, of rain and of sunshine, of rich earth and of amazing flowers, of handsome trees and of dancing fishes, of contemplative animals and of whistling winds, of dry and wet seasons, of cold and hot climates. But it is a banquet that works, this banquet we call creation, the human planet. It works for our benefit if we behave toward it as

112

reverent guests. God has declared that this banquet is "very good" and so are we, blessings ourselves, invited to the banquet. To recount just a few of these remarkable gifts of creation ecstasies that God has given us, let us recall the following elements at table with us: nature; friendship; thinking; sexuality; the arts, from those of conversation and car repair to the arts of dance and opera; good work; non-competitive sport. (14.45-53) The list of divine blessings that we call creation and that can rightly be called a banquet goes on and on. Yes, we can conclude that God is indeed a good host/hostess, welcoming us to creation and its multiple gifts and blessings.

As if this were not enough for us, God the host has set another table for us: the Eucharist is an opportunity to eat cosmic bread and drink cosmic blood, to say "thank you" for the banquet of our lives. In this instance God—the host—in an amazing act of imagination— actually becomes the food and the drink at table.

But the gradual unfolding and revelation of the holiness, that is the hospitality, of God does not stop here. Hospitality is about a relationship—one cannot be hospitable without guests. God not only plays the host for us and becomes the banquet for us; God also has become guest for us. This is one of the deep meanings of the Incarnation, that God let go of hosting long enough to become guest as well. It is as if the human race could understand the hosting side of hospitality, but the guesting side was becoming more and more difficult to grasp. Love is not just setting the table and giving out food; love is also the receiving end of the banquet. And for this the human race begged an Incarnation, a fleshy enactment of the guesting side of God, of holiness and of hospitality. Jesus was an excellent guest, a true revelation of God's guesting side.

> Meal-sharing in fellowship, whether with notorious tax-collectors and sinners or with his friends, casual or close, is a fundamental trait of the historical Jesus. In that way Jesus shows himself to be God's eschatological messenger, conveying the news of God's invitation to all—including especially those officially regarded at the time as outcasts. (34.216)

Schillebeeckx recognizes a "marvelous abundance" that comes into play when Jesus offers fellowship at table, an abundance that is surely that of the "eschatological abundance" that the prophets envisioned. (Amos 9:13-15) The messianic banquet is celebrated by Isaiah in the following manner:

On this mountain,
Yahweh Sabaoth will prepare for all peoples,
a banquet of rich food, a banquet of fine wines,
of food rich and juicy, of fine strained wines.
On this mountain he will remove
the mourning veil covering all peoples,
and the shroud enwrapping all nations,
he will destroy Death forever. (Isa. 25:6-8)

Not only is Yahweh the host and hostess, but God also prepares the meal as the keeper of the vineyard.

That day,
sing of the delightful vineyard!
I, Yahweh, am its keeper;
every moment I water it
for fear its leaves should fall;
night and day I watch over it. (Isa. 27:2,3)

Thus wisdom who beckons us to "come and eat my bread, drink the wine I have prepared," as the prophets invite us to celebrate the hospitality of our God. And this hospitality can rightly be called the holiness of God.

Jesus' frequent parables about hosting and guesting, his laments at the failure of guests to appear (Matt. 22:2-10; Luke 14:16-24), his own attendance at wedding feasts and his dining with poor and rich alike, his promise that the hungry and thirsty will be sated, all this preoccupation in the gospels with banqueting and with guesting provides additional revelation of the holy hospitality of our Creator God. The psalmist sings of such divine hospitality as well.

You prepare a table before me
under the eyes of my enemies;
You anoint my head with oil,
my cup brims over.

Ah, how goodness and kindness pursue me,
    every day of my life;
My home, the house of Yahweh,
    as long as I live! (Ps. 23:5,6)

Here the house of Yahweh is equated with our whole life experience, all the hospitality of Dabhar is conjured up, all the blessings of the Via Positiva are celebrated. The expression "to anoint one's head with oil" is a "gesture of hospitality in the East."[11]

114

We see from the prophets and from wisdom writers that the banquet God extends to humankind is not an elitest one—the poor are fully represented there, the outcasts and the forgotten ones. "The poor will receive as much as they want to eat," sings the psalmist. (Ps. 22:26) And where the poor have been excluded, some cosmic readjustment will be in order. Mary tells us this: "He has pulled down princes from their thrones and exalted the lowly. The hungry he has filled with good things, the rich he has sent away empty." (Luke 1:52,53)

What is the appropriate response from deep within the human person to this banquet of blessings that the divine Dabhar spreads out and continues to spread out so lavishly? The response is the deepest prayer there is: thank you. Thankfulness, gratefulness. As Brother David Steindl-Rast points out, in our English language there is no such thing as being half full of thanks or gratitude: we are either thank*ful* or grate*ful* or we have not yet experienced the Via Positiva. True holiness, full hospitality, leads to gratitude. Appreciation becomes the awesome, reverent mystery that it is. Not control; not project-planning; but being still with the gift. Savoring. Thanking. Our thanks at the pleasure that the blessings of creation are about is itself our return of blessing for blessing. As Mechtild of Magdeburg put it, "I bless God in my heart without ceasing for every earthly thing." Not only is our thanks for every creature, it is also with every creature—though at some times we are more verbally articulate than at others. "This is why God gave us a mouth—to praise God with inconceivable praise, in common with all creatures, with all our doings, and at all times," says Mechtild. If the Via Positiva touches us at all in our depths, then it touches us where we are capable of thanks. Of praise. Of blessing. Of Eucharist. This is why Meister Eckhart can say with all accuracy, "If the only prayer you say in your whole life is 'thank you,' that would suffice." For there is no deeper, no more adult nor fuller response to our first path, the path of Via Positiva, than this. The thanks we have to give is a cosmic thanks, a thanks from the depths of the cosmos that we are for the cosmos in which we live. No one sings such thanks and praise more authentically than the psalmists of ancient Israel.

> Praise God in his temple on earth,
> praise her in her temple in heaven,
> praise him with blasts of the trumpet,
> praise her with lyre and harp,
> praise him with drums and dancing,
> praise her with strings and reeds,
> praise him with clashing cymbals,
> praise her with clanging cymbals!
> Let everything that breathes praise Yahweh!
> (Ps. 150:1,3-6)

Numerous indeed are the psalmists' songs of praise to the Creator God, praise that is a response to cosmic beauty and not merely to anthropomorphic salvation. The psalmist recognizes that humanity's struggles and beauty are integral to those of all God's creation.[12]

But thank you by words and even thank you by silence is not enough. God went to great lengths to reveal to us that true holiness is hosting (creating) and guesting (receiving gratefully). Guesting alone is not enough, and hosting alone is not enough. We are to be guest and hostess. This means that, in addition to thanking by receiving, there exists thanking by sharing or hosting. The guesting is to feed the hosting. Why do parents bring children into the world if not to share the guesting at God's banquet of life? Why would anyone baptize a child if not to share the guesting at the banquet of faith? We host because we have first been guests; as John puts it, "First God has loved us." And in this sharing as much as in the guesting is full thank you and authentic holiness. Today, under the pressure of ecological crises, we are becoming more and more aware that humanity has not been a good guest on this earth of late. We have some severe disciplining to undergo if we are to recover the art of savoring, which is what guesting is about. And we must let go of much that is humanly chauvinist if we are to recover the truth of hosting all beings. "God has compassion over all of her works," say the scriptures; "I welcome *all* the creatures of the world with grace," shouts Hildegarde. Cosmic hospitality requires a deeper and deeper reverence for all that is and all that might be. It will therefore require a substantial preparation, as all true hospitality does. No small part of that preparation will be worked out in Paths II and III that follow, the Via Negativa and the Via Creativa respectively.

10 SIN, SALVATION, CHRIST FROM THE PERSPECTIVE OF THE VIA POSITIVA: A THEOLOGY OF CREATION AND INCARNATION

On that day, says Yahweh,
I will make the heavens drop rain
And they shall make the earth fruitful
And the earth shall produce corn, new wine, and oil;
And they shall make Jezreel fruitful.
                —*Hosea 2:23,24*

Now in the people that were meant to be green there is no more life of any kind. There is only shrivelled barrenness. The winds are burdened by the utterly awful stink of evil, selfish goings-on. Thunderstorms menace. The air belches out the filthy uncleanliness of the peoples. The earth should not be injured! The earth must not be destroyed!
                —*Hildegarde of Bingen*

I am the vine,
you are the branches.
Whoever remains in me, with me in him,
bears fruit in plenty.
                —*John 15:5*

One God, the maker of all; this is the first and foremost article of our faith. But the second article is the Word of God, the Son of God, Christ Jesus our Lord, who . . . in the end of times, for the recapitulation of all things, is become a man among men, visible and tangible, in order to abolish death and bring to light life, and bring about the communion of God and people.
                —*St. Irenaeus*[1]

Christianity became the greatest moral and political revolution in the history of the human race. It . . . preached the equality of human souls—the true basis for all other equalities, political, social and economic.
                —*Otto Rank (29.146f.)*

117

Christology is creation underlined, concentrated, and condensed: Faith in creation as God wishes it to be.
   —*Edward Schillebeeckx*[2]

A true transformation of our culture would require reclaiming the erotic as power-from-within, as empowerment.
   —*Starhawk (38.138)*

Humanity's recapitulation is renewed growth.
   —*St. Irenaeus*

If being is by nature holy there is no salvation except of *everything* that exists.
   —*Teilhard de Chardin (40.139)*

Jesus Christ is the living voice of Israelite wisdom.
   —*Eugene La Verdiere*[3]

This, then, is salvation: When we marvel at the beauty of created things and praise their beautiful Creator.
   —*Meister Eckhart*

Creation and Salvation come together in the man Jesus Christ. The specific divine activity is one of creation, in the sense that the sovereign freedom it brings into being, something *completely new (bara)*.
   —*Edward Schillebeeckx*[4]

Christ sustains the universe by his powerful command.
   —*Hebrews 1:3*

It is not true that the creation-centered spiritual tradition, because it begins our spiritual journey with blessing and not sin, therefore has nothing to say about sin or about salvation or about Christ. I would maintain that just the opposite situation prevails: Where a religious tradition begins with sin and centers its energies almost exclusively around sin and redemption from sin, then sin gets distorted and indeed trivialized; salvation loses its meaning—a point that biblical theologian Claus Westermann makes repeatedly; and then Jesus is rendered impotent and consequently a Christ of power emerges in what is often a docetistic christology that forgets or denies the human side of Jesus and abounds in Christology. Hence the work of God the Creator and God the Holy Spirit is downplayed if not forgotten altogether. From each of the four paths whose journey we enter into in this book there is much light shed on the meanings of sin, of salvation, and of who Jesus Christ is. We shall outline a few of these insights at the end of each path as we do here in response to our journey through Path I, the Via Positiva.

About Sin.   Sin, one learns from reflection on the Via Positiva, would consist in injuring creation and doing harm to its balance and harmoniousness, turning what is beautiful into what is ugly. In this sense all ecological damage is a sin against the Via Positiva and, as both Hildegarde and the wisdom theologians point out, such sin is a break, a rupture, in creation itself. It represents the most basic injustice, that of humanity to its own source, the earth. Hildegarde writes:

> Now in the people
> that were meant to green,
> there is no more life of any kind.
> There is only shriveled barrenness.

> The winds are burdened by the utterly awful stink of evil,
> selfish goings-on.
> Thunderstorms menace.
> The air belches out the filthy uncleanliness of the peoples.

And she exclaims, "The earth should not be injured! The earth should not be destroyed!" There is no trivializing of sin here—instead there is the hearty recognition of humanity's power to corrupt even its home planet. The sinful consciousness that lies behind ecological sin is that of a dualistic mentality that treats other creatures in a subject/object fashion of manipulation and control. This dualism accounts for the sin of putting the egological ahead of the ecological. It is, when one thinks of it, a rather substantial sin of omission to omit the cosmos itself.

Another sin of omission that is named for us in the Via Positiva is the sin of limiting, always guarding or policing, pleasure. This sin of omitting Eros or love of life from our lives expresses itself in a preference for Thanatos, love of death. Thanatos represents the preoccupation with death, with the putting off of death, or with clinging to death-filled objects. By sinning in this way we refuse to fall in love with life, to love what is lovable, to savor life's simple and non-elitist pleasures, to befriend pleasure, to celebrate the blessings of life, to return thanks for such blessings by still more blessing. Another sin or missing of the mark would be introverted living,

119

whether by individuals or groups or ideologies which refuse the cosmic banquet and cosmic potential that the divine Host/Hostess has laid out for all peoples. Included here would be the sin of adults who directly or through their institutions from family to school to church to nation do not pass on a cosmic awareness to the younger generation, nor love of beauty and the art of savoring it. Indeed, the loss of beauty as a significant theological category for the past few centuries has proven to be profoundly sinful. The sin of consumerism is a child of the sin of omission of Eros. When religion fails to celebrate authentic Eros in our lives, we fall into ersatz pleasures which are subject/object pleasures that can be bought and sold but do not satisfy.

How often Jesus complained, "O you of little trust." The failure to trust, which usually begins with a failure to trust oneself, would be a sin against the Via Positiva. With this lack of trust there happens the refusal to grow and to expand into full acknowledgement of one's royal personhood. A forgetfulness of the Via Positiva leads to what Carol Christ and other feminist writers have called "a uniquely female form of sin through self-negation." (10.19) This sin consists of the refusal to love oneself well, the refusal to celebrate both one's dignity and one's responsibility. When people sin in this way they become suckers for hero-worship, for projecting onto others their own dignity as images of God. Whether these others are matinee idols or religious ones, whether alive or dead, makes no difference. The sin of refusal to acknowledge one's own dignity remains the same. Without healthy self-love there will be no other love. Hildegarde talks about the sin of drying up, of losing one's "greening power" and "wetness." This sin has everything to do with the triumph of death, Thanatos, over life, Eros. Drying up represents the end of blessing, the death of fertility, the choking of earth, of plants, of animals, of humans. It is the ultimate ecological disaster, for in it the microcosm of the human person refuses to ripen and therefore to live. With it all light and all life are snuffed out and the wonderful ways of the Via Positiva, the great delight that creation is meant to give to the Creator God and to all creatures, is forgotten.

About Salvation. One's soteriology or grasp of salvation is going to be related to one's understanding of sin. What light does the Via Positiva shed on our efforts to revivify the meanings of salvation? One scholar tells us that for St. Francis salvation meant "enchanted existence."[5] There is an awakening of Eros, of love and awareness of life, in the Via Positiva that is truly salvific, healing for individuals and society alike. Beauty becomes an experience again and constitutes a vocation in the long, twenty-billion-year vocation of the cosmos to become ever more beautiful. With a realization of beauty and its potential nearness to all, people become social once again. As Meister Eckhart put it, "This then is salvation: to marvel at the beauty of created things and praise the beautiful providence of their Creator."

Salvation is about healing, and just as the cosmos itself can be ruptured and torn apart by injustice, so too it can be healed by all human efforts to bring justice, which is balance, back to human relationships to earth, air, fire, water, and one another. Just as dualism and subject/object living is sinful according to the Via Positiva, so too harmonious living and lifestyles of simplicity represent salvific action on humanity's part. The healing process of making whole and integrating also includes a return to one's origins, and the Via Positiva offers deep invitations to examine anew our preexistence, both in the historical unfolding of the cosmos and in the Creator's heart. With this examination comes a greater reverence for our uniqueness, and therefore a greater reverence for that of God's other creatures. This reverence is itself salvific.

If drying up and embracing Thanatos represents an ultimate sin against the Via Positiva, then the letting go of death and opting for Eros represents a profound healing and salvation from sin. St. Irenaeus and Julian of Norwich both call this a "second creation," a kind of rebirth for humanity. This recapitulation of heaven and earth, of uniting Creator and creation, constitutes a "fresh start" for humanity, according to Irenaeus.[6] "Renewed growth" is Irenaeus's definition of recapitulation or salvation.[7]

If the omission of Eros is a great sin, then the return of Eros is deeply salvific and, in Starhawk's words, empowerment. The salvific return to Eros is a return to blessing, a return to play, a return to living the kind of existence that Meister Eckhart called "without a why." Such an understanding of salvation would put a lot of people back to work—specifically artists, clowns, ritual-makers, storytellers, and celebrators of various kinds. It would also allow those who are overworking to open up work to the underemployed or unemployed. And it would allow all to live on less. Norman O. Brown puts it this way:

> The question confronting mankind is the abolition of repression—
> in traditional Christian language, the resurrection of the body....

The life insfinct, or sexual instinct, demands activity of a kind that, in contrast to our current mode of activity, can only be called play.[8]

About Jesus Christ. What is a savior? The opposite of a destroyer. Jesus Christ is a creator, present with the Creator from the beginning. "In the beginning was the Dabhar." The presence of Dabhar with the Creator was a playful presence, as we read in Proverbs:

I was by his side, a master craftsman,
delighting him day after day,
ever at play in his presence,
at play everywhere in his world,
delighting to be with the sons of men.
(Prov. 8:30, 31)

Jesus comes announcing life, not death. "I come that they may have life and have it in abundance." Like wisdom, his is the way of the Creator, the way of Eros and life. It is a way of abundant blessing and overwhelming fertility, unimaginable greenness, one might say. In the Hebrew scriptures, personified wisdom talks of being a vine "taken root in a privileged people." (Sir. 24:17-21) Jesus also talks of himself as a vine and source of fertility. "I am the vine, you are the branches. Whoever remains in me, with me in him, bears fruit in plenty." (John 15:5) Like the wisdom of old that accompanied all Dabhar, all creation (Ps. 78:2), Jesus "expounds things hidden since the foundation of the world." (Matt. 13:35)

Out of the mouths of babes he heard wisdom, for he was always looking for wisdom in order to grow in wisdom (Luke 2: 40,52), and he promised nothing but blessing—the beatitudes. He spoke wisdom, but more than that he played the role of wisdom, the post-prophetic prophecy, the royal person calling all to their royal personhood. And he paid the ultimate price for such extravagant democracy, for such criticism of manmade monarchies, for such blasphemy and such panentheism.

Ironically, Jesus, who comes to announce the presence of the kingdom/queendom of God, is mocked at the end of his life with a crown of thorns and an inscription that he is "king of the Jews." Yet he came not to be king himself—he rejects those temptations in Luke 3:21-4:14—but to redefine kingship and to redistribute it so that everyone realizes that he or she is king or queen, a royal person with dignity and responsibility to the cosmos. Even his executioners are invited to this royal personhood. Jesus is a royal person par excellence, calling especially the poor to their royalty. His very name, Christ, "the anointed one," reminds us of that special blessing he receives from Yahweh and he extends to all. "The King of the chosen people is divinely anointed [in Hebrew a 'messiah,' an anointed one]; he is the recipient of God's blessing, and this blessing ensures the prosperity of his people."9 He calls all royal persons to be in him as he is in them—a christological panentheism that puts an end to all theisms once and for all. He is the food of the royal voyager that, once taken in, gives out nourishment and hope. He is reported to have said,

> The bread of God is that which comes down from heaven
> and gives life to the world.
> I am the bread of life.
> He who comes to me will never be hungry;
> She who believes in me will never thirst.
> (John 6: 33,35)

Like wisdom, the perfect hostess (Prov. 91, 92), he reveals in a banquet context the mysteries of our origin and of God. Thus Jesus, weak and imperfect as he is and we are, "is the power and the wisdom of God." (1 Cor. 1:25) He shows us a way to God which is grounded in the Via Positiva—God's and our love of creation. A way of Eros.

So great were his love and trust of creation that death itself could have no dominion over him. Death is overcome in resurrected life. Eros will have the final say. This "son of Adam, son of God" (Luke 3:38) fully incarnates the Dabhar, the ever-flowing, cosmos-filling, creative energy of the Creator. Yet he becomes fully flesh as we are, pitching a tent in our midst. Thus God is not incarnated as the Perfect One but, since Jesus is "alike us in every way save sin," as the imperfect one. The divinely imperfect one, or if you will the Imperfect Divinity. Here lies the scandal of the Incarnation and the cross—a revelation of the imperfection and limits of God and how badly God has need of us.10

He is called Emmanuel, the ultimate with of God, the ultimate divine preposition made flesh and fully human. He is "he-with-us," William Blake declares, "because he did not abhor the uterus."11 Fully mammal, fully a product of twenty billion years of evolution as are we, fully among us as is the reign of God. He is the New Adam, the "eldest of many brothers" (Rom. 8:29), the beginner of the new race which is the old race with a fresh start, a new creation, a glorious new birth. He is a cosmic Christ, as we have seen, fully present to all of creation, drawing heaven and earth together in a celebration of the unity of all things, a recapitulation. He is the image of God par excellence, and so he calls us back to our own origins in the Godhead. Here he is prophet, reminding us of our royal personhood, including our dignity and responsibilities. In him is found the revelation of creation and especially human creation "as it was meant to be," as Schillebeeck puts it. Having emptied himself of all divine privileges and prerogatives in order to share our human state fully (Philem. 2), he is the revelation of the guesting side of divine hospitality. He does not stop there, however, but reveals the hosting side of the divinity as well. Still playing with divine holiness in its deepest sense, he also becomes food for the banquet. In utter confusion that only divine play could muster, Jesus the Christ plays host, guest, and food for the eschatological banquet. What an uneasy eagerness there is here to get us humans to respond once again to divine hospitality. He calls us also to follow him, to guest, host, and Eucharist to one another, to be alive, to be eaten and consumed. If every human person is truly made after this person's image, then hospitality becomes the empowerment of every individual: we can all do it, we are reassured. We can trust and our trust will heal us.

Jesus is also lover and pray-er of nature. Mountains, deserts, parks, lakes welcomed him for days at a time as he suffered his fame and his loneliness and his beauty and his decision-making in all these sacred temples. His biggest and most innovative decision was the manner in which he chose to preach. He chose the way and the lifestyle of the storyteller, the parable-maker who fashions a new creation out of the holy materials of the only creation we all share in common: the birds, the lilies of the field, the fishes caught, the fig tree in bloom, the sheep versus the goats, the leaven in the bread, the mustard seeds of the world, and the rains that fall on unjust and just alike. His reverence for nature was so great that the creatures of nature were indeed his teachers, his professors, who he recognized instinctively were looking "on him with affectionate looks" and with truth to tell.

In his prayer he learns to pray to a Creator God as "Abba," or "Papa," thus personalizing as no religion ever had the intimate bond between creature and Creator. His panentheistic Father/Mother God is forever a personal God. Jesus emerges from his prayer a teacher, a rabbi, albeit by way of parables in preference to classrooms. He teaches a blessing theology, how to receive blessing and bestow it, that culminates in the blessings of the Beatitudes. He also insists that the blessings are for all, especially the lame and sick, the poor and the widowed. Royal personhood is no longer restricted to any blood line. We have here what Otto Rank calls the greatest human revolution ever preached, that of the "equality of soul." The Eros he preaches includes a revolution in time-consciousness, for as Herbert Marcuse says, time is "the deadly enemy of Eros." His is a kingdom-come theology, a proclaiming of Good News and even Better News than creation had ever heard before. The News that humanity could, after all, learn here and now to enjoy creation rightly. But to do so, other journeys would still need to be made. Thus, Path II that follows.

PATH II
BEFRIENDING DARKNESS,
LETTING GO AND LETTING BE:
THE VIA NEGATIVA

emptying silence being emptied pain sinking nothingness sin, salvation, Christ - the cross

One of the most remarkable and provocative statements in all of Jung's work is his comparison of Ignatius of Loyola to Meister Eckhart when he declares that what distinguishes the two is that "Ignatius has no Via Negativa."[1] This is no small criticism of Western spirituality since the sixteenth century, the period when Ignatius lived, for as the great Catholic historian M. D. Chenu says, "The church has been Jesuit for three hundred years." If both Jung and Chenu are correct, then, it means that the Catholic Church has been without a Via Negativa for three hundred years. And, since mainstream Protestantism is hardly more steeped in spirituality than Catholicism, it means that the general religious attitude of Western Christianity has been without a Via Negativa in the modern period. (Exceptions would have to be made for the more radical Protestant groups such as Quakers, Mennonites, and Moravian Brethren, and perhaps for some minority Catholic groups such as the Catholic Worker Movement.)

What—if anything—did religion substitute for a Via Negativa? Asceticism was more often than not the response in Catholic spirituality; the effort at using will power to control one's feelings replaced a Via Negativa. Mortifications replaced meditations. Where meditation was encouraged it was so often of an active kind that it could easily drive out any temptations to contemplation. Meister Eckhart eight centuries ago offered the critical objection to asceticism when he said, "Asceticism is of no great importance, for it creates more self-consciousness instead of less and reveals a greater ego rather than a lesser one." The religious acquiescence to "more self-consciousness" and bigger egos in a historical period of rising capitalism, industrial birth, mass armies, and civilian targets in modern warfare did not go unrewarded by the secular guardians of

129

the status quo. When the Via Negativa is ignored, the prophetic voice is invariably silenced. Life becomes superficial, easily manipulated, and ultimately as boring as it is violent. And, above all, cheap. For while the Via Positiva teaches us the cosmic *breadth* of living, of our holy relationship to stars and atoms, to royal persons and to blessed bodiliness, the Via Negativa opens us to our divine *depths*. When one has suffered deep pain and allowed the pain to be pain, one can visit the Grand Canyon and learn that it has nothing on the human person who is even deeper and more powerfully carved over millions of years by the flowing tides of pain.

When the mystical tradition of the *Theologica Germanica*, for example, was lost in Protestantism, what took the place of the Via Negativa was an exaggerated fall/redemption preoccupation with sin, so that one's sinfulness became the proper object of meditation. Another expression of shadow and darkness that Protestantism meditated on was the Catholic Church, so that a letting go of that church became for some Protestants their almost-exclusive expression of letting go. With the ecumenical movement in our time, many persons from Protestant traditions are seeking a deeper Via Negativa. They are often having trouble finding it, however, because few Protestant theologians understand the tradition of a healthy Via Negativa such as is available in the creation spirituality of Meister Eckhart.[2]

One could have predicted the loss of the Via Negativa in the West because of the fact that the Via Positiva and a spirituality of pleasure and hospitality were so profoundly silenced for so long. There is no Via Negativa without a Via Positiva. How can one let go of what one has not fallen in love with? The depth of nothingness is directly related to the experience of everythingness. The void is the convex of the concave surface of the cosmos. We learn we are cosmic beings not only in our joy and ecstasy but also in our pain and sorrow. The salvific rebirth of Eros will surely usher in an era of profound darkness as well. The cataphatic God—the God of the Via Positiva who is drawn to the light—and the apophatic God—who is the God of darkness—are, after all, the same God. And we, who in our recesses experience light *and* darkness, fullness *and* emptiness, are as deeply dialectical and both/and as is our God.

The creation-centered spiritual tradition, as we have seen, does not neglect the Via Positiva. Nor does it lack a profound Via Negativa. We will journey this spiral journey in this section, Path II, and will be guided along the way by the following themes:

11. Emptying: Letting Go of Images and Letting Silence Be Silence.

12. Being Emptied: Letting Pain Be Pain: Kenosis.

13. Sinking into Nothingness and Letting Nothingness Be Nothingness.

14. Sin, Salvation, Christ in Perspective of the Via Negativa: A Theology of the Cross.

Christians will recognize in this path a theology of the cross as they recognized in Path I a theology of creation and Incarnation.

11 EMPTYING: LETTING GO OF IMAGES AND LETTING SILENCE BE SILENCE

God is not found in the soul by adding anything but by a process of subtraction.
> —*Meister Eckhart*

Language cannot do everything—
chalk it on the walls where the dead poets
lie in their mausoleums.
> —*Adrienne Rich (30.19)*

I feel closer to what language can't reach.
> —*Rainer Maria Rilke (8.101)*

You cannot get it by taking thought;
You cannot seek it by not taking thought.
> —*a Zenrin poem*[1]

O silence, golden zero
Unsettling sun

Love winter when the plant says nothing.
> —*Thomas Merton*[2]

This word is a hidden word
and comes in the darkness of the night.
To enter this darkness put away
all voices and sounds
all images and likenesses.
For no image has ever reached into the soul's foundation
where God herself
with her own being is effective.
> —*Meister Eckhart*

Be still
Listen to the stones of the wall
Be silent, they try
To speak your

Name.
Listen
To the living walls.
Who are you?
Who
Are you? Whose
Silence are you?
     — *Thomas Merton*[3]

We can know the dark, and dream it into a new image.
    — *Starhawk, (38.xvi)*

Then alone do we know God truly, when we believe that God
is far beyond all that we can possibly think of God.
    — *Thomas Aquinas*[4]

The ground of the soul is dark.
    — *Meister Eckhart*

I said to my soul, be still,
and let the dark come upon you
which shall be the darkness of God.
    — *T. S. Eliot*[5]

If we allow the night,
if we allow what she is in the darkness to be,
this knowledge, this that we have not yet named:
what we are. Oh, this knowledge of what we are
is becoming clear.
    — *Susan Griffin (20.168)*

Yet no matter how deeply I go down into myself
my God is dark, and like a webbing made
of a hundred roots, that drink in silence.
    — *Rainer Maria Rilke (8.15)*

Nothing in all creation is so like God as stillness.
    — *Meister Eckhart*

Blessed be
     the beds that bring us down
     to worship one another
     in the night—
Never, oh never naked
     enough
     to know the
     Being of the other.
        —Lee Pieper[6]

In this temple of God, in this the divine dwelling place, God
alone rejoices with the soul in the deepest silence. There is no
reason for the intellect to stir or seek anything, for the Lord
who created it wishes to give it repose here.
        — Teresa of Avila[7]

Tao is beyond words
And beyond things.
It is not expressed
Either in word or in silence.
Where there is no longer word or silence
Tao is apprehended.
        —a Taoist text[8]

The Enlightenment—the en·light·en·ment—has rendered all of us
who live in Western civilization citizens of the light. And of lights.
Questers after left-brain—which is light-oriented—satisfaction. The
invention of the light bulb and electricity and neon lights and handy
light switches was a marvelous outgrowth of the Enlightenment's
technological achievements. And with the light bulb there came also
the radio, so that now not only were our eyes attracted to what is
outside of us but our ears were as well. With television we experience a new kind of light machine—one that combines eyes *and* ears,
light and radio, to allure us out of ourselves. Then came color
television, whose light is a bright, bright light of rainbow varieties,
ever more alluring and more demanding. Religion too has become
very light-oriented in the West. The religion of Positivism is almost
all light. And the sentimental hymns that ignore the dark or reduce
it anthropomorphically to human sin and therefore to salvation
contribute to the excessive lighting of our world.

What price have we paid as a people for all this light? We have become afraid of the dark. Afraid of no light. Of silence, therefore. Of image-lessness. We whore after more—more images, more light, more profits, more goodies. And, if Eckhart is correct about the power of subtraction versus the power of addition, our souls in the process shrivel up. For growth of the human person takes place in the dark. Under ground. In subterranean passages. There, where "no image has ever reached into the soul's foundation," God alone works. A light-oriented spirituality is superficial, surface-like, lacking as it does the deep, dark roots that nourish and surprise and ground the large tree.

The wonderful working mysteries that are our bodies are filled with darkness. Our heart works just fine—in the dark. Our livers, our intestines, our brain, all the beautiful and harmonious and working parts of our blessed bodies go about their everyday business—at night and during the day—completely in the dark. Isn't that wonderful? Doesn't that thought—a dark mystery worth meditating on, the beauty of our body's insides—fill you with wonder and gratitude and praise for what amazing things can happen in the dark?

There can be little question that part of the flight from darkness in the modern period of Western culture has been the flight from mortality and the fear of death, of letting go of this life. Otto Rank sees this fear of death as the most basic characteristic of a patriarchal society. It has much to do with our hatred of animals, of the earth, of life in fact. This fear drives out any Eros or love of life. What is the dark? Starhawk, in her fine tribute to the holiness of darkness, *Dreaming the Dark,* says that the dark is "all that we are afraid of, all that we don't want to see—fear, anger, sex, grief, death, the unknown." (38.xiv) The way of the unconscious mind or the "right brain" is the way of darkness. "The depths of our beings are not all sunlit; to see clearly, we must be willing to dive into the dark, inner abyss and acknowledge the creatures we may find there."[9]

How does one learn to recover the darkness and to befriend it again? And how does a people learn this? First, it is healthy to reflect on how in fact our lives are already bound in darkness without our having to perform any extraordinary manipulations. For example, we all began in the dark. Our loving parents presumably conceived us in the dark nights of their lovemaking. We ought to celebrate that dark sacrament of marriage's most intimate moments much more sensually and honestly than we do. Furthermore, we lived apparently quite contented lives for nine full months in the dark. The womb was dark and not fearful. These are our origins, the

135

very holy origin of our original being, our original blessedness. There is no underestimating the importance of our meditating on our dark and silent origins if we are to make touch with our spiritual depths.

The sun does not penetrate all of space. Much of space is dark. Much of the birth of the cosmos itself was done in the dark—the sun has not always existed. The seed under ground is growing in the dark no less than the fetus in the mother's womb. All mystery is about the dark. All darkness is about mystery. The Enlightenment left us with a pernicious notion that we were to conquer mystery itself just as we were to conquer the land and animals and our feelings. We were robbed of savoring mystery and its darkness. We need to retrieve our rights to mystery and to the darkness in which it is so often immersed and enmeshed.

We have touched on the dark mystery of our origins, of our preorigins, of our birth, of all of living at the depths of mystery, and not just light or knowledge or problem-solving. We also are wrapped in mystery and darkness when pain and suffering come our way, when the death of a loved one or of a relationship or our own dying confronts us. Our dyings may include changing jobs or locales or friends or relationships. Always it takes place with darkness and mystery. Today we are confronted with a new level of darkness that is without precedent: that darkness that Jonathan Schell calls "extinction"—the very death of birth, the end of all human life and existence that nuclear extinction makes possible. If we do not face frontally this unimaginable darkness and befriend it, enemy that it is, we shall surely pay the price all those pay who repress the shadow: it shall return to haunt us and break into our light-of-day giddiness, our blind feeding of a bloated war machine that can culminate in authentic darkness for the earth itself. If a nuclear war takes place, the sun itself will be blotted out for three days, animals will be permanently blinded, a very unfriendly darkness indeed will pervade the earth.

In addition to meditating *on* our very real relationship to darkness and to its ever-present companion, mystery, we also need to let go of all meditations, all images, all likenesses, all projections, all naming, all contact with isness. The need for silence that Zen speaks of, that wisdom literature celebrates, that Eckhart praises, and that Merton calls for is not just about oral silence. Silence means the letting go of all images—whether oral ones or auditory ones or visual ones or inner ones or cognitive ones or imaginative ones. Whether of time or of space, of inner or of outer. It is a radical letting go of language. A letting language go. A concentration on what is non-language, non-music, non-self, non-God. It is being. A being still. Eckhart puts it this way:

> One should love God mindlessly, without mind or mental activities or images or representations. Bare your soul of all mind and stay there without mind.

In this sinking into silence and non-imaging we do not have to be afraid, for God is "superessential darkness," and to make contact with the darkness is to make contact with the deepest side of the Godhead. "Love God as God is a not-God, a not-mind, a not-person, a not-image," counsels Eckhart.

Letting go of busyness and allowing silence to be silence means letting go of the busy work of projecting. As Eckhart says, "When you come to the point when you are no longer compelled to project yourself into any image or to entertain any images in yourself, and you let go of all that is within you, then you can be transported into God's naked being." We are indeed capable of such blankness, emptiness, silence. But we need to desire it deeply, to pray for it, and even to let this letting go become our prayer. Thus Meister Eckhart confessed that he "prayed God to rid me of God." One must recognize the importance of letting go in this radical way of the silence-of-no-images if one is to befriend the dark. And there can be no symbols or images that are allowed to hang around—not even our names and symbols for God can go unchecked. We pray even to let go of God. Here if anywhere lies "sheer abandon."

How do we go about letting go of images, images for ourselves and images for others and images for God? First, this presumes that we do indeed entertain images in the first place; it presumes that the Via Positiva has been entered into deeply enough that we have imbibed of the excitement of living and relating and that therefore images do flow in us. One does not let go of images by concentrating on letting go of images. One does not let go of a pink elephant in one's head by trying to let go of a pink elephant in one's head. Rather, one lets go by breathing deeply in and out, by entering into the music of one's body—its breath, the tympanum of one's heartbeat or lung beat, by concentrating on what is most immediately present. Zen sitting or yoga posturing can help some people to do this letting go. For others, just being, just sitting can work. For still others the moments following ecstatic experiences in nature or music or sexual sharing or poetry afford the correct setting for letting go and for silence of the deepest sort. For others a group meditation, as at a Quaker meeting or a monastic meditation period, is a fine occasion for such letting go. All of us, when circumstances imprison us and force us to let go of our light-of-day plans, learn anew what silence means. This may happen in a hospital following an accident or during an illness, in prison if that is where we are, in moments of deep sorrow following the loss of a loved one or of a loved relationship. And it may happen in praying scripture with the heart and not just the head. Or in communing with the deep silence of the cosmos and its children, whether of the two-legged or four-legged or finned or winged variety. For most of us a combination of almost all the above ways of letting go and letting silence be silence can be expected to prove fruitful at different periods in our lives.

One example of the ways in which Western religion has thoroughly misunderstood the Via Negativa as a letting go of images is in the iconoclastic movements of Protestantism, where the German term *keine bild* (no image) was taken to mean "Destroy art." This association of images with external images tells us much about Western culture. But the real meaning in the *Theologica Germanica*, for example, of "no images" is the meaning Eckhart holds: that persons need to let go at times of all images if we are to birth authentic ones with our lives and work and prayer and art.

Psychologist Carl Gustav Jung admits that it took a creation-centered mystic to teach him this valuable art of letting go, an art that Eastern mysticism does not ignore. In commenting on the Taoist text *The Secret of the Golden Flower*, he asks, "What did these people do in order to achieve the development that liberated them? As far as I could see they did nothing but let things happen." And he goes on,

> The art of letting things happen, action through non-action, letting go of oneself, as taught by Meister Eckhart, became for me the key opening the door to the way. We must be able to let things happen in the psyche. For us, this actually is an art of which few people know anything. Consciousness is forever interfering, helping, correcting, and negating, and never leaving the simple growth of the psychic processes in peace.[10]

Letting go is indeed an art. It is the surest meditative art of the Via Negativa. With good reason Jung laments its rarity in Western, patriarchal culture and religion.

If it is true that the ground of the soul is dark, then the human race cannot continue to afford to flee the darkness and to embrace an Enlightenment that does not include an Endarkenment. If we were able to invent the light machine called television which captures every eyeball that enters a room, why do we not invent dark machines that suck people into mystery on their entrance into a room? If we are to "allow the night" and overcome "this fear of the dark," as Susan Griffin counsels (20.168, 122), then spirituality should lead the way by itself, proclaiming the truth and the practice of a healthy Via Negativa. Such a journey will not consist of manufacturing religious exercises but of letting go and letting be, of breathing deeply, of trusting the empty spaces and the silences. Of sinking, therefore, and not of climbing.

The image of our spiritual journey as one of sinking is a familiar one in the creation-centered tradition. John the Scot in the ninth century wrote of "the supernatural falling of the most purified souls into God Himself,"[11] and Mechtild of Magdeburg writes of "sinking and cooling." Eckhart picks up on this image when he says that "we are to sink eternally from letting go to letting go into God." We sink into depth and in this depth we find God, who dwells especially in the depths and in the dark. God who is indeed a "superessential darkness." (Eckhart)

12 BEING EMPTIED: LETTING PAIN BE PAIN: KENOSIS

If we could learn to learn from pain
even as it grasps us. . . .
—*Adrienne Rich (30.10)*

She [Marie Curie] died a famous woman denying
her wounds
denying
her wounds came from the same source as her power.
—*Adrienne Rich (30.3)*

From suffering I have learned this: That whoever is sore
wounded by love will never be made whole unless she embrace the very same love which wounded her.
—*Mechtild of Magdeburg*

Suffering is the badge of the human race.
—*Mahatma Gandhi (22.287)*

I feel her pain and my own pain comes into me, and my own
pain grows large and I grasp this pain with my hands, and I
open my mouth to this pain, I taste, I know, and I know why
she goes on.
—*Susan Griffin (20.219)*

What do we know of the inner mechanisms of Mozart the
creative genius? Only one thing is certain: depression or psychic
suffering does not diminish his productivity, unlike other creative people, but increases it qualitatively and quantitatively.
—*Wolfgang Hildesheimer*[1]

Remember this: All suffering comes to an end. And whatever
you suffer authentically, God has suffered from it first.
—*Meister Eckhart*

The life in me trickles away,
    days of grief have gripped me.
At night-time, sickness saps my bones,
    I am gnawed by wounds that never sleep.
It has thrown me into the mud
    where I am no better than dust and ashes.

I cry to you, and you give me no answer;
    I stand before you, but you take no notice.
        —Job 30:16, 17, 19

I am worn out with groaning,
every night I drench my pillow
and soak my bed with tears;
my eye is wasted with grief,
I have grown old with enemies all around me.
        —Ps. 6:6, 7

One should identify oneself with the universe itself. Everything that is less than the universe is subjected to suffering.
        —Simone Weil[2]

When Christ was in pain we were in pain. All creatures of God's creation that can suffer pain suffered with him. The sky and the earth failed at the time of Christ's dying because he too was part of nature.
        —Julian of Norwich

It is one thing to empty. It is an even deeper thing to be emptied. Pain does this. It empties us, if we allow it to.

Today in America—and every day in America—seventy-six million Valium will be swallowed. In addition, some thirty million people will glue themselves to soap operas on television. It would seem that our culture is not well adapted to deal with pain. Pain is today's unmentionable reality, much as sex was unmentionable in the Victorian period. And pain is everywhere—deep, ineffable, unfathomable, cosmic pain. And it needs to be named for what it is so that we can pray our pain, i.e., enter into it. That is the only way a dentist resolves the pain of a toothache—by entering into its source in an inflamed cavity. Covering our pain up with drugs, alcohol, soap operas, or shopping is no release from the pain. It is more acquiescence, of a perverse kind, to the pain. It is letting pain run our lives instead of letting Eros and our love of life run our lives.

Much of a society's values and realities can be surmised by listening to its youth. The youth in our culture are committing suicide at record rates. Suicide is the number two killer among American youth —and perhaps number one, since number one is car accidents and we will never know how many of these accidents are in fact suicides. Pain reaches deeply into women's lives, as Carol Christ observes.

> At a very young age a girl realizes that being female means understanding that her brothers have a right to demand more of their mother's attention, that her father will not play ball with her. Being female means that even if she gets A's, her career will not be as important as that of a boy who gets B's. Being female means that *she* is not important, except in her relationships to boys and men. (10.15)

Facing the darkness, admitting the pain, allowing the pain to be pain, is never easy. This is why courage—big-heartedness—is the most essential virtue on the spiritual journey. But if we fail to let pain be pain—and our entire patriarchal culture refuses to let this happen—then pain will haunt us in nightmarish ways. We will become pain's victims instead of the healers we might become. And eventually pain's perpetrators. Both Adrienne Rich and Mechtild of Magdeburg in their observations in the beginning of this section have the insight to pain: enter in; befriend it. Jesus had the same insight: love your enemies. Pain is our enemy, but that is no excuse to run from embracing it, kissing it long enough so that we might truly let go of it. There is no way to let go of pain without first embracing it and loving it—not as pain but as a sister and brother in our dialectical living of both pleasure and pain. Eros does not come without a price. Every rose has its thorns. The Japanese poet Kenji Miyazawa left us a powerful image of dealing with pain when he said that we must embrace pain and burn it as a fuel for our journey. The image that comes to my mind on hearing this advice is the following: we pick up our pain as we would a bundle of sticks for a fireplace; we necessarily embrace these sticks as we move across the room to the fireplace; then we thrust them into the fire, getting rid of them, letting go of them; finally we are warmed and delighted by their sacrificial gift to us in the form of fire and heat and warmth and energy. This is the manner in which we can and indeed must deal with our pain. First comes the embrace, the allowing of pain to be pain; next comes the journey with the pain; then the letting go, but in a deliberate manner, into a fire, into a cauldron where the pain's energy will serve us. And finally comes the benefit we do indeed derive from having burned this fuel. Pain is meant to give us energy. What might some of this energy look like?

First, pain helps us to understand other people in pain. Pain is profoundly social, it is eminently shareable, and it is no coincidence that the privatizing of pain, the covering up of pain in our culture, parallels the privatizing of body and pleasure and spirituality in our culture and its religions. A healthy experience of letting pain be pain is always a schooling in compassion. For when a person has suffered deeply even once and has owned that suffering, that person can never forget and never fail to recognize the pain of others. Pain is the most legitimate school for compassion that I know of. Dorothy Day, arrested for picketing with militant suffragists in 1918, was thrown into jail for the first time. She writes of what she learned from this pain.

> The blackness of hell was all about me. The sorrows of the world encompassed me. I was like one gone down into a pit. Hope had forsaken me. I was that mother whose child had been raped and slain. I was the mother who had borne the monster who had done it. I was even that monster, feeling in my own heart every abomination.[3]

Here lies compassion, the growing imagination to identify with others.

Secondly, pain helps us to understand pleasure and to criticize it. The Via Negativa relates back to the Via Positiva—not only by carving us into deeper people and ridding us of layers on layers of cover-ups of both pleasure and pain, but also by allowing us to experience how the true pleasures in our lives are of the simplest, most shareable kind. Pain destroys the illusions of false, that is elitist, pleasures. It burns from the inside out. It therefore sensitizes us to what is truly beautiful in life. Molly Rush, the grandmother of seven who was jailed for protesting the Trident submarine, an invention that carries within itself more destruction than has resulted from all human wars combined, including the atomic bombs of World War II, had such an experience of awakening to pleasure while she underwent the sufferings of prison life. She writes:

> Last October I found myself out in a scrubby prison yard, discovering amidst the mud eighteen varieties of wildflowers. Some of them were almost too small to see until you'd gone around that yard a hundred times. Maybe the hundredth time you would have caught five of them. After several days, you could count eighteen. . . . Most of the

143

time we never see the flowers around us, but when that's about all there is to see, they become precious.

When asked what she most learned from her Plowshares action and her jailing, she replied, "I have a greater sense of the preciousness of life."[4] The psychological term for how it is that the Via Negativa can in fact increase our sense of pleasure at the basics of life is deautomatization.[5] We become, as adults—children do not lack this as a rule—automatized to the beauty and form and shapes and colors and smells that are around us all the time; we lose our sense of pleasure, of the preciousness of life. Unwished-for pain, provided we pray it or enter into it and do not cover it up and run from it, can often bring that love of life back to us.

The poet Rainer Maria Rilke, who himself underwent a profoundly painful childhood, having been locked in the attic by his mother for long periods of time, and having been sent to a military school even though he was a sensitive child, learned something of praise and pleasure from his journeys into pain. He writes:

Oh, tell us, poet, what do you do?
                    I praise.
But the deadly and the violent days,
how do you undergo them, take them in?
                    I praise.
But the namelessness—how do you raise
that, invoke the unnameable?
                    I praise.
What right have you, through every phase,
in every mask, to remain true?
                    I praise.
—and that both stillness and the wild affray
know you, like star and storm?
                    Because I praise.[6]

And, for the very same reasons, Meister Eckhart can say that "Everything praises God. Darkness, privations, defects, evil too praise God and bless God."

A third way in which pain enlivens us and gives us energy is that embarking on pain and making that journey toughens us up. It makes us stronger by testing us and demanding discipline of us that we did not know we were capable of. Here the image of the athlete that Paul uses is in some way a valid one—not in the way in which the patriarchal ascetic tradition employs it, however, as a conscious effort to control one's passions. But in the natural flow of events in our lives wherein living life fully requires strength to endure pain and suffering. One point that feminists Adrienne Rich and Carol Christ make about men who discover their gentle sides in our culture is that too often these men mistake gentleness for passivity and weakness. Sensitivity, which includes sensitivity to pain, also demands strength. A new kind of strength, it is true; the strength of endurance and perseverance; the strength that solitude requires; the strength that vulnerability is about. This strength does not come from willing it or gritting our teeth. It comes from undergoing pain—unwished-for, unplanned, unheralded pain. There is a strength learned from suffering that cannot be learned any other way. For suffering tests the depth of our love of life and relationship even when and especially because relationships are so often the cause of our suffering. Suffering converts the fuel of Eros into the energy of living Eros out in our personal and social lives. As Susan Griffin puts it, "Beauty demands a more arduous process." (22.192) Beauty and terror, as Simone Weil noted, are related. Prettyness does not demand arduousness, but beauty does. Beauty is hard. Hard as hell, the *Song of Songs* says. Beauty is not learned or valued without the suffering that makes us big enough and strong enough to be proper vessels of the beautiful.

Still another energy derived from suffering is the manner in which letting pain be pain links us with others. All social movements and organization were born of pain. Not privatized pain or pain kept to oneself or the wallowing in one's own pain, but pain shared. Unemployment shared. Unjust taxes shared. The evil, bitter taste and experiences of racism, of sexism, of ageism—all shared. Today it is the pain of nuclear war that people enter into by meditation and reflection and storytelling that is birthing that social movement that can—if it is not too late—finally put an end to war as a means for solving human conflict. Nonviolence is born of the shared experience of the pain of violence. We can become so alone, so deeply alone and emptied in our pain, that we have to go out to others with whom we can share this dark, dark journey. And this makes social linkage possible and vivifies it with an energy that no one can take from us. Mechtild of Magdeburg saw this clearly when she wrote,

When I can no longer bear my loneliness I take it to my friends. For I must share it with all the friends of God. "Do you suffer?" "So do I!"

145

Liberation begins at the point where pain is acknowledged and allowed to be pain. From there pain becomes shareable. And, where possible, resolvable.

Still another way in which pain energizes us is in opening us up. While we learn that we are citizens of the universe, capable of the cosmos, in the Via Positiva, this same truth is reestablished in the Via Negativa. Our pain is a cosmic pain—and for this reason Simone Weil advises us to "identify with the universe itself." This cosmic relationship heals, for "everything that is less than the universe is subject to suffering." All creatures of the universe suffer pain—pain unites us. This understanding is very different from what Descartes taught a few centuries ago when he said that because in his estimation animals did not have souls but were machines, you could only damage an animal but never really hurt one. It is another and very dangerous form of human chauvinism to say that only humans suffer pain. It makes no sense, it returns no energy to us, it forces us to introverted efforts at problem-solving such as drugs or drink or constant crying, if we try to deal with our suffering only from the point of view of our manmade or ego-constructed worlds. Pain, like pleasure, is a cosmic experience. It urges us to return to cosmic celebration, cosmic healing, cosmic connection-making, cosmic rituals, cosmic awareness. Here the cosmic Christ plays a special role, for in this figure we have an affirmation of the cosmic pain of God. As Julian of Norwich notes, the entire cosmos responded to the crucifixion of Jesus Christ. This pain cut through human chauvinism and united all creatures; it also cut through human, in the sense of ego, understanding of time and space. Julian says:

> I saw a great oneing between Christ and us because when he was in pain we were in pain. All creatures of God's creation that can suffer pain suffered with him. The sky and the earth failed at the time of Christ's dying because he too was part of nature.

In our depths we are one with all creatures and all of God, not only in pleasure as in the Via Positiva, but also in pain as in the Via Negativa. All creatures suffer, not just human ones. That means we can all contribute to bearing one another's burdens.

It follows from these examples of the gifts that the Via Negativa brings that suffering is not, as the fall/redemption tradition emphasizes too much, the wages we pay for sin. As Tanquerry puts it, "God has made suffering the wages of sin."[7] Suffering is built into the birth process of the entire cosmos. It has to do with sacrifice and yielding, with receiving and birthing forth. It is cosmic not only in its dimensions but in time, that is to say that suffering has accompanied all the birthings of the universe right up to the labor pains of the most recent mother birthing her human child. Some suffering—that which leads to birthing—can be a blessing.

In this entire reflection on letting pain be pain, I must emphasize how important it is that we not glorify pain or cling to our pain or wallow in our pain. That is not letting pain be pain—that way lies letting pain be our boss. That way lies sado-masochistic manipulation. The purpose of letting pain be pain is precisely this: to let go of pain. We are not asked to cling to our pain, to wallow in it, to build our lives around it. What we must do ultimately is to let go of pain. Ideally, by entering into it we become able to breathe so much freedom from within the pain that the deepest kind of letting go can truly occur. For this to happen, the naming of the pain, the letting it be pain for a while, is essential. For the Via Negativa is not an end in itself; it is only part of a four-part cycle repeated endlessly— "eternally," Meister Eckhart says—in our lifetimes. There arrives the time when we need to let go even of letting go, when we let the Via Negativa itself go. But that awaits Path III, and there is still more exploring of Path II to attend to.

13 SINKING INTO NOTHINGNESS AND LETTING NOTHINGNESS BE NOTHINGNESS

Love the nothing, flee the self.
—*Mechtild of Magdeburg*

Nothingness spreads around us. But in this nothing we find what we did not know existed.
—*Susan Griffin (20.159)*

All creatures are a mere nothing. I do not say that they are something very slight or even something, but that they are a mere nothing. All creatures have been drawn from nothingness and that is why their origin is nothingness.
—*Meister Eckhart*

You played heroic, necessary
games with death

since in your neo-protestant tribe the void
was supposed not to exist

except as a fashionable concept.
—*Adrienne Rich (30.55)*

To reach satisfaction in all
desire its possession in nothing.
To come to possess all
desire the possession of nothing.
To arrive at being all
desire to be nothing.
To come to the knowledge of all
desire the knowledge of nothing.
—*John of the Cross*[1]

Women's experience of nothingness is more far-reaching than men's. Women's experiences of nothingness begin at birth and continue throughout their lives.
—*Carol Christ (10.15)*

God is a being beyond being
and a nothingness beyond being.
God is nothing. No thing.
God is nothingness.
And yet God is something.
　　　　—*Meister Eckhart*

Do you wish to have love? If you wish to have love, then you must leave love.
　　　　—*Mechtild of Magdeburg*

Irradiated by the fire of its long love, overpowered by the embrace of the Holy Trinity, the soul begins to sink and to cool—as the sun sinks down from its highest zenith into the night. Thus, too, do we sink with soul and with body.
　　　　—*Mechtild of Magdeburg*

If you would swim on the bosom of the ocean of Truth, you must reduce yourself to a zero.
　　　　—*Mahatma Gandhi*

Are you willing to be sponged out, erased,
　　cancelled,
　　　made nothing?
Are you willing to be made nothing?
　　dipped into oblivion?
If not, you will never really change.
　　　　—*D. H. Lawrence*[2]

Outside of God, there is nothing but nothing.
　　　　—*Meister Eckhart*

When one learns letting go and letting be, when one learns sinking, when one learns emptying and being emptied, one necessarily comes face to face with nothingness. Our experiences of nothingness can be personal or political; they can be at times the most affirming and unitive experiences of our lives and at other times the most devastating and earth-shaking experiences. What is certain is that our nothingness experiences are never superficial. They are always rock-bottom, radical, of our roots. Learning to befriend the dark means learning to befriend nothingness, to reverence it. To let nothingness be nothingness. To trust nothingness. For in the ulti-

149

mate of darknesses, in what Eckhart calls our "unknowing knowledge," wisdom itself is often tasted. The experience of nothingness that one might touch based on the emptying meditations we discussed under Theme Eleven may be very quiet, a kind of blank space or empty mirror, experience of what-is/what-is-not wherein everything is and everything is not. Or, based more on the being emptied, Theme Twelve, pain and suffering may render our nothingness experience quite hurtful, shocking, and even violent. In this case very often our most spontaneous response will be anger—"Why me? Why now?" In any instance, no matter how the nothingness experience comes about, we need to recall how holy nothingness is, how it deserves our respect and attention, how nothingness needs to be allowed to be in our lives. Its presence will change us in unfathomable and surprising ways. We shall be recreated as everything is created, *ex nihilo,* from the nothingness.

Our nothingness experiences are substantive of our deep living and indeed of our recovering Eros in our spiritualities. Yet for centuries we in the West have been deprived of a healthy understanding of nothingness. Feminist Carol Christ cries out for the deeply felt need for naming our nothingness experiences once again.

> Women must even read themselves sidewise into analyses of the experience of nothingness. Women need a literature that names their pain and allows them to see the emptiness in their lives as an occasion for insight rather than as one more indication of their worthlessness. Women need stories that will tell them that their ability to face the darkness in their lives is an indication of strength, not weakness. (10.17)

Christ's first conclusion in her study on various women writers' spirituality is that "the *experience of nothingness* is central in each." (10.119, italics hers) Nothingness is part and parcel of every authentic liberation movement. Martin Luther King, Jr., talked about his civil rights movement journeying "from nothing",[3] and his mentor, Mahatma Gandhi, referred to the political implications of nothingness on many occasions.

> True individuality consists in reducing oneself to zero. The secret of life is selfless service. The highest ideal for us is to become free from attachment. (22.93)

Erikson comments that for Gandhi this "zero position" meant his escaping the establishment and that this freedom from society gave

Gandhi "the Archimedean point for total national renewal."[4] Erikson further analyzes the power behind the nothingness experience of Gandhi under the title "Leverage of Truth," the conclusion to his study *Gandhi's Truth*.

> Out of the acceptance of nothingness emerges what can be the most central and inclusive, timeless and actual, conscious and active position in the human universe. . . . Actuality, however, is by no means a mere denial of nothingness. . . . Actuality is complementary to nothingness and, therefore, deeply and unavoidably endowed with the instinctual energy and the elemental concern of generativity.[5]

One reason why nothingness is a prerequisite for liberation is that in a real sense those who commit themselves to liberation must come to that "zero point" wherein they have "nothing to lose." This means that, compared to the truth of the justice they seek, of the God they incarnate, there is nothing to lose, that outside of this truth there is nothing. As Eckhart puts it, "Outside of God there is nothing but nothing."

Mechtild of Magdeburg, who was also involved in social change, befriended nothingness and, like Gandhi, linked it directly to the service of neighbor. She counsels:

> Love the nothing, flee the self.
> Stand alone, seek help from no one.
> Let your being be quiet,
> be free from the bondage of all things.
> Free those who are bound,
> give exhortation to the free.
> Care for the sick, but dwell alone.
> When you drink the waters of sorrow
> you shall kindle the fire of love
> with the match of perseverance—
> This is the way to dwell in the desert.

The image of the desert is a familiar one for the prophetic mystics like Mechtild and Eckhart, who derive it from certain translations of the prophet Hosea. A visit to the desert is a letting go of all things that occupy one; therefore the desert represents a "no-thing" or a nothingness experience. One is refreshed in this desert; there one derives energy to carry on the struggle for greening and liberation.

What are some other experiences of nothingness that unite us and energize us? Consider the following: If you are thirty-nine years old, meditate on forty years ago. There was a time when each of us was nothing. It is important that we make contact with our origins, and our origins are quite literally *ex nihilo,* from nothing. Every experience of nothingness, then, can prove to be a healing experience for us, one that makes us whole and returns us to our primary origins. Without making this connection with the nothingness from which we spring, we fail to appreciate how unique each one of us is and how unique every being with whom we share the cosmos is. We lose reverence for being. When we fail to make this connection, we live our lives in jerks instead of in a flowing manner, and we will resist and indeed put to death those who remind us of our origins. Few have celebrated the darkness of our origins more beautifully than the poet Rilke.

> You darkness, that I come from,
> I love you more than all the fires
> that fence in the world,
> for the fire makes
> a circle of light for everyone,
> and then no one outside learns of you.
>
> But the darkness pulls in everything:
> shapes and fires, animals and myself,
> how easily it gathers them!—
> powers and people—
>
> and it is possible a great energy
> is moving near me
>
> I have faith in nights. (8.21)

Rilke's faith in nights, his love of the dark, is related to the cosmic womb of our origins, where all is drawn in, where we can celebrate our cosmic existence together.

A nothingness experience is also a deep experience of nothingness. It is an experience which is now verified by modern physics. As the poet Angelus Silesius put it in the seventeenth century, "There are no objects for compassion because there are no objects." By dropping or letting go of worlds of subjects/objects, we sink into a consciousness of interdependence and indeed of transparency. Our experiences of transparency and synchronicity are experiences of no-thing-ness, and vice versa. As we allow this truth to penetrate us more and more deeply we begin to realize the truth of compassion: to relieve another person's pain or to celebrate another's joy is to relieve one's own pain and to celebrate one's own joy. Here the unnatural boundaries between inner and outer, personal and social, I and you, truly melt, and we return to a micro/macrocosmic relation to existence.

An experience of no-thing-ness that we frequently encounter but seldom relate to the Via Negativa is the letting go and the sinking that occurs in laughter. Laughter is a kind of letting go of ourselves brought about by paradoxical or seemingly incongruous images. Susan Griffin bears rich testimony to this gleeful "revelation."

> She lets herself fall. She falls into the room of her wants. . . . This room filled with darkness. Where we go into darkness. Where we embrace darkness. Where we lie close to darkness, breathe when darkness breathes and find darkness inside ourselves. The room of the darkness of women. Where we are not afraid. Where joy is just under the surface. Where we laugh. Where laughter fills us utterly when we see what we thought was horrible. Where our demands are endlessly received. Where revelation fills us with glee. (20.157)

The Buddhist tradition, too, with its koans pays tribute to the act of laughter as an act of the Via Negativa. Jesus' parables are not without their gleeful side, and neither is the preaching of Meister Eckhart. A healthy Via Negativa will always include a powerful sense of humor, a recognition of how deep down we are divine jokes, cosmic jokes, and even our pain is not to be taken too seriously. To do so would deny pain its transparency.

Pain and anger too can sometimes be so great in us that the only name for them is no name—thus, nothingness. Pain and suffering can be so great that they are, like God, ineffable. Pain can be so deep, so dark, so silent, so untouchable, and so unresolvable that it can appropriately be called nothing. We touch the void in our pain. The void is simply the concave surface whose convex is cosmos. A spirituality that opens us to cosmic joy and beauty also renders us vulnerable to an experience of the void. Cosmic nothingness. It helps at such times of ineffable pain to realize that others too suffer from such kinds of pain, that nothingness is very much a shared and shareable experience. But nothingness must be named if it is to be shared. Once when I was in such bottomless pain I had an image of falling down a deep, deep well that got darker and darker, more and more endless. Along the walls of the well an occasional person smiled as I fell but these persons were incapable of extending a hand to break my fall. Nevertheless, just those smiles helped a bit to sustain my sinking, my undergoing what Rich describes as to "sink and float." (30.7)

One of the differences between Jewish thinking and Hellenistic thinking is that in biblical faith our trust extends even to nothingness. Our Creator is author of all things, even of nothingness. Our falls into nothingness can be and must be trusted—we can learn to let ourselves fall, to let ourselves sink. Isn't this what the seed does as it falls into the ground, eventually to sprout new life? Our Creator God is a God of nothingness as well as of isness. A both/and God calling us to both/and living. The Via Positiva is cheapened without the Via Negativa, and the Via Negativa without the Via Positiva becomes sick asceticism, more power-as-control instead of less in the universe. The dark night of our souls is a special occasion for divine birth and opportunity, provided we let the darkness be darkness and the nothingness be nothingness, at least for a while. Without nothingness there will be no creation or re-creation. Only reproduction, reshuffling of what is and has been. Music editor Irving Kolodin comments on Beethoven's spiritual experience of nature as of 1802, an experience of the Via Positiva.

> He conceived joy and the fulfillment of it in the "Temple of Nature" as an outward, direct, physical experience—the pleasure that comes from a sunny day in the country, feeling its warmth, hearing the bird sounds, the music of a village band, even, at day's end, the threat of thunder in the distance. This is normal and natural for anyone.

But the next six years were to constitute a "spiritual upheaval" for Beethoven, a true Via Negativa. For in those years, he learned that he was going deaf. Imagine a musician going deaf—a dancer without legs, a painter with no eyes, a public speaker with no voice. Here surely we have an experience of nothingness. Beethoven struggled in his "Heiligenstadt Testament" with this crisis: "O Providence, let for once a pure day of joy be mine, so long is true joy's inward resonance a stranger to me. Oh when, Oh when, O God, can I feel it once again in this Temple of Nature and of Humanity. Never? No—Oh that were too cruel." Ultimately, Beethoven's resolution to this crisis of nothingness was indeed new birth, the birth of his *Pastoral* Symphony, no. 6. This represents, says Kolodin,

> the more exalted privilege of one who could no longer hear to speak of how a day in the country *feels*, to fix forever the senses it stimulates, the sights it conveys—in short, not to reproduce but re-create.[6]

154

In the creation-centered spiritual journey, then, nothingness is an essential part of the deep and fruitful journey. There will be no creativity or New Creation without the Via Negativa. Without the silence that constitutes the letting go of images, without the emptying and the being emptied that full living brings, without sinking into nameless nothingness, we do not grow. For our souls grow by subtraction and not by addition, Eckhart warns us. Also, there is no strengthening of our spirits for the battles that await us in group movements and liberation struggles without acknowledging the "zero point" from where all new creation emerges. The journey to nothingness is described by Susan Griffin and John the Scot as "falling," by Adrienne Rich and Meister Eckhart as "sinking," and by Mechtild of Magdeburg as "sinking and cooling." Just as the Via Positiva was an experience of light and of heat, so for Mechtild the Via Negativa will be an experience of yielding to darkness and to coolness. She compares this sinking to the sinking of the sun at dusk and the consequent cooling of the day. But sinking in the waters is also a cooling since the waters are cooler—and darker— the more deeply we sink down into them. In all these images of sinking there is little trace of will power, but rather of the deep breathing, the deep relaxing and letting go that a healthy Via Negativa is all about.

This affirmation of the dark journey is very different from the fall/ redemption approach to the Via Negativa, an approach that is filled with will power, with terms like "mortification," meaning "to put to death," and "penances" and even "annihilation." For example, the eighteenth-century French preacher Bourdaloue, whose work was so popular that a collection of his sermons went through fifteen editions in his century alone, says the following: "The great advantage of religious profession is Christian abnegation. What is the Gospel if not a law of renunciation of oneself, death of oneself, a perpetual war against oneself?" He waxes eloquent as well on the advantages of "blind submission, humiliating exercises and lacerations of the flesh." Is it any wonder that a spirituality so devoid of the Via Positiva and therefore so violent toward body, self, and creation would contribute so little to society that the century would almost have to end with a revolution? The distortion of the Via Negativa by the fall/redemption tradition parallels not only the loss of cosmos in that tradition, as we saw in Path I, but also the loss of moral outrage at social sin. It represents that dichotomy that Gandhi decries in Augustine between the political and religious orders of society.

155

> One of the main reasons for this distinction was that the religious order alone regulated the rites and ensured the possibility of redemption. ... The Augustinian contrast meant that the political order could never be elevated, but could only be endured.... Aquinas, unlike [St.] Augustine, stressed the vital role of the political order as necessary for the attainment of the highest earthly good.[7]

When one gets down to asking the pressing question, Why has Western Christian spirituality been satisfied to wrap itself almost exclusively in the fall/redemption mantle and thereby fail to teach an authentic Via Negativa to believers?, one of the responses surely lies here: that politically it serves many powerful interests of the status quo to neglect the deep personal and social implications of a Via Negativa. To neglect what re-creating a society worthy of our deepest selves would be about. To confuse people's minds over their self-doubts instead of unleashing them with their creative powers—surely our generation, with its well-paid electronic preachers preaching guilt and patriotic positivism, is not the first to so have been rewarded by the powers-that-be for remaining silent about the human person's immense capacity for suffering. For naming that suffering. And therefore for moving beyond the suffering.

14 SIN, SALVATION, CHRIST IN THE PERSPECTIVE OF THE VIA NEGATIVA: A THEOLOGY OF THE CROSS

To make any progress we must not make speeches and organize mass meetings but be prepared for mountains of suffering.
—*Mahatma Gandhi*[1]

We need to think about extinction in a meaningful way.
—*Johnathan Schell (33.139)*

Do not be afraid.
—*Jesus*

The cross does not offer us any explanatory model that would make us understand what salvation is and how it itself might be salvation. Instead it invites us to participate in a process within which we can actually experience history as salvation.
—*Jon Sobrino (36.227)*

My Father is the vinedresser.
Every branch that does bear fruit he prunes
to make it bear even more.
You are pruned already,
by means of the words that I have spoken to you.
—*John 15:1-3.*

Here we are preaching a crucified Christ; to the Jews an obstacle that they cannot get over, to the pagans madness, but to those who have been called, whether they are Jews or Greeks, a Christ who is the power and the wisdom of God. For God's foolishness is wiser than human wisdom, and God's weakness is stronger than human strength.
—*1 Cor. 1:23-25*

What is this darkness? What is its name? Call it: an aptitude for sensitivity. Call it: a rich sensitivity which will make you whole. Call it: your potential for vulnerability.
—*Meister Eckhart*

This earth is my sister; I love her daily grace, her silent daring, and how loved I am, how we admire this strength in each other, all that we have lost, all that we have suffered, all that we know: we are stunned by this beauty, and I do not forget: what she is to me, what I am to her.
— *Susan Griffin (20.219)*

Oh, where can I go from your spirit,
Or where can I fall from your face?
If I climb the heavens, you are there.
If I lie in the grave, you are there.
If I take the wings of the dawn
And dwell at the sea's farthest end,
Even there your hand would lead me,
Your right hand would hold me fast.

If I say: "Let the darkness hide me
And the light around me be night,"
Even darkness is not dark for you
And the night is as clear as the day.
— *Ps. 139:7-12*

When the sixth hour came there was darkness over the whole land until the ninth hour. And at the ninth hour Jesus cried out in a loud voice, *"Eloi, Eloi, lama sabachthani?"* which means, "My God, my God, why have you deserted me?" But Jesus gave a loud cry and breathed his last. And the veil of the temple was torn in two from top to bottom.
— *Mark 15:33,34,37,38*

Be the same as Christ Jesus who, though his state was divine, still did not cling to his equality with God, but emptied himself to assume the state of a slave. He became as people are and, being as all people are, he was humbler yet; he even accepted death, death on a cross.
— *Phil. 2:5-8*

Suffering is part of your training. God is treating you as his sons or daughters.
— *Hebrews 12:7*

As we saw at the conclusion of our journey through Path I, a creation-centered spirituality, just because it does not begin its

158

theology with sin and salvation, does not thereby remain silent about such topics. As we conclude this journey through Path II, the Via Negativa, it will be good to pause and ask the question, What light is shed on a theology of sin, salvation, and Christ as a result of this befriending of darkness?

About Sin. Essentially, what the Via Negativa is about is learning receptivity. "Everything that is to be receptive must and ought to be empty," observes Meister Eckhart. The emptying we do of language and images and noisiness or the emptying that comes our way by events of suffering or of ecstasy—and often these are the same events—all this carves spaces within ourselves that make receptivity bigger and bolder and more full of surprises than we could ever imagine. Sin against the Via Negativa would consist in the refusal to let go, the refusal to admit the need for receptivity in our lives and therefore the refusal to develop receptivity. An example of the need for receptivity and relaxing and of our innate resistance to both is found in this description of the birthing process written by a long-time maternity nurse.

> The transition stage of labor is the interval during which the cervix goes from 7-8 centimeters to complete dilation (10 centimeters). During this time the mother usually notes a drastic change and may respond by getting very anxious, and if she is not properly supported and prepared, *she may feel panic.* As in the early stages of labor, *she can assist only by relaxing.* If she loses control, fights the contractions, she will increase her own fear, which in turn increases her discomfort. For most women, this is the most difficult stage because the interlude seems to threaten the loss of control and, momentarily at least, to be without fruit.[2]

This description of the woman who panics and thereby increases her own fear describes for me the history of spirituality the past few centuries in the West. With women's experience so profoundly exiled, there has been no one to counsel relaxing and birthing, and so the Via Negativa was distorted by those threatened by a "loss of control" into becoming a barren asceticism. The naming of the feeling of "panic" is important—all sinking usually has a note of panic about it, and the Via Negativa, which calls us to the deepest sinkings of all, is no exception. Here the refusal to trust, to trust the buoyancy of the water, of the darkness, of the pain, of the nothingness, of the God of nothingness, of our own body, own air, own lungs, own trust—all this is sinful because it stifles our spiritual growth. We are advised in this description of labor that the only assistance we can

159

offer is that of "relaxing." A compulsive, competitive, workaholic culture like ours has not rewarded us for relaxing or for developing those skills of meditation, of massage, of quiet and solitude that are so integral to the holy art of relaxing. To refuse such arts or to stifle them in educating self or others is sin against the Via Negativa.

Clinging is sin in the Via Negativa. Clinging to ego and therefore refusing to let it go for deeper and more transcendent experiences, clinging to control, to will power, even to religious control, to ascetic control in the name of spirituality, clinging to our sacred images of our sacred selves—all this can be sin against the spirit of the darkness and of sinking. There is in this path of letting go and letting be very sound and deep insight about the sins of addiction on which a consumer society by definition establishes itself. Whether our addictions are to Atari games or to making more money, to shopping or to bigger and bigger TV sets, to attending workshops or to alcohol or to drugs, to our anger at our parents or others, our spirit wants to be set free. It wants to let go. Letting go is so essential when we learn to realize that it is not letting go *of things* that is important, but the letting go *of attitudes* toward things. "There where clinging to things ends is where God begins to be," notes Meister Eckhart. A fall/redemption tradition, by devaluating the spirituality of matter, has led people to believe that spiritual depth consists in letting go of things. Spiritual conversion requires a more radical action than that: it requires a letting go of the attitude of addiction. And this way lies freedom, which, with receptivity, marks the goal of the Via Negativa.

Another sin against the Via Negativa is the sin of projection. Projection is the refusal to let be. To let others be different, be surprising, be themselves. This refusal to let be comes from an inner refusal to let oneself be, to be with oneself—the essential spiritual gift learned from solitude. It is when we are so dissatisfied with being ourselves or so not at home with our deepest self that we must always be projecting onto others our ways, our attitudes, our fears, our disappointments. This is a deeply devisive attitude and a grave sin because it disrupts all authentic pleasure, all authentic communication, all authentic relating. Behind it lies the refusal to let go of dualisms and therefore to acknowledge the differences among creatures and within creatures that in fact make up the glory of creation. The irony of projection is that it is only when we cease projecting that we relax enough and breathe deeply enough to fill up with enough space and air to allow ourselves to "sink and float"

(Rich), and as we sink deeper into the darkness of less and less projection we experience what is in fact the unity of all things, the darkness that Rilke praises for its capacity to "pull in everything." Barry Lopez makes note of the importance of our ceasing to project. Although his discourse applies to our killing of wolves, the insight is applicable to all humanity's temptations to kill, including the wars we so creatively prepare for.

> Killing wolves has to do with murder. Historically, the most visible motive, and the one that best explains the excess of killing, is a type of fear: theriophobia. Fear of the beast. Fear of the beast as an irrational, violent, insatiable creature. Fear of the projected beast in oneself.... At the heart of theriophobia is the fear of one's own nature. In its headiest manifestations theriophobia is projected onto a single animal, the animal becomes a scapegoat, and it is annihilated. (24.140)

One is moved to reflect on how many other fears—the fear toward people of the opposite sex, the fear of people of a different sexual lifestyle, the fear of people of a different race or political system or language—are sins all committed in the name of projection.

The refusal to let go of our projects at times and of our projections feeds our temptations to climb, for climbing has a projected goal known as "the top of the ladder." The Via Negativa teaches us that sinking is more holy than climbing. Depth is more godlike than height. The Creator God, a great underground river, awaits our sinking more than our climbing. The reason we can trust the sinking so deeply is that, at the bottom, "my ground and God's are the same." (Eckhart) God is already at home in a deep, deep way. But we need to return home to make contact with that depth. As Eckhart puts it, "God is at home; it is we who have gone out for a walk." The Via Negativa is about returning home. Sin is about our missing the mark, wandering about in a superficial or "outer" fashion of living above ground, and climbing to even higher ground.

We also need to let sin be sin for a while. To allow sin its rightful and even instructive place in our own and others' lives. Not to do this is to multiply the sin. Allowing mystery to be mystery is equally essential to deep, spiritual living. Lopez celebrates what he calls "this tolerance for mystery" which "invigorates the imagination." (24.285) We kill the imagination by refusing to let mystery be mystery in our lives.

Another sinful attitude that the Via Negativa lays bare is the refusal to let pain be pain, the refusal to admit pain, to allow pain, to listen to pain. Or to mystery, to darkness, to the unknown. Too much armor, too heavy defences, too thick walls prevent the vulnerability which is such an occasion of grace in the Via Negativa. We sin against the Via Negativa by refusing to develop our capacities, in this instance our capacities for endurance, our strength for the journey, our strength to endure the pain. The strength called for in the Via Negativa is not a stoical strength of gritting the teeth nor a macho strength of controlling the situation: it is a vulnerable strength, the strength to absorb, to receive the dark with the light, the pain with the pleasure, a strength to keep on falling. It is a strength born of sensitivity, a refusal to live with insensitivity, with coldness of heart, with the god of protection, the idol of invulnerability. To be able to undergo what Gandhi calls the "mountains of suffering" is to discover a new source and a new level of strength. The strength of emptiness, nothingness, the zero point. This strength shatters our very definitions and projections of what it means to be strong.

About Salvation. Salvation, we learn from the Via Negativa, is not a salvation *from pain* but *through pain*. Both Adrienne Rich and Mechtild of Magdeburg, cited on the opening page of Theme Twelve, along with Jesus Christ, speak eloquently to this truth: the need to love our enemies, embrace our fears, enter the darkest of the dark. The very act of entering darkness to befriend it becomes a profoundly healing event. Why is this so? Why are there so many levels of healing or salvation to our befriending of the dark?

The salvation or healing that the Via Negativa is about presents itself in both a personal and a social manner. Of course, since the personal at its depth *is* social and the social when it is not idolatrized is deeply personal and caring of the individual, this kind of holistic salvation should not surprise anyone. In fact, it ought to constitute a requisite test of all claims to salvation. A personal salvation by itself is not truly salvific, for people in the deepest recesses of their personhood are social. Since they are in deep communion with others, it is their very relationships that beg for healing. Relationships constitute part of the healing of every person. The depth of the personal anguish for healing that the Via Negativa arouses is well attested to by the psalmist.

> The enemy pursues my soul;
> he has crushed my life to the ground;
> he has made me dwell in darkness
> like the dead, long forgotten.

Therefore my spirit fails;
my heart is numb within me. (Ps. 143:3,4)

Like water I am poured out,
disjointed are all my bones.
My heart has become like wax,
it is melted within my breast.
Parched as burnt clay is my throat,
my tongue cleaves to my jaws. (Ps. 22:14-16)

By the very acknowledgment of our darkness and of our pain we are saved, that is, healed. By refusing to cover up the cosmic despair and the cosmic anguish that life rains on us we make healing possible. We allow an entrance into the wound to take place. By letting pain be pain we allow healing to be healing, and instead of healing our projections or our imaginary darknesses we heal what is truly in pain, what is deeply and irretrievably dark. Too quickly has the fall/redemption tradition instructed us in the idea that the Via Negativa psalms are "penitential psalms." Psalms such as 6, 32, 38, 51, 102, 130, 143 are far bigger than sin and penance meditations. They cover the full range of the Via Negativa experiences of sinking and letting go, of tasting darkness and nothingness, pain and emptying.

As was mentioned above in Theme Thirteen, another reason the Via Negativa fully entered into brings salvation is that such a journey returns us to our origins. Our origins of darkness, of mystery, of deep contentment in the womb. But also to our pre-origins, to our nothingness that preceded our holy and blessed conception. Such an invitation to make the journey full circle is a salvific one for us adults especially, for by making the full connections in our lives we become healed, whole, saved, and holy. There is no way to heal without making such full connections.

Forgiveness is another word for letting go. We are saved by forgiveness, the power to forgive ourselves, to allow ourselves to be forgiven, which matures into the power to forgive others and allow them their time to be forgiven. Forgiveness is about letting go of guilt—some imagined, some real—and about letting go of fear. There is no healing, no salvation, without forgiveness. And with forgiveness all things become saved and healed once again. Creation is restored.

Sacrifice is another kind of salvific power recovered in the Via Negativa. A sacrifice is a holy offering, traditionally a burnt offering, an offering that is consumed by fire. "To be alive is to be burning," Norman O. Brown says, and to sacrifice is to be so in love with being

163

alive that one is willing to let go: to consume and be consumed, burn and be burnt out of Eros and not out of nihilism or despair. This kind of willingness paradoxically requires an *un*willingness, a letting go of will power and projects, in order to see creation ablaze. Here lies the sense of sacrifice regained. It is not an appeasement of the gods or of God, but a burning out of our own reluctances to let go. Sacrifice too can save and heal and make warm once again.

The trust that is demanded in the darkness of the Via Negativa also heals. "Go your way, your trust has saved you." Trust makes whole. Not only the trust of ecstasy and delight as in the Via Positiva, but trust of the darkness, the sinking and the nothingness of the Via Negativa. Trust in Path II invites us into mystery again, to taste and explore it and to let go of making a problem of it. Mystery heals. Unites. Saves. Trust drives out fear, and when we let go of fear we are ready to live fully, love fully, and be instruments of healing or salvation. The fear of death itself—that dark mystery about which we who still live and bury our dead know so little—is let go of. By becoming skilled in our many letting-gos we are preparing for a gentle death, a relaxed entry into another realm, another transparent and divine kingdom and queendom. When death no longer has dominion over us we are ready for all heaven to break loose on this earth. This is part of that salvific gift of *strength* that the Via Negativa has carved into our selves. Strength is, after all, a letting go of weakness, of self-pity, of puerile shame, of fear to be different or to be ourselves. Such strength saves. Not only oneself but others. The Via Negativa also teaches the salvific power of waiting. There are times in our lives when waiting is best and the most healing thing we can do for ourselves or for others. Lopez says that our times require an "unfamiliar patience," and Simone Weil writes about "waiting for God." Such patience is part of the letting go and letting be that is the Via Negativa experience.

Not only the person undergoes the trials of the Via Negativa. The people do too. Especially the poor in society, the downtrodden, who must face their darkness more directly than the comfortable who can more easily cover up the darkness and the fears it generates by their ready access to things or objects or busyness. The psalmist sings of the people's need for healing.

The Lord has never despised
nor scorned the poverty of the poor.
From him he has not hidden his face,
but he heard the poor man when he cried. . . .

The poor shall eat and shall have their fill.
They shall praise the Lord, those who seek him. (Ps. 22:24-26)

The author of the Lamentations celebrates the social catastrophe of the fall of Jerusalem. In doing so, he allows healing and salvation a way into the people's grief and sorrow.

Yahweh, remember what has happened to us;
Look on us and see our degradation.

Our inheritance has passed to aliens,
our homes to barbarians.

We are orphans, we are fatherless;
our mothers are like widows. (Lam. 5:1-3)

From the emptiness of despair there lies only one cry left—a cry of hope for healing and salvation.

Happy were those killed by the sword,
happier than those by hunger,
spent and sinking,
deprived of the fruits of the fields.

With their own hands, tender-hearted women
have boiled their children;
these have been their food
in the disaster that fell on the daughter of my people. . . .

And still we wore out our eyes,
watching for help—in vain. (Lam. 4:9,10,17)

For Israel the exile is an exile in the desert. It is the desert. The wasteland. The silence that appears to be barren. Not even God talks in the silence of the letting go of the temple and of Jerusalem. And yet in this waiting the word of Yahweh is hoped for, the fruitful, creative energy of God that can recycle even despair into possibility, even chaos into creation, and nothingness into something wonderful.

Joy has vanished from our hearts;
our dancing has been turned to mourning. . . .

But you, Yahweh, you remain for ever;
your throne endures from age to age.

You cannot mean to forget us for ever?
You cannot mean to abandon us for good?

Make us come back to you, Yahweh, and we will come back.
Renew our days as in times past. (Lam. 5:15, 19-21)

The sin that is considered the cause of Jerusalem's downfall might well be the sin of refusal to let go. In our times, salvation would include a recognition of the need to let go: the letting go of crazy military projections and nuclear madnesses; the letting go of nation-states and their rights to control us; the letting go of narrow and parochial political systems and unjust economic systems. The letting go of war itself as a totally unreasonable and humanly insulting way to solve differences; therefore the recognition of the obsolescence of war that the nuclear age is trying to teach us before it is too late. The letting go of patriarchy which creates one-sided citizens of women and men alike and culminates in violent living and violent relationships. The letting go of satisfaction with the way things are for the poor, the homeless, the starving, the ignorant, the sick—yes, and with the way things are with the too-wealthy, the too-powerful, the too-knowledgeable. Clearly the political implications of salvation as liberation are tremendous for the Via Negativa. We will want to explore these insights in greater depth when we arrive at Path IV, the Via Transformativa. What we learn here is that salvation and liberation have everything to do with letting go.

About Christ. If the fall/redemption tradition in Christianity has made people conscious of anything at all, it is surely that of the cross of Jesus Christ. But to discuss the cross outside of the context of creation and Incarnation, to expound on the Via Negativa outside of the Via Positiva, invites severe distortion of the Good News. Clearly the cross as a symbol of the ultimate letting go, that of death and death as an outcast and misunderstood criminal, has no parallel for its remarkable power to awaken and to bring about healing and redemption. But as Jon Sobrino insists, the power of the cross is not in its being an object to meditate on so much as in the truth that "it invites us to participate in a process within which we can actually experience history as salvation." (36.227) The cross is a process, or better, a culmination of a process, in Jesus' life and for that reason—because Jesus' life represents the fullest creation-centered and deepest of the spiritual journeys of humankind—the cross symbolizes our own spiritual journey in deep and divine ways. The cross represents a turning point in a journey of a royal person preaching the "kingdom/queendom of God," that is, a person who came to share the Good News that all people, especially the outcasts and down-trodden, are royal persons. To preach this news, this *metanoia*, or transformation of consciousness, was to upset many people who felt *they* were custodians of creation and *their* kingdoms were the important ones. Jesus was not politically naive; he knew what Herod had done to John the Baptist's preaching of new and fresh news; he knew what the religious guardians of Israel had done to prophets, turning them into martyrs. And yet he did not shirk his divine task, the preaching of the Good News to the poor. He did not refuse to go to Jerusalem though death was in the air. "The basic fact that he did go knowingly and willingly" to his death is "beyond doubt," notes Albert Nolan (27.115). And why did he do so?

> Jesus seems to have been faced with the alternatives of remaining in hiding to avoid death or coming out of hiding to face death. . . . If he came out of hiding in order to preach he would sooner or later be caught and silenced—unless his death itself could become a way of awakening faith in the kingdom. . . . Jesus died so that the kingdom might come. (27.114f.)

Here, then, lies one of the deepest lessons and indeed salvific powers of grace from the death of Jesus: that neither he nor we can be true to the kingdom/queendom of God, that is we cannot live out our vocations as royal persons who awaken others to their royal personhood, without a willingness to let go radically. To let go even of our fear of death, of our clinging to this life, to the light and the pleasure of the Via Positiva. Jesus says, "The person who saves her life will lose it; the person who loses her life will save it." There is no Via Positiva fully lived without a Via Negativa, a deep letting go, an entry into darkness and doubt and uncertainty and danger. Like Gandhi and Martin Luther King, Jr., Jesus knew that the only way to live life fully was to let go of it radically. And this has everything to do with letting go of the fear of death. As Nolan puts it,

> To save one's life means to hold on to it, to love it and be attached to it and therefore to fear death. To lose one's life is to let go of it, to be detached from it and therefore to be willing to die. The paradox is that the man who fears death is already dead, whereas the man who has ceased to fear death has at that moment begun to live. A life that is genuine and worthwhile is only possible once one is willing to die. (27.113)

Jesus confronts the fear of death head on. And he invites us to do the same—not by meditations that project us on a cross and not by mortifications that have us create our own crosses in our privatized basements, but by living the Good News, the kingdom/queendom of God. If one cannot live without letting go of the fear of death, is it possible to be married without letting go of the fear of the failure of the marriage? Is it possible to be a priest without letting go of the fear of leaving the priesthood? Is it possible to be a male without letting go of the fear of losing one's maleness? Is it possible to be American without letting go of America? Here lies the process by which all of us will experience history—our own and the human race's —as salvific.

The salvation that Jesus brings is primarily liberation from the fear of death. The author of the book of Hebrews puts it this way:

> Jesus, by his death, took away all the power of the devil, who had power over death, and set free all those who had been held in slavery all their lives by the fear of death. (Heb. 2:14-15)

When Otto Rank says that Jesus and Paul brought the greatest social revolution the world has seen, he is responding to this same Good News that Hebrews speaks about. To free *all* those held in slavery by fear of death is to free *all*, for according to Rank the human preoccupation with immortality, with escaping mortality, grounds all human fears from the fear to create to the fear to let go. Fear of death is the cause of so much sin: power over others, thus sadism, the fear of Eros and of living, thus the sins against the Via Positiva, consumerism, hoarding. Jesus' liberation, then, is of the most radical and the most universal kind. Were we truly to enter into its depths, we would cease our questing for pyramids of immortality in money, fame, power, militarism; we would cease the sexism and racism by which we need to project our death fears onto those different from and supposedly less immortal than ourselves. And we would become the images of God, the birthing, creative, co-creators we were all meant to be. Truly there is Good News wrought by the cross of Jesus Christ in all this. As Paul put it, "This doctrine of the cross is the power of God." (1 Cor. 1:18)

Jesus instructs us by words and by example that we can and indeed must let go in the most radical fashion. He states that the kingdom will come only by letting go, i.e., that like a seed it must first die darkly in the black soil underground. (Mk. 9:30-34) He does something still more in the parable of the Transfiguration. He actually shows the bright side, the beauty side, to letting go and to facing death. In Mark's Gospel the Transfiguration story begins with Jesus linking the kingdom of God to the tasting of death, the entering into the Via Negativa. "And he said to them, 'I tell you solemnly, there are some standing here who will not taste death until they see the kingdom of God come with power." (Mark 9:1) Jesus takes three witnesses of his fear of dying, Peter, James, and John, on the seventh day—an allusion to the refreshment the Creator sought after creation of the world. His transfiguration and his clothes turning dazzingly white (9:2,3) are paralleled in Mark's account of Jesus' crucifixion. "And they crucified him and divided his garments among them." (15:24) Gernando Belo writes that "the garments stand, by metonymy, for the body"[3]—thus Jesus became "too white," or "overly white," i.e., white as a ghost at facing his death. The word usually translated as "bleacher" or "fuller" (*gnapheus*) can also mean an instrument of torture, and as a verb it can mean "to tangle, tear, or lacerate." Elijah, a helper to the Jew in need, appears at the Transfiguration and is called upon at the crucifixion in Mark's Gospel. Jesus' words on coming down the mountain reveal that suffering was indeed on his mind: "How is it that the scriptures say about the Son of man that he is to suffer grievously and be treated with contempt?" he asks.

We learn from Jesus' Transfiguration that all beauty involves letting go. That the Via Positiva does come up against boundaries and limits, intimations of mortality. But that this too can be beautiful. Chaim Potok relates asking his father about death when, at age six, he saw a dead bird.

> "Why?" I asked.
> "That's the way the Ribbono Shel Olom made his world, Asher."
> "Why?"
> "So life would be precious, Asher. Something that is yours
> forever is never precious."[4]

Jesus was not unacquainted with the tradition of the suffering servant in Isaiah 53, and he is said in Luke's Gospel to say following his resurrection: "O foolish ones and slow of heart to believe in all that the prophets have spoken! Did not the Christ *have to* suffer these things before entering into his glory?" (Luke 24: 25,26)[5]

Jesus is a model and a teacher of letting go. He too frequents the desert in order to let go. He lets go of images of what a messiah ought to be, of what kingship ought to be, of how a man should relate to a woman, of how women should be treated. He finds it necessary to empty himself on many occasions, and people's strong responses to him, whether negative or positive, create many more letting-gos. It should not be forgotten that Jesus was by birth from the middle class of his culture. He was not born or brought up poor. Yet he chose

169

to identify himself with the outcasts of society, he chose to let go of privileged position in his society. Nolan puts this fact very well:

> The remarkable thing about Jesus was that, although he came from the middle class and had no appreciable disadvantages himself, he mixed socially with the lowest of the low and identified himself with them. He became an outcast *by choice*. (27.27; italics his)

Like the artist that he was, Jesus resisted success as his society wanted glibly to define it. He stuck to the truth of his prophetic insight, which was that hearts had to be changed if society was to be loving and just. He rejects Peter's "confession" on his behalf in Mark's Gospel with such vehemence because he is rejecting a "power Christology," as Father Schillebeeckx puts it.

> Mark is clearly campaigning against various forms of [a premature] "power" Christology. . . . Mark countenances no Christ-mystique, except the Jesus mystique of following after the earthly, suffering Jesus, who puts all his trust in the coming of God's rule.[6]

Jesus does not demand of others what he has not demanded of himself. Letting go characterizes his life and therefore his instruction to others. A fall/redemption interpretation of the miracles of Jesus tends to define a miracle as a victory or intervention against nature, as for example in the miracle and fishes story of Mark, Chapter Six. But as Nolan points out, the real miracle that Jesus wrought was not a quantitative magic trick of turning five loaves and two fishes into thousands. The true miracle was that *Jesus got people to let go*, to share with one another.

> The event itself was not a miracle of multiplication; it was a remarkable example of sharing. The "miracle" was that so many men should suddenly cease to be possessive about their food and begin to share, only to discover that there was more than enough to go round. There were, we are told, twelve baskets of scraps left over. Things do tend to "multiply" when you share them. (27.51-52)

The early church learned this same lesson of letting go from Jesus. "Everything they owned was held in common. . . . All those who were owners of lands or houses would sell them and bring the money from them, to present it to the apostles; it was then distributed to any members who might be in need." (Acts 4:32,34,35) This does not mean early Christians rendered themselves destitute— but that they did indeed let go of "their surplus, the extras which they did not really need." (27.52)

Jesus came preaching forgiveness of sins, forgiveness of one's enemies, letting go of guilt and of the projection of guilt. "Let him who is without sin throw the first stone." This forgiveness invariably resulted in deep healings that were as physical as they were psychic, emotional, and spiritual for Jesus' listeners. But, amazingly, Jesus does not draw attention to himself in this regard. He stresses how this power of forgiveness and of healing, powers of empowering others to let go, are given to all people. "A feeling of awe came over the crowd when they saw this, and they praised God for giving such power to people." (Matt. 9:8) Jesus' faith and trust in the arrival of God's power of healing and forgiveness, the divine power to let go, arouses it in others. "Your sins are forgiven . . . your trust has saved you; go in peace." (Luke 7:48,50) The Good News in the creation tradition of reading the gospels is not in the fact of sin—that is not news and is not good. It is in the power and empowerment of the forgiveness, i.e., the letting go of sin. Those who favor the fall/redemption tradition need to meditate long and hard on this fact. Instead of translating the word *metanoia* as "Repent!," as so many fall/redemption translators have done, we need to understand that its fuller meaning is a letting go, a change of heart and of vision in order to envision more fully, a letting go of parochial world views in order to experience the kingdom/queendom of God.

One deep "letting go" that Jesus' crucifixion demands of us is letting go of our projections onto an all-powerful God. The real scandal of the cross, as theologian Jon Sobrino sees it, is in the fact that God did not intervene to save the divine son from the awful death of the cross. Jesus died a disastrous death, and his divine father/mother let it happen. (36.186-192) Jesus redefines the power of love—it is not so great as we had presumed because it is a power of love and not a power of thunderbolts and interferences in nature's. processes. We hear echoes of Eckhart here, who prays an ultimate Via Negativa prayer when he says, "I pray God to rid me of God." To let God be God requires considerable letting go through our lifetimes, as it did for Jesus whose prayer in Gethsemane began with an earnest desire that the cup pass from him but ended with a resolve that his will be so emptied as to become the divine will. The despair of the cross, the darkness of the event, the suffering God who allowed the suffering of the divine son to be suffering—all these are powerful images of letting go.

Jesus Christ, who underwent a divine void, a letting go of divinity in order to be fully human (Phil. 2), a *kenosis*, becomes the model

171

and exemplar of what a "virgin," that is a truly emptied person, is like. A truly emptied person is so vulnerable to beauty and truth, to justice and compassion, that he or she becomes a truly hollow and hallowed channel for divine grace. Jesus emptied and he was emptied, and thus he becomes a source of wisdom, a royal person, a prophet through whom the divine Dabhar can gush and flow with intensity and sensitivity. Through him God, the underground river, bursts above ground into human lives and human history. But only because Jesus, so fully grounded himself, is a hollow conduit in full contact with the divine source and wellspring underground. And we too are invited to be patterned after this same emptied and hollowed image of God.

For this to happen a constant letting go, a constant pruning (John 15:1-6) will prove necessary for us as it was for Jesus. Pruning creates strength, richness, depth, though temporarily pruning hurts and conjures up doubt and fear. It takes a wise gardener to know when and how and how much to cut back a beautiful rose. It takes a wise parent to prune each child according to the needs of that child. So it takes a wise individual to prune himself or herself according to one's unique needs and timing. But from this letting go we become a much richer and stronger people. More often than not it is events that come our way in our lives that prune us or urge us to prune ourselves. One might say that it is, as Jesus put it, his words, the ever-flowing energy of Dabhar, that forces this pruning. (John 15:3)

But the gospel story—at least in the creation-centered spiritual tradition—does not end with the cross. Neither do our journeys end with the Via Negativa. The emptying and letting go of the cross was a prelude to an ever greater birth, just as our letting-gos are followed by creativity. In moving on from the Via Negativa we journey into Path III, the Via Creativa. We take delight in letting go even of letting go.

PATH III
BEFRIENDING CREATIVITY,
BEFRIENDING OUR DIVINITY:
THE VIA CREATIVA

divinization as co-creators art as meditation trusting images discipline, dialectic, trinitarian God as Mother, as child sin-salvation, Christ—the Resurrection

We have now traveled along two paths in the creation-centered spiritual journey, that of the Via Positiva and that of the Via Negativa; that of cosmic blessing and our own royal personhood, a celebration of the cataphatic God, and that of darkness, silence, and emptiness, that of the apophatic God. Because this tradition pays equal heed to both the Via Positiva and the Via Negativa, it celebrates the union of the two in the Via Creativa. In letting both pleasure and pain happen, both light and darkness, both naming and unnaming, both cosmos and void, we allow a third thing to be born: and that third thing is the very power of birth itself. It is Dabhar erupting out of humanity's imagination. It is the image of God, the image of the Creator, coming alive and expressing its divine depths and divine fruitfulness. It is our creativity which is the full meaning of humanity's being an "image of God."

The poet Novalis writes: "All the hazards of life are elements out of which we can fashion whatever we like." There is a necessary link between darkness, nothingness, and creativity. All creation is *ex nihilo*, out of nothing. Creation is birthing something where previously there was nothing. Darkness is the origin of everything that is born—stars born in the darkness of space, our ideas and images born in the darkness of the brain, children born from the darkness of their mothers' wombs, movements of liberation born from the darkness of slavery and pain. But creativity is also born of pleasure and delight and for the sake of pleasure and delight. Thus the fall/redemption tradition has robbed us of our *imago dei*, our power and love of creativity. One can read Father Tanquerry's 750-page manual on spirituality and never see creativity celebrated once. Creativity cannot happen where there is no Via Positiva, where the cosmos itself is not taken cognizance of, where it is not

175

celebrated. For creativity is a cosmic energy; it is the cosmos birthing itself. And creativity cannot happen where true nothingness is not allowed and where the fear of the dark dominates over a reverence for the dark and what can be birthed in the dark. Asceticism, by denying us a true Via Negativa experience, kills creativity. It is the father of all modern-day abortions, this aborting of human imagination.

Meister Eckhart relays the following dream: "I once had a dream in which I, even though a man, was pregnant like a woman with child. I was pregnant with nothingness; and out of this nothingness God was born." Here we have an amazing confession for our times: First, it is possible for the human person, the male in this case, to let go of excessive sexual stereotypes. Second, men can birth and must birth and have no need to fear birth. Patriarchy has feared birth immensely and has invested much in trying to control it. A study done a few years ago in America found that 80 percent of six-year-olds but only 10 percent of forty-year-olds were creative. Thus between six and forty creativity is killed in our culture; this means, theologically speaking, that God is killed, God is aborted in a culture where imagination and juicy creativity are not celebrated. For as Eckhart points out, the birthing we all do is nothing less than the birthing of God's word, God's Dabhar, God's Son. To abort this process is to abort the divinity in us and to render the worlds in which we live boring and one-dimensional, flat and juiceless. This way we invite violence. Such a world rewards only imagination used for making missiles and counter-missiles, bigger and bigger bombs and faster and faster "delivery systems." Such a world culminates in displaced creativity, that is, in sadism and its necessary counterpart, masochism.

In this third path we will explore the following themes along the journey known as the Via Creativa:

15. From Cosmos to Cosmogenesis: Our Divinization as Images of God Who Are Also Co-Creators.

16. Art as Meditation: Creativity and Birthing as Meditation, Centering, a Return to the Source.

17. Faith as Trust of Images: Discipline—Yes! Asceticism—No!

18. Dialectical, Trinitarian: How Our Lives as Works of Art Spiral Beauty Back into the World.

19. God as Mother, God as Child: Ourselves as Mothers of God and Birthers of God's Son.

20. Sin, Salvation, Christ in the Perspective of the Via Creativa: A Theology of the Resurrection.

Christians will recognize in this path a theology of the Resurrection as they recognized in Paths I and II theologies of creation, Incarnation, and of the cross respectively.

15 FROM COSMOS TO COSMOGENESIS: OUR DIVINIZATION AS IMAGES OF GOD WHO ARE ALSO CO-CREATORS

Contemporary creativity consists in activating, expressing, and fulfilling the universe process, the earth process, the life process, and the human process within the possibilities of our historical moment.
— *Thomas Berry*[1]

The greatest formal talent is worthless if it does not serve a creativity which is capable of shaping a cosmos.
— *Albert Einstein*

To act is to create and creation is for ever.
— *Teilhard de Chardin (40.141)*

We shall have a creative Kingdom!
— *Mechtild of Magdeburg*

Do you create or do you destroy?
— *Dag Hammarskjöld*

The Creator is Author of all arts that are truly arts.
— *John the Scot*

The soul among all creatures is generative like God is.
— *Meister Eckhart*

By the grace of God I have not been fruitless.
— *Paul, 1 Cor. 15:10*

God alone has this power of creative attention, the power really to think into being that which does not exist.
— *Simone Weil*

It is the imagination that gives shape to the universe.
— *Barry Lopez (24.285)*

While in classical Catholic theology it was supposed that faith resides in the intelligence, it may be more realistic... to say that faith resides in the imagination.
— *Gregory Baum*[2]

God is our Creator. God made us in His image and likeness. Therefore we are creators.... The joy of creativeness should be ours.

> —*Dorothy Day*[3]

Think of the love that the Creator has lavished on us by letting us be called God's children; and that is what we are.... My dear people, we are already the children of God.

> —*John 3:12*

I saw no difference between God and our substance, but, as it were, all God.... Yet God is God and our substance is a creature in God.

> —*Julian of Norwich*

Divinity is aimed at humanity.

> —*Hildegarde of Bingen*

God's method, the only method his love would allow, is to create a being that might create himself in order truly to become god, a being in the image and after the likeness of the Creator.

> —*Claude Tresmontant*[4]

God became a human being in order that human beings might become God.

> —*St. Irenaeus*

The Word was in people for this purpose, that it might divinize them.... The Word had to become man in Jesus for this reason, that people both in spirit and in the flesh, from within and without, behind and before, and in all places might have testimony (of this goal of divinization).

> —*Hans Denck*[5]

Everyone moved by the Spirit is a son or daughter of God.... The Spirit itself and our spirit bear united witness that we are children of God. And if we are children, we are heirs as well: heirs of God and co-heirs with Christ, sharing his sufferings so as to share his glory.... The whole creation is eagerly waiting for God to reveal his sons and daughters.... From the beginning till now the entire creation, as we know, has been groaning in one great act of giving birth.

> —*Rom. 8:14, 16, 17, 19, 22*

Path III

We are fellow workers with God.
—I Cor. 3:9

In a conversation we had two summers ago, the eighty-four-year-old creation theologian and historian Father M. D. Chenu, a French Dominican, made the following observation: "The greatest tragedy in theology in the past three centuries has been the divorce of the theologian from the poet, the dancer, the musician, the painter, the dramatist, the actress, the movie-maker." Chenu was lamenting the hegemony of fall/redemption theologies that have not given the *imago dei* prominence in their spiritualities and have therefore denied creativity its place of prominence in our spiritual lives. The artist has indeed been cut off more and more from church life, and as a consequence church life has been cut off more and more from life itself. The loss of cosmos in religion that we considered in Path I has been hastened in the West by the loss of those who birth cosmos, namely the artists in our midst. With this loss, as Rank observes, neurosis has increased in both society and religion. And in the artist too, for art has invariably found its roots in religious vision, as was the case in ancient Greek drama, in Chartres cathedral, in black spirituals. A secular society that is devoid of spiritual vision will not produce art but entertainment and will soon succumb to the selling of the artist's soul. Einstein saw this when he declared that "The purpose of both art and science is to keep alive the cosmic religious feeling."

It is not enough, in our naming of our deepest spiritual journeying, to call for a return to cosmic vision as we did in Theme Four above. For the cosmos does not just sit there. The cosmos is in motion; more than that, the cosmos is in birth. We need to move from cosmos to cosmogenesis. We need to take prideful wonder in and responsibility for what the human species can itself birth back to the cosmos. We need to face up to the truth that we are agents of cosmogenesis. Like all beings, beginning with the very first fireball twenty billion years ago, we humans are generators of new dimensions to the cosmos. But we, latecomers to this universe, are graced with a unique capacity for birth or destruction: from our nothingness experiences we can indeed birth almost anything. The cosmos waits to see what it is we commit our visions to. Thomas Berry puts the situation this way:

We see the universe more as cosmo-genesis than as cosmos. We perceive a long sequence of emergent creative activities over vast periods of development leading up to our present. We see ourselves also as emergent creative process rather than as fixed and established in a clearly defined mode of being and of functioning.[6]

Teilhard de Chardin waxes poetic about the same reality.

Something is afoot in the universe, a result is working out which can best be compared to a gestation and birth: the birth of a new spiritual reality formed by souls and the matter they draw after them. Laboriously, by way of human activity and thanks to it, the new earth is gathering, isolating and purifying itself. No, we are not like flowers in a bunch, but the leaves and flowers of a great tree, on which each appears at its time and place, according to the demands of the All. (40.49)

We now have an inkling of the unbelievable fertility of the universe, of the constant birthings of atoms and molecules, eggs and spermatozoa, of cells and living organisms in water and on land in this so-far-unique of all cosmic places, the Earth. When Eckhart says the human soul is "alone generative as God is," he is not denying the generativity of all of creation. He is, however, underlining a unique breakthrough in nature that is found in the human imagination. If we think the human species is fecund in its capability to reproduce sexually, with the production of from 300 to 400 eggs in each woman's lifetime and of four hundred billion sperm in each male's lifetime, then how much more fertile is one human imagination? What limits are there to the images that one person gives birth to in a lifetime? And what does it mean that the human person is not only capable of birthing images but of executing them as well? What does it mean that not just the human individual but people can get together to share images, refine them, knead them? What limits are there to the human capacity to birth new images, new creations of beauty and surprise, of wonder and justice, of gentleness and play?

Perhaps humankind had to go through its childhood and its ego-exaggerating adolescence before it could come to the point of creative maturity. Perhaps we had to let this adolescent period which we now call the Enlightenment carry us to the brink of nuclear holocaust before, staring extinction in the face, we could wake up to our divine and demonic powers of creativity. Perhaps we would not face the awesomeness and the responsibility of our creativity until it faced us as an equal, a lethal child bent on destroying its parent, a power greater than we are that we ourselves unleashed. When Eckhart reminds us that "We are heirs of the fearful creative power of God," he is unveiling the truth of our deep, creative selves. Like a volcano that spews hot lava from the steaming bowels of the earth, we have powers of birthing that are as destructive as they are awesome. Art is not a genteel thing. Creativity is not tiptoeing through the tulips; it is not a Donny and Marie Osmond entertainment program. Creativity—whether we are talking of the powers to make a Trident submarine or the nuclear missiles that go on it, or the power to create a symphony, or the power to build a table for the living room or to write a poem to a loved one—creativity is so divine that it is awesome. Truly it is a "fearful creative power," as Eckhart pointed out. We need, both as individuals and as peoples, to face creativity and the fears it conjures up straight in the face. Naked. And learn reverence for it, a deep, divine, "fear of the Lord" reverence. We need to befriend creativity, embrace the shadow it extends over all of us, and love it as we have never learned to love any enemy or any friend in our whole lives. We need to wrestle with creativity today the way Jacob wrestled with the angel.

For if we do not, our creativity will destroy us, if not in the form of nuclear war, then in the form of multiplication of McDonald's hamburger stands and agribusiness conglomerates, of pornographic magazines and sentimental news broadcasts. Consumerism after all is a kind of creativity, albeit a perverse one. We cannot redirect this perverse way of birthing without ourselves being equally committed to the enterprise of giving birth. Is our creativity to be for life or for death? For people or for profits? For justice or for forgetfulness? Hammarskjöld's question is such a precise one when he asks, "Do you create or do you destroy?" for it implies that the human species is made of such stuff that there is no halfway point between destruction and creativity. Creativity, the divine power of Dabhar, is so powerful and so overwhelming in us that we simply cannot deny it, cannot keep it down. If we are not consciously bent on employing it for life's sake, it will emerge on its own for the sake of destruction. Today it is one of religion's most pressing responsibilities to make creativity, this "fearful creative power of God," conscious to all humankind, and to assist all efforts at good will in humans to redirect our capacities for generativity toward goals that are worthy of our species and are a blessing to this planet. We do not have much time left. And religion's sin of omission and of silent complicity during the centuries in which human/divine creativity was used to kill, to perpetrate sadism, to justify slaughter, to wipe out millions of species—this must be confessed openly. The fact that I am the first theologian that I know of in the West to have named the Via Creativa as an essential ingredient to the spiritual journey does not give me comfort. It frightens me. It disturbs me that the Pentagon has more at stake in birthing than does the Vatican. However, this situation is breaking down rapidly, and more and more spiritual seekers are finding the truth of the image of God in themselves and the potential of divine—as distinct from demonic—creativity for all of us. And more and more theologians are recovering the human imagination as a proper locus for the divine spirit to play in. But their effort is severely hampered still by the Enlightenment educational structures that continue to dominate the universities and seminaries where theologians teach. We shall deal with how a breakthrough in education can take place when we discuss Art as Meditation in our next section.

A sound theology is an indispensable antidote to humanity's fear of its own creativity. Psychologist Otto Rank has dealt brilliantly with some of the fears that lurk behind our fear of creativity—fear of death, of life, of suffering, of pleasure, of androgeny, of guilt—and I have interacted with him elsewhere on these topics.[7] However, in this study we have laid bare other fears that prevent our creativity: fear of the cosmos on the one hand, and of the void and nothingness on the other. When either an in-depth Via Positiva or an in-depth Via Negativa is lacking, there can be no creativity. But now, in discussing the Via Creativa, we must face still another fear: our fear of the *imago dei*, the image of God in us and in all people. The fear of our own divinity so haunts us that religious leaders and thinkers rarely if ever preach this truth—and in ignoring it leave the field of creativity open to the demonic sellers of military weaponry and of creativity-for-destruction or for bigger and bigger profits, which is also a form of destruction. Meister Eckhart was not so reticent to speak to our divine powers: "Now the seed of God is in us. The seed of a pear tree grows into a pear tree; the seed of a hazel tree grows into a hazel tree. The seed of God grows into God." The fact that we "grow into God," that we are ourselves part of the cosmogenesis and its patient and evolutionary ways, is attested to by Paul as well. "And we, with our unveiled faces reflecting like mirrors the glory of the Lord, all grow brighter and brighter as we are turned into the

183

image that we reflect: This is the work of the Lord who is Spirit."
(2 Cor. 3:18) The psychology of trust and growth that, as we have
seen in Theme Five, is the mainstay of creation-centered spirituality
and culminates in our growth into our own divinity. And divinity
means creativity.

For who is God if not the Creator? And, when we are each called
an "image of God" in Genesis, God is understood there as the
Creator God. Since we are images of God, our growing into this
image, our growing "brighter and brighter into the image," as Paul
puts it, consists in our growing more and more brightly into birthers
and creators like God. It means our accepting the truth of our selves
as co-creators with God. This truth recalls on the one hand our
immense dignity and on the other our awesome responsibility.
When Paul speaks of the "glory of the children of God," he is talking
about the restoration of this *doxa* or glory or beauty of the image of
God that is in each of us. The divine image gets tarnished from
misuse and egotistical use, from greed and forgetfulness, and it
needs restoring.

Meister Eckhart explains what it means to be an image. "An
image receives its being immediately from that of which it is an
image. It has one being with it and it is the same being." (17.408)
We, who are the Creator's image, share one being with the Creator.
Like God, we need to create. Hildegarde of Bingen explains the
passion God holds for us, the divine images, and how this passion is
meant to "serve all the world" through our creative work. "With my
mouth," God says, "I kiss my own chosen creation. I uniquely,
lovingly, embrace every image I have made out of the earth's clay.
With a fiery spirit I transform it into a body to serve all the world."

The biblical teaching on creativity, namely that every human
person is endowed with the divine power of birthing, is absolutely
essential if we are to redeem the words "art" and "artist" from an
elitist and anthropocentric culture. The Hebrew Bible and Jesus and
Paul democratize the meaning of art and artist, and here lies the
truth to Otto Rank's statement that we have in Jesus and Paul the
most radical revolution the world has ever seen. For if each person is
endowed with the seed of God and the image of God and the power
of divine creativity, then no person has the right to project onto
someone else his or her responsibility for creativity and for carrying
out the ongoing birth of the cosmos. Russia's attempts to silence the
prophetic artist and America's efforts to buy out the talented and
allow only a chosen few to be called "artists" crumble impotently

when held up to the "unveiled faces reflecting like mirrors the glory of the Lord" that Paul sings about. It is in unveiling our faces, in letting out our deepest selves in the self-expression that our adult work and play is about, that we all become baptized artists. Perhaps we can say that the letting go and letting be of Path II lead to a letting out which is Path III. The artist in each one of us needs to be let out of the closet. It deserves to be shared, to be wondered at, to be celebrated, and to be criticized. This letting out may take the form of storytelling and conversing; doing carpentry or repairs; writing or dancing; painting or parenting; singing or clowning. If what is let out truly flows from our depths, then it is flowing from God's depths too, and the divine creative energy of Dabhar that alone inspires the universe is happening through us. Meister Eckhart sees this divine emergence through our human creativity as a breakthrough in time and space.

> Everything which God created millions of years ago and everything which will be created by God after millions of years—if the world endures that long—God is creating all that in the innermost and deepest realms of the human soul. Everything of the past and everything of the present and everything of the future God creates in the innermost realms of the soul.

It should be emphasized that Eckhart is not talking only of the soul of a Mozart or a Mahler, of a Dostoyevsky or a Dickinson, but of the soul of every human person. This nonelitist understanding of human creativity is found as well in the creation spirituality of Pablo Casals, who, while blessed with musical genius, does not find it necessary to put down the image of God in others.

> I have always regarded manual labor as creative and looked with respect—and, yes, wonder—at people who work with their hands. It seems to me that their creativity is no less than that of a violinist or a painter. It is of a different sort, that is all.

There are indeed "different sorts" of creativity—but one Dabhar, one divine energy of creation that finds unique expression in the human gift for birthing. Casals continues in his praise of the carpenter's creativity: "If it had not been for my mother's conviction and determination that music was my destiny, it is quite conceivable that I would have become a carpenter. But I do not think I would have made a very good one."[8]

Theology, and with it Western culture, has not only lost sight of the essential democratization of human creativity that the doctrine of the *imago dei* is about, but it has also lost the sense of pleasure and delight that birthing is all about. Where art has been allowed to be elitist, culture becomes bored and violent. Where art is recovered as being an essential human activity, ecstasy returns. And wonder. And surprise. And God, as Eckhart points out, is the first to partake of such deep pleasure: "In this power of birthing, God is as fully verdant and as wholly flourishing in full joy and in all honor as she is in herself. The divine rapture is unimaginably great. It is ineffable." The human rapture too is of a great and deep kind. Dorothy Day recognized this truth.

> God is our creator. God made us in his Image and likeness. Therefore we are creators. He gave us a garden to till and cultivate. We became co-creators by our responsible acts, whether in bringing forth children, or producing food, furniture or clothing. The joy of creativeness should be ours.[9]

We have here another instance of the interpenetration of all three paths of the spiritual journey, for not only are the Via Positiva and the Via Negativa essential to birthing a Via Creativa, but in the experience of the Via Creativa itself we re-experience, though in fresh and ever-deepening ways, themes of the first two paths. We have already considered how cosmos becomes cosmogenesis in the Via Creativa. We have just seen how pleasure and ecstasy and with them cosmic hospitality are drunk deeply anew in the Via Creativa. Simone Weil testifies to how important the Via Positiva is to the artist when she says, "Every true artist has had real, direct, and immediate contact with the beauty of the world, contact that is of the nature of a Sacrament." There is a hint here of the diaphanous and transparent experience that panentheism is always about. We shall explore more implications of panentheism in the Via Creativa when we discuss Theme Nineteen below. In creating we are also reminded in a deep and unforgettable way of the theology of blessing. "In the birth," Eckhart declares, "you will discover all blessing." But, "neglect the birth and you neglect all blessing." (17.291) A student of mine recently wrote of the truth of this insight in reflecting on her own life experience:

> When I have been attentive to the creative gifts within me, I have been free to pray and grow as a human being. When I have cooperated in the denial of those gifts, or when I have chosen to set them aside, I have withered. My love of life has suffered. I have stopped

praying, I have become small and cynical or I have driven myself to the point of exhaustion and burnout. I have become a compulsive worker trying to make up in my work what I have denied in my most creative self.

One reason that there is so much blessing to be experienced in creativity is that, as Eckhart puts it, there is "equality of God within ourselves." This equality with God, what Paul and John call our being sons and daughters or children of God, amounts to the greatest of all the blessings of life. To create is to experience the likeness to divinity.

The soul longs for the greatest of all blessings that the divine nature can accomplish. This is that the divine nature should bring itself forward and accomplish a comparison of the soul with itself, that is, with the divine nature. The greatest blessing in heaven and on earth is based on "equality." (17.366f.)

The recovery of faith in our creativity and in the artist within each of us and the artists among all of us is no small thing. It has to do with the rekindling of the spark of hope and vision, of adventure and blessing, that a tired civilization needs. Indeed, according to Whitehead, such a rekindling would constitute the rebirth of civilization which, in these last days of patriarchal competition and war-consciousness, has all but died.

Art heightens the sense of humanity. It gives an elation of feeling which is supernatural. A sunset is glorious, but it dwarfs humanity and belongs to the general flow of nature. A million sunsets will not spur on men towards civilization. It requires Art to evoke into consciousness the finite perfections which lie ready for human achievement.... Thus, in its broadest sense, art is civilization. For civilization is nothing other than the unremitting aim at the major perfections of harmony.[10]

Both the individual and the community come alive by this rekindling of the divine spark or seed or image in each of us. This is no small blessing for the individual or for society or for the ongoing cosmos itself. If we fail to love it well, it will return with cosmic fury to teach us, if nothing else, a respect that will never be forgotten.

187

16 ART AS MEDITATION: CREATIVITY AND BIRTHING AS MEDITATION, CENTERING, A RETURN TO THE SOURCE

We are too exclusively bookish in our scholastic routine. The general training should aim at eliciting our concrete apprehensions, and should satisfy the itch of youth to be doing something. . . . In the Garden of Eden Adam saw the animals before he named them: in the traditional system, children named the animals before they saw them.

Alfred North Whitehead (45.285)

Art proceeds from a spontaneous instinct like love does; and it must be cultivated like friendship.

— Raissa Maritain

Every artist may not be a special kind of person. But every person is a special kind of artist.

— Eric Gill

A Poet, a Painter, a Musician, an Architect: the Man or Woman who is not one of these is not a Christian.

— William Blake[1]

I had been trying to give birth to myself; and in some grim, dim way I was determined to use even pregnancy and parturition in that process.

— Adrienne Rich[2]

The street cleaner has to take his task of sweeping as the starting point for meditation. So, likewise, must the potter take his task of producing clay utensils on his potter's wheel and the cobbler, his handicrafts. Here, again, therefore, it is evident that one may do what he will so long as he is clearly aware of what he is doing. Every activity is of equal value as a basis for a dharana exercise.

— Claudio Naranjo[3]

When a man is deprived of the power of expression, he will express himself in a drive for power.

— José Arguelles

The craftsman does not always build toward a prior vision. Often images come in the process of working. The material, his hands—together they beget.
    —M. C. Richards (31.115)

Whatever I want to express in its truest meaning must emerge from within me and pass through an inner form. It cannot come from outside to the inside but must emerge from within.
    —Meister Eckhart

Religious truths have not been expressed throughout time as mathematical formulas, but in art, music, dance, drama, poetry, stories, and active rituals.
    —Starhawk[4]

The idea of "professional artist" should be tossed away. Everyone should feel as an artist does. Everyone should be free to let his or her inner mind speak to her. And everyone is an artist when she does this.
    —Kenji Miyazawa[5]

If you do not express your own original ideas, if you do not listen to your own being, you will have betrayed yourself.
    —Rollo May[6]

The too perfect cease to create.
    —Nicolas Berdyaev[7]

Gardening is an active participation in the deepest mysteries of the universe.
    —Thomas Berry[8]

We are God's work of art.
    —Eph. 2:10

One hundred years ago the painter and poet William Blake lamented the ever-increasing violence of industrial society with these words: "Art degraded, Imagination Denied, War Govern'd the Nations."[9] The dominance of war and war mentalities, of war budgets and wars inside as well as outside us, of war as Atari games and war as pro football games—all this is the price we have paid in the West for denying imagination, repressing or forgetting it, and thereby degrading art. No small part of the blame for this denial of imagination in the West must be laid at the feet of organized religion which, if it has taught meditation at all of late, has seldom if ever taught art as meditation. Rather too much meditation has been of an introverted, introspective kind wherein one takes another's symbols or images—for example those of St. Ignatius—and is taught to imagine "getting in the boat with Jesus" or to sit with the image of Christ on the cross. Now such meditations, which psychologist Claudio Naranjo calls "introvert meditations," have a certain place in certain people's lives at certain times. They are by no means, however, the only form of meditation; nor are they the most fulfilling form, either for the person or for society. They do not lead very readily to new birth and new creation.

What meditations do lead to fuller living and deeper spiritual celebration of both pain and joy? Art as meditation does. Listen, for example, to the experience of St. Hildegarde of Bingen.

> When I was forty-two years and seven months it happened that a light of great flashing poured down from the open sky, setting on fire my entire head, all my breast and my whole heart. Suddenly I was tasting a discerning of the meaning of books, of the psalter, the Gospels, of other Catholic writers, of the Old and New Testaments. . . . Beaten down by many kinds of illness at the same time, I decided to put my hand to writing. Once I did this, a deep and profound exposition of books came over me. I received the strength to rise up from my sick bed, and under that power I continued to carry out the work to the end, using all of ten years to do it.[10]

Here we have remarkable testimony from as remarkable a person as the West has yet produced—a playwright and painter, a musician and mystic, a doctor and healer, a physicist and botanist, a political activist and prophet—about the power of art as meditation. It was in her commitment to "putting her hand to writing" that not only was her health restored (read: salvation happened) but others' as well. In the writing and painting that followed that decision to enter art as meditation many, many others have been healed and today are being healed. I know this because I have of late done many workshops using slides of Hildegarde's amazing mandala drawings as well as passages from her writings and have experienced with others the deep, deep healing that follows.

The healing that was effected by art in Hildegarde's case is of great significance for our times as well. Spirituality plays an indispensable role in recovering art for the global civilization that our world cries for at every plane of existence today, whether economic, political, religious, or ecological. Ingmar Bergman laments the divorce of art and spirituality from the viewpoint of what it has done to art in the West. "It is my opinion that art lost its basic creative drive the moment it was separated from worship. It severed an umbilical cord and now lives its own sterile life, generating and degenerating itself." Not only is religious faith sterile without art, but art grows sterile when divorced from spirituality. Without spirituality recovering art for all peoples, especially the poor and powerless, art will continue, in Blake's words, to be degraded, part of the problem of elitism rather than its solution. But equally, the obverse is the case as well. Until art is allowed its full and proper place in spiritual meditation, meditation itself will remain elitist, a complex and convoluted exercise for an elite minority of professional pray-ers who are as often as not members of what William Callahan calls "multinational religious orders."

There was a time in our not-so-distant past, previous to industrial society and to electronic society, that art as meditation could be almost taken for granted. The ability to grow one's own garden, to play a basic musical instrument, to sew, tell stories, relate to animals and to nature's seasons was widespread. But industrial society and urban living have changed much of this, and today we must make a conscious effort to develop the unconscious, the right brain, our mystical lives, by self-expression or art. Gandhi recognized this when he urged his Indian peoples to return to spinning and, as Erikson puts it, "elevated the spinning wheel to significance as an economic necessity, a religious ritual, and a national symbol."[11] Art as meditation was one of the ways Gandhi devised to employ and to spiritually energize his people. Today in America words and word machines, and now picture machines—television and film—for all the wonders they bring us, too often operate on an introverted meditation model. That is to say, they bring us *their* images— and who the "they" are is of vital significance: is it multinational corporations whose purpose is mainly to sell us a product wrapped around a news program or a sports event or a sitcom? These images come from outside in, as do all commercials of every kind.

As Eckhart points out so clearly, outside/in dynamics are not the stuff of which deep living is born. This is not at all an adequate kind of meditation for nourishing self or society. Says Eckhart, "Whatever I want to express in its truest meaning must emerge from within me and pass through an inner form. It cannot come from outside to the inside but must emerge from within." What emerges from within is art. Art is inborn within us. Art is not the same as stream-of-consciousness spontaneity. It "passes through an inner form," as Eckhart observes. Perhaps that form is dancing or clay or paints or a musical instrument or dramatic technique. Art as meditation is not meditation without form, but it is meditation wherein the form serves the inner truth and not the other way around. Ritual and worship are equally meant to be prayerful expressions of the people— liturgy means "the work of the people"—that is an outward-flowing expression of the inner events of the people which find an outlet in a group form. Too many revisions of prayer books, whether of Catholic, Episcopal, or Protestant denominations, in our day ignore this fact and presume that more "relevant" prayers from outside a group of people will somehow renew worship. What will renew worship and indeed all prayer is the calling forth from the inside of a people whatever they want to express in its truest meaning, as Eckhart puts it.

What churches need to do now to renew self and society is to take spirituality seriously; this means taking art seriously. Not art for the sake of art; not art for the sake of making banners or teapots; not art for sale. But art as prayer, art as meditation. Only art as meditation allows one to let go of art as production à la capitalism and return to art as process, which is the spiritual experience that creativity is about. Only art as meditation reminds people so that they will never forget that the most beautiful thing a potter produces is . . . the potter. Every church ought to have clay and paints, body movement and music, ritual-making and body massage and gardening as meditation. Thomas Berry comments on what is learned when children learn gardening, for example.

> Gardening is an active participation in the deepest mysteries of the universe. By gardening our children learn that they constitute with all growing things a single community of life. They learn to nurture and be nurtured in a universe that is always precarious but ultimately benign. They learn profound reasons for the seasonal rituals of the great religious traditions.[12]

Not only churches but education itself can and need to be revitalized in the same manner. The notion that education is about educating the left brain alone is obsolete and inherently violent. It does violence to the individual and ultimately to society itself. Teachers of all disciplines—sciences, arts, religion, history—need to recover the power of art as centering and ongoing creating of the cosmogenesis for which we are all responsible. If education is to be an instrument in social transformation, education itself must be transformed. It must allow art as centering to breathe life into whole curricula and whole educational systems. It cannot be presumed that those whom our society has knighted as art teachers are the proper ones to lead the recovery of art as spirituality, whether in churches or in educational systems. I have often found that graduates of our specialized art or music conservatories are among the most Newtonized (and by that I mean inculcated with parts-mentality) people I know. We need to look hard and long and to encourage those unique persons who, while loving their craft, have not also split their souls. The artist needs as much redemption by way of spirituality as spirituality needs by way of art in our times.

The single largest obstacle in teaching adults to meditate by means of art is getting them to let go of judgemental attitudes toward their self-expression. These judgemental attitudes have been passed down to most members of our society from the youngest age: "You can't sing," or, "You don't dance well," or, "You can't draw at all." Books exist to assist this process, such as *Drawing on the Right Side of the Brain*, that are very helpful.[13] To do clay in the dark for the first time, for example, destroys all temptations to make comparisons with others' work and in the process creates a powerful group bonding experience. It is good to begin art as meditation experiences with a letting-go exercise of breathing in and out in order to let one's powers be free to give their full attention to the images within that are needing to be born. Of course it should be emphasized that art as meditation presumes, as all of creation spirituality does, trust. A trust that out of silence, waiting, openness, emptiness one can and will give birth to images. The facilitator in such a prayerful exercise must believe deeply and therefore trust each individual present to be capable of birthing his or her own symbols or images or pictures. Such a leader allows silence to be silence. Is this after all not the root meaning in our language of the verb "to believe," namely to leave be or let be? More of this leaving or letting be is needed in worship and in education if the people of our society are to come to shared truth.

In inviting one another to art as meditation, it is important that the group leader, especially at the beginning stages, make clear that one thing we all need to let go of in our society is expressing ourselves almost exclusively in words. Rainer Maria Rilke was fond of saying that words are the last resort for expressing what happens deep within oneself. By letting go of our overdependence on words we allow images, symbols, pictures to emerge, and we express them by drawing, painting, body movement, music, poetry, etc. Art as meditation takes one on deeper, more communal journeys than words can ever do. (Storytelling is more than words, it is words serving the form of stories, thus pictures of our lives; and poetry is more than words, it is the retrieving of language and of the symbolic energy that words ought to possess.)

Since we have been using art as meditation as an essential ingredient in our educational and spiritual program at our Institute in Creation-Centered Spirituality for five years now, I would like to share a few stories of results from our experience and then follow these with some comments from the most recent class of students who took painting as meditation. A young man, a farmer from an Evangelical background, approached me a month after classes began and said, "I am a mystic. Every small farmer is a mystic. But I have been astounded that I have experienced more mysticism—more experiences of transcendence and of unity, more and deeper making of connections—on the dance floor, taking dance as meditation, than I have ever experienced in my whole life." There was the thirty-seven-year-old mother and housewife who said on taking clay as meditation that clay "totally transformed my marriage. The first day we had clay and I returned home, when I touched my husband's skin it was like touching it for the very first time." I like to point out to people to whom I tell this story that clay is much cheaper than a marriage counselor and much more fun. The Creator has given us art to heal one another with—and what have we done with it? We either reduce it to entertainment or buy it or sell it or project onto others whom we label "artists" our own responsibility for it. That is why art as meditation is so democratizing a movement: it returns responsibility to each of us for the images we believe in. And with the responsibility goes the fun. Art empowers. There is insight in this woman's remark about the art of lovemaking and sexuality that is so often distorted in a pornographic or sex-as-consumerism society. Lovemaking ought to be as much an act of art as meditation as any other expression of "whatever we want to express in its truest meaning" (Eckhart). It has every right to be as playful, as sensual, and as unitive as all our other mystical experiences.

Once when our students were sharing their experience with art as meditation, a clay student told the following story: "I fought the clay and fought the clay for six weeks," he confessed, "and every-thing I made fell apart. One day I got so tired of fighting the clay that I quit fighting it, and lo and behold what I made held together." Then a piano-as-meditation student spoke up: "A similar thing happened to me," she said. "I fought the keys and fought them for seven weeks. One day I was so tired I put my head down on the keys and fell asleep. When I woke up I began—for the first time—to play the piano!" There is deep testimony here to one reason why art is so powerful a form of healing: neither the clay nor the piano keys nor the body in dance nor the colors in painting nor the back in massage will tolerate subject/object relationships. The holy matter with which all art interacts has a good opinion of itself—no one instructs it in original sin ideologies—and as a result it demands relationships of equality. With clay and dance, music and painting, one actually learns the wisdom of fifty-fifty relationships, of give-and-take, of action and receptivity. Nothing less holds together. Everything less, all our attitudes of war and control over self or others or matter itself, is enervating. And fails to yield fruit. The word "craft" means power. The power that is practiced and refined in art as meditation is not and can never be a power-over or a power-under; it is the ultimate affront to sado-masochistic relationships of power. It is power-with. Adrienne Rich has seen this truth vividly when she writes:

> the passion to make and make again
> where such unmaking reigns
>
> the refusal to be a victim
>
> *we have lived with violence so long* (30.64)

Birthing requires the refusal to be a victim, and it will help bring about the end of our long living with violence. And it is the process of interacting with materials of art that brings this truth about, this passion to make and make again in a society that has enthroned unmaking or the making by others instead of making ourselves.

Following are some testimonies of students who took painting as meditation recently in our ICCS program under the able tutelage of our instructor, Blanche Marie Gallagher, BVM. Giving these testi-monies are one mother, one Lutheran minister, two priests, and two Catholic sisters. One thing that strikes me in studying these reflec-tions is how much light is shed on each of the paths, not only Path III, but Paths I and II as well, by art as meditation. Comments one meditator:

All of creation seems to be made up of lines, colors, and space. I am made up of body, heart, and soul. Creation also has what I have, and I have what creation has. Together we discover the inherent beauty and grandeur in both.

I see a leaf, a balloon, a tree, a stretch of water, and I pass it by because it has no meaning to me in my haste to go on to other, more important realities. They allow me to pass by, not infringing, for they know their own beauty and realize that if it is not I, then another will come eventually. They maintain their identity no matter how often they are passed by. Not so with me! I do not know my own identity and beauty, and that is why I seek what seem to me more important realities.

Suddenly I am faced with the things of creation. I must begin to recognize their lines, their colors, their space. They begin to speak to me of their beauty, their meaning. . . . I struggle to bring into form the lines, the color, the shape that together articulate the beauty of creation. Slowly, painfully, things come together, I speak to them of my fear; they speak to me of their beauty. I forget the problems and difficulties of life. I desire only to paint this beautiful part of creation. In doing so I become more aware of myself. . . . I feel a tranquility I have not know before. Time passes quickly without notice. The time is a prayer. (Robert McNeil)

Painting is teaching me about trust. I want the painting to be realistic as my left brain tells me. But whenever that happens I am denied the richness of letting go and trusting my inner images. Only in trusting myself and the paint do I discover *anew* the creation—including myself. In letting go and trusting my images I discover that I have something significant to offer this life. The only way this will happen is when I yield to my images, trust and listen to them.

There is so much joy in not having to use words to convey meaning and truth. Sometimes I paint in silence and other times I listen to classical music. Experiencing this new kind of time is almost always relaxing and healing. One of the reasons this is true, I believe, is that it is vastly different from the feeling of guilt, trying to please others, that has driven me in the past. I am beginning to respond to an inner "drive" within *me* that is very old; it is inscribed in my archetypal depths.

In the final analysis painting, like faith, is about seeing. It is a seeing that invites us all to greater depths of knowledge and wisdom about who we are in this vast cosmos. (John Mix)

After I finished my paintings and matted them, I received many compliments. This was both surprising and pleasing to me, and

I realized that I had been an enabler. I had helped others to admire something; I had made them happy. This in turn made me happy. I'm glad I let go. (Bernadette Poor)

Inadequate as my entry into art is, I find a great desire to produce something beautiful, and when I have no idea how to express a leaf or a tree, it makes me remember how marvellous creation is and how much beauty we forget every day. And the next time I pay more attention. (Sean Cahill)

Colors were not only related to meditation but became the meditation. Following a relaxation exercise when there were no words, no body movement, the colors would speak from the silence and often the confusion inside. The green, the red, the yellow of the mandala speak for the heart and respond to the God of all creation. (Helen Murphy)

The first obstacle for me to face in my Painting as Meditation course was and is fear—fear of doing something totally new, fear of being inadequate and inept, fear of doing it "wrong," fear of making a mistake, fear of being laughed at, fear of not being in control of what's happening to me, and fear of facing myself. ... What if there is no real me—only a Phony—or what if they and/or God don't like this imperfect self that I reveal?

Taking the risk to choose to let go and be vulnerable with watercolor, paper, and brush is leading me to try to take the risk to let go more and be more open and vulnerable in my prayer and meditation. This is because I found that I didn't die when I made that risk with paper, watercolor, and brush. To the contrary, I came very much more alive.

In painting connections were being made between myself and earth, air, water, and fire—through the flipping of air onto my paintings, through painting the lake, through painting the candle flame, through rituals. I felt connected to God and my parish community as well.

Painting the self-portrait I relaxed and breathed slowly, trying to center myself within and then breathe the inner self out onto the paper. In accepting myself lovingly I started to learn how to center, how to be present to God within me without talking or using words, so that my breathing in and out becomes a recollection of the Presence of God and so does each heartbeat.

Praying, centering, meditating—all involve relaxing and becoming still. So, I found out, do drawing and painting. (Marilla Barghusen)

I believe what is evident from these simple testimonies of ordinary folk who found themselves in ICCS this year is the power of art as meditation. It is interesting how many refer to the art process as itself a discipline for letting go. All meditation forms are about

197

letting go, and art as meditation is no exception to this rule. C. G. Jung talks about how to let things happen in the psyche and how to overcome a "veritable cramp of consciousness" caused by a "web of fantasies."

> The way of getting at the fantasies is individually different. For many people, it is easiest to write them; others visualize them, and others again draw and paint them with or without visualization. In cases of a high degree of conscious cramp, oftentimes the hands alone can fantasy; they model or draw figures that are often quite foreign to the conscious mind.
>
> These exercises must be continued until the cramp in the conscious mind is released, or, in other words, until one can let things happen, which was the immediate goal of the exercise. In this way a new attitude is created, an attitude which accepts the non-rational and the incomprehensible, simply because it is what is happening.[14]

Art is the basic form of meditation in the creation-centered tradition. With art as meditation we truly listen to the cosmos within us and around us and give birth to the ongoing cosmogenesis of our world and worlds. With art as meditation creation as blessing is rediscovered and our trust in letting go is affirmed. By turning to art as meditation we insure our continual greening, our continual being young, our childlikeness. Gustav Mahler wrote a letter to a friend while working on his Fourth Symphony and confessed the following:

> This one is quite fundamentally different from my other symphonies. But that *must be*; I could never repeat a state of mind—and as life drives on, so too I follow new tracks in every work. That is why at first it is always so hard for me to get down to work. All the skill that experience has brought one is of no avail. One has to begin to learn all over again for the new thing one sets out to make. So one remains everlastingly a *beginner*!... It is and always will be a gift of God— one that, like every loving gift, one cannot deserve and cannot get by asking.[15]

To create is always to learn, to begin over, to begin at zero. Part of the discipline of art as meditation is the discipline of struggling always from the beginning—"In the beginning," one might say. Given the wisdom and power of art as meditation, there is little wonder that creation-centered mystics/prophets like Mechtild of Magdeburg, Hildegarde of Bingen, and Meister Eckhart found the need to create to constitute the very substance of their spiritual journeys. We have seen how Hildegarde's writings and paintings literally moved her from her sickbed. Mechtild testifies how she was advised by many that to publish a book was vanity. She replies, "I am forced to write these words regarding which I would have gladly kept silent out of fear of vainglory. But I have learned to fear more the judgment of God should I, God's little creature, keep silent." The keeping silent, the burying of our images and talents, is not what the Creator God desires of us. This Jesus taught time and time again. Eckhart felt the same need not to keep silent that Mechtild felt; every artist/mystic feels this.

> Human beings ought to communicate and share all the gifts they have received from God. If a person has something that she does not share with others, that person is not good. A person who does not bestow on others spiritual things and the joy that is in them has in fact never been spiritual. People are not to receive and keep gifts for themselves alone, but should share themselves and pour forth everything they possess whether in their bodies or their souls as much as possible.

But how will we share the gifts and joy within ourselves if we do not spend silent time in an effort to image them, to birth them? How will we ever be spiritual if we do not recover art as meditation? And once we do, what might the community pleasure and the restructuring of human societies be like? Who could ever imagine?

It should be pointed out that not only is art meditation when we birth art—though this is a primary sense of art as meditation that we have often neglected in the West of late—but art is also meditation when we truly commune with either what we have birthed or what another has birthed. Philosopher Gabriel Marcel calls this "admiration" or "wondering at," and about this kind of art as meditation he says:

> I have always felt that admiration was of the same order as creation. ...In reality any creation is a response to a call received, and it is receptivity that we should stress here while pointing out that a serious error is made whenever receptivity and passivity are confused, as it seems to me they are in Kant, for example.[16]

The Catholic monk Thomas Merton, who himself practiced many forms of art as meditation, especially in the eight final and most prophetic years of his life, also speaks to the experience of art and meditation.

> Art enables us to find ourselves and lose ourselves at the same time. The mind that responds to the intellectual and spiritual values that lie

hidden in a poem, a painting, or a piece of music, discovers a spiritual vitality that lifts it above itself, takes it out of itself, and makes it present to itself on a level of being that it did not know it could ever achieve.[17]

If it is true, as Paul says, that "we are God's work of art," then everything we have said about art as meditation applies to the delight, wonder, admiration, surprise that God takes at our birth and continual unfolding. We are related to God as a painting is related to a painter, as a clay pot to a potter, as a book to its author. This bespeaks no mildly intimate relationship.

17 FAITH AS TRUST OF IMAGES: DISCIPLINE? —YES! ASCETICISM—NO!

You must give birth to your images. They are the future waiting to be born.... fear not the strangeness you feel. The future must enter into you long before it happens.... Just wait for the birth.... for the hour of new clarity.
—*Rainer Maria Rilke*[1]

Beauty demands a more arduous process.
—*Susan Griffin (20.192)*

The discipline comes in when we have to pay attention to what we don't like, aren't interested in, don't understand, mistrust ... when we have to read the poetry of our enemies—within or without.
—*M. C. Richards (31.64)*

The greatness of an artist lies in the building of an inner world, and in the ability to reconcile this inner world with the outer.
—*Albert Einstein*

Asceticism is of no great importance for it creates more, instead of less, self-consciousness.
—*Meister Eckhart*

Those who would storm the heavenly heights by fierceness and ascetic practices deceive themselves badly. Such people carry grim hearts within themselves; they lack true humility which alone leads the soul to God.
—*Mechtild of Magdeburg*

Art is the product of labor.
—*Pablo Casals*[2]

To be religious is to give your life so that the world may be more beautiful, more just, more at peace; it is to prevent egotistical and self-serving ends from disrupting this harmony of the whole.
—*Arturo Paoli*[3]

I am like a cypress ever green,
all your fruitfulness comes from me.
　　　—Hos. 14:9

A real artist is nothing if not a workingman and a damn hard
one.
　　　—Edward Weston

We ordinary people must forge our own beauty. We must set
fire to the greyness of our labor with the art of our own lives.
In this kind of creation, every day becomes a pure enjoyment.
　　　—Kenji Miyazawa[4]

The habit of art is the habit of enjoying vivid values.
　　　—Alfred North Whitehead (45.287)

When one moves from an introspective psychology to a cosmic one
and from a static cosmos to an emerging one and from a repression
of human creativity to a welcoming of the divine power of creativity
in humans, one unleashes much that is hidden. Much that is charged
and exciting. When Augustine and other fall/redemption theologians talk about the divine trinity in people, it is often presented as
a psychologized and introverted relationship. But when Meister
Eckhart or any representative of the creation-centered spiritual tradition speaks of creativity, he is speaking of the basic dynamism of
the universe in which humanity plays such a powerful role. "God's
generating is his indwelling and God's indwelling is his generating,"
says Meister Eckhart. The powers we humans have to give birth to
our images are in fact the very divine power of the universe itself
and, more than that, of the divinity itself. Since our souls are not
bound by our bodies, all time and cosmic space are affected by the
images we choose to ride and play with. This is why Eckhart can
ask, "What is it that remains?" and then answer his question this
way: "What is inborn in me remains." Eckhart is not trying to satisfy
a cheap yearning for immortality by this question and answer.
Rather, he is revealing a truth of the universe: That which comes
from deep within plays a role in the time and space of the universe
so powerful that it in fact cuts through our ordinary notions of time
and space. It outlives us all. It contributes to the gradual unfolding
of God, of people, of the cosmos.

　　In each of the paths we have traveled we have uncovered a

meaning of faith as trust that has often gone unnoticed during the fall/redemption hegemony in Christianity. In Path I we saw that the world, meaning the cosmos, and including our bodies and passions and all creation blessings, was "thoroughly worthy of trust" (Von Rad); in Path II we saw that darkness and even nothingness can be trusted and are trusted by a faithful person. In Path III we learn that our images are trustworthy. Every person needs to learn to trust his or her own images. It is precisely out of this trust that the artist in us is born. Without this trust all newness, all adventure, all hope, all divinity is aborted or stillborn. Acedia reigns. And with this boredom comes violence, as Arguelles insists: "Those who are deprived of the power of expression will express themselves in a drive for power."

Images are not always easy to trust, for they bear within themselves, precisely because they are new, a capacity to disturb the peace, to question the peace, to rock the status quo, to wonder about the way things are, to suggest that at times chaos—which precedes birthing—is holier than the order that currently reigns. It is in this sense that biblical scholar Walter Brueggemann observes that "Every totalitarian regime is frightened by the artist.... Indeed, poetic imagination is the last way left in which to challenge and conflict the dominant reality." (5.45) The potential conflicts that we conjure up in our minds and hearts, conflicts of a personal as well as a social kind, all become rationalizations for our not creating, excuses we can hide behind. And, in a very perverse way, we even enlist God in our efforts to cease creating, that is, to cease the birthing of God. As we have seen, Mechtild of Magdeburg, when criticized for writing a book although she was not a cleric and did not have a lot of formal theological education, trusted her own images. Her trust outweighed her and her society's fears, guilts, pettiness, temptations to comfort. Vulnerability is no excuse for not creating, just as fear is no excuse for lack of courage and despair is no excuse for lack of hope. Fear produces courage, which in fact happens in the midst of fear. Despair produces hope, which is born out of the depths of despair. And vulnerability produces creativity, which requires a capacity to get hurt. Our images can indeed hurt us. But only temporarily. To kill or forget or neglect our images is far more lethal; that way lies the way of dying while still living, of drying up, as Hildegarde of Bingen warns. The very pain that trust of images brings about can be a renewing pain, a pain of new birth and new creation, a salvific and healing pain that ushers us into deep and wonderful relationships

203

with others and with times and spaces and even places that bring'
about transcendence.

We need to ride our images as one would ride a giant eagle,
soaring up and down wherever they take us. And if they prove to be
wrong images, from which we fall and hurt ourselves, that is okay
too. For our creativity does not consist in being right all the time but
in making of all our experiences, including the apparently mistaken
and imperfect ones, a holy whole. Jesus, after all, rode his images to
the cross, to his very death. And beyond this apparent failure, to the
empty tomb and to resurrection. Who knows what lies behind and
beyond our images until we trust them enough to ride them fully,
even into the darkness and into the depths like a seed in the soil?
Perhaps we will never know the gift that our images are until we
ride them through to the other side, and only from that perspective
will we see them for the first time. ·

One reason for trusting our images is that we ourselves are trusted
images. We are God's images, and God trusts us with that divine
power of imagination. We have been entrusted by God with our
capacity to imagine and to birth. If we are truly "God's work of art,"
as Paul says we are, if we are truly God's extrovert meditation, then
surely we have no excuse for not trusting the creative powers within
us. Imperfection is no excuse; failure is no excuse; sin is no excuse;
suffering is no excuse. Who, after all, has the right to be excused or
to excuse him- or herself from the divine plan for the universe? And
when did God—as opposed to society and its leaders—ever excuse
any one of us from being an active, energetic image of God?

The image I use for the process of imaging is popcorn popping.
When one corn begins to pop all the others soon chime in. I believe
that learning to trust just one image and play it out releases all the
other images to assert themselves as well. When this happens a
great feeling of wonder and delight comes over one. But then come
the hard choices that must be made, the choices of some images
over others. I believe that many times we fail to create because we
fail to choose one image in preference to another. Without such
choices, however, nothing is born. A mother does not give birth to
all babies but to her particular baby, who in turn will relate to all
babies. Part of trusting images and riding or living them is choosing
which ones we most need to ride. Behind the trust of images lies a
trust in self—that one is capable of making an adequate decision
about which images to throw one's lot in with. Path III, more than
Paths I and II, is a time for decision-making, for commitments to

204

certain images and not to others. It is a time for letting go of letting go. The Zen artist Kenji Miyazawa described the process this way:

> You experience something deeply. Later, you picture it in your own mind; you idealize it; you cooly and sharply analyze it; you throw all your passion and power into it. Then you fuse all these things together into one. If you do this without self-consciousness, the depth and the power of creation will be much greater.[5]

Our images are our children. Like our children they will prove to be demanding on us and our time. And, like our children, they will demand to be trusted. Our children are our images but by no means our only ones, nor are they, in all cases, our best ones.

When Miyazawa praises the need for operating "without self-consciousness" he is underlining one of the significant distinctions between creation spirituality and fall/redemption spirituality. The former is an aesthetic spirituality that requires discipline to utter the beauty in ourselves. The latter is an ascetic spirituality that calls for mortifications (which literally means "to put to death or deaden"). The former is more spontaneous and childlike and unself-conscious. The latter is will-oriented and therefore self-conscious and self-consciously adult. The creation tradition criticizes asceticism as not being the correct way to carry on God's Dabhar or creative energy, for what evidence do we possess, after all, that God is herself ascetic? Rather the evidence we have from creation's beauty and richness is that our God is a God in love with beauty, with delight and the sharing of it. Or, as Eckhart puts it, "God is voluptuous and delicious." Mechtild of Magdeburg, as is evident in the quote at the beginning of this section, criticizes asceticism for its lack of humor and delight. Eckhart criticizes it for its lack of unself-consciousness.

> Asceticism is of no great importance. There is a better way to treat your passions than to heap on them practices which so often reveal a great ego and create more instead of less self-consciousness. And that is to put on them a bridle of love. The person who has done this will travel much further than all those the world over practicing mortifications together would ever do.

What is a "bridle of love"? A bridle is a steering instrument. We are to steer, not control or abuse, our passions, according to Eckhart. We are to make them work for us, to discipline them so that they take us where we need to go, as is the case with a bridle on a charging horse. Notice that the bridle is itself a bridle of love. We discipline by way

205

of love, not by way of threat, intimidation, or control. The creation-centered way of spirituality is one of discipline, not of asceticism.

What is discipline? The word "discipline" comes from the word "disciple." A disciple is one who is allured or attracted by another. Jesus' disciples were persons who met him, saw him interacting with others, heard him speak, and were thereby attracted to him. Being attracted to him, they committed themselves to his company to learn more of the beauty they had intuited. This is the way it is with other artists as well. The pianist is somehow attracted to the music of the piano, and so the long hours of hard work at the instrument, until the back aches and the arms twinge and the fingers swell to become more muscular—all this pain is not counted. It is not called "mortification" or "asceticism." It is discipline, a loving relationship that brings out the best in us.

Discipline is about work and about hard work. But the disciple does not count the pain or dwell on it, for, as Jesus observed in John's Gospel, the mother's joy at the birth overshadows the pains that precede it. Pablo Casals writes about the discipline of the artist which constitutes the hidden work behind the childlike sharing.

> There is of course no substitute for work. I myself practiced constantly, as I have all my life. I have been told I play the cello with the ease of a bird flying. I do not know with how much effort a bird learns to fly, but I do know what effort has gone into my cello. What seems ease of performance comes from the greatest labor.... Almost always, facility results only from maximum effort. Art is the product of labor.[6]

It is very important that we recover a spirituality of discipline that is very unlike a spirituality of asceticism on the one hand or a pseudospirituality of fear of labor on the other. The fact that the creation tradition is not ascetic does not mean that creativity is as easy as falling off a log or just "being spontaneous." In fact, creativity requires hard work, sweat, sore limbs, bloodied fingers, callouses, aching muscles, hurting eyes, and just being tired. Ask any dancer, any musician, any writer, any mother or father, any painter, any sculptor. But, when the relationship is truly one of discipline devoted to the fashioning of images one loves, then the pain is let go of because the joy and delight are so great.

I am convinced that one reason why asceticism has reigned so supremely in Western spirituality for the past few centuries is the fascination the West has had for the mechanistic during this period. An ascetic spirituality is a kind of mechanistic spirituality: behind rules of self-abnegation there lies a hidden assumption that something good will result from not indulging in pleasure, that by controlling matter we somehow arrive at our divinity. The awful truth is that in our quest to control matter we have arrived in our century more at the demonic of atomic discovery and release than we have arrived at the divine. A passage from a Newtonian, mechanistic universe to an Einsteinian one marks well the passage from an ascetic to an aesthetic spirituality.

Spiritual writer and feminist Carol Christ astutely comments on how important asceticism appears to an all-male spirituality. As the world became more and more Newtonian in the past three centuries, so too did it become more and more masculine. And male-dominated spirituality seldom questioned its mechanically oriented, ascetic emphases. She writes:

> After achieving power and respect, men may come to experience their power as illusory. They may then open themselves to a deeper experience of power "not as the world knows it." As literatures of both East and West indicate, the male mystic's quest is arduous and difficult.

In contrast, because "women never have what male mystics must strive to give up," they have less need for asceticism. It is logical to conclude, as Christ does, that "mystic insight may be easier for women to achieve than men." (10.17f.) Thus it is not only Einstein who throws us into a more disciplined and a less ascetic spirituality; it is also the women's movement, the feminist awakening among women and men. And, by inference, the awakening of all disadvantaged peoples. Asceticism is a luxury for those with power. It is not even a consideration for those without power. Why? Because their lives already contain enough crosses and pain, sufficient experiences of nothingness and the void, to empty even God of God. The issue for the poor is survival and creativity: how to survive with what minimal gifts one has been left. And how to make something with the simplest of materials and out of the nothingness of one's existence. Here lies new birth and new creation.

18 DIALECTICAL, TRINITARIAN: HOW OUR LIVES AS WORKS OF ART SPIRAL BEAUTY BACK INTO THE WORLD

By their fruits you shall know them.
—Jesus

The key word is paradox. As a fool I sidestep the either/or choices of logic and choose both.
—Ken Feit (professional fool)

Feminine wisdom is a paradoxical wisdom which never juxtaposes opposites into "either-or" pairs but gathers them into "both-and" relationships.
—Ann Ulanov[1]

What I know about centering makes it impossible for me to pretend that trust is either objective or subjective; the practice of centering casts upon such dualisms another light. . . . Polarities . . . map our being: feminine and masculine, child and adult, birth and death. They are dynamics by which we live. Eliminate one, and the other fades. Paradox and metamorphosis are laws.
—M. C. Richards (31.65, 96.116)

This, therefore, is the salvation of Christians, that believing in the Trinity, that is in the Father and the Son and the Holy Spirit, and baptized into it, we believe without doubt that there is one and the same true and singular divinity and power, majesty and substance.
—Council of Rome, 382 A.D.

In the history of mysticism [the mystical experience of Trinitarian Mysticism] has not had the prominence one might expect in view of the importance of the mystery in saving history.
—Karl Rahner[2]

And when light and darkness mate
Once more and make something entirely transparent,

. . . .
Then our entire twisted nature will turn
And run when a single secret word is spoken.
   —*Novalis (7.42)*

God is beauty.
   —*Francis of Assisi*

Grace pours all beauty into the soul. . . . The soul means the world.
   —*Meister Eckhart*

The springs that moved Berlioz, in fact, were just the springs that moved his great contemporaries. The essence of their revolt was an insistence upon the truth that beauty is coextensive almost with life itself.
   —*Ernest Newman*[3]

We ordinary people must forge our own beauty. We must set fire to the greyness of our labor with the art of our own lives. . . . What is the essence of this art of living? Of course, even this art should have beauty as its essence.
   —*Kenji Miyazawa*[4]

The poor need not only bread. The poor also need beauty.
   —*Monsignor Hildebrand*

Real beauty is my aim.
   —*Mahatma Gandhi (22.252)*

In the Orthodox spiritual tradition, the ultimate moral question we ask is the following: Is what we are doing, is what I am doing, beautiful or not?
   —*Carolyn Gifford (Orthodox theologian)*[5]

The Baptized "in whom dwells the Word, possesses the beautiful form of the Word; he is assimilated to God and he is beautiful himself." It is then rightly that Heraclitus said: "People are gods and gods are people." This mystery is indeed revealed in the Word: God in people and people, God.
   —*Clement of Alexandria*[6]

The teleology of the Universe is directed to the production of Beauty.... The type of Truth required for the final stretch of Beauty is a discovery and not a recapitulation.... Apart from Beauty, Truth is neither good, nor bad.... Truth matters because of Beauty.
    —*Alfred North Whitehead*[7]

The basic dynamic of the creation-centered spiritual tradition is dialectical, as distinct from dualistic. Dualism creates a consciousness, and with it institutions and structures, of either/or. One is either good or bad, male or female, strong or weak, spiritual or sensual, for example. Dialectical consciousness is about both/and thinking, both/and relationships. One can be both good and bad, male and female, strong and weak, spiritual and sensual. One reason why the creation tradition is so deeply grounded in dialectical as distinct from dualistic consciousness is that the way in which humans see themselves as related to nature is one of the most basic of all relationships. Frederick Turner laments what he considers to be the basic spiritual principle of Western civilization, that of the "enduring opposition of man and nature." It is clear from Path I, with its consciousness of panentheism, that the creation-centered spiritual tradition rejects this fundamental dualism of man (or woman) versus nature. "We are nature seeing nature," as Susan Griffin so aptly puts it. (20.226) How can separation—which all dualism presumes—continue in such a situation?

Indeed, this separation that lies behind all dualism is what the creation-centered tradition considers to be original sin or the sin behind sin. Not only Meister Eckhart but Mary Daly and Susan Griffin see the sin behind sin as dualism or separation. Eckhart observes that, in Genesis, all of creation was called "good" and "very good" except when God separated earth from sky. "The separation was not called good," he comments. Susan Griffin titles an entire book within a book "Separation." She names patriarchal efforts to separate man from woman, work from effort, womb from body, mind from body, the wild beasts from his world, space from space, time from time, matter from reality, truth from feeling, death from life, energy from matter.[8] Feminist theologian Beverly Harrison seconds this commitment of feminist thought to dialectical consciousness when she says simply, "A feminist theology is not a theology of either/or."[9] Nicholas of Cusa was a champion of dialectical as distinct from dualistic thinking. The former he calls "copulative theology," whose basis is a "reconciliation of mind and nature, of intellect and sense." He opposes this theology to all theology that is merely "disjunctive, negating and divisive."[10] Comments Cusa scholar Ernst Cassirer, "The spirit of asceticism is overcome; mistrust of the world disappears. The mind can come to know itself and to measure its own powers only by devoting itself completely and unconditionally to the world."[11]

A dialectical consciousness is essential for the way we begin to see the world and ourselves as integral to it. It is also what living in the world is all about; it is what creativity, birthing, art are all about. If the great mystery of sexuality teaches us anything—and already we have seen how it teaches wisdom and cosmic awareness among other things—it surely teaches us the primordial truth that all dualism forgets: that one plus one equals three. That life is born of tension and struggle and difference. That life is not born by virginal withdrawal but by active coupling. Whether the coupling is that of a positive/negative charge that gives birth to an electrical current; whether it is that of oxygen and hydrogen that births the great miracle of the universe called water; whether it is that of the musician coupling with her images of notes and forms; whether it is the sculptor coupling with her wood; whether it is husband and wife coupling in their love and birthing a child; whether it is a widow coupling with memories of a deceased husband: all love is born of the conflict that dialectical consciousness acknowledges. Dualism wants to control conflict, to deny tension and difference. And in the process of such denial nothing is born. It is all stillborn. Frederick Turner comments on how this sad attitude controlled the Puritans who first came to America: they had an opportunity to become vulnerable to a new religion which was very ancient, that of the Native Americans, and to create anew. Instead, their Christianity "could not issue into anything regenerative" and was reduced to "merely mimicking actions original to the mighty days of the ancients."

Of themselves they could initiate nothing of significance. Indeed, we now know they did not. Their brief and bitter hour here ... is but a sad, microcosmic recapitulation of the history that Christianity had already enacted in the Old World. ... repeating helplessly its negative achievements: the suppression of dissenters, the search for and destruction of alien enemies; and the costly self-repression that would finally sunder the very sect itself. To have been genuine reformers,

211

they would have had to accept the New World. But nothing in their history told them how this might be done. (41.213)

All art in our personal and collective histories tells us how this might be done, this assimilation of what is different, what is surprising, what is at first feared. It is of this union of seeming opposites that all creation is renewed.

One way in which we all experience dialectical moments is in laughter and foolishness. The spiritual fool Ken Feit, by inviting people to celebrate a "fool's mass" instead of merely a formally correct mass, was a priest of paradox and imagination. His eating of an animal cracker shaped like a lion and roaring immediately afterward left lessons for all to experience in how to accept what is different, be vulnerable to it, and be transformed. Just as he transformed the animal cracker from cracker to food, so the animal transformed him from person-in-charge to a roaring lion. In biting off just a tiny piece of the same animal cracker his response was a meek "meow," a pussycat transformation, a subtle suggestion of cosmic history, for lions and pussycats are related. All laughter recalls the dialectic for us, and it is no coincidence that Cotton Mather and the unfortunate band of Puritans that Turner weeps for are not known for their humor. A dialectical consciousness is a letting go, a paradoxical, a humorous consciousness. Dualism is deadly serious, for it must always be in charge, in control. The laments that Turner sheds over the fall/redemption history of Puritan America are by no means shed for the Puritans alone but for their victims, the Native Americans and black slaves and all of us who have been influenced by a tradition that cannot create. To refuse to create is profoundly destructive. To reject dialectic for dualism is to reject Chartres cathedral for MX missiles.

We have already seen a powerful dialectic at work in the very journey we have taken along the creation-centered spiritual path. For the Via Positiva and the Via Negativa, the God of light and the God of darkness, the befriending of pleasure and the befriending of pain, are themselves dialectical. By admitting both experiences into our spirituality we have been invited on the third path, the Via Creativa. Alfred North Whitehead celebrates what he calls the "discord" that alone can accomplish beauty in the universe. Discord is to be valued, he insists, for without it there is no new beginning, no fresh start. "The contribution to Beauty which can be supplied by Discord—in itself destructive and evil—is the positive feeling of a quick shift of aim from the tameness of outworn perfection to some other ideal with its freshness still upon it."[12] The dialectical process is not a "tame" process. The beauty we birth is not birthed antiseptically or without discord. Beauty and terror, as Simone Weil used to observe, come together. There is something awesome, awful, powerful about new creation. Nature and its renewal are not superficial. Eckhart is reminding us of the same dialectical need not to exclude evil or tragedy from our birthing processes when he says that "All things praise God and bless God. Evil too praises God." Whitehead distinguishes between what he calls "tragic evil" and "gross evil." Tragedy is not in vain, he insists, for from it a deeper beauty is forged. The Resurrection, after all, could not have happened without a crucifixion. There is no Easter without a Good Friday. Whitehead sees it this way:

> As soon as high consciousness is reached, the enjoyment of existence is entwined with pain, frustration, loss, tragedy. . . . Each tragedy is the disclosure of an ideal:—What might have been, and was not: What can be. The tragedy was not in vain. This survival power in motive force, by reason of appeal to reserves of Beauty, marks the difference between the tragic evil and the gross evil.[13]

Tragic evil, then, is redemptive. It is redeemed by beauty, one might say. But to achieve its power, evil itself must become part of our dialectical way of living; it cannot be controlled by dualistic relationships to it. Beauty is born of the coupling of love of life and its harmonies with pain at life and its discords.

The creation-centered mystic Mechtild of Magdeburg images the dialectical grounding for her spirituality in a wonderful way when she says the Creator has given us two wines to drink from: the white wine of bliss and harmony and ecstasy and the red wine of pain and suffering and loss. To fully live, to live spiritually, therefore, is to drink of both wines in our lifetimes. Twentieth-century artist Philip Guston talks of the struggle between the lyrical and the abstract in his work. "It has taken me years to understand that such conflict is welcome; one thing fires the other."

St. Augustine and the fall/redemption religious tradition developed a psychological theory of the Trinity based on Augustine's introspective psychology. What we need today is a cosmic and creativity-oriented understanding of the Trinity based on the expanding cosmos within and without us. As is seen in the dogmatic declaration from the Council of Rome on the opening page to this section, Christians boast that they believe in a triune God. The Trinity is an article of faith, surely one of the very most fundamental articles of faith, in which Christians say they believe. And yet, that belief is very often a mere reciting of a doctrinal statement with the head and with the lips. Has it begun to enter believers' hearts and right brains what is truly powerful in the trinitarian formula? Can it be denied that what is being celebrated here is the truth that the ultimate energy of the universe is dialectical and therefore creative? Dualism and separation are the original sin, the sin behind sin, because they refuse to give birth, they refuse to spiral and to carry on the divine process of cosmogenesis that is the Creator's divine force of Dabhar. What is being celebrated in trinitarian doctrine is the truth that neither the universe nor the Creator is static; they are unfolding, pulsating, passionate, loving, creating, breathing, spiraling. And that humankind's imaging of such a creating triune God must also be an imaging of generation and creativity. Eckhart captures the urgency of this doctrine when he says, "Our name is that we must be born. And the Creator's name is: to bear." Just as God is in continual process of birthing God—the spirit flows from the Father *and* the Son, as traditional doctrine insists—so too are we humans to be in the process of birthing ourselves, our lives, our society, our cosmos. The trinitarian doctrine that spirit must proceed from *both* Father and Son and not from Father alone or Son alone is an indisputable reminder that only both/and, only a dialectical and therefore creating consciousness, can constitute an imitation of the divine.

As we see in the opening lines to this section, theologian Karl Rahner laments that a trinitarian mysticism has remained undeveloped in the West. The reason for this can be found principally, I believe, in the fact that a dualistic consciousness propagated by fall/redemption theologies as well as by Newtonian science and patriarchal privilege, has downgraded the truth of dialectical consciousness. Similarily, the truth of the spiritual way of the artist within and among all peoples has been downgraded. When "left-brain-itis" prevails either in education or in religious dogma, there is no birthing, no expansion of divine mystery. The same non-activity occurs when "right-brain-itis," superstition or sentimentalism that fails to couple with a firm intellectual life, dominates. In the wedding of left and right brain in both theology and education we would all re-experience divine mysteries such as the Trinity.

The Trinity itself gives us form and insight into other trinities which will in turn generate life and divinity into the cosmos. For example, instead of the dualism of soul versus body, we can live a dialectic of soul/body and thereby birth spirit. Spirit and life are birthed by soul *and* body—not exclusively by soul nor exclusively by body. Art is a marriage of left *and* right brains, not of right brain exclusively. A true artist is an intellectual who has ideas to share. By the same token, a true intellectual is an artist with ideas, passionately in love with their wonder and their consequences for humankind. A trinitarian model would bring together again the artist and the thinker, and from this coupling adventures in ideas would awaken us all. A trinitarian rather than dualistic approach to work and art and play would recognize how these three—work, art, play—are essential to human expression and to the ongoing growth of the cosmos and of human society. Unemployment itself would be addressed at its roots, which can be found, among other places, in our culture's far-too-narrow definition of work. As if what the clown does or the musician does or the meditator does is not work. Or as if what we call work has nothing in common with play. Recovering the holy trinity of work, art, play will be to recover the dignity of humanity in its likeness to a triune God who works and creates and plays. The trinity of social justice, art, and spirituality needs to be recaptured so that it can be lived. The absurd divorce of spirituality from social justice or of workers for social justice and peace from art could only happen in a dualistic world view. When we play again at this trinity we will have regained the power and passion and imagination that social transformation requires.

Some people today are lamenting that "the ecumenical movement is dead." What is dying and is boring is not the movement within ecumenism but the lack of it. And this comes from people's being satisfied with what is basically a dualistic approach to ecumenism. In this model, which our psychologically oriented society calls "dialogue," representatives of different traditions talk to each other with a certain tolerance and desire to understand one another. This represents a first step to ecumenism, and it is clearly an improvement over centuries of battles waged between foes. But we must move today from dialogue to common creativity. Ecumenism is not about talking together or putting out position papers together but about creating together. What can two parties, Protestant or Catholic, Christian or Buddhist, scientist or theologian, artist or mathematician, create together? That is the question that the universe and the human race and God the Creator put to all of us. It is a question of how deeply we care about birthing and how deeply we

215

can create with those who differ from us by interacting in dialectical and not merely dualistic ways. The universe was not created by tolerant dualisms but by mutual interpenetrations. Of course this implies letting go: hydrogen must let go of its hydrogenness and oxygen of its oxygenness when the two come together and create water. Letting go is demanded as much of religious traditions as it is of individual religious believers.

A dialectical life is necessarily a trinitarian life. It has no choice. Birth inevitably happens from both/and living and both/and relationships. If one were to devise a way in which to best kill creativity, one would be hard put to invent anything more surely effective than to instruct persons in dualistic thinking and dualistic feeling and dualistic living. The problem with this is that it kills God, it kills the spirit, it kills the human person who cannot live humanly without creativity. Theologian Edward Schillebeeckx calls the trinitarian formula of faith in God, hope in Jesus, and love for neighbor "the characteristic primitive Christian structure of the life of graće."[14] A theology without a dialectical pattern does not give us a theology of grace. It is grace-less. In such a theology grace becomes a commodity, a spiritual consumer item, and church becomes a supernatural vending machine. In such a situation religion itself becomes a repository for dualism and a legitimization for its subsequent violence.

I am convinced that fall/redemption theologies in the West have lost the sense of the Trinity. In skipping over God the Creator they minimize a theology of Dabhar and render it open to trivialities: a theology of words about God. Fall/redemption theology has also allowed psychology to play too great a role, and Freud's well-grounded objections to the religious people he met who prayed to God as surrogate father are evidence of this. Today's trend to pray to God as surrogate friend or lover or companion are little improvement over what Freud encountered seventy-five years ago. A trinity without God as Creator is no trinity at all. Furthermore, fall/redemption theologies have a strong tendency to become Christolotrous and to zero in almost exclusively on Christ as Redeemer. In the process docetism is committed—the heresy that denies the human side of Jesus. Seldom if ever does the fall/redemption tradition develop, for example, the role of Jesus as prophet, or the sensual or the artistic side of Jesus. With docetism, all sensitivity to the suffering of creation itself is lost, since only Jesus as Son of God occupies such a believer. When the first two persons of the Trinity are so shabbily dealt with, it is no wonder that a theology of the Holy Spirit goes undeveloped, unpreached, unlived. The spirit of birth and of creativity and imagination cannot be born in a theology that does not relate God the Father and God the Son with passionate interaction. It is well known that Karl Barth spent fifteen years trying to write a volume on the Holy Spirit and eventually gave up. Fall/redemption theologies never have had much to say about the Holy Spirit—how could they, since there can be no Via Creativa without a Via Positiva? Besides, a preoccupation with pessimism, sin, or asceticism renders the Via Negativa superficial. With the exile of the Holy Spirit the world becomes a "non-sacramental" world, in Frederick Turner's phrase (41.175), nothing new happens, and the victimization of the "unsaved" raises its head with sadistic fury that only repressed creativity could muster. Prophecy is silenced.

Because the creation-centered spiritual tradition does not ignore or gloss over God the Creator, because the creation tradition is not Christolotrous or docetistic, it can be trinitarian. It is trinitarian in the most radical sense of trinitarian consciousness. It insists on the play of the spirit in the world, our world and our worlds. The worlds we give birth to as much as the worlds we are born into. This tradition challenges us to become instruments of that spirit, channels for its grace and its beauty. Co-creators with God. How is this best accomplished? By making a work of art of our lives.

If it is true, as Eckhart testifies, that "Grace pours all beauty into the soul," then beauty is the essence of the lives we give birth to and of the persons we give birth to, beginning with ourselves. As Miyazawa puts it, "What is the essence of this art of living? Of course, even this art should have beauty as its essence." The word "beauty," like the word "cosmos," has not been a significant one in the Western vocabulary of the past few centuries. In fact, Newtonian physics, by presumably solving the "problem" of the universe; patriarchal culture, by investing all truth into "clear and distinct ideas" (Descartes); and religion by reducing faith to intellectual assent (Augustine), have denigrated beauty. Recently I asked a most prominent Catholic theologian what role beauty played in his ethics, and his answer was, "None. Beauty is purely subjective and in the mind of the beholder." What a pity that even theologians are still clinging to the dualistic Newtonian universe of subjective/objective illusion, and that they are so untouched by feminist thought. Susan Griffin warned that this would happen: "But 'beauty,' they argued, is only a relative term, and beauty, they said, has been said to exist only in the eye of the beholder." (20.119) This is a facile and tired way to dismiss beauty. One reason beauty is so glibly dismissed is that harmony and cosmos are so little dealt with. Beauty alerts us to our cosmic connections—but not if we so live in our heads that only our heads constitute the cosmos. Kenji Miyazawa advises one to "discover the galaxy within yourself and remain aware of it" if one wants to be an artist of life.

> What then is the art of living? It is simply this: an expression of cosmic feeling—through the earth and its products, through people and their activities, and through our own individuality. And the way we create is this: Using our emotions and intuitions, we affirm real life all the time, while all the time heightening and deepening our experience of it.

Beauty was lost in the West when the cosmos was lost, and as Rank says about this latter loss, we all become neurotic with it. We also become willing victims of the consumer society's efforts to sell us ersatz beauty, as for example by way of perfectionism of luxury living.

Beauty has to do with seeing all of life as blessing, with returning blessing for blessing, with forging blessing of pain and suffering and tragedy and loss. Beauty needs to be made and remade. It is the vital work of the artist within ourselves. Beauty needs to be forged between warring parties, whether these war within us or around us. Beautiful is what a movement of oppressed peoples is about, as in the slogan, "Black is beautiful," or in Gandhi's statement, "Real beauty is my aim." Beauty is what the royal person is about, recognizing it and then birthing it. Beauty is what our lives are about. What the scriptures call *doxa* or glory can rightly be translated as "beauty." God and God's Son are ultimately attractive and alluring because of their beauty. True beauty and truthful beauty, as Whitehead points out, "is a discovery and not a recapitulation." We have lost beauty as a theological and educational category in the West to the extent that we have lost the dialectical birthing process, the artistic energy. For beauty is born and not made. There lies its marvel, its surprise. But all experience of beauty is experience of cosmic wholeness, of harmony. Beauty is a microcosmic intuition of a macrocosmic reality: Blessing does prevail, life and death, pain and joy, dark and light, conflict and resolution of conflict, commitment and letting go, are all connected.

If grace pours *all* beauty into the soul, then it is clear that the dialectical or creative person is one who at times feels inundated by beauty, overcome by it, barely able to tolerate its power and brilliance. When we touch the artist in ourselves we touch this empty channel, the open conduit for the spirit to work through. We ourselves become like the universe we have learned to love, transparent and diaphanous. Beethoven described the experience this way in a conversation with Bettina von Arnim:

> Every real creation of art is independent, more powerful than the artist himself, and returns to the divine through its manifestation. It is one with man only in this, that it bears testimony to the mediation of the divine within him.[15]

We become instruments of divine grace and beauty, and that is enough for the Holy Spirit to spiral beauty back into the world through us. It is our lives, more than any particular work of art in our lives, that most put us in touch with the communion of saints which is the communion of beauty-birthers. If we are returning harmony back to the universe then we are truly co-creators with the God of the cosmos.

I believe that beauty is better understood as an adjective than as a noun. Rather than pursuing the question, What is beauty? I believe it is more useful to ask the question, What are beautiful experiences you have had? And how can we forge more beauty from our common sharing of this planet? An inevitable consequence of asking such a question is the truth that beauty is simple and it is shareable. My most recent beautiful experience was taking a break from writing this book to walk in newly fallen snow, the first real snowfall of this season. What beauty! Sticking to all the branches of the trees, covering all of creation under a common blanket of white and warmth. Think of how the cosmos yearned for twenty billion years to show off this one day of a snowfall's beauty! In the microcosmic experience of a local snowfall's beauty there lies a hint that the entire effort of the universe has been and continues to be one of cosmic beauty and harmony. And one returns to the discord refreshed and made a believer, one who wishes to contribute to the ongoing beautifying of the universe. Cynicism dies. Hope reigns because beauty is possible. For beauty *is*.

19 GOD AS MOTHER, GOD AS CHILD: OURSELVES AS MOTHERS OF GOD AND BIRTHERS OF GOD'S SON

I (Yahweh) groan like a woman in labour, I suffocate, I stifle.
    —*Isa. 42:14*

For Zion was saying, "Yahweh has abandoned me,
    the Lord has forgotten me.
Does a woman forget her baby at the breast,
    or fail to cherish the son of her womb?
Yet even if these forget,
I will never forget you.
    —*Isa. 49:14,15*

Yahweh says: . . .
Like a son comforted by his mother
    will I comfort you.
    —*Isa. 66:12,13*

What does God do all day long? God gives birth. From all
eternity God lies on a maternity bed giving birth.
    —*Meister Eckhart*

When Ismael was a child I loved him,
    and I called my son out of Egypt.
I was like someone who lifts an infant close against her cheek;
    stooping down to him I gave him his food.
    —*Hos. 11:1,4*

Enough for me to keep my soul tranquil and quiet
    like a child in its mother's arms,
as content as a child that has been weaned.
    Israel, put your dependence on Yahweh,
    now and for ever!
    —*Ps. 131:2,3*

God is not only fatherly. God is also mother who lifts her loved child from the ground to her knee. The Trinity is like a mother's cloak wherein the child finds a home and lays its head on the maternal breast.
—*Mechtild of Magdeburg*

God is the true Father and Mother of Nature.... God almighty is our loving Father, and God all wisdom is our loving Mother.
—*Julian of Norwich*

If anyone does not confess that God is according to the truth Emmanuel and for this reason the holy Virgin is the mother of God (for she begot carnally the word made flesh who is from God), let him be anathema.
—*Council of Ephesus, 431 A.D.*

Mary, ground of all being, Greetings!
Greetings to you, lovely and loving Mother!
—*Hildegarde of Bingen*

Mary,
You birthed to earth your son,
You birthed the son of God from heaven by breathing the spirit of God.
—*Mechtild of Magdeburg*

What good is it to me if Mary gave birth to the son of God fourteen hundred years ago and I do not also give birth to the son of God in my time and in my culture?
—*Meister Eckhart*

We are the mother of Christ when we carry him in our heart and body by love and a pure and sincere conscience. And we give birth to him through our holy works which ought to shine on others by our example.
—*Francis of Assisi*

In creating a situation in which they could nurture and rear infants safely and effectively, women became the civilizers, the inventors of agriculture, of community, some maintain of language itself.
—*Adrienne Rich*[1]

The creative process has feminine quality, and the creative work arises from unconscious depths—we might say, from the realm of the mothers.

—*C. G. Jung*[2]

No man is sterile. Every soul is pregnant with the *seed* of insight. It is vague and hidden. In some people the seed grows, in others it decays. Some give birth to life. Others miscarry it. Some know how to bear, to nurse, to rear an insight that comes into being. Others do not....

—*Rabbi Heschel*[3]

We are all meant to be mothers of God. For God is always needing to be born.

—*Meister Eckhart*

I, God, am your playmate! I will lead the child in you in wonderful ways for I have chosen you.

—*Mechtild of Magdeburg*

Unless you adults turn and become like children, you will never receive the kingdom/queendom of God.

—*Jesus*

When we say God is "eternal," we mean God is eternally young.

—*Meister Eckhart*

It will come as no surprise to anyone to suggest that the fall/redemption spiritual tradition which has ignored creativity as our divine birthright and responsibility has not invested heavily in preaching to us about the motherhood of God. The patriarchal tradition has pretty much ignored the implications of God's motherly side and of our responsibility to develop the mother in ourselves, whether we are women or men, married or celibate, heterosexual or homosexual. If Eckhart is correct when he declares that "We are all meant to be mothers of God," then it follows that we are all meant to be mothers. There is a potential mother, as Heschel insists in the prologue to this section, in each and every person. After all, does birth happen from a single parent? Does the father alone birth the child? Every artist—and as we have seen this means every person made in the image and likeness of God—is called to mother. As Jung

222

put it, creativity arises "from the realm of the mothers." The putting down of motherliness—which can, ironically, express itself in a pseudoelevation of literal motherhood, as in sentimental celebrations of "Mother's Day" in a patriarchal culture—accompanies the putting down of the artist within and among us.

The feminist movement and with it the creation-centered spiritual tradition have celebrated and retrieved the nonliteral meaning of motherhood. Adrienne Rich, who defines feminism as "developing the nurturing qualities of women and of men," has, like Eckhart, awakened our consciousness to the question, What is nurturing? What would it mean to live in a nuturing society, one where even men nurtured self, one another, and others? Surely it would mean from a theological point of view the recovery of the tradition of God as Mother. The tradition of the motherhood of God is rich not only in those Western sources I have cited at the beginning of this theme but also in the matrifocal religions of the Wikke and Native American traditions and indeed wherever religion preceded patriarchy. Frederick Turner, for example, celebrates the depths of the "aboriginal mother love" which is so much richer than Western mother love and which he finds in Native American religion.

The motherhood of God is celebrated wherever panentheism is celebrated, wherever images of roundness and encircling take precedence over linear imaging. Hildegarde says, "Divinity is like a wheel, a circle, a whole." Julian's image of "a mother's cloak" is deeply maternal. Julian frequently uses the image of being enclosed, as when she says, "The deep wisdom of the Trinity is our Mother, in whom we are enclosed." Or, as we saw in Theme Three, that we are "body and soul enclosed in the goodness of God." Eckhart too, when he speaks of how all creation "flows out but remains within," is arousing in us a maternal symbol of panenthesim and enclosure. He applies this reality not only to our enclosure in God but also to our relationship to what we give birth to. In other words, the work of every artist, divine or human/divine, is a maternal work. One is never separated from what one has birthed, or as Isaiah puts it, "Does a woman forget her baby?" It is telling too how Julian and Eckhart and Mechtild all rely on the image of "flowing out," for this too is a maternal symbol. Birth for them is not a trauma and certainly not an event for an operating room; rather it is a "flowing out." Julian writes, "God is the true Father and Mother of Nature and all natures that are made to *flow out of God* to work the divine will will be restored and brought again into God." (Italics mine.)

223

There is something flowing about the maternal side of God and of existence; this flowing is the opposite side of what Ma in *The Grapes of Wrath* called the "jerky" dynamic of the male. There is also implied here a respect and dialectical reverence for nature's birthing processes rather than a dualistic or panicked approach to them. St. Hildegarde also images God on many occasions as panentheistic and therefore maternal. She writes of "this circle of earthly existence," just as Eckhart preached about "the circle of being in which all beings exist." And Hildegarde says, "God hugs you. You are encircled by the arms of the mystery of God." This is motherly talk. It is enveloping, embracing, welcoming, inclusive, cosmic, and expansive. God is a welcoming mother in this tradition.

I wonder, when meditating on these beautifully panentheistic and maternal images for God, if the reason pantheism has been such a threat to patriarchal religion is that it comes so close to panentheism that it also comes close to reminding persons that God is as much Mother as Father. When I reflect on the burnings at the stake and the condemnations of persons from Giordano Bruno to Eckhart to thousands of older women who were dismissed as witches, and also on the genocide against Native American peoples, I wonder if such violence can only be understood by grasping the truth of how the repressed mother in male-dominated Western society and religion is powerful indeed. There lies the dark side to our history.

But the brighter side is upon us as well. With the feminist movement urging us on to recover the traditions of God's motherhood, with creation-centered spirituality replacing fall/redemption models, with the scientist and the artist awakening to mystical awareness, is it not possible that this almost demonically powerful repression is yielding, so that the mother may see the light of day and lead us to a fuller kind of living? One where nurturing and trust, where earthiness and democratic panentheism, where circles instead of ladders arouse our images. And where creativity is welcomed, encouraged, nourished, and celebrated in the name of the Creator of all.

The conclusion to be drawn from our being "enclosed" in the Trinity is not that we are withdrawn narcissistically in a womblike state of bliss and security. Rather, the conclusion Julian of Norwich comes to regarding the motherhood of God focuses on *service*. "The mother's service is nearest, readiest, and surest: nearest because it is most natural, readiest because it is most loving, and surest because it is truest." It includes the pain, risk, and courage that all birthing is about: "We know that all our mothers bear us for pain and for death," she remarks. The service she has in mind is a service of compassion, for motherhood is about "compassion and grace." A return to the motherly side of God would be a return to compassion as a way of life. It would also be a return to wisdom as distinct from mere knowledge or information-gathering. Wisdom and compassion; compassion and wisdom: wouldn't such energy revitalize Western religion and civilization, forge new links with non-Western traditions, create gentler and more dialectical relationships to earth, to body, to pleasure, to work, to the artist within and among us? God as mother, Julian insists, is "all wisdom."

Mary, the mother of Jesus, teaches us that not only is God mother, but God is also child. And we are to be the mothers of God. She alone is *Theotikos*, the literal mother of God. But by her example the Good News comes upon us that we too are mothers of God whenever our birthings bear the fruit of wisdom or compassion, as hers did in the person of Jesus Christ. Jesus, though a male, shocks the world by his constant growth "in wisdom and in grace" (Luke 2.52) and by his preaching of the maternal side of God, that is, of compassion. "Be you compassionate as your Creator in heaven is compassionate," he insists (Luke 6:36) as a summary of all his teaching. And he was killed for teaching this, namely that the Creator is maternal as well as paternal. To birth wisdom or to birth compassion is to birth God. Here lies the deepest of all meanings behind cosmogenesis, the unfolding birth of the cosmos, and here we, as co-creators with God, have so significant a role to play. It is here that all art, all work, all self-expression, all sexuality, all creativity, all the divine power of the human who is a royal person finds its fullest expression. The birthing of our life as a life of beauty and a work of art is necessarily a birthing of God in the cosmos. This is why Eckhart laments in so poignant a way our missing our vocations as mothers of God. He writes, "Is your heart troubled? Then you are not yet a mother. You are only on the way to giving birth. You are only near to birth." Without creativity, which is our divinity and the expression of the image of God in us, we are sad and live with troubled hearts as individuals and as a people. Only the deepest recovery of our motherhood, one that births God by birthing lives and works of wisdom and compassion, will satisfy. In this birth, Eckhart promises, "you will find all blessing. But neglect this birth and you neglect all blessing."

To suggest that Mary and ourselves birth God is to suggest that God can be a baby, a child, a new creation. It is to suggest that in

225

some sense God is not born yet. And that is indeed the case. Wherever compassion and wisdom are lacking, wherever justice and delight are missing, there the full presence of God does not yet exist. In the creation-centered tradition there is ample awareness of the childhood of God. But patriarchy, if it has acknowledged God's childlikeness at all, has done so only in the sentimentalized context of a "sweet baby Jesus." Its truer meaning, that God must be born and must be allowed to grow up into human society and social structures, and that humanity is responsible for the birthing and the nurturing of God—all this has for rather obvious reasons not been heralded as integral to the Good News of late. But in fact it is among the Best News one could imagine.

The Incarnation is a shock and therefore a mystery, because it suggests that God would come in a male form to announce divine compassion and wisdom. After all, one would have expected God to be incarnated as a woman. The God of the Bible is full of surprises![4] It is also a shock and a mystery because it suggests that God needs to be born and can be a child. Eckhart says God is *novissimus*, the newest thing there is. "When we say God is eternal," Eckhart remarks, "we are saying God is eternally young." The eternal youth of God is a sight to behold, to meditate on, and to imitate. With this in mind Mechtild of Magdeburg celebrates the playfulness and child-likeness of God, who tells her, "I, God, am your playmate!" And what this means is that God will draw out the child in us: "I will lead the child in you in wonderful ways." And play with us God does. "God takes the soul to a secret place, for God alone will play with it in a game of which the body knows nothing." The timelessness and ecstasy, the suspension of ego and bodily self-consciousness that all play is about, are hinted at in these rich images. And Mechtild repeats the line as if she could not get enough of it: "God says, 'I am your playmate! Your childhood was a companion of my Holy Spirit.'"

This theme of playing with God is familiar to any pray-er of wisdom literature, for wisdom in the scriptures is always playful. (See Prov. 8:30,31.) One of the most poignant passages in all of scripture is when Jesus laments the inability of his religious con-temporaries to dance and play.

What descriptions I find for this generation? It is like children shouting to each other as they sit in the market place: "We played the pipes for you, and you wouldn't dance; we sing dirges, and you would not mourn." . . . Yet wisdom has been proved right by her actions. (Matt. 11:16, 17, 19)

226

In this kingdom of heaven, as in the kingdom/queendom of all creative spaces, it is the child who shall stand out and set the tone for all. Greatness is to be found in something the child has.

> At this time the disciples came to Jesus and said, "Who is the greatest in the kingdom of heaven?" So he called a little child to him and sat the child in front of them. Then he said, "I tell you solemnly, unless you change and become like little children, you will never enter the kingdom of heaven. And so, the one who makes himself as little as this little child is the greatest in the kingdom of heaven." (Matt. 18:1-4)

How do adults make themselves childlike without being childish? Play is the key. And art is the result of play. The ability to feel connections that perhaps have never been felt before, to see them with wonder and surprise, with amazement and laughter, with lost time and unself-consciousness—here lies the often-missing ingredient to birthing creatively. The nineteenth-century poet Baudelaire could say, "The artist is one who can recover childhood at will," thus emphasizing Jesus' teaching that adults who lose the child in them will never participate in the God-given delight of cosmogenesis. Norman O. Brown also comments on how "Art is a way of life faithful to the natural instincts and therefore faithful to childhood."[5] A paternalistic culture is dangerous because it takes itself so seriously and in the process aborts all imagination and all ways out of our folly and man-made problems. Eckhart recognized this essential relationship between the abortion of imagination and the lack of the child among us when he observed that "Some people do not bear fruit because they are so busy clinging to their egotistical attachments and so afraid of letting go and letting be that they have no trust either in God or in themselves." The child is not afraid of letting go; in fact children go out of their way to experience ecstatic highs, whether by hanging upside down, by running about in circles until they drop, or by holding their breath. At least children used to do these things, up to the time when an all-adult and all-male world invented Atari games to shoot down galaxies and called this play. The poisoning of play is one of the greatest of the sins of patriarchy. Jesus warns, at the same place in the gospel where he insists that God's kingdom is of childlike adults, that scandal to these little ones is among the most heinous of all crimes. The scandal of changing play to war, Eros to Thanatos, that our consumer society is now engaged in cannot go unnoticed by the cosmos as it groans to give a more delightful birth.

Path III

What is certain is that the cosmos is not yet done with its work. Twenty billion years have not completed by any means its longing for beauty. The cosmos is still birthing, still expanding, still calling us to birthing and expansion. The human race, the most recent and most surprising child of the cosmos, is called to take a conscious role in this birthing process. That is what recovering the motherhood of God and the mother of God role for all people is about. Theology promises that the Creator, who is not yet done with her work, desires additional delight still for the cosmos. And we, artists all, are to be instruments of that delight which is the delight both of wisdom and compassion.

20 SIN, SALVATION, CHRIST IN THE PERSPECTIVE OF THE VIA CREATIVA: A THEOLOGY OF RESURRECTION

Man's capacity for evil, then, is less a positive capacity, for all its horrendous activity, than a failure to develop man's most human function, the imagination, to its fullness, and consequently a failure to develop compassion.
        —*Denise Levertov*[1]

What masochism means is "I can't."
        —*Karen Horney*[2]

Art in a wide and general sense, as a part of everyday life, has lost its place in our world.
        —*Erich Fromm*[3]

The artist's gift is always to creation itself, to the ultimate meaning of life, to God.
        —*Ernest Becker*[4]

Neither power alone nor reason alone creates the works of art and poetry . . . the Spirit creates them individually and universally, powerful and full of reason at the same time.
        —*Paul Tillich*[5]

Beauty constitutes the only finality here below. . . . Beauty is eternity here below.
        —*Simone Weil*

Anyone who lives art knows that psychoanalysis has no monopoly on the power to heal. . . . Art and poetry have always been altering our ways of sensing and feeling—that is to say, altering the human body.
        —*Norman O. Brown*[6]

They are truly monks when they live by the labor of their hands, as did their Fathers and the Apostles.
        —*Rule of St. Benedict*

The sin against the Holy Spirit is the sin against new life, against self-emergence, against the Holy fecund innerness of each person. It can be committed quite as easily against oneself as against another.
　　　　　—M. C. Richards (31.59)

Humankind, full of all creative possibilities, is God's work. Humankind alone is called to assist God. Humankind is called to co-create. With nature's help, humankind can set into creation all that is necessary and life-sustaining.
　　　　　—Hildegarde of Bingen

God is the Creator, and the very fact that we were begetting a child made me have a sense that we were made in the image and likeness of God, co-creators with him.
　　　　　—Dorothy Day[7]

The theology of creativity will necessarily be the theology of the Holy Spirit re-forming us in the likeness of Christ, raising us from death to life with the very same power which raised Christ from the dead. The theology of creativity will also be a theology of the image and the likeness of God in humanity.
　　　　　—Thomas Merton[8]

The artist is no more and no less than a contemplative who has learned to express himself, and who tells his love in colour, speech, or sound: The mystic, upon one side of his nature, is an artist of a special and exalted kind.
　　　　　—Evelyn Underhill[9]

This, then, is salvation: When you marvel at the beauty of created things and praise the beautiful providence of their Creator.
　　　　　—Meister Eckhart

Is the inventor of the ear unable to hear?
Is the creator of the eye unable to see?
　　　　　—Ps. 94:9

The Lord God formed (*yasar*) the human from the clay of the ground. Then he breathed a breath of life into his nostrils and in this way humanity became a living being.
　　　　　—Gen. 2:7

230

God created people in the image of himself, in the image of
God he created them, male and female he created them.
    —*Gen. 1:27*

Using many parables like these, Jesus spoke the word to them,
so far as they were capable of understanding it. He would not
speak to them except in parables.
    —*Mark 4:33, 34*

Christ is the image of the unseen God,
    the first-born of all creation.
    —*Col. 1:15*

It is to the glory of my Father that you should bear much fruit,
    and this will prove you are my disciples. . . .
I commissioned you to go out and to bear fruit,
    fruit that will endure.
    —*John 15:8,16*

I have long been dissatisfied with the dominant definition of sin preached by the fall/redemption tradition: namely, that sin is "privation of good." Something about the gas chambers at Auschwitz or about the crucifixion of Jesus or about the massacres of American Indians told me that sin was more than a "privation of good." My personal breakthrough on the subject of sin and the powerful insight about sin that accompanies a recovery of the Via Creativa occured a few winters ago. I was reflecting on Father Bill Callahan's advice that we should "pray the news and not just watch the news" when two disturbing events occured simultaneously. One was the news that rioting prisoners in the New Mexico penitentiary had killed one of their brothers by driving a metal pipe in one ear and out the other; the second bit of news was that here in Chicago, where I was living, John Gacy, who tortured and murdered thirty-three young men, was going on trial. It was not an easy week to "pray the news." But it did indeed occur to me that sin is not privation of good so much as it is *the misuse of good*, the misuse of the greatest good of the universe, which is that image of God in humanity, our imaginations. Other species of animals kill to eat or protect their young or their territory, but humankind is the only species we knows that kills sadistically, that is, to get pleasure from the killing. Sadism and its counterpart masochism are born of misplaced imagination. I believe that the fall/redemption tradition in spirituality never named this deeper understanding of sin because it never considered human creativity to be that essential to the ongoing power of the universe. As so it forgot what a power—divine and demonic—human imagination can be. The Via Creativa lays bare the immense demonic power that is coiled up in the very divine power, namely the imagination, of humanity. The divine and the demonic are very close together; only a thin line separates them/us. We who are indeed capable of divinity are also capable of the demonic. And the deepest of all demonic activity is the use of our divine imaginations to invent destruction. More than destruction, as Jonathan Schell points out, we have now invented nuclear war which can birth *extinction* for the human race and other living species of our unique and beloved planet. This is sadomasochism at its fullest extreme; this is evil. As Oppenheimer said after the dropping of atomic bombs on Japan, "Now we scientists know sin."

At the same time that patriarchal society has neglected creativity and mothering as fundamental spiritual and cultural values, it has elevated sadomasochism to positions of glory in just about all of our institutions, from medicine to education to religion to government to the military to sports to business. Pornography, which is the cultural institutionalization of sadomasochism, is now a five-billion-dollar-a-year business in America, and sadomasochistic magazines are available at almost every newsstand in our country. It is hinted at in the media and of course sold on cable television. But the sexual or bedroom sadomasochism that sells so well in our culture is only the tip of the iceberg compared to the boardroom sadomasochism that asserts itself in top governmental decision-making about who will control whom, in hospitals and medical establishments of power-over, even in churches where the male or the celibate, for example, is to have power-over women or laypersons. Sadomasochism prevails wherever humans exploit the earth, the animals, the fishes, or one another.

Feminists, who have woken up to the prevailing presence of sadomasochism in Western civilization, have the power to wake others up to this sinful consciousness as well. Adrienne Rich, for example, in her study on motherhood, *Of Woman Born*, talks of what she calls the "essential dichotomy: power/powerlessness." Sadomasochism is dualism lived out as a way of life, i.e., a perverse spirituality. Power over others, she believes, assures the control that many people need. "The powerful (mostly male) make decisions for the powerless: the well for the sick, the middle-aged for the aging, the 'sane' for the 'mad,' the educated for the illiterate, the influential for the marginal." Yet there remains a relationship between the powerful and the powerless, between the sadist and the masochist. "Powerlessness can lead to lassitude, self-negation, guilt, and depression," and at the same time power can generate "a kind of willed ignorance, a moral stupidity, about the inwardness of others, hence of oneself."[10] The sadist has no inner life and no sensitivity to anyone else's. We can see how, in the unveiling of misused creative power as sin, all kinds of other sins that so haunt our culture come to the fore. But Rich does not limit her powerful critique just to the sins of individuals. She sees sadomasochism as dominating our institutions. "The identification of womanhood with suffering—by women as well as men—has been tied to the concept of woman-as-mother," she asserts,[11] and in no place was this suffering more assured than in maternity wards of the past century.

> At the onset of labor, the woman was placed in the lithotomy (supine) position, chloroformed, and turned into the completely passive body on which the obstetrician could perform as on a mannequin. The labor room became an operating theatre, and childbirth a medical drama with the physician as its hero.

Yet even today the relationship between woman and doctor has seldom changed very much. "No more devastating image could be invented for the bondage of woman: sheeted, supine, drugged, her wrists strapped down and her legs in stirrups, and the very moment when she is bringing new life into the world."[12]

Psychoanalyst Karen Horney defines masochism as "I can'tism." Whenever we say "I can't," as in the expression, "I can't be creative," or, "I can't change anything," or "I can't be mystical," we are setting ourselves up for the sins of the sadist, who is always wanting to tell us, "You can't, but I can." In this regard it is important to meditate on how much of the advertising that keeps consumer society going is sadomasochistic. "You can't make friends, but our toothpaste can for you." Mechtild of Magdeburg puts the lie to all temptations to masochism when she says simply, "God has given me the power to change my ways." All liberation movements, whether of women or men, of Third World or First World, of blacks, Hispanics, Native Americans, gays, or lesbians, share this energy in common: they are made up of persons who were instructed by those with power to be at home without power. And they are saying, "No! I can, *we* can, express ourselves and our ways." In this sense every liberation movement is about the release of the artist within people, that part of us which expresses our deepest self. It is all part of the Via Creativa. And the primary sin in the Via Creativa when it comes from the outside is sadism; but from the inside, the internalizing of the sadist's message, there happens the sin of masochism. Of acquiescing to the lie that "I can't."

The Via Creativa lays bare the sins of sadism and of masochism. In Western culture and church life the sin of omission of creativity has been especially pronounced of late. One example is that, as Father Schillebeeckx points out, there was not one artist as observer or participant at the Second Vatican Council. The results of this omission are clear to see in the sentimental music that has dominated Catholic liturgy for the past twenty years. The exile of the artist from ecclesial spirituality continues. The Via Creativa helps us to name the sins of repression of imagination, of abortion of creativity, of exploitation or persecution of the artist among us and within us. If Erich Fromm is correct that "art in a wide and general sense, as a part of everybody's life, has lost its place in our world," then he is naming the sin of killing the artist. Where art has no role to play in education, religion, science, the media, and where it has been replaced by entertainment, sin abounds. Sins of unemployment, boredom, and the violence that accompanies boredom. Loss of art is a social sin. With that deprivation our work life becomes distorted and violent, and so too does our leisure time. Life becomes ugly—without meaning—and acedia or boredom sets in. Atari games that announce the killing of galaxies take over. Or titillating sex. Or titillating news. Or titillating anything. Life can no longer be lived or celebrated in depth. Superficiality reigns.

Another sin in the Via Creativa is the refusal to make connections. I understand creativity as our power to make connections[13], the lack of creativity renders us locked up, privatized, sectarian, defensive because we have no healthy outlet for the divine Dabhar in us that desires to connect with the cosmos and the cosmos yet birthing, and therefore with all things. Just as obsessive control is a sin against the Via Creativa, so too is the obsessive preoccupation with security. Security becomes an idol when creativity is banished. For, as we have seen, vulnerability is the matrix for creative birthing. Security obsessions become sources of killing the artist. As Jung puts it, "Security and peace do not lead to discoveries." Boredom and acedia do not lead to breakthroughs.

If sadomasochism born of the misuse of imagination is sin in Path III, what is salvation in such a context? It is art, creativity, the awakening of possibilities and imagination for possibilities. This heals. Rich writes, "The most important thing one woman can do for another is to illuminate and expand her sense of actual possibilities." Here lies the end of masochism, the end of passivity. *"To refuse to be a victim:* and then to go on from there."[14] The refusal to be a victim constitutes the conversion, the metanoia of the masochist or anyone who has been taught in a sadistic culture to be masochistic. Ironically, this refusal also constitutes the beginning of new life for the sadist, insofar as the sadist without a masochist is a lonely person and possibly ready for change.

If repression and killing of the artist within and around us, ugliness and boredom, acedia and the refusal to make connections, idolatrous securities and obsessive control are sins against the Via Creativa, what would constitute salvation in Path III? One meaning of salvation that is uncovered in the Via Creativa is the awakening to our divinity. To recover our divinity and the doctrine of our deification and divinization is itself salvific. It awakens us to possibilities; it arouses us from boredom, pettiness, acedia. In the midst of cynicism and negativism, our being images of God comes as Good News. It is not static news, it is news about our potential for action and for new birth. We do not take glory in it; rather we are moved by it to act out our powers of new images. Thomas Aquinas identifies acedia or spiritual torpor as a "contraction of the mind."[15] The news of our divinity is the opposite: it brings about an expansion of the mind, of the person, and of the societies we choose to create after our own images. Nicholas of Cusa calls God the "absolute art" who chose to make an image that was less perfect but which "had the power of constantly heightening itself and of making itself more and more similar to the original." This divine choice—to make humans capable of growing into their divinity by way of divine imagination—in turn gives God, the Only or Prime Artist, great delight.[16] It ought to delight and heal us also. Of course when the creation spiritual tradition celebrates humanity's divinity, it does not deny that ours is a created divinity, while God's is an uncreated divinity. But ours is divinity nonetheless. To remain silent on this important doctrine, as most of the fall/redemption tradition has done for centuries, is to invite the demonic. Divinity repressed, which is creativity repressed, will not stay down for long. Like a cork held under water, it must assert itself in some form or other. When religion forgot the Good

News of our divinity, our demonic side came to the fore. Or, as Ernest Becker puts it, "if we don't have the omnipotence of gods, we can at least destroy like gods."[17] To bring the Good News of our divinity is to restore us and our relationship to creation. Dialectical consciousness is itself a form of healing and redemption. Perhaps the most gross of all dualisms is the dualism between the divine and us. As if we hold no divine blood in us, as if we are creatures only and not creators. Co-creators with God.

Recovering the theme of our co-creativity with God is itself salvific and redemptive. This theme too awakens us to be the instruments of divine grace that we are called to be. It renders life powerful, meaningful, worthy of sacrificing for. It overcomes boredom and superficiality. Will not all healing come from the deepest resources of individuals and of collective humanity? If creativity is such a deep resource, are not those who arouse us to our capacity as co-creators initiating our salvation and redemption? The divine creation and redemption, after all, have never ceased. "Language about God's creative work, initial or continuing," says biblical scholar John Reumann, "can also be sued reflectively by faith to describe redemption, past, present, or future."[18] God's creative and redemptive work continues, and it is evident that in creating humanity God wanted that creativity and healing to be carried on with special gusto and energy through humanity being true to itself, which means being true to its divine capacity for creativity. If "creation is a redemption from chaos," as Reumann says, then the news of our being co-creators is the news of our being agents of redemption. Since creativity is so redemptive, we ought to be celebrating "redemptive creativity."

Furthermore, the Via Creativa alerts us to how salvific beauty is. Beauty saves. Beauty heals. Beauty motivates. Beauty unites. Beauty returns us to our origins, and here lies the ultimate act of saving, of healing, of overcoming dualism. Beauty allows us to forget the pain and dwell on the joy. Beauty, as Simone Weil says, "is eternity here below." Beauty leads to gratitude which, as we saw in Theme Nine above, is the deepest and most adult of all prayers. In her autobiography, Dorothy Day recounts her experience of gratitude and prayer.

> I was surprised that I found myself beginning to pray daily.... Over and over again in my mind that phrase was repeated jeeringly, "Religion is the opiate of the people."

"But," I reasoned with myself, "I am praying because I am happy, not because I am unhappy. I did not turn to God in unhappiness, in grief, in despair—to get consolation, to get something from Him." And encouraged that I was praying because I wanted to thank Him, I went on praying.

Day recalls how it was her lover Forster's "ardent love of creation" that brought her to the Creator. And she "cried out to him, 'How can there be no God, where there are all these beautiful things?' "[19] Paul celebrates beauty, or glory (*doxa*) as being the proper inheritance of all those called to the "beauty of the children of God." We are heirs to a promise, to an image of God restored. For him the beauty of humanity shines forth in Jesus Christ, who is the "eldest of many brothers and sisters." (Rom. 8:14-30)

The Via Creativa also alerts us to how the recovery of mother-hood in a patriarchal society is profoundly salvific. Otto Rank, who loved artists and worked to heal their pain in our culture, was not himself a Christian, but he considered this contribution to be among the greatest of the "revolution" wrought by Jesus and Paul. To Rank, the history of civilization has meant the "gradual masculinization of human civilization." But in the historical context of an ever more powerful patriarchy, Jesus born of Mary appears. Mary, "heavenly Queen," represents the prepatriarchal spirituality. "Christianity does not represent a mere parallel to those ancient conceptions but rather a revival and re-interpretation of the original mother-concept which had given way to the masculinization of Eastern civilization," Rank asserts. (29.237) The fear of motherhood, the suspicion of creativity, the displeasure with birthing processes that characterize patriarchal cultures are exposed. And with this exposure comes the salvific power of rebirth, of motherhood for everyone. Eckhart immediately sees the connection between Mary's vocation in being impregnated with the Holy Spirit and that of the artist in each of us.

The work that is "with," or "outside" or "above" the artist must become the work that is "in" her, taking form within her. In other words, to understand one's vocation as an artist we should interpret the verse "The Holy Spirit shall come upon thee" (Luke 1:35) to mean: "The Holy Spirit shall come from within thee."

Eckhart rejects all temptations to see the work of the spirit in ladder or hierarchical terms. It is from deep within that all holy birth takes place, be it that of a mother with child or of any other less literal birthing we undertake. And this Good News, that the Holy Spirit births from deep within us, is truly salvific. It breaks through any temptations we harbor to worship a "God outside." Or a superman outside. Or a corporation outside. It insists that the deepest mystery and gift of the cosmos, our own creativity, is as near as our depths.

Mahatma Gandhi was another male who brought salvation or healing to our patriarchal times by way of encountering the mother in himself. According to Erik Erikson, it was Gandhi's mother who first taught him "a certain basic religiosity—the undogmatic sense of being carried along by a demanding and yet trustworthy universe."[20] In other words, the sense of cosmic trust and panentheism came from his mother. Gandhi, Erikson concludes, "prided himself on being half man and half woman," and in this he was returning to the deepest sources of Indian religion and culture, for "a primitive mother religion is probably the deepest, the most pervasive, and the most unifying stratum of Indian religiosity." Erikson sees a prophetic challenge here to the excessive maleness of Western, military-minded culture wherein "the renunciation of armament" is comparable to "an abandonment of malehood." Here lies healing and salvation for many levels of relationship, suggests Erikson, since a "relative devaluation of the martial model of masculinity" may open the way to fuller interchange between men and women.[21] The nonviolent methods for social change that Gandhi espoused and Martin Luther King, Jr., developed in an American context come from the realm of the mothers, and they are, as Gandhi said, a special gift to the West from Eastern religion. It should be noted too what an important role art as meditation played for Gandhi, who wanted to bring back the spinning wheel to every Indian's home. It is said that Gandhi elevated the spinning wheel "to significance as an economic necessity, a religious ritual, and a national symbol,"[22] and he was a champion of art as meditation for his people and saw this kind of empowerment as salvific vis-à-vis the encroachments of Western industrialization and mass technology.

The Via Creativa assures us that faith, that is *trust*, saves as much in Path III as in Paths I and II. In Path III trust is salvific because it demands that we trust our images and ride them where they must go, and that we take responsibility for them and where they take us. The Via Creativa also invites us to trust our vocation as artists, as new imagers and new birthers, as resurrected people capable of sharing resurrection news. Part of the salvation that faith brings is trust in the truth that wisdom already is. Wisdom has been present from before the beginning of the world. Wisdom consists among other things in the recovery of the maternal, compassionate side of God—and this heals. It also consists in play and delighting before the cosmos—and this heals. Otto Rank declares that there exists a profound "purposelessness" in all true art (28.103). The passage from neurosis—and I understand neurosis to be a social as much as a personal state today—to health, from dis-ease to wholeness, occurs with the recovery of play. "The neurotic must first learn to live playfully, illusorily, unreally, on some plane of illusion—first of all on the inner emotional plane. This is a gift which the artist, as an allied type, seems to possess from the outset." (28.109) This gift of play is a special gift of wisdom bequeathed in the Via Creativa. It corresponds to Eckhart's advice that we learn "to live without a why, work without a why, love without a why." Play is always without a why.

Still another salvific contribution from the Via Creativa is that it saves us from too much preoccupation with salvation itself. During the patriarchal period, when men could not believe in their own powers of motherhood, of nurturing, of birthing and crafting without guilt, redemption religion took over. In freeing us of this preoccupation with salvation as deliverance, the Via Creativa actually allows the healing power of the Holy Spirit to return to our lives. And with it we re-experience the blessing that birthing can be. And the joyful salvation that creativity brings.

Who is Jesus Christ in light of the Via Creativa? And what light does Jesus himself shed on our invitation to enter deeply into the path of creativity? The first and most conspicuous point to be made of Jesus in Path III is that Jesus was a poet, a storyteller, an artist. He was not a priest or a theologian or an academician or a dispenser of sacraments primarily, but an awakener to the sacrament of the cosmos, of the kingdom/queendom of God in which all persons are immersed and which immerses all persons. Fall/redemption theologies that have reduced Christianity to the cross alone—"Christ is the cross and nothing but the cross," a theologian shouted in a discussion this past week—and have forgotten Jesus' life and works and his Resurrection as well have robbed us all of realizing the powerful significance of Jesus' choice of action as an artist. This was a deliberate choice by Jesus, namely to speak in parables, and it was an immensely creative choice. It is distinctly Christian in many respects. Docetistic and Christolotrous spiritualities have had nothing to say about this very significant choice of Jesus the artist. Yet we know for a fact that the parables of Jesus are the closest we will ever come to his exact words, his exact images, his exact message. Behind them all lies what Brother David Steindl-Rast has rightfully called "a poetic mind who sees everything in the world as symbol if only we have the eyes to see."[23] Behind this unique method of parable-telling that Jesus chose there lies trust: Jesus' trust in his own, unique images—leaven and a dragnet and a mustard seed and a pearl and a coin lost around the house symbolizing the kingdom/queendom of God, for example. And there lies Jesus' trust of his listener. For Jesus proves by his parables how much he trusts in the power of images and in their capacity to arouse truth to the open-hearted, open-minded hearer. Parables are nonelitist. Jesus trusts the intelligence of his listeners as well as their integrity. As Albert Nolan puts it,

> Nothing could be more unauthoritative than the parables of Jesus. Their whole purpose is to enable the listener to discover something for himself. They are not illustrations of revealed doctrines; they are works of art which reveal or uncover the truth about life. (27.122)

Most of the time Jesus' parables end with a question or imply a question. Not answers. His choice of parables reveals the universality in Jesus' consciousness, for one does not have to be a Jew or a Christian to enter into the images and questions Jesus' parables raise. He appeals to "the divine authority within each person." (Steindl-Rast) Yet Jesus' parables and art are not for entertainment. They invite the listener to change his or her life, to metanoia, to transformation. And they invite a whole society to let go and start over again, trusting its images and its power for creativity.

Jesus the royal person is artist. So too was King David, who "sang the songs of Israel" (2 Sam. 23:1) and composed songs, psalms, and religious poetry. The prophets too were artists, as we shall see in Path IV below. Jesus, by trusting his own vocation as artist and imager, invites all of us to do likewise. It is not enough that prayerful Christians meditate *on* the Christ: this is introvert meditation, and while it has a certain part to play, it is not enough. Jesus never told people to meditate on him but to do the works he does, which are "works of the Creator." Instead of being an *object* of introvert meditation, Jesus ought to be a *model* of extrovert meditation, that is, of how the true son or daughter of God comes as an artist to awaken others from their slumber and death.

Jesus, a true son of God, comes preaching in parables. He also comes preaching that it is okay to be divine and human at the same time. In fact, by being so fully divine and human himself, he incarnates both/and, the dialectical process, and enfleshes it in his own person. His cross too becomes a powerful dialectical symbol—it is ugly and outrageous, but it is also his "glory." Easter too is dialectical—it is not a triumph devoid of the wounded body and death. By teaching every person not to fear death any longer, Jesus frees every person to be creative, dialectical, and divine. When Rank calls Jesus' revolution the greatest the world has seen, he is talking of this freedom from the fear of death and therefore the freedom Jesus promises to every human person who must create. Consider, for example, how creativity-oriented is the Jesus of John's Gospel who says:

> I am the vine, you are the branches.
> Whoever remains in me, with me in her, bears fruit in abundance....
> It is to the glory of my Father that you should bear much fruit,
> in this way you will be my disciples....
> I commissioned you to go out and bear fruit,
> fruit that will last. (Jn. 15. 5,8,16)

Eckhart, commenting on this passage, points out that the fruit that lasts is "that which is inborn in me." What is creative, what comes from our inner depths, this is what endures; beauty endures.

Julian of Norwich understood this essential meaning of the Incarnation so well: "Our nature which is the higher part is joined to God in its creation, and God is joined to our nature, which is the lower part in taking flesh. And so in Christ our two natures are united." The entire creation tradition celebrates how true it is that "God became human in order that humans might become divine." (Irenaeus) This—the release of the divine Dabhar through human creativity—is the primary focus of the Incarnation and not a wiping away of original sin. The Via Creativa is among the best of the Good News there is to announce! Humanity and divinity are fully united in this New Adam, this New Creation, who is in fact the "first-born" and eldest brother of each of us, who are also called to be New Persons who will see the world newly, respond creatively, be resurrected from dullness and boredom and violence. Jesus is explicit about why he chose to be an *artist* or parable-teller. He relates his motivations to those of the prophet Isaiah.

> The reason I talk to them in parables is that they look without seeing and listen without hearing or understanding. So in their case this prophecy of Isaiah is being fulfilled: "The heart of this nation has

grown coarse, their ears are dull of hearing, and they have shut their eyes, for fear they should see with their eyes, hear with their ears, understand with their heart, and be converted and be healed by me." (Matt. 13:13-15. Cf. Isa. 6:9, 10)

Not only does Jesus awaken us to our divine creativity, but he awakens us to the motherly side of the divine. He teaches that we are redeemed, made whole by recovering the compassionate side of God. He calls himself a mother hen who weeps over her lost chicks as he weeps over Jerusalem. This and other dimensions to Jesus' aroused consciousness about the mother in him gave impetus to a rich tradition of Jesus as mother which is found in Julian of Norwich, Thomas Aquinas, St. Anselm, and many medieval mystics. Jesus, in his desire to heal and to see forgiveness happen so that God's Dabhar and continual creation can happen, assures us that it is okay to be divine and motherly. "It's okay to disturb the universe... because I did. It is your nature to do so since you are a son/daughter and image of God like myself. This is creation's way. Enjoy it. Take responsibility for your images and creations." Jesus forgives us the guilt and the fear that hamper our capacity to give birth. He forgives us our divinity. Thus Jesus invites people to renew a tarnished, guilt-ridden, lacking-in-confidence image of God. Namely, ourselves. All persons are "the image and glory of God" (1 Cor. 11:7, 8; cf. Gen. 1:27, 28), but Jesus comes to remind us of what this means, to reawaken us to our beauty (*doxa*) and our responsibility for beauty. An image of God who is also beautiful is not passive and is not despising of self or of one's gifts. An image of God does what God does, which is to birth beauty in all its forms. This is what Jesus did. It is also what Jesus was. Christ is "the beautiful one" about whom the prophet spoke:

He shall bloom like the lily,
and thrust roots out like the poplar,

his shoots will spread far;

he shall possess the beauty of the olive
and the fragrance of Lebanon. (Hos. 14:6, 7)

The creation mystics Julian and Mechtild, among others, celebrate the beauty of the Christ. If "God is beauty" (St. Francis), then is not the Son of God a beautiful one, an incarnation of divine beauty? Does not Christ teach us what true beauty means and where to truly look for it? The beauty the world sees is so often superficial, the "outer" beauty that can be bought and sold. But Jesus, the New

Adam, represents the inner person who is also the heavenly beauty (1 Cor. 15:47-49) Jesus is the one who shows us what it means to be beautiful and make of our lives a work of art and beauty. How harmony, compassion, care, passion, freedom, relating, are the essence of the beautiful. Cleanliness, money, possessions, honor, prestige, security are not where beauty is to be found. Jesus died confused and dirty, ugly, bloody, and naked. But beautiful. And his Resurrection announces how beauty and not ugliness, life and not death, rebirth and not killing will in the end triumph as they did in the beginning. Christ, the "resurrected one" who had to leave us in order to send the spirit, urges us to throw off all temptations to masochism or sadism. He converts the sadist by first converting the masochist, the one who says "I can't" inside himself. He calls us to co-creation with God. An immense dignity and power that are ours not by our work but by God's grace and gift. A son or daughter of God must needs be a creator with God.

And Jesus comes as wisdom. As wisdom he plays before us as every artist does. He played in his choice of place in which to preach the Good News—from boats, in parks, on the seashore, in the fields, in people's homes. He plays with his audience and with his enemies, trying to love them and trust them into their own conversion. He plays, as every artist does, with his images. And he invites us to do the same. He plays even with death. He lost that gamble on Good Friday, but on Easter Sunday the last play of the game was his to enjoy. And ours. Creativity is about wisdom; and wisdom is about creativity. Scripture teaches this. Jesus, wisdom incarnate, lived it. The poet William Blake once suggested that the true son of God will come as an artist. That is exactly how Jesus did come. But fall/redemption interpretations of the scriptures have left out the Via Creativa and have missed the point just as the children did who were called to dance and mourn in the market place. (Matt. 11:16-19) To recover the Via Creativa would mean a rebirth of the Good News.

It will also mean a rediscovery of a lost significance of the cross of Jesus Christ. Too many people, when they hear the word "creativity," imagine that a life of creativity is a life of tiptoeing through the tulips, a life of "doing nothing" or of pure enjoyment. In fact, such people only reveal their ignorance of birthing. For all birthing involves labor pains. All creativity involves destruction and deep suffering. It was precisely Jesus' creative re-working of Israelite religion that led to his crucifixion and death. As Henry Miller put it,

243

"such a person must go again and again to the stake and the gibbet."[24] Because the artist does not dwell on the pain—as an ascetic so often does—but on the ecstasy of birthing, as Jesus did, the price the artist pays for creativity often goes uncounted or becomes distorted—as is the case in too much of the fall/redemption remembering of the cross of Jesus Christ. A significant contribution to salvation that is made by Jesus' crucifixion is his invitation to be courageous enough to create. And to pay the price. And to believe that the many crucifixions involved do not add up to even one resurrection.

PATH IV
BEFRIENDING NEW CREATION:
COMPASSION, CELEBRATION,
EROTIC JUSTICE,
THE VIA TRANSFORMATIVA

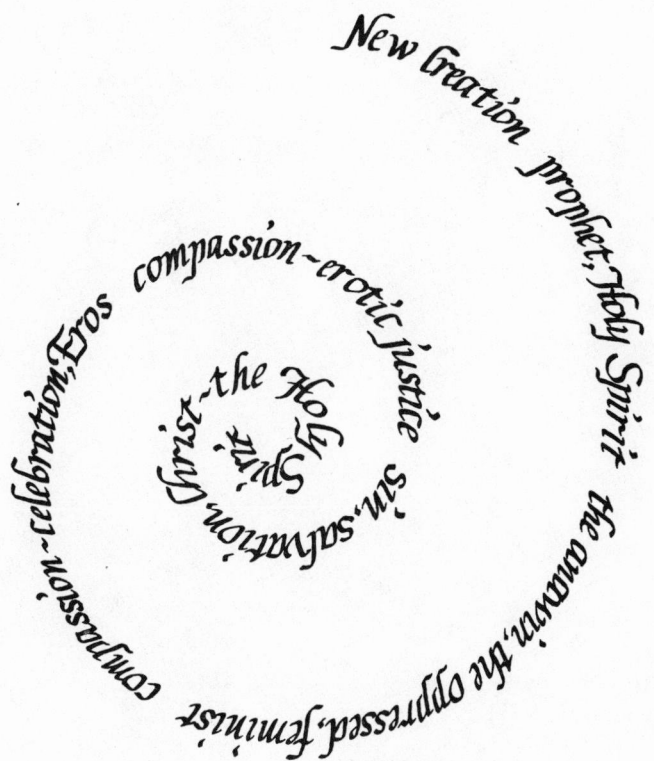

W e have seen how the spiritual journey of the Via Positiva and Via Negativa, when entered into fully, culminates in the Via Creativa. But we are also aware that not all creativity is for the beautiful. Creativity itself needs criticism and direction. Path IV, the Via Transformativa, provides the basis for that judgment and that direction. It also returns us to the beginning of our spiral journeying, for the New Creation that the Via Transformativa is about is creation renewed, seen anew, and righted from its state of sinful or unjust relationships. It is the cosmos mended and made whole again; it is the return of wisdom and of celebration and play. All this adds up to compassion, for compassion is the goal, the fullest energies of the human/divine marriage in the creation-centered spiritual tradition. Our creativity in all instances is to be put to the use of compassion. When it is not, then racism and sexism, militarism and giant capitalism will co-opt the image of God in people and use creativity not to return blessing for blessing with but to curse and destroy. Much creativity, after all, went into Hitler's ovens for efficient human extermination at Auschwitz; and an immense amount of creativity and skill goes into planning and building a Trident submarine today. This is creativity, but it is not new creation. It is, potentially, the end of all creation as humanity knows it and shares in it. Clearly our creative energy needs some steering and some directions to follow if it is to save and liberate and not enslave and destroy.

The creation-centered spiritual tradition considers *compassion* rather than *contemplation* as the fulfillment of the spiritual journey that takes one back to one's origins in renewed ways. It considers justice to be absolutely integral to the spiritual journey. We saw how

247

in Path I justice is integral to the cosmos and its order and harmony; so in Path IV, justice and the creating of justice and the struggle against injustice are the very lifeblood of this spiritual way. Eckhart said, "The person who understands what I say about justice understands everything I have to say." Every creation-centered wayfarer ought to be able to utter such a statement. The creation tradition cannot imagine a spirituality without justice or one that consigns justice to a weekend outing. Justice lies as the fulfillment of the need to birth oneself—all are to be birthed into justice-making instruments for the work of the spirit. The fourth path lays bare how the creation-centered tradition is the way of the prophets. The *anawim*—the forgotten and oppressed persons in society—are creation-centered, as we shall see. In addition to the evidence I will present for the truth of this statement, there is the following: The creation-centered spiritual tradition has itself been oppressed time and time again in Western Christianity. While many saints, such as Irenaeus, Hildegarde, Francis, and Aquinas, are included among its chief exponents, at the same time many so-called heretics have suffered needless and violent treatment—such persons as Pelagius, John the Scot, Meister Eckhart, Giordano Bruno, Teilhard de Chardin, to name a few. And most creation-centered mystics have been conveniently ignored—among them persons like Hildegarde, Mechtild, Eckhart, Julian of Norwich, Nicholas of Cusa, and Irenaeus—because their way of life did not conform comfortably to the dominant religious world view of the fall/redemption ideology. This ideology, which has served patriarchy and the marriage of empire and church so well ever since the fourth century, has always been in power. It chose to condemn or ignore the creation tradition, condemning even Thomas Aquinas three times before it canonized him—a curious fact that Meister Eckhart did not let his inquisitors overlook when he was put on trial. Thus we see that not only is the creation tradition the spirituality of the oppressed in a theoretical sense, but those who have espoused it even to this day have found themselves reduced to the powerlessness of the oppressed. From that position of nonpower creation spirituality derives its greatest wisdom, and its greatest contribution to social and ecclesial transformation. One can only pray that creation spirituality will always be a minority and remnant church, lest success render its identification with the *anawim* only theoretical.

In this fourth path we will explore the following themes along the journey known as the Via Transformativa.

21. The New Creation: Images of God in Motion Creating a Global Civilization.

22. Faith as Trusting the Prophetic Call of the Holy Spirit.

23. A Spirituality of the Anawim: Feminists, Third World, Lay, and Other Oppressed Peoples.

24. Compassion: Interdependence, Celebration, and Recovering Eros.

25. Compassion: Interdependence and Erotic Justice

26. Sin, Salvation, Christ in the Perspective of the Via Transformativa: A Theology of the Holy Spirit.

Christians will recognize in this path a theology of the Holy Spirit, whom Eckhart calls the "Spirit of Transformation," as they recognized in Paths I, II, and III theologies of creation, Incarnation, the cross, and the Resurrection, respectively.

21 THE NEW CREATION: IMAGES OF GOD IN MOTION CREATING A GLOBAL CIVILIZATION

The Kingdom/Queendom of God is not just words, it is power.
—*1 Cor. 4:20*

God appears to you not in person but in action.
—*Mahatma Gandhi*[1]

Our art must be the foundation of the coming culture.
—*Kenji Miyazawa*

Art is civilization.
—*Alfred North Whitehead*

Politics have a very close affinity to art.
—*Simone Weil*

I get exalted by metamorphosis, when one thing becomes another. That's the miracle, and I wouldn't stop with a picture unless it performed that transformation. An artist is a cannibal. He eats, mangles the world, and gives it back in a new form.
—*Philip Guston*

The new meaning of soul is creativity and mysticism. These will become the foundation of the new psychological type and with him/her the new civilization.
—*Otto Rank*

Art seduces us into the struggle against repression.
—*Norman O. Brown*[2]

The theoretical intelligence merely contemplates the world, and the practical intelligence merely orders it; but the aesthetic intelligence creates the world.
—*Friedrich Schelling*[3]

Let no one think that the birth of humanity is to be felt without terror. The transformations that await us cost everything in the way of courage and sacrifice. Let no one be deluded that a knowledge of the path can substitute for putting one foot in front of the other.
—*M. C. Richards (31.8)*

For now I create a new heaven and a new earth!
> —*Isa. 65:17*

Nobody puts new wine into old wineskins; if he does, the wine will burst the skins and the wine will be lost along with the skins. No! New wines demand new skins!
> —*Jesus, in Mark 2:22*

For anyone who is in Christ, there is a new creation; the old creation has gone, and now the new one is here. It is all God's work.
> —*2 Cor. 5:17,18*

Then I saw a new heaven and a new earth. The first heaven and the first earth had disappeared now.
> —*Rev. 21:1*

One reason why we do not hear of either the Via Creativa or the Via Transformativa in fall/redemption theology is that Augustine makes a dangerously dualistic distinction between action and contemplation. For him, "wisdom belongs to contemplation, knowledge to action."[4] Gandhi, who insists that God comes in action, shares the creation-centered belief that wisdom is part of creating. If contemplation be pitted against action, as it is in Augustine's viewpoint, then contemplation cannot represent the fullest spiritual energy of the human person.[5] In addition, fall/redemption spirituality, with its dualistic attitude that projects heaven into life-after-death and ignores realized eschatology, also ignores the Good News of the Holy Spirit's birthing of a New Creation. Yet today all people are challenged to be instruments for this new age, this new creation. Without a New Creation, which means a new heart and a new consciousness in people and in new social structures, humanity will exterminate itself and put an end to twenty billion years of providential art and history. We humans, for whom the planet has indeed become a global village, are required to create a new civilization that is worthy of our dignity as royal persons and our responsibility as divine co-creators. If we do not create a global civilization where peace and justice reign and where the spirit of delight and celebration can be made to happen, then we have no one to blame but ourselves. For we do choose the religious and social structures we prefer, and we choose the gods and idols we worship.

Path IV

The transformation of the person and of society that the New Creation is about presumes the Via Creativa. This in turn presumes the Via Negativa, which today stares every citizen of the world in the face as an omnipresent nuclear cloud. And this presumes the Via Positiva, a passionate love of isness, of the mystery of creation. Creativity will mark the New Creation just as it marked the original, ongoing creation. It is a creativity that is nonelitist and has never ceased. The New Creation will call forth a great outburst of creative energy from all beings and certainly from all peoples. This is where Miyazawa, Whitehead, Richards, Rank, and Weil—whom I cited above —all agree: Art will indeed characterize the new civilization. Not elitist art, but art as meditation and spirituality, the art of our lives. We must first confess how distant we are from such a civilization. Mahatma Gandhi was once asked, "What do you think of Western civilization?" and he replied, "I think it would be a good idea." A civilization built on dualism and war within and between persons, one that puts its most creative minds and ifs best engineers to sadistic work building more and more destructive weapons, is no civilization at all. It needs a radical transformation from the heart outwards. It needs to outgrow and outlaw war just as in the last century it outlawed slavery. The human race has outgrown war; but it hardly knows it yet. The new civilization will value the creativity of each person and therefore will consider the artist a worker. In this way unemployment will be ended and vast amounts of new employment will be created. Then all of our social systems, from religious ones of worship to educational, governmental, political, economic, and artistic ones, will need to be recreated after the true image of God; that is, after the true creative powers of people. As one psychologist puts it, the next step will move us beyond

> not only "cure" but beyond "personal growth" into the development of a new communal climate. . . . New ways of communicating, new values, new priorities over institutions such as marriage, schools and government, new vocational requirements, new reward systems—all are part of a necessary change in the spiritual atmosphere of our society.[6]

Thomas Berry believes that the history of creativity has led the cosmos, through its most recent creators, the human species, to the place of transformation where we now find ourselves. After all, history is creation history and not just salvation history. Or, to put it differently, there is no salvation without creation. Berry distinguishes four "macro-phase" expressions of human creativity:

252

1. The tribal-shamanic phase, for example that of Native American peoples or the Matrifocal religions, which derives its deep inspirations from the "ultimate mystery of the universe."

2. The classical religions phase, which developed throughout Eurasia and Central America and which was dominated by a space-rather than a time-consciousness.

3. The scientific-technological phase ushered in by modern science and technology, wherein time and space have frequently been "conquered."

4. The emerging ecological phase, which seizes us "by a new revelatory experience that is coming to us in the new origin story."[7]

Berry does all a great service by naming these periods of creativity, for by doing so he reminds us how today's creativity is part of a historical process and that, while we rely on what has preceded us and need to birth out of all three of the past eras of creativity, still what we birth is new. The New Creation is calling us forth even as it is remolding us from the inside so that we can birth its new images and restructure society accordingly. Berry talks about what he calls "the more basic arts" which we will need to develop in order to be instruments of this emerging ecological phase. Among these are the following:

> The shaping of the human world itself, identifying values, establishing a civilizational discipline, molding a language that can carry our deeper interpretation of human experience, activating a communion with the divine, providing an educational program in which succeeding generations can achieve an expanding life pattern along with an interpretative vision of life meaning.[8]

When one meditates on this agenda, one has to shout: Who can possibly talk of unemployment? All this would be new employment and "good work," to use Schumacher's phrase. The best possible work: that of being instruments of a new creation.

But we must not deceive ourselves into believing that transformation is easy work. It is not, as Richards puts it, "without terror." But then again, no creativity is, and no creation ever has been. Gandhi warned, too, that the most important thing was not to prepare speeches or to organize marches but to prepare oneself for "mountains of suffering."[9] And Whitehead also admonishes that New Creation does not come cheaply or without confusion and doubt. In fact, he wisely attributes the cynicism and pessimism and languor—what spirituality calls acedia—of middle-class persons in the present challenge to fear and insecurity at the prospect of "a renewed exercise of the creative imagination."

> The middle-class pessimism over the future of the world comes from a confusion between civilization and security. In the immediate future there will be less security than in the immediate past, less stability. It must be admitted that there is a degree of instability which is inconsistent with civilisation. But, on the whole, the great ages have been unstable ages. (45.299)

There will be plenty of Via Negativa, of letting go and letting be, of letting pain be pain and suffering be suffering, in this process of personal and social transformation. But we have one another for support in our weakness, from which all grace flows. And we have the work of the Holy Spirit, the spirit of transformation.

First, a lively faith and trust assure us that the work of the New Creation is the work of the Creator. Paul writes, "It is the same God who said, 'Let there be light shining out of darkness' who has shone in our minds to radiate the light of the knowledge of God's glory, the glory on the face of Christ." (2 Cor. 4:6) All the previous three paths, beginning with the energy of Dabhar itself, pulsate and culminate in the Via Transformativa. We have not been left orphans. In the Hebrew Bible the "technical term" for creation, *bara,* is used for the making of heaven and earth, of sun, moon, and stars, of light and darkness, of nations, of humanity, and of a clean heart. "In the Bible it [*bara*] seems to connote the idea of making something wonderful, new, astonishing."[10]

Is not the excitement and joy of the New Creation what will see us through the labor pains, just as Jesus observed was the case in a mother's getting through a difficult childbirth? The New Creation, Paul assures us, is "God's work." (2 Cor. 5:17) There is a new "rule," Paul says, for those who will form the people of God: it is "to become an altogether new creature." (Gal. 6:15,16) The New Creation takes place within our consciousness, and it demands nothing less than, in Paul's words, "a spiritual revolution." He says, "Your mind must be renewed by a spiritual revolution so that you can put on the new self that has been created in God's way, in the goodness and holiness of the truth." (Eph. 4:24) To put on this new self we must let go of the old self. The old wineskins, the old civilization, the old mindsets will not suffice for the New Creation. "You must give up your old way of life; you must put aside your old self, which gets corrupted by following illusory desires." (Eph. 4:22) This new self will be characterized by the letting go of dualisms, by the celebration of differences, by the emergence of God's creative power.

> You have stripped off your old behaviour with your old self, and you have put on a new self which will progress towards true knowledge the more it is renewed in the image of its creator; and in that image there is no room for distinction between Greek and Jew, between the circumcised or the uncircumcised, or between barbarian and Scythian, slave and free man. There is only Christ: he is everything and he is in everything. (Col. 3:9-11)

The image of God is truly an image in motion. A growing into the image. An alive art that is involved in actions of transformation. We are called "to become true images of God's Son" and therefore images of the New Creation. (Rom. 8:29) For what Christ promised was nothing less than "the new heavens and new earth, the place where justice will be at home." (2 Pet. 3:13) A place, better a space, where peace and beauty, justice and compassion, celebration and respect for differences will find a home. A place where everyone, as Meister Eckhart put it, will be a mother of God.

I believe that the key to befriending the New Creation is learning to befriend the first creation. Given the wealth of scriptural theology dedicated to the New Creation, only some of which I touch on in this section, I am continually amazed at the silence in organized religion about New Creation. In my four decades as a Roman Catholic I have never once heard a sermon on the "New Creation." Why is this? Obviously, a fall/redemption spirituality that has not learned to love creation is going to be deeply suspicious of talk about a "new creation." Yet Christians and others should not be afraid. of terms like "new age." Newness is a divine attribute. Surely the human race is as idolatrous towards inherited and familiar institutions and patterns of living as it ever could be about new patterns. The "new" can in fact prove to be quite old. For example, a "new" theology of original blessing is in fact far more ancient than the familiar theology of original sin. Awakening people to newness is the baptismal experience of rebirth. It is metanoia, waking up. What is newest about our times is the global demand on our consciousness. The global pain, the global interconnections of beauty and pain. The invitation to create a global civilization of love/justice and ecological harmony is a new invitation. And so too are the global means to carry out this New Creation.

Clearly we have our work cut out for us. But the spirit of God who wants creation to thrive is with us. The kingdom/queendom of God is among us; and it is a kingdom not just of words but of power. The New Creation will be God's work *and* our work. We will truly be co-creators in this process of transformation.

22 FAITH AS TRUSTING THE PROPHETIC CALL OF THE HOLY SPIRIT

There is the grain of the prophet in the recesses of every human existence.
— *Rabbi Heschel*[1]

Every totalitarian regime is frightened of the artist. It is the vocation of the prophet to keep alive the ministry of imagination, to keep on conjuring and proposing alternative futures to the single one the king wants to urge as the only thinkable one.
— *Walter Brueggemann (5.45)*

We struck the religious imagination of an angry people.
— *Mahatma Gandhi*[2]

Society must be transfigured by a new type of social personality, a new humanity appropriate to a new earth.
— *Rosemary Ruether (32.211)*

The spirit of the Lord Yahweh has been given to me,
for Yahweh has anointed me.
He has sent me to bring good news to the poor,
to bind up hearts that are broken;

to proclaim liberty to captives,
freedom to those in prison;
to proclaim a year of favour from Yahweh,
a day of vengeance for our God,

to comfort all those who mourn and to give them
a garland in exchange for ashes.
— *Isa. 61:1-3*

Path IV

The word of Yahweh was addressed to me, saying,
"Before I formed you in the womb I knew you;
before you came to birth I consecrated you;
I have appointed you as prophet to the nations.

There! I am putting my words into your mouth.
Look, today I am setting you
over nations and over kingdoms,
to tear up and to knock down,
to destroy and to overthrow,
to build and to plant."
          —*Jer. 1:4,5,10*

Blessed are you when people abuse you and persecute you
and speak all kinds of calumny against you on my account.
Rejoice and be glad for your reward will be great in heaven!
This is the way they persecuted the prophets before you.
          —*Matt. 5:11,12*

When people grow and become rooted in love and in God, they
are ready to take upon themselves every attack, temptation,
vexation, and painful suffering willingly and gladly, eagerly
and joyfully, as the prophets did.
          —*Meister Eckhart*

My heart is moved by all I cannot save:
so much has been destroyed

I·have to cast my lot with those
who age after age, perversely,

with no extraordinary power,
reconstitute the world.
          —*Adrienne Rich (30.67)*

Any religion which professes to be concerned about the souls
of men and is not concerned about the social and economic
conditions that can scar the soul, is a spiritually moribund
religion only waiting for the day to be buried.
          —*Martin Luther King, Jr.*[3]

During the fall/redemption hegemony in Western Christianity the
word "prophet" was seldom invoked except to describe a kind of

unique and solitary individual, a loinclothed John the Baptist in the desert, who invoked oaths and curses on the world. The word "prophesy" usually meant "to foretell the future." And the question of faith was seldom, Is Jesus a prophet who calls us all to be prophets? Yet the birth of the Christian spiritual movement was inaugurated by the Pentecost experience of the power of the Holy Spirit to cut through human divisions and rivalries. The Pentecost experience of the earliest followers of Jesus after he left them was a startling one of the end of the Tower of Babel and all the divisions that it stood for.

> Now there were devout people living in Jerusalem from every nation under heaven, and at this sound they all assembled, each one amazed and astonished. "Surely," they said, "all these people speaking are Galileans? How does it happen that each of us hears them in his or her own native language? ... Everyone was amazed and unable to explain it; they asked one another what it all meant. Some, however, laughed it off. "They have been drinking too much new wine," they said. (Acts 2: 3-8, 12, 13)

What some took as drunkeness Peter insists was in fact the coming of the Spirit. A spirit so holy that it would make all persons prophets— imagine that! Not just the prophetic "greats" of Israelite history, Isaiah and Jeremiah, Hosea and Amos, were now called to be prophets, but all persons. And Peter invokes the prophet Joel to make his point.

> These men are not drunk, as you imagine; why, it is only
> the third hour of the day. On the contrary, this is what
> the prophet spoke of:
> In the days to come—it is the Lord who speaks—
> I will pour out my spirit on all humankind.
> Their sons and daughters shall prophesy,
> your young men shall see visions,
> your old men shall dream dreams.
> Even on my slaves, men and women,
> in those days, I will pour out my spirit. (Acts 2:15-18; see Joel 3:1-5)

It is no small matter in the history of civilization to learn that ordinary people are all called to a prophetic vocation. This could truly be the energy that brings about a New Creation, were it believed in, that is, *trusted*. Faith in Path IV means trust in our prophetic vocations. It is a trust not based on human apprehension or human power but on the grace of the Holy Spirit, which is truly poured out on all humankind.

259

Path IV

But what does it mean to be a prophet? Who is a prophet? A prophet is one who carries on the Dabhar, that is the creative energy or word of God, when it has been stimied or stifled by injustice or laziness or too much belief in the immortality of what already is. The prophet in each of us is our social conscience, our heartfelt concern about the loved ones of God who suffer needlessly. "Prophetic inspiration," Rabbi Heschel writes, "is for the sake, for the benefit, of a third party. It is not a private affair between prophet and God; its purpose is the illumination of the people rather than the illumination of the prophet."[4] The prophet in us says, "NO! This is not the way the Creator wanted the universe to respond to the the blessing that creation is. We can—we must—do things differently." Heschel says that "The major activity of the prophet was *interference*."[5] To interfere with the way things are going, whether in terms of militarism among nations, sexism in churches, racism in education, or dualism in self and society—the prophet criticizes and places himself or herself in opposition and therefore in a position of interfering with what is happening. Jeremiah talks of "tearing up and knocking down"—a Via Negativa that must precede the "building up and planting" that creative transformation is about. Brueggemann interprets this to mean that the prophet is sensitive to the discontinuity of history: how things need to break and be broken if New Creation is to emerge.[6] The interference and therefore the discontinuity that are the prophet's concern are most evidently an interference in unjust situations and a break with the continuous injustice that is rained on, for example, women or artists, the earth or animals, Native Americans or Third World peoples. The prophet does not hesitate to break with the recent past in order to regain an older past when the just harmony and order ruled the cosmos.

The prophet knows something about trusting anger, trusting one's moral outrage, trusting what is intolerable. And molding that anger and outrage into creative possibilities. When Eckhart says that "all deeds are accomplished in passion," he is underlining how important a blessing anger and outrage can be. The fall/redemption tradition has made far too much of anger as a sin. In fact, anger is often necessary to see one through the interference that must be accomplished. Anger, after all, is proportionate to one's love. Gandhi at one point called his work useful because it "struck the religious imagination of an angry people."[7] Poet Audre Lorde believes that trusting "the chaos ourselves" is the key to vitality and creation. And this is the essential role of poetry.

As we get in touch with the things that we feel are intolerable in our lives, they become more and more intolerable. If we just once dealt with how much we hate most of what we do, there would be no holding us back from changing it. This is true with any kind of movement. This is the way in which the philosopher/queen, the poet-warrior leads.[8]

It is no wonder that Brueggemann sees the prophetic role as one of a "ministry of imagination." It is imagination that steers the sparks of anger in the direction of transformation and new creation. In this sense we need to realize that every prophet is an artist. And every true artist is a prophet. Psychologist Claudio Naranjo has called extrovert meditation or art as meditation "the way of the prophets."[9] Why is this so? Because, as we saw in Path III, creativity is a process and way of uniting, of bringing together disparate—or disputing—parts and recreating a whole of them. The prophet recycles the anger of oppressed peoples, not into sublimation or passivity but into ways of transformation, self-expression, and New Creation. This rebirth is the work of the Holy Spirit, the great transformer. The finest preparation for the prophet's daily task of awakening and interfering is art as meditation. This is also the finest refreshment for tired and misunderstood prophets who need their own filling up and rejuvenation. Nonelitist art, with its sensuousness and immediacy of contact, is the prophet's best friend.

Theologian Krister Stendahl complains that Christianity has for too long talked about Paul's conversion as if his was a typical religious conversion like those UHF channels trumpet to us in our living rooms. Rather, Stendahl argues, Paul's transformation was a "prophetic call." Paul did not change his religion from Jewish to Christian; rather he changed his work, and his inner person was transformed from the sin of persecuting early Christians to being an apostle of Christ. "There is hardly a thought of Paul's which is not tied up with his mission, with his work. The 'I' in his writings is not 'the Christian' but 'the Apostle to the Gentiles.' That is why I say call rather than conversion." (39.8,11f.) Paul's prophetic call, like every Christian's and ultimately every person's, is a call to transform the world from slavery and bondage to freedom and justice. And, as in the case of Paul, it is a question of our work. An entire spirituality of work is found in the four paths that have led us to consider our prophetic vocation here as Theme Twenty-One. How is my work a prophetic work contributing to the dismanteling of the Tower of Babel, contributing to interference with injustice and with the planting of new seeds of harmony and cosmic order? This is the question behind all work which is meant to be Dabhar, God's word/work carried on in us. Or as Meister Eckhart puts it, "When word and work are returned to their source and origin, then all work is accomplished divinely in God." The prophet celebrates the return of God's word (creative energy) and work by way of human work.

> Yes, as the rain and the snow come down from the heavens and do not return without watering the earth, making it yield and giving growth to provide seed for the sower and bread for the eating, so the word that goes from my mouth does not return to me empty, without carrying out my will and succeeding in what it was sent to do. (Isa. 55:10,11)

Prophecy is about a return of blessing, our returning blessing for blessing. It presumes the kind of faith, that is trust, that we have named for each of the four paths. The prophet in us calls forth the excellence and beauty in each of us, it calls forth the best that we can give, the best that we can enjoy (Path I), the best that we can let go of (Path II), the best that we can create (Path III), the best that we can give to birthing the future by transforming the past (Path IV). Heschel says that the prophetic seed lies in the "recesses" of each person—but what are the recesses? I believe that the four paths represent the recesses of each person: pleasure and suffering, birthing and transforming. That is why the spiraling movement of the creation-centered journey necessarily leads to prophecy: because it is not a superficial journey but the deepest of all journeys. It is a journey to the recesses and beyond. It is necessarily, then, a journey of the prophet in each of us.

It is interesting to consider the etymology of the word "prophet" in Hebrew and its derivative words. Words that are related to *nabiy* (prophet) include *nabat*, to scan, look intently at, to regard with pleasure, favor or care, to behold, consider, see. This comes amazingly close to Path I. Another related word is *nabab*, to pierce, to be hollow, to empty. Here we have Path II. Another derivitive is *nebayoth*, meaning fruitfulness, from the verb to germinate, to utter, to bring forth fruit. And the related word *nebek* means to burst forth, like a fountain or a spring. In these words we clearly have Path III. The related word *nabach* means to bark like a dog. Thus the prophet is a watchdog, a nay-sayer, an interferer when prowlers are about (Path IV).

I believe it is important today to understand "prophet" not just in terms of individuals, as if four billion people were to become individualized prophets, but as movements. Prophetic movements are evidently the way the Holy Spirit is calling persons to their prophetic vocations and the prophetic dimensions to their work in our time. The various modern liberation movements, from the Gray Panthers to women's liberation, from Alcoholics Anonymous to Overeaters Anonymous, from base communities to nuclear freeze, from black and red liberation to lesbian and gay liberation—the prophet in each of us recognizes the work of the spirit in each of these movements. And to put our work and energy into selected prophetic movements—for no one person can immerse himself or herself in all—is to guarantee a kind of contribution on our part that is not messianic or ego-tripping. Also, I believe that not only does every individual have a prophetic vocation but that, more accurately, every individual has prophetic vocations. As times change and we change and our responsibilities in a changing culture change, we are called to let go sometimes of past prophetic calls and to immerse ourselves in new ones. I know of no better way to stay young and, in Hildegarde's word, green. As she puts it, the work of the Holy Spirit is the work of greening the universe.

The prophet is nonelitist in his or her empathy and understanding and in the means he or she chooses to arouse the people. The prophets present a street spirituality, one that the nonprofessional person can understand. This is why, as Brueggemann points out, the prophet must be an artist who calls forth symbols of justice and injustice that are universally recognizable. In this regard, as in so many others, wisdom and prophecy are alike in the Jewish spiritual tradition. As one scholar puts it, "Wisdom acts like a prophet, walking through the streets and urging her doctrine on the people."[10] Consider, for example, the following statements on wisdom and on the prophet respectively:

Wisdom calls aloud in the streets,
    she raises her voice in the public squares;
she calls out at the street corners,
    she delivers her message at the city gates,
"You ignorant people, how much longer will you cling to your
    ignorance?" (Prov. 1:20-22)

The word that was addressed to Jeremiah by Yahweh, "Go and stand at the gate of the Temple of Yahweh and there proclaim this message. Say, 'Listen to the word of Yahweh, all you people of Judah who enter

by these gates to worship Yahweh.' Yahweh Sabaoth, the God of
Israel says this: 'Amend your behaviour and your actions and I will
stay with you. . . .' " (Jer. 7: 1-3; cf. 5:1)

A creation-centered spirituality is nonelitist because creation belongs to all and not just to those who rule human affairs. And it is
nonelitist because it appeals to all and not just to the professional or
ruling classes. In this regard a hard question needs to be put today
to *all* professionals, be they educators, theologians, doctors, artists,
lawyers, judges, engineers, architects, businesspeople, sociologists,
economists, and scientists. Whom are you serving?

One of the surest ways of being able to answer this question is in
terms of another: What language do you use in this service? If only
professionals can understand your language then it is most likely
that you are not being prophetic or wise, not being "in the streets"
with your particular gift of work and word. Theological educators
write books on justice for the poor in language that even professional theologians can barely understand. Ridiculous! If a teacher is
not smart enough and in touch enough with the nonelite peoples to
communicate his or her knowledge to them, then that person is in
the wrong vocation. Professional status and professional ego trips
are no excuse for elitist language; they are an invitation to professionals to start getting prophetic within their own profession—to
start transforming that particular profession so that it serves the
oppressed and ceases to legitimize the oppressor. Many professionals today will find their prophetic calling precisely in de-elitizing
their own profession. Of course, like all the prophets, they must be
willing to pay a price for doing such work.

The spiraling journey of creation-centered spirituality finds its
fulfillment in persons responding to their prophetic vocations. The
prophet falls in love with creation and especially with the little ones,
the *anawim*, of creation (Path I); she then experiences the bottomless depths of pain that wrench at the beauty and dignity of have
and have-nots alike (Path II); from the nothingness experience she
recreates, working from the best that both left brain and right brain
can offer (Path III); yearning for a New Creation, she launches her
creativity in the direction of healing by way of compassion, celebration,
and social justice (Path IV). In this manner she interferes with
pessimism, cynicism, and despair, and channels moral outrage into
rebirth.

23 A SPIRITUALITY OF THE <u>ANAWIM</u>: FEMINISTS, THIRD WORLD, LAY, AND OTHER OPPRESSED PEOPLES

Only when redemption in Christ is understood as historical, as an affirmation of God's original intention for creation, rather than a rejection of creation, will it become possible to see the great New Testament theme of equality in Christ as a mandate, not merely of flight from the world, but of transformation of the world in the direction of justice.

—Rosemary Ruether (16.161)

Knowledge is not the conformity of the mind to the given, but an immersion in the process of transformation and construction of a new world.

—Gustavo Gutierrez[1]

My soul proclaims the greatness of the Lord
and my spirit exults in God my saviour,
because he has looked upon his lowly handmaid. . . .
He has pulled down the princes from their thrones
and exalted the lowly.
The hungry he has filled with good things,
the rich he has sent away empty.

—Mary, in Luke 1:46,47,52,53

From coast to coast, desert to woodland, the Native peoples perceive themselves to be an integral part of Creation.[2]

There is no such thing as "my" bread. All bread is *ours* and is given to me, to others through me and to me through others. For not only bread but all things necessary for sustenance in this life are given on loan to us with others, and because of others and for others and to others through us.

—Meister Eckhart

The oppressed must realize that they are fighting not merely for freedom from hunger, but for . . . freedom to create and to construct, to wonder and to venture.

—Paulo Freire[3]

First, it is imperative in the name of the gospel to make the underdeveloped masses aware of their human dignity, of their rights to a better life, one which is worthy of the human person. The second point is to stir the consciousness of the rich at home and abroad.
    —Dom Helda Camera[4]

He defended the cause of the poor and the needy. . . . Is not this what it means to know me? It is Yahweh who speaks.
    —Jer. 22:16

Gandhi identified himself completely with the poor and the weak, with *Daridranarayan* (God as manifested in the meek and the wretched). . . . Self-realization is impossible without service of, and identification with, the poorest.
    —Raghavan Iyer (22.6,237)

It was the great mass of the poor, the workers, who were the Catholics in this country, and this fact in itself drew me to the Church [in the 1930's].
    —Dorothy Day[5]

The Christian Gospel promised to the poor a kingdom of their own—a dream of Caesar's which could not be fulfilled realistically. Where Caesar had failed politically and economically, Christianity succeeded spiritually. The dispossessed founded a religion whch solved for them their problems through a timeless and spaceless ideology establishing them as a powerful class with an entirely new psychology.
    —Otto Rank (28.141)

Black folk find white folk afraid of their bodies. Blacks bring their bodies even to worship—especially to worship with.
    —Nathan Jones[6]

Why are white people so afraid of the homosexual? In Native American languages we don't even have a word for the homosexual. In fact, it is well known among us that the most spiritual people are often homosexuals and these people have often been counselors to our greatest chiefs.
    —José Hobday

Time and again when I lecture on the themes and paths of creation-centered spirituality people respond by saying, "Why haven't I heard this side to the Christian tradition before?" "Why did I have to wait fifty years of my life to hear this kind of spirituality?" "Why is it that fall/redemption theology has so dominated in the West?" There are no doubt many replies to so basic a question, but a fundamental answer has to be this: It has served the purposes, conscious and unconscious, of empire builders and patriarchy and certain political and economic systems to encourage a fall/redemption instead of a creation-centered spirituality. Fall/redemption ideologies help to keep the poor poor. They do not encourage the trust, the creativity, the moral outrage, the prophetic call and bonding for social transformation that the oppressed need to hear. In fact, fall/redemption theology is a theology of the oppressor. Creation-centered spirituality is a spirituality of the oppressed and of those who have learned, as Jesus did, to identify with the oppressed in order that the oppressed might liberate themselves and eventually even the oppressor might become liberated. If global citizens are eager today to create a global civilization that is based on justice and on the elimination of war and the obscene national expenditures that go towards militarism the world over, then they should heed Gandhi's advice. He believed that the "prime cause of modern wars" was "the inhuman race for exploitation of the so-called weaker peoples of the earth." (22.208) To listen to the *anawim*, to the so-called weaker peoples of the earth, requires that we let go of oppressive spiritualities that appeal to right-wing ideologues. Historian Carroll Quigley, in his book *The Evolution of Civilizations*, points out that "right-wing" spirituality, which emphasizes an inward soul and "the perfect rationality of God," has "worked historically through Augustine of Hippo, who was a Platonist in philosophy although a Christian in religion."[7] Throughout this book we have seen thinkers as diverse as Ashley Montagu and Susan Griffin, Mahatma Gandhi and William Eckhardt, Michael Polanyi, and Rosemary Ruether decry original sin ideologies, dualism, privatization and cosmosless psychologies, fear of the body, and distrust, that has been taught Western culture through its right-wing spiritual tradition. In short, we have seen all along how different creation spirituality is from fall/redemption spiritualities. Perhaps we have even understood how it is that so many creation-centered saints and thinkers have been forgotten, repressed, and condemned by fall/redemption ideologues. This entire book has been an exposition of a spirituality of the *anawim*, of the oppressed.

In this section I will deal more explicitly with why this is so and with some examples of how creation spirituality is indeed the spirituality of the *anawim*.

When one meditates on the groups who have been oppressed and put down in the West and then listens to the reasons given by their oppressors as to why they have been put down, an amazing common thread runs through all the arguments. Whether we are listening to reasons why women are put down, or homosexuals, or Jews, or Native Americans, or blacks, the invariable argument is that in some way these people are or do something against nature. They are "naturally below" those who pronounce their fate. For example, the notion that women are to be submissive to men is given by Paul and Deutero-Paul as the "order of creation." (1 Cor. 11:2-16) The hierachy of male over female is the order of nature, we are told. (16.142f.) After all, women are "misbegotten males" (Aristotle and St. Thomas Aquinas) who are "made of blood-without souls" (John Marston) and, unlike men, are not made in the image and likeness of God (St. Augustine). Homosexuals are persons whose sexual activity is "contrary to nature," we are told. And the question that preoccupied the theorists while Native Americans were being slaughtered and enslaved was whether Indians are human (i.e., have souls) or not. As Native Americans put it, the Spanish conquistadors reached

> a conclusion that Native peoples did not have "souls," and therefore it was perfectly all right to enslave or murder them. Much of that same kind of thinking is alive and well today in such countries as Paraguay, Brazil, Chile and others where Native peoples are still hunted down and killed. . . . The question at this point that needs to be addressed is, what kind of theology were the institutional churches propagating that could lead to such a dehumanizing analysis of missions of peoples? And, is that kind of theology still functioning in the churches in the 1980's?[8]

A missionary in Brazil told me the story of a bounty hunter in the Amazon who was paid to kill Indians. In a recent interview about his work, he said he once shot an Indian who did not die at once but appeared to be in pain and suffering, "just as if he were a human being." Jews, we were instructed, were "those lustful Jews" (St. Augustine) and blacks were "natural slaves" (à la Aristotle) who fit beautifully into the "obviously natural" system of slavery. Plants and animals too are without souls (Descartes).

What we have in each of these instances is one group, namely the dominant political group—white heterosexual males, usually economically privileged—setting itself up as the criterion for what is and is not natural, for what is and is not creation as God meant it to be. We have a colossal lack of respect for the diversity of nature itself, a profound failure to admit hospitality and to celebrate the diversity of nature or creation. How ironic it is that a spirituality that ignores creation and those who study it and refers to nature exclusively as "fallen" invokes "the natural" as the standard of morality. One has to ask how much creativity, how much imagination, how much good work for human dignity and justice and celebration has been wasted by this wanton arrogance on the part of ruling groups. For does Aristotle or Augustine or Aquinas know enough about "nature" or "creation" to condemn others in creation's name? I take just one example, that of the homosexual. Science, whose task it is to study nature or creation, has arrived at the fact that about ten percent of any given human population will be homosexual. (Moreover it has found that other species of birds and animals also practice homosexuality.) Thus we can only conclude that homosexuality is indeed "natural" for ten percent of the human race. And we are quite utterly ignorant still about bisexuality as well. The political question comes down to this: does the majority, for example the 90 percent who consider themselves heterosexual, have the right to dictate what the minority does and to tell the minority that it is "unnatural" and "contrary to nature"? Gandhi warns of the violence behind such arrogance when he says, "Numerical strength savours of violence when it acts in total disregard of any strongly felt opinion of a minority." (22.142) It is especially striking to hear what those who put others down say about the unnaturalness of these others when one considers how as a rule the spirituality of the oppressor avoids the cosmos altogether.

A spirituality that ignores the imagination can never be a spirituality of the oppressed. Imagination—along with one's body—is all the poorest of the poor have left to them. They possess no bank accounts, no real estate, no tanks, no clout. What they possess is what God has given them: a body and the image of God in them; imagination, which is divine power to birth anew. They need and deserve a spirituality that will empower them by way of imagination to release the divine energy in them to create their world and work anew. They deserve a creation-centered spirituality. Gandhi was not mistaken in saying that for the poor the economic is the spiritual and God appears only as bread and butter. (22.35)

In reminding us of what the basics of living are about, the *anawim* return us to true humility, i.e., earth and earthiness (see Theme Three). The *anawim* are an authentic source of revelation; they are our primary spiritual directors; they reveal where the kingdom/queendom of God is hidden (see Matt. 25). And they challenge all to metanoia, change of heart and lifestyle.

A panentheistic spirituality that encourages a nondualistic and nonmechanistic relationship to nature will also encourage democracy. It will not see the world in terms of ladders but as concentric, interacting circles of energy. Starhawk points out how appealing the mechanistic concept of nature as dead and inert and machinelike was to the political, social, and economic powers of the past few centuries.

> The principle of immanence was identified with radicalism and lower-class interests.... Such ideas were termed *enthusiasm*, and a vigorous campaign was carried out by the state, the established Church, and the new scientific institutions against them. Enthusiasm was associated with radical activism and rebellion. (38.217)

She is supported in this thesis by David Kubron, who also points out some of the political implications of a nontheistic spirituality. He writes that the

> conception of the world's being inherently active, full of Gods, and constantly charging helped develop people's self-confidence, and perhaps better encourages them ... to step forward to act, to transform the world, rather than to remain passive in the face of the great social transformation then sweeping England.[9]

The spiritualities of Native Americans and of Third World peoples, of feminists and of blacks, of homosexuals and of the handicapped, are creation-centered spiritualities. I have learned over the years from interacting with all kinds of persons in teaching, lecturing, retreat, and workshop settings that this is in fact the case. I recall, for example, how this summer I did a workshop on "Native Ways and Creation-Centered Christian Ways" at a beautiful gathering of 1500 Native Americans at the Tekekwitha Conference in Spokane, Washington. Following the dialogue between myself and Native American priest Father Ed Savilla, a Navajo woman stood up and declared, "This one-hour presentation has healed forty years of my life. I always had this split in me between Native ways and Christian ways, and now I know the split has been between Native ways and St. Augustine." She was seconded by numerous other Native Americans. I have presented creation-centered spirituality to gay and lesbian groups and have found the same deep resonance. I have written about how the four paths help name the homosexual's journey in a special way.[10] Artists, who have been the *anawim* for centuries in the West, find a home in creation spirituality—and more than a home, a new energy for their work and holy vocation. And, of course, feminists not only find a home here, but they are the principal group today who are recovering and recreating the creation-centered spiritual tradition.

There can be no question that the creation tradition is the feminist tradition in the West. Feminism of its very nature is prophetic during a patriarchal period of history. Accordingly, feminists have been treated very often the same way as prophets were treated by those in power with power. Consider how many persons on the Family Tree of Creation Spirituality (see Appendix A) are women or were spiritually educated, as Eckhart was, by women. And consider their fate—how few are known to us, how St. Hildegarde is hardly known even by Benedictines; how Mechtild and Julian of Norwich have been roundly forgotten in our religions, how Eckhart and John the Scot (and Aquinas too) were condemned, for example. Women's religions such as those Starhawk is recovering in her works are deeply prepatriarchal: they have existed for tens of thousands of years longer than the patriarchal religions that dominate the globe today. Native American spiritualities come from the same period, and it is astounding and uncanny how Hildegarde of Bingen's pictures, painted in twelfth-century Germany, are profoundly Native American. What unites the Native American to the twelfth-century German is the ancient creation-centered tradition.

When I read feminist thinkers and poets like Adrienne Rich, Susan Griffin, Rosemary Ruether, Starhawk, Carol Christ, and Beverly Harrison, I find all the themes of creation-centered spirituality that we have treated in this book. In their works, all four paths of the spirituality journey are named and celebrated. I am a spiritual theologian, and there is simply no doubt in my mind or heart that what feminism is doing today is bringing back the creation tradition. The *anawim* are being heard from at last. One hopes it is not too late. And one hopes that the dominant powers in religion and society and in the hearts and minds of persons everywhere will let go of their arrogance enough to listen to this recovery of wisdom in

271

our midst. One hopes that all peoples will welcome the prophets among us. And today in no small measure these prophets are feminists.

I have taught Third World peoples—Africans, Latin Americans, Asians, and the Irish. Among them all I have found a confirmation of their deepest cultural heritage in their learning of the creation spiritual tradition. Latin American theology at its best is today groping for a spirituality that supports its justice orientation. It needs and deserves to create its world view with the help of creation-centered spirituality. Latin American theologian Jon Sobrino writes as follows:

> Wittingly or unwittingly, then, the church is in the process of giving renewed value to an authentic theology of creation. . . . And in so doing, we look where theology has all too often failed to look, i.e., at the very fact of living and managing to stay alive, at work, and at the use of nature and its resources in the service of human beings. . . . It would be illusory, useless, and even blasphemous to claim to bear witness to God without engaging in practical activity to repair creation. Faced with the basic primary needs evident on our continent, all experience of God and all witnessing by the church must logically start there.[11]

Gandhi, whom I have cited often in this book, is of course a Third World person who, by his education and profession, bridges First and Third worlds for us. He is deeply creation-centered, not least in his insistence that nonviolence, a healthy kind of letting go and Via Negativa, must be practiced as the true asceticism of our time. It was Gandhi who, for all his awareness of the suffering that accompanies the prophet of social transformation, still summarized his work in these words: "Real beauty is my aim." (22. 271) It is indeed the Third World that can recover beauty for humankind as an operable political and economic and spiritual category. For what is more ugly than the oppression of a royal person, an image of God, a living, creative brother or sister? And what is more beautiful than to awaken people to their own dignity and the rights that accompany such dignity? Is this not the work of the cosmos—to share the blessings of creation with others? Has this not been the untiring work of twenty billion years of creation's amazing unfolding, an unfolding that brings us face to face today with a choice between extinction and creativity, life and death, blessing and curse? The psalmist sings of this happy liberation.

Blessed the person who has the God of Jacob as a helper,
Yahweh maker of heaven and earth,
Yahweh forever faithful, gives justice to those denied it,
gives food to the hungry,
gives liberty to prisoners.

Yahweh restores sight to the blind,
Yahweh straightens those who are bent over,
Yahweh protects the stranger,
he keeps the orphan and widow. (Ps. 146:5-9)

First World peoples often forget that the majority of persons in the world are peasants. Does creation spirituality speak to peasants more than fall/redemption spirituality? And do peasants have much to teach others about creation spirituality? John Berger, in his sensitive and powerful work on French peasants, *Pig Earth*, makes clear that this is the case. The peasant's love of the earth, at-home-ness with sensuality and birthing processes, sense of folk art and of the art of survival, cosmic and compassionate consciousness, and sheer toughness and ability to let go teach us much about living creation spirituality. Berger, for example, describes how the cow giving birth represents an unforgettable cosmic event to the peasant.

She mooed making a sound I've never heard a cow make on other occasions—not even when in pain. . . . A sound stronger than complaint, and more urgent than greeting. . . . He fetched the straw to bed the calf on. For him these moments are moments of triumph, moments of true gain; moments which unite the foxy, ambitious, hard, indefatigable cattleraiser with the universe which surrounds him.[12]

Spiritualities that ignore the cosmos might take a lesson from peasant spiritualities.

Black spirituality is grounded in creation; the religion of Africa is cosmic. It is based on imagination, participation, music, prophetic outrage, and exodus symbols. It is telling that in theologian Nathan Jones's fine book on ministry in the black community, the second chapter is entitled, "Seizing the Beautiful: Black Aesthetics and the Learning Process."[13] In a workshop I gave recently at a Lutheran seminary in which I presented the four paths of Eckhart and creation spirituality, a black student came up and said, "I am a street person. I've been in this seminary for four years, and that man Eckhart names the truth of my life. There's more fire in this message than in all my four years of studying in this school." The creation tradition can not only dialogue with black spirituality but can create with it. For it is already present deeply within black religious experience. Black theologian Cornel West, for example, considers two fundamental elements in the Christian gospel to be "the dignity of persons and the depravity of persons." How does he define depravity? As the refusal to let go and to be transformed and to transform. "The depravity of persons is their proclivity to cling to the moment, to refuse to transform and to be transformed." He opts for a Christianity that flows from the "prophetic stream" of the Bible and that is "dialectical" in nature.[14] The Black Theology Project of 1977 decried a "piecemeal Christianity" that creates a false dualism between "spiritual" and "physical" needs of peoples.[15] And black theologian James Cone points out how a futuristic eschatology instead of a realized eschatology played into the hands of slavemasters who wanted their slaves to look forward to a liberated existence only in the life after this one.[16] Black spirituality is a lively and vibrant aliveness: "To be spiritual is to be alive, to be capable of moving and of responding to movement."[17] The whole person responds in black worship. "There is no understanding of black worship apart from the rhythm of the song and sermon, the passion of prayer and testimony, the ecstasy of the shout and conversion as the people project their humanity in the togetherness of the Spirit."[18] There is earthiness and passion in such a spirituality, as there is in the creation-centered tradition of the West we have been considering.

The Celtic spirituality of Ireland, Scotland, Wales, Appalachia is a deeply creation-centered spirituality. Yet, under the onus of being a colonized nation, Ireland itself has often had its Celtic heritage wiped out, and the dominant spiritual influence in the Irish church since the seventeenth century has not been creation theology but Jansenism—a seventeenth-century export from France denuded of its rather impressive political consciousness. The oppression of Celtic and creation-centered spirituality in the Western church dates back as far as Pelagius in the fourth century and extends to John the Scot, who was an Irishman of the tenth century condemned in the thirteenth. Yet it was the Celts who settled along the Rhine and deep into Germany and northern Italy who laid the spiritual groundwork for the great creation-centered Rhineland mystics including Hildegarde, Mechtild, Eckhart, and even Francis of Assisi. A spiritual renewal in Ireland will mean a recovery of creation-centered spirituality—a tradition that Irish poets and bards and writers have impressively carried on well into our century.[19]

Within church circles the unordained ones are very often the *anawim*. The creation-centered tradition is fundamentally a lay spiritual tradition. Study the Family Tree of Creation Sprituality (see Appendix A) and you will observe a great number of unordained persons including St. Benedict, St. Francis, John the Scot, Pelagius, all the Catholic women, and of course the plethora of lay persons, especially artists and scientists, of the past few centuries who have kept this tradition alive. The creation tradition is essentially nonclerical because it recognizes existence, life itself as the primary sacrament. This sacrament requires awareness and wakefulness, not ordination, to bring about its proper distribution and to elicit the sacrament from children and adults, workers, artists, lovers, citizens. Once the sacrament that creation is is well founded, then other sacraments—for example, the seven stages of maturation and unfolding that the Catholic Church celebrates—take on their deeper meaning. To say that creation spirituality is nonclerical and a lay spirituality does not exclude religious or ordained persons from participating.

Creation spirituality is a lay spirituality because it cares profoundly about *work*, which is, after all, what most adults do with their lives. It cares about *pleasure* and its wise and celebrative possibilities. It cares about sexuality and sensuality. It cares about nature, science, economics, and politics, that is, about people being in the world as agents of transformation. It cares that all of nature and history are sources of revelation.

It is no secret that the models of sanctity that the patriarchal period of Christianity has held up to us have rarely been laypersons. The ideology behind the canonization of saints has been profoundly oriented towards clerical and fall/redemption theology. One obvious example would be Bonaventure's *Life of St. Francis*, which was written immediately following Francis's death and which had the desired effect of contributing to his canonization. It had the undesirable effect, however, of rendering him dualistic, afraid of women and of body, for example. This in turn sentimentalized Francis so that much of the hagiography of Francis has failed to make clear the prophetic dimensions to his living. In a considered article on "The Social Function of the Canonization of Saints," Pierre Delooz asks some important questions. "What kind of sanctity is wholly acceptable? . . . To whom is canonization useful? Certainly not to the person who has been canonized. . . . Canonization serves to reinforce the authority of the one who canonizes."[20] He demonstrates that while for a thousand years in the church it was the "ordinary believers" whose role was decisive in canonization, the process became more and more clericalized and centralized until finally only the central hierarchy of Rome held the power. What was the result of this clericalization? "For some centuries now it has no longer been possible to envisage a canonization without an accompanying pressure-group, having at its own disposal a supply of specialists, time and capital." It turns out that "the ideal lobby" is religious congregations. "It is almost impossible for any layman to be able to meet" today's conditions or have the money necessary to support such a clericalized process. Delooz concludes that "The channels of bureaucracy have made it so difficult for a lay person to be canonized that *the perception of sancity has itself been affected.*"[21] It has become a clerical prerogative to define the very meaning of holiness for us. That is not the creation spirituality way of holiness as cosmic hospitality. (See Theme Nine.) Facts and figures substantiate the clerical hold on sanctity that Delooz is talking about. From the tenth to the twentieth centuries the Catholic Church has canonized 351 men and 75 women (an 82 percent to 18 percent ratio); in the same period it has canonized 332 clergy and 81 laity (an 81 percent to 19 percent ratio). Among the laity canonized only very few were married. The last layperson to be beatified, G. Moscati, who was beatified by Paul VI, was a celibate! I suggest that there is an ideology—a fall/redemption ideology, that cannot deal with the holiness of sexuality, among other things—behind this sad situation. To correct it, Delooz urges "a different model of power. If this new model of power appeared, it would bring with it, I suspect, a different model of saint." Yes, the creation-centered spiritual tradition would surely bring new models of power and of holiness. The *anawim* would be heard from once again as they were in Jesus' and Mary's day.

24 COMPASSION: INTERDEPENDENCE, CELEBRATION, AND THE RECOVERY OF EROS

One thing is sure: man today must be obsessed; if he is, there is still hope. If he is passionate, meaning *com*-passionate, ... there is hope.
　　—Elie Wiesel[1]

Be you compassionate as your Creator is compassionate.
　　—Jesus, in Luke 6.36

The most that we can do for one another
Is let our blunders and our blind mischances
Argue a certain brusque abrupt compassion.
　　—Adrienne Rich[2]

The whole idea of compassion is based on a keen awareness of the interdependence of all these living beings, which are all part of one another and all involved in one another.
　　—Thomas Merton[3]

I am a part and parcel of the whole, and I cannot find God apart from the rest of humanity.
　　—Mahatma Gandhi (22.93)

All things are interdependent.
　　—Meister Eckhart

There is a tendency for living things to join up, establish linkages, live inside each other, return to earlier arrangements, get along, whenever possible. This is a way of the world.
　　—Lewis Thomas[4]

The air, blowing everywhere, serves all creatures.
　　—Hildegarde of Bingen

Whatever God does, the first outburst is always compassion.
　　—Meister Eckhart

To rejoice at another person's joy is like being in heaven.
　　—Meister Eckhart

A true transformation of our culture would require reclaiming
the erotic as power-from-within, as empowerment.
        —*Starhawk (38.138)*

The dichotomy between the spiritual and the political is false,
resulting from an incomplete attention to our erotic knowledge.
For the bridge which connects them is formed by the erotic. . . .
the passions of love in its deepest meanings.
        —*Audre Lorde*[5]

God is voluptuous and delicious.
        —*Meister Eckhart*

The fullness of joy is to behold God in everything.
        —*Julian of Norwich*

Those whom the gods love grow young.
        —*Oscar Wilde*

Come, Love! Sing on! Let me hear you sing this song—sing for
joy and laugh, for I the Creator am truly subject to all creatures.
        —*Mechtild of Magdeburg*

Christianity stripped its world of magic and mystery, and of
the possibility of spiritual renewal through itself. . . . It had
rendered its people alienated sojourners in a spiritually barren
world where the only outlet for the urge to life was the restless
drive onward.
        —*Frederick Turner (41.82)*

Since a love of life may ultimately be all that we have to pit
against our doom, we cannot afford thoughtlessly to tear aside
any of its manifestations.
        —*Jonathan Schell (33.8)*

In a recent edition of *The Oxford English Dictionary* we are told that
the notion that compassion is about a relation among equals is
"obsolete" and that compassion is about superior/inferior relationships.[6] This shocking misdefinition of the single most important
word in Jesus' vocabulary is evidence indeed of the death of God in
our language and therefore our culture. This reduction of compassion to dualistic, philanthropic, sentimental, and indeed sadomasochistic relationships tells us much about our culture at the same time

that it leaves us ignorant about compassion. Since for the Jew—and therefore also for Jesus—compassion is the fullest divine attribute there is, to distort compassion or kill it is truly to distort and kill God. It is also to distort and kill the universe insofar as humanity relates or can relate to it, for Jesus calls on persons to be "compassionate as your Creator is compassionate," and according to Jewish teaching what most characterizes God's compassion is that it extends to "all she has created" and not just to other humans. Our befriending of all the cosmos is our way of compassionately relating to the microcosm that is self and the macrocosms in which self is immersed and to which self gives birth. Jewish prophet that she is, Adrienne Rich, like Jesus, reminds us that the best we can do is to argue a certain compassion, however modest.

But compassion requires equality, not subject/object relationships. Spiritually minded persons must redeem the word "compassion" from our very language. And of course this redemption can come only from understanding compassion and practicing it. The key to understanding compassion is to enter into a consciousness of interdependence which is a consciousness of equality of being. Creation-centered mystics, for whom compassion is the fullest expression of the spiritual journey, insist on interdependence being the basis of all relationships. Hildegarde of Bingen, for example, says that "God has arranged all things in the world in consideration of everything else." And Meister Eckhart says that "one creature sustains another, one enriches the other, and that is why all creatures are interdependent." In a Newtonian era of a billiard-ball universe, these claims by creation mystics would have seemed unbelievable. And, of course, in a theology that can only dwell on the fallenness of creation they appear incredible.

But in a post-Newtonian science and in a post-Augustinian theology the cosmic principle of interdependence is making more and more sense; it is becoming easier and easier to believe. Physicists like Fritjof Capra and Brian Swimme, biologists like René Dubos and Lewis Thomas, ecologists like Jacques Cousteau and Thomas Berry all see interdependence as a basic law of our cosmos. Barry Lopez points out that it was "the inclination of white men to regard individual and social motivations in themselves as separate" that led them to misunderstand the native peoples along with the rest of creation. For the Indian, "Each of the animals—mosquitoes, elk, mice—belonged to a separate tribe. Each had special powers, but each was dependent on the others for certain services." It was

279

precisely that "strong sense of the interdependence among all creatures" that allowed the Indian to "fit into the universe" and derive meaning and value in life. (24.105, 104) Lopez, after living among wolves for some time, concludes that a combination of "social pressure and interdependence" keeps the wolf pack together. Two persons who sit together in the same room are exchanging water vapor within thirty minutes. This is interdependence. To take a deep breath is to breathe in some of the breath that Jesus breathed on the cross, we are assured by scientist Brian Swimme. This is interdependence. Every square mile of soil on our earth contains particles from every other square mile of soil on our earth, says biologist John Storer. This is interdependence. Mystic and scientist alike are urging humanity to a new level of consciousness, a new awareness of the interdependence of all things "which are all involved in one another and all part of one another," as Thomas Merton put it. To wake up to this new scientific knowledge and ancient religious myth would mean to transform and recreate all our institutions and systems: nations, economics, politics, worship, education. It would mean to righten relationships, which is the true meaning of "righteousness" in the scriptures.[7]

How can this happen? Can humanity awaken to interdependence, which is the basic consciousness of compassion? Can this happen swiftly enough so that we do not first destroy creation by our dualisms and nationalisms and our various parochial and parts-mentalities? Meister Eckhart has an answer to this question. He says, "What happens to another, whether it be a joy or a sorrow, happens to me." Jesus had a similar answer when he said, "Whenever you do it to one of these little ones, you do it to me." And poet Angelus Silesius reacted in the same way: "There are no objects for compassion because there are no objects." Adrienne Rich responds similarily when she says, "They are luckiest who know they're not unique." What each of these persons is pointing out is that we live in an illusion of separateness and ego differentiation, but in reality we are already united, already part of one another, especially where our depths or recesses lie. "In our joy and in our sorrow," as Eckhart puts it. What happens there to another happens to me. What happens in the Via Positiva and the Via Negativa and the Via Creativa for another happens *to me*. And Jesus adds, "and to God also." God is in our depths of pleasure and of pain and of birthing the cosmos. But to fully enter into this reality one must let go of ego's ways of relating. One must move from "I" to "we," not by adding anything but by simply letting go.

What is being said is that compassion—interdependence—already is the universe. We do not have to make it anew. Compassion, one might say, is a grace and not a work. This is very good news indeed. Our work comes in entering into this truth and then struggling to rebuild or start anew in building human institutions that themselves relate interdependently and encourage interdependent relationships. When I talk of letting go of ego or letting go of knowing one is unique, as Rich puts it, I am not talking of cutting oneself off from self. In fact, I am talking of befriending the deeper self within us, of befriending our passions, our deepest feelings of ecstacy and of pain. The author of *Proverbs* puts this well when he says, "If a person is mean to herself, to whom will she be good? She does not even enjoy what is her own. No one is meaner than the person who is mean to herself." (Pro. 14:5,6) Jesus understood the same truth when he said: "Love others as you love yourself." We need to love ourselves well, compassionately. We need to befriend the depths or recesses of ourselves, whether these be of pleasure, pain, or birthing. Compassion, then, is not only about waking up to a consciousness of interdependence; it is also about living out interdependence. It is the action born of the truth of cosmic interdependence. And those actions fall into two basic kinds: celebration and justice-making.

To celebrate from deep within our deepest selves is a way of avoiding being mean to oneself. We have a word in our language for passionate celebration, but it has been co-opted of late by the multibillion-dollar pornography industry. I am certain that, as in the case of consumerism and the word "pleasure" (see Theme Two), the reason the pornography industry has priority on the word "erotic" is that our spiritual traditions in the West have lost passion for passion and passion for Eros. Spiritual persons need to redeem the word "erotic" before it is too late. This is what the black feminist poet Audre Lorde does in a brilliant and beautiful article called "Uses of the Erotic: The Erotic as Power."[8] She points out that what distinguishes the erotic from the pornographic is that true love includes feeling and not just sensation. To recover the erotic is to recover feeling. But in a patriarchal society the erotic "becomes misnamed by men" and our economic systems themselves divorce us from feeling because "it defines the good in terms of profit rather than in terms of human need." Human need is about feelings, feelings of our self-worth (royal person); of our cosmic interconnectedness; of our emptiness and pain; of our power to give birth and to be

281

instruments of change and transformation. Lorde points out that a culture cut off from an erotic base "robs our work of its erotic value, its erotic power and life appeal and fulfillment." She sees the erotic as integral to the Via Creativa—which it surely is. "Erotically satisfying experiences" can include, "dancing, building a bookcase, writing a poem, examining an idea." A feminist spirituality as distinct from a patriarchal one will value the erotic and teach us disciplines of erotic celebrating, creating, and justice-making. "When I speak of the erotic, then, I speak of it as an assertion of the life force of women," Lorde comments.

A similar understanding of Eros is given by Ann Ulanov. She defines eros in the following manner:

> The psychic urge to relate, to join, to be in-the-midst-of, to reach out to, to value, to get in touch with, to get involved with concrete feelings, things, and people, rather than to abstract or theorize.[9]

Ulanov agrees with Lorde who says that "the erotic cannot be felt secondhand" when she maintains that "feminism wisdom is personal, never impersonal."[10] Here, as Lorde insists, lies the healing to feelings of powerlessness; here lies authentic empowerment. As a man I have to ask, are we men totally devoid of the erotic? Or do we only act as if we were? Make laws as if we were? Build institutions as if we were? Construct MX missiles and Trident submarines and make "war games" as if we were? Who will redeem us men from our compulsion to control the erotic, to banish it to unhappy bedrooms, to stifle it in boardrooms and classrooms and say that truth comes from "clear and distinct ideas" and footnotes and budgets and price lists—but not from celebration?

The creation-centered spiritual tradition calls women and men alike to celebrate Eros and the erotic Creator of Eros. For the God of this tradition is not an unmoved mover, a perfectly in-control patriarch in the sky. Rather, as we saw in Theme Two and elsewhere, the Creator God is a God who delights, who truly participates, who urges us to develop the art of savoring. Eckhart says that this God, who is "voluptuous and delicious" and the maker of all that is voluptuous and delicious, dances and becomes tickled with joy. This God is a very youthful God, for "when we say God is eternal we mean God is eternally young." Mechtild sings of this same theme, how God is our "divine playmate" who calls out the child in each of us. We read in wisdom literature about the play of God and we have considered the play of God as artist in Theme Nineteen above. Artist, child, and Eros go together—and if our God is artist and child, then ours is truly an erotic God. Does not God the Mother play? What kind of mother would it be who never played with her babies? Does not God the Lover play? What kind of lovers would they be who did not play together? Surely the *Song of Songs* celebrates the holy playfulness of lovers. This erotic and sacred book, because of the sacredness of erotic play, is not compelled to name God even once. Is there a musician who does not play with the piano keys, the notes, the counterpoint, and harmonies? Is there a thinker who does not play with ideas? As the psalmist asks the question, "Does the maker of ears not hear?" so we need to ask the question, does the maker of play not play? Does the maker of Eros not join in the erotic?

Ashley Montagu, in his study on *Growing Young*, reveals an amazing finding in contemporary science: Of all the animal species we know, the human is unique in its capacity to continue play into adulthood. An insect never plays; a chimpanzee plays hard as a youngster but loses play as an adult; an adult can play right up to death . . . and with death. But how human are we? How many of us and how many of our institutions render us insectlike in our lack of letting go, lack of celebration as a value and as an authentic source of truth and truthful relating?

Montagu believes that youthfulness in an older person "is a gift." It is also a work of art, perhaps the work of art that our life is meant to be, as we saw in Path III. "Growing young into what others call 'old age' is an achievement, a work of art."[11] Like any work of art, to grow young takes discipline, time, and attention. Eckhart also talks of how the gift of youthfulness is the first gift of the spirit.[12] Surely Hildegarde is stressing the same basic theme when she encourages one and all to stay green, wet, moist. In fact, Thomas Berry has correctly called Hildegarde's mysticisim an "erotic" mysticism that binds earth to Creator in a luxuriant way.[13] Hildegarde compares the relationship of Creator with creation to that of lover with lover or husband with wife. "The entire world has been embraced by this kiss," she notes.

To recover the erotic is to recover play and the child in ourselves and in all creation, including the Creator. Perhaps the time has come to play with God more than to pray to God, and in our play true prayer will emerge. And we will emerge as younger, fresher, greener. For if we who are God's image can learn to trust the erotic God then this very trust will draw the Eros out of us and into the task of transforming our worlds in a manner patterned after God's playful image. Eckhart's term for play—"to live without a why, to work without a why, to love without a why"—speaks to the heart of erotic celebration. Such a celebration need not be an expensive party or a formalized ritual. More often it is a response to the pathos, tragedy, and joy of the moment. It is nonelitist ritual. An occasion to celebrate our being first of all; and then our joys; and then our suffering. All of it needs to be remembered and let go of and therefore celebrated.

Playfulness is itself a way of resolving deep pain and division. There are Eskimo tribes, for example, who when a war with another tribe is brewing hold a poetry contest between the two best poets of each tribe. The jury is made up of equal numbers of members from each of the tribes. The winning poet wins the war for both sides. Here is an instance of art as healing and of what William James called the "moral equivalent of war." Our so-called defense departments, so creative at building sadistic weaponry, lack imagination when it comes to moral equivalents for war. Richard Sorenson describes how the agricultural people of New Guinea called the Fore deal with aggression in a child "by affectionate playfulness" or by "diversionary playful activity or amusement." Play is meant to be a way out of aggression. But our culture, which does not value playfulness or Eros, has forgotten that, and so we lock ourselves into trillion-dollar military budgets, and imagine we can buy security.[14]

Compassion is about celebration because it is about what people and other creatures do or ought to do with one another when they find themselves together in one common soup. The cosmos can and needs to be imaged as a cosmic womb, a cosmic soup, in which all creatures swim. The cosmos is God's womb, the divine womb. The Jewish word for compassion is derived from the word for womb— compassionate consciousness and womb consciousness go together in all religions' imaging of compassion, both East and West. If it is true that all of us creatures are swimming in one divine soup or womb, then what ought we do with one another? I suggest that we are to relate erotically. That is, celebrate. Play is circular, curved, Sara-circle-like among children, and wherever adult ritual has not lost its celebrative and erotic energy. Where people come together to meet eye to eye, which means with feeling and potential feeling or vulnerability. Interestingly, the Jewish word for celebration, *kagiyaah,* is related to *kag,* to draw a circle or go round; to *kagur,* to be girded; to *kug,* a circle; to *kugah,* a dial. A patriarchal time of linear events and linear thinking was not a celebrative time. Einstein's curved time and curved space invite us into cosmic celebration once again. And so too does all art worthy of the name. Musician Robert Schumann wrote the following to a friend:

> It is precisely from music that philosophers could learn that it is possible to say the profoundest things in the world while preserving the appearance of frivolous youthful levity; for that is just what music does when, pretending to be a playing child with a brimfull heart that it is almost ashamed to reveal to the wise and learned, it mischievously hides behind its tinkling musical figures . . . with wonderful sound-meanings which knock at every human heart with the quiet question 'Do you understand me?'[15]

Of course, while befriending Eros and disciplining ourselves to its development, we need to keep a dialectical attitude about us. There will be times in our love of Eros and for the sake of Eros that we will need to let go of Eros. That emptying will prove in time to be a deep preparation for a fuller celebration, a richer sharing of Eros.

COMPASSION: INTERDEPENDENCE AND EROTIC JUSTICE

Many are called
but most are frozen
in corporate or
collective cold,
these are the stalled
who choose not to be chosen
except to be bought and sold.
                    —Lee Carroll Pieper[1]

In the face of suffering, one has no right to turn away, not to see. In the face of injustice, one may not look the other way. When someone suffers, and it is not you, he comes first. His very suffering gives him priority. . . . To watch over a man who grieves is a more urgent duty than to think of God.
                    —Elie Wiesel[2]

Is not one of the problems of religious life today that we have separated ourselves from the poor and the wounded and the suffering? We have too much time to discuss and to theorize, and we have lost the yearning for God which comes when we are faced with the sufferings of people.
                    Jean Vanier[3]

Compassion means justice. . . . The person who understands what I have to say about justice understands everything I have to say.
                    —Meister Eckhart

All of creation God gives to humankind to use. If this privilege is misused, God's justice permits creation to punish humanity.
                    —Hildegarde of Bingen

God is justice.
                    —Julian of Norwich

If you love the justice of Jesus Christ more than you fear human judgment, then you will seek to do compassion.
—Mechtild of Magdeburg

What does the Lord require of you but to do justice and to love kindness and to walk humbly with your God?
—Mic. 6:8

One of the most disastrous errors in the history of Christianity is to have tried—under the influence of Greek definitions—to differentiate between love and justice.
—José Miranda (26.61)

As a rule it was the pleasure-haters who became unjust.
— W. H. Auden

But a Samaritan on the road was moved with compassion when he saw this victim. He went up to him, bandaged his wounds, pouring oil and wine on them. Then he lifted him up to his own donkey, carried him to the inn and looked after him. . . . Go and do the same yourself.
Luke 10. 33-35, 37.

Awakening to the cosmic/earth/human process whereby all things have a genetic relationship with each other is the most significant intellectual achievement of humankind since the higher civilization came into being some 2500 years ago. Nothing can be itself without being in communion with everything else, nor can anything truly be the other without first acquiring a capacity for interior presence to itself.
— Thomas Berry[4]

It is impossible, I think, taking our nature into consideration, that anyone who fails to realize that he or she is favored by God should have the courage necessary for doing great things.
—St. Teresa of Avila[5]

If the first response to interdependence and to our sharing the common, grace-filled soup of the cosmic womb is to celebrate, the second response is to heal. Wherever dependence reigns instead of interdependence, healing is in order. Wherever independence of an impersonal kind reigns, healing is in order. Since the most basic kind of false dependencies and false independencies are those of injustice, justice-making is the primary kind of healing. Compassion is about both celebration and justice-making. But since both come from the same root depths of a person, they are connected. One reason the West has had as little Via Transformativa as it has is that it has not practiced the Via Positiva deeply enough. People, after all, are changed more by pleasure than by any other means.

If W. H. Auden is correct when he observes that "As a rule it was the pleasure-haters who became unjust," then only a civilization that fosters erotic celebration can usher in a new era of justice-making. Compassion is about justice-making as much as it is about celebration for the very same reason, that "What happens to another, whether it be a joy *or* a sorrow, happens to me." Another's pain is my pain; my pain is others' pain. To relieve another's pain is to relieve one's own, and to relieve the pain of God, who shares in all the pain of the universe. The recovery of the concept of justice came with Enlightenment figures like Voltaire, and we are deeply indebted to him for this contribution. For just as the celebrative side of compassion is a right-brain response to the interconnectedness of our world, so too the justice side of compassion might be understood as a left-brain response to the interconnectedness of our world. But something has been missing in the way patriarchy and the Enlightenment have been defining justice for us. Justice has remained too abstract, too distant, and, ironically, too subjective to move most people. In the name of an abstract justice, communist countries have resorted to moving people by coercion and capitalist countries have resorted to moving people by advertising and consumerism. It is apparent that neither ideology has found justice to be moving in itself.

A prophetic contribution that feminists bring to both Marxist and capitalist efforts to create society is the recovery of Eros. Both giant capitalism and state-run bureaucratic socialism suffer from the same lack of Eros—of nearness, of feeling, of care and intimacy with the unemployed and the employed as well as with earth, waters, air, plants, animals, bodies. If it is true that Eros is in a special way "woman's power," as Lorde puts it, then feminism will furnish a powerful healing to the new civilization we are called to create. For partriarchal philosophies have left Eros out of justice. We need an erotic justice. A justice that moves peoples. How is that possible?

Justice moves us first because injustice moves us. An erotic justice means first of all getting in touch with our feelings about injustice. Do we have such feelings? Do we allow them to be? Do we have feelings toward unemployed people? Toward prisoners who become more violent in a violent prison system? Toward the local grocer whose small business is swallowed up by a multicorporate monster? Injustice is not an abstraction: it is about the draining away of Eros and joy from people's lives. This is how the prophet Isaiah felt it in what can only be described as a cosmic, erotic picture. Isaiah writes:

> The wine is mourning, the vine is pining away,
> all glad hearts are sighing.
> The merry tambourines are silent,
> the sound of revelling is over,
> the merry lyre is silent.
> There is lamentation in the streets: no wine,
> joy is lost,
> gladness is banished from the country.
> Nothing but rubble in the city.... (Isa. 24: 7-9, 11,12)

Lorde assures us that "the erotic cannot be felt secondhand."[6] So too the pained and suffering victims of injustice need to be touched. It is distance that allows the bomber pilot to drop napalm from 42,000 feet and say he got a kick out of seeing villages go up in flames. Nearness, had he been on the ground to see and smell and touch and look into the eyes of the burnt children and old people, would have transformed him. The First World keeps its distance too readily from the Third World: criticisms of "multinational corporations" or of "right-wing dictators" do not transform First World peoples until they talk to victims whose relatives have been tortured or who live in cities with 90 percent (sic) unemployment, or until they walk through the streets of Calcutta over bodies that are lined up side by side begging for alms. Then, transformation begins. This is where prophetic movements today, such as the Center for Global Service and Education at Augsburg College in Minneapolis or the Ministry for Money Center in Washington, D.C., are doing so valuable a work of transformation. In addition to formulating theory about injustice and justice they invite First World persons to participate in an experience of Third World peoples. Life transformations happen, and with them energy and imagination for returning home, simplifying one's own lifestyle, and helping others to do the same. These are movements of erotic education, education in erotic justice. For Eros has the power to wake us up, to see passion happen again, feeling return, hope and transcendence come alive. It makes compassion possible, returning it from what I have called its "lonely exile." Here lie authentic conversions, changes of heart and work and lifestyle, so that one becomes committed to working for social transformation in whatever profession one is involved in. Of course, one does not have to travel to Mexico or to India to experience the Third World. One can live in Harlem or the Bronx, on an Indian reservation or in a feminist drop-in center, at a Catholic Worker house or in a Los Angeles barrio, in an Appalachian mining town or in the city of Detroit. The Third World has in great measure come home to the First World. To admit its existence, to experience it, is to initiate erotic justice. Every parish or synagogue ought to sponsor such a Third-World visit for a few of its parishoners and then listen to their stories and process their meanings on their return. This would be an investment in erotic justice which is compassion.

An erotic justice flows from a panentheistic theology wherein all creation is in God and God is in all creation. For if God truly loves all creation, even erotically loves all creation, so that God in loving creation is loving herself, then when creation is in pain God is in pain and feels that pain. For good reason Starhawk has written that theism in the West has created a cold and abstract kind of justice.

> The conceptions of justice in the Western, patriarchal religions are based on a worldview which locates deity outside the world. Of course, within each tradition there are exceptions, but in the broad view of Christianity, Judaism, and Islam, God is transcendent, and His laws are absolutes. . . .

She calls for a recovery of the sense of an immanent justice based on "the interwoven chain of relationships that link all forms of life." In other words, compassion in a unique contribution of feminist religions.

> The major difference between patriarchal religions and the evolving Goddess religions— . . . is the worldview that includes regarding divinity as immanent: in the world, not outside the world. (37.416f.)

Rabbi Heschel understands justice as awakening to injustice when he defines it as "the active process of remedying or preventing what should arouse the sense of injustice." Though he does not use the word "erotic" in his definition, it is telling that he does talk of "arousal." Justice is aroused by passionate caring. Heschel continues, "What is uppermost in the prophet's mind is not justice 'an ideal relation or static condition or set of perceptual standards' but the presence of oppression and corruption. The urgency of justice urges an urgency of aiding and saving the victims of oppression."[7] Furthermore, if it is true that the prophet's main activity is "interference," as we saw in Theme Twenty-Two above, then is it not a great act of interference in a dualistic and flat and patriarchal culture to announce the Good News that Eros is a blessing far too beautiful to be left to pornographers to peddle? To lead the oppressed and eventually the oppressor into celebration is a mighty interference indeed in a cultural situation where flatness reigns. But Heschel warns that the bearers of justice are not the bearers of glad tidings to everyone equally. The art of letting go must be learned in a new way by those who have more than enough.

"There is enough for everyone's need," Gandhi warned. "But not for everyone's greed." The first reaction to justice as compassion is not necessarily a welcoming one on the part of all persons. Heschel explains why this is so. "The claim of one person to attain justice is contingent upon the assumption that there is another person who has the responsibility to answer it. Justice, then, is an interpersonal relationship, implying both a claim and a responsibility."[8] An erotic justice, however, will employ imagination in addressing the responsibility dimension of justice. Confrontation is usually a shallow and imagination-less approach to justice-making. Eros as love of enemy will inspire the kind of imagination that allows transformation to happen, even transformation of the oppressive systems or guardians of said systems. Here lies the power of Gandhi's nonviolence as a prophetic method for change. Gandhi does not define justice-making as winning/losing but as loving people into transformation; this love includes, for a period, absorbing their hatred. Gandhi's method is erotic, based on what Erik Erikson describes as "seasoned playfulness." Interestingly, Erikson calls for "an enlightened eroticism" which also includes "the enlightened sacrifice of it" as integral to creative nonviolence in the future.[9]

Examples of erotic justice can be found among the creation mystics. This is no surprise since it is evident that Eros, deep feeling, accompanies the prophet in each of the four paths of the creation-centered spiritual journey. Mechtild of Magdeburg, for example, celebrates an erotic justice when she writes about "the play of love" which alone "transforms." She says, "Compassion means that if I see my friend and my enemy in equal need, I shall help both equally." And "Justice demands," she continues, "that we seek and find the stranger, the broken, the prisoner and comfort them and offer them our help." Notices that she emphasizes *seeking out* the pain in our society and not just waiting comfortably for it to pass over our color television tube or to come our way on the golf course. The term "seeking out" is used in erotic biblical wisdom literature, as for example in the *Song of Songs* when a lover seeks out her beloved. It is part of the nonelitist and "street spirituality" we have seen previously that is characteristic of both the prophets and the wisdom writers. St. Hildegarde too presents an erotic justice when she describes the relationship of Creator to creature as one of "lover to lover" or "husband to wife." Injustice for her constitutes a rupture in that relationship.

Eckhart tells us that "In compassion peace and justice kiss." The erotic marriage of peace and justice, of rest and equality, of the pleasure of relationship and the righting of relationship—this is the work of the compassionate person. It is God's work. And our work at it, even when we appear to fail, is itself still one more good reason for celebration. All this passion—passion for pleasure and the sharing of it—all this passion deserves to be celebrated, honored, and then let go of. Eros deserves a home among spiritual people once again.

26 SIN, SALVATION, CHRIST IN THE PERSPECTIVE OF THE VIA TRANSFORMATIVA: A THEOLOGY OF THE HOLY SPIRIT

A radical conversion of the non-poor is needed today."
    —*Maria Augustine Neal*[1]

At Catholic Worker we sought a 'Green Revolution'—a kind of society where it would be easier for people to be good."
    —*Dorothy Day*[2]

Those who say religion has nothing to do with politics do not know what religion means."
    —*Mahatma Gandhi*[3]

A spirituality that preaches resignation under official brutalities, servile acquiescence in frustration and sterility, and total submission to organized injustice is one which has lost interest in holiness and remains concerned only with a spurious notion of 'order.' "
    —*Thomas Merton*[4] *(Bystander*, p. 16)

I say more: the just man justices;
Keeps grace: that keeps all his goings graces;
Acts in God's eyes what in God's eye he is—Christ.
    —*Gerard Manly Hopkins*[5]

It is important to revive and revitalize the biblical meaning of judgment (*krisis*) as that establishment of justice which by necessity means mercy for the wronged and loss for those who have too much.
    —*Krister Stendahl (39.100)*

Justice is a constitutive element of the Gospel.
    —*Synod of Rome, 1971*

Who is the Holy Spirit? The Holy Spirit is a compassionate outpouring of the Creator and the Son.
    —*Mechtild of Magdeburg*

Is not this the sort of fast that pleases me
—it is the Lord Yahweh who speaks—
to break unjust fetters
and undo the thongs of the yoke,

to let the oppressed go free,
and break every yoke,
to share your bread with the hungry,
and shelter the homeless poor. . . .
        —*Isa. 58:6*

Unrolling the scroll, Jesus found the place where it is written:
"He has annointed me to preach the good news to the poor; He
has sent me to proclaim release to the captives; And recovering
of sight to the blind; To set at liberty those who are oppressed,
To proclaim the acceptable year of Yahweh."
        —*Luke 4:17-19*

Jesus was, in his divinely mandated (i.e., promised, anointed,
messianic) prophethood, priesthood, and kingship, the bearer
of a new possibility of human, social, and therefore political
relationships.
        —*John Howard Yoder*[6]

Jesus repeatedly addresses himself to the individual in terms
of re-creation. When he approaches the poor, the oppressed,
and the sinner, he does not simply console them in their plight;
he proposes to re-create their present situation and thus do
"justice" to them. This is the quintessence of Jesus' understanding of the kingdom.
        —*Jon Sobrino (36.120)*

Jesus of Nazareth is the fulfillment and quintessence of the
prophetic tradition."
        —*Walter Brueggemann (5.97)*

Come, you whom my Father has blessed, take for your heritage the kingdom prepared for you since the foundation of the
world. For I was hungry and you gave me food; I was thirsty
and you gave me drink; I was a stranger and you welcomed me.
. . . I tell you in all seriousness, in so far as you did this to one
of the least of these brothers or sisters of mine, you did it to me.
        Matt. 25: 34, 35, 40

Joy was in fact the most characteristic result of all Jesus'
activity amongst the poor and the oppressed.
     —Albert Nolan (27.41)

Hildegarde of Bingen warns that those who lose their juiciness,
wetness, greening power, fall into a "dryness of carelessness."
Carelessness—not caring, apathy, coldness of heart, loss of passion—
all these are deeply sinful. In the Bible it is coldness of heart, not
hate, that is the opposite of love. This is why Dante makes ice and
not fire represent the lowest pit of hell. Not caring, losing all
passion, here lies the way to no compassion and therefore to sin.
The cold heart is the birthplace of the great sin of omission in Path
IV, the omitting of compassion, which is both celebration and justice-
making, from our lives. The Creator God is not without passion,
either for life and celebration or for justice. To settle for a heart that
is indifferent to the sufferings of others is to refuse to imitate the
Creator. This rejection of God in our lives marks the beginning of
cynicism and with it despair. To refuse to use our creativity to
transform with or to settle for superficial uses of our imagination
and artistry—this would be a sin against the fourth path. To refuse
or run from our vocation to be prophetic would also be to "miss the
mark," that is, to sin against the fourth path. To forget or repress
Eros and its powers for bonding and awakening and celebrating is
also to "miss the mark" or to sin.

When one meditates on sin in the light of Path IV, one is awakened
by the fact that sin, after all, is nothing trivial. Injustice is not a
trivial matter. It can build ovens of genocide, it can wipe out whole
races and whole cultures and whole peoples. And it has. Injustice is
not just the lack of justice; it is the use of creativity to lord over
others, to kill, to be sadistic, to refuse to celebrate. Moreover, as we
saw in Path I, injustice is a rupture in the order, harmony, balance,
and survival of the universe itself. The psalmist laments how human sin actually undoes the cosmic order.

Do Justice for the weak and the orphan,
defend the afflicted and the needy.
Rescue the weak and the poor;
set them free from the hand of the wicked.

295

Path IV

Unperceiving, they grope in the darkness
and the order of the world is shaken. (Ps. 82:3-5)

Violence and dualism, the refusal to do compassion and justice, contribute to the very shaking of the world's order and foundations. Behind this sin lies the basis of all sin, the dualism that human, sexual, racial, economic exploitations are all about. No one can live in an isolated, privatized religion or world any longer. Interdependence is too much a reality of every nation today and of all global struggles for growth and peacemaking. Privatized salvations sin against the cosmos itself. They blind us to the levels of ecological justice as well as human justice that we must be about. Hildegarde of Bingen warned us eight centuries ago of the price we would pay for indifference or injustice to the creation. "All of creation God gives to humankind to use. If this privilege is misused, God's justice permits creation to punish humanity." Creation itself will not tolerate indifference or injustice for long; creation-itself will struggle for a balance and harmony even if humankind refuses to do so. The earth, for example, if it is abused by the dumping of too-rich fertilizer, will simply refuse to yield its fruits. Hildegarde warns of the price the human race must pay for such nontrivial sinning. "As often as the elements of the world are violated by ill-treatment, so God will cleanse them through the sufferings and the hardships of humankind." Three Mile Island, Love Canal, acid rain—these are all creation's way of awakening us to the ecological sins caused by greed and insensitivity to creation. To leave justice out of what believers mean by love and to leave New Creation out of the gospel message are sins of omission that are laid bare in Path IV.

To leave justice out of our meaning of love is itself a sin of omission; so too is leaving out the preaching of the New Creation that believers are to bring about, a sin of omission; so too is the failure to live lives of transformation and of being transformed—or indeed of being "reborn" only once instead of many, many times. And, since every theme in the creation-centered tradition has deep social and personal implications, to leave these themes out of our theology constitutes a real sin of omission. Themes like earthiness, for example; or creativity; or divinization; or cosmos; or original blessing—it is very likely that the reason religion has been so loudly silent on these deep and ancient theological themes is that the Via Transformativa has not always been welcomed by political and religious powers-that-be.

What light does the Via Transformativa shed on the topic of salvation? According to biblical scholar Helen Kenik, the New Creation represents a New Exodus, a new liberation event, a new salvation experience for God's people. This is proclaimed in Isaiah, chapters 51 and 52. In those chapters we read of the creation themes of cosmos and justice, of royal person, and of the end of lament and the birth of "everlasting joy" that comes with the advent of peace and justice. As one scholar has put it, Second Isaiah "links creation and redemption so closely together that one is involved in the other. Yahweh's creative acts belong to the history of salvation. . . . His redemptive acts are acts of creation; and his creative acts are acts of history."[7] Yahwah the Creator is also the Deliverer.

> Send justice like dew, you heavens,
> let the clouds rain it down.
> Let the earth open up
> so salvation will spring up,
> Let deliverance too bud forth
> which I, Yahweh, shall create. (Isa. 45:8)

Yahweh, the author of the first creation, is author too of this second or new creation. Understandably, because justice and creation are so intertwined (see Theme Four), so too are justice and the righting of creation, that salvation and liberation of creation. The God of justice is the God of salvation.

> Was it not I, the Lord?
> There is no god but me,
> a God of justice, a saviour.
> There is no one but me. (Isa. 45:21)

Just as injustice is the basic rupture of creation and the basic sin against creation, so justice is salvation. Justice will bring blessing and fruitfulness once again.

> Faithfulness will spring from the earth
> and justice look down from heaven.
>
> The Lord will make us prosper
> and our earth will yield its fruit. (Ps. 85:11, 12)

What the Via Transformativa makes abundantly clear is the biblical teaching that in fact there is no such thing as privatized or individualized salvation. The prophets of yesterday and today find it necessary to constantly remind God's people of this fact. Mahatma Gandhi, Dorothy Day, Martin Luther King, Jr., all had to fight this battle with religious people who had mistakenly understood salvation as personalized righteousness. King speaks, for example, of his efforts to educate the black ministers of Birmingham in the civil rights movement.

> I stressed the need for a social gospel to supplement the gospel of individual salvation. I suggested that only a "dry as dust" religion prompts a minister to extol the glories of heaven while ignoring the social conditions that cause men an earthly hell.... I asked how the Negro would ever gain his freedom without the guidance, support and inspiration of his spiritual leaders.[8]

Because Gandhi was creation-centered and believed in cosmos and how "nature and society are both subject to a single law of justice and unity," he resisted the distinction between secular and profane politics that Augustine taught. Gandhi complained that Augustine's distinction meant that "the political order could never be elevated, but could only be endured." (22.252, 46) Gandhi, like King, Day, and Jesus, believed we are here to transform the social order and not merely to endure it in a passive or cynical way. The spirit of transformation, which is bigger than all of us, works through us to righten human and social relationships. We become vehicles of divine salvation. It is interesting that just as King and Day had to struggle with the tendency to privatize salvation in Christianity, so too Gandhi had to struggle with this same temptation in Hinduism. "The problem in India, as Gandhi saw it, was to adapt the older notions of *moksha* and *tapas*—the pursuit of individual salvation through specific austerities and prolonged contemplation—to the practical needs of a society in which men were more concerned to escape than to alter the conditions of worldly life." (22.234f.)

Christian biblical scholars have also had to fight this very same fight. "Righteousness and justice," says Krister Stendahl, "are the one and only justitia." (39.101) For too long in the West our Bibles have translated "justitia" as "righteousness" or as "justification" and missed the meaning of salvation in Christ. As John Yoder puts it, "justification" in Paul's letters to the Galatians and the Ephesians means "making peace" or "breaking down the wall" between peoples. This conjures up the Pentecost event, the work of the Holy Spirit in breaking through the Babel of confusions and dualisms among persons. Biblical scholar Markus Barth writes, "Justification in Christ is thus not an individual miracle happening to this person or that person, which each may seek or possess for himself. Rather justification by grace is a joining together of this person and that person, of the near and far; . . . it is a social event."9 Stendahl, like many other scholars, sees Augustine as the one who began the Western preoccupation with individualized salvation. Augustine "turned in on himself, infatuated and absorbed by the question not of when God will send deliverance in the history of salvation, but how God is working in the innermost individual soul." (39.17) Path IV invites all persons to recover their role as instruments of the New Creation, agents of justice and transformation in a salvific history of renewal and rebirth of justice and compassion. This is good news to us all. But it is also a Great Reminding of our immense responsibility for the universe. Never has this fact been more vivid than in our time when "salvation from extinction by nuclear weapons," to use Schell's phrase, is demanded. (33.197) Only humans—whose creativity made nuclear weapons—can incite the same and even greater creativity to dismantle them and put an end to war itself. Such a passage of humanity from immature warring to mature settling of differences would constitute a profound salvation indeed.

Other insights on salvation in light of Path IV include the salvation and healing that Eros brings. When Jung says that a "greater and stronger life urge" is what moves people to a new level of consciousness so that their problems are seen differently and thereby become healed, he is speaking of salvation, salvation by way of celebration, by way of Eros. This way lies empowerment, as Starhawk insists, for this way lies the unleashing of power from within that is meant to be a power for transformation of self and others. The Via Transformativa reminds all people that they are already empowered to be instruments of transformation. This is evident in our experiences of Eros and celebration as much as in other forms of healing.

Eckhart says that compassion brings salvation, and one reason for this is that salvation always involves in some manner a return to our origins. But since our origins were always compassion—this is the origin of the earth and the origin of our birth—to make contact with compassion is to make contact with our deepest past. This is salvific; it heals; it unites; it energizes and empowers one to make the future present as deeply as the past is present. It therefore brings about salvation by opening up a compassionate future.

To unleash the prophet who is present in the recesses of every individual existence is to unleash the spirit's work of New Creation, of new possibilities for letting go and birthing, for being transformed and for transforming. In a culture that has lost its sense of Eros and celebration, the true prophets will come celebrating. Celebrating sensuality and earthiness, passion and compassion, failures and imperfections, space, time, being, foolishness, our capacity to laugh, let go, and be young again. Play itself becomes a salvific act, an essential ingredient in the creativity that alone gives birth to deep transformation. The healing of child and adult is no less significant a salvific healing than is the healing of rich and poor, of black and white, of men and women, of Third World and First World.

If Jesus is truly a son of God then he is a son of the Compassionate One, and all his life and work and death and teachings find their culmination in the Via Transformativa. We shall touch on certain of these aspects of Christ in light of Path IV here. First, it should be pointed out that Jesus' birth comes about not through an ordinary father but through the Holy Spirit. This makes his birth a cosmic event, as was the original birth of creation. This makes Jesus not only a prophet of the New Creation but the New Creation itself. As New Testament scholar Raymond Brown puts it, "Mary is a virgin who has not known man, and therefore the child is totally God's work —a new creation."[10] This spirit that begot Jesus resembles "the Spirit of God that hovered over the waters before creation" in Genesis 1:2. The earth was void and without form when that Spirit appeared; just so Mary's womb was a void until through the Spirit God filled it with a child who was His Son." Furthermore, Mary and the rest of us are surprised by this event—with Jesus there is "the surprise of creation."[11] Not only does a new creation begin with the birth of Jesus, but at the end of his life Jesus sends the spirit of new creation on to others. "He breathed on them and said: 'Receive the Holy Spirit.'" (John 20:22) This is the spirit who will make all things anew.

Jesus, who is a new creation, calls all persons to reconciliation with themselves, with one another, and with creation. The first of these, reconciliation with oneself, authentic self-love, must not be underestimated. Jesus taught people to love themselves, forgive themselves, recognize the divine beauty and royal personhood in themselves. This is where learning to love God begins, as psychologist Otto Rank testifies: "Being loved by God, manifesting itself as love for God, can only be experienced on the basis of self-acceptance." (29.191) Jesus frees people from self-hatred and from masochism. He frees them to feel compassion toward themselves. Thus, he frees us from pessimism, which, as Rank indicates, is the basis for sadism.

Self-hatred is the basis for hating others or the world at large. For self-hatred, being really unbearable, is easily justified by making the others and the world bad so they can become the object of hatred instead of the own self. Thus, pessimism may be called the philosophy of hatred, or, as Nietzsche termed it more subtly, of "ressentiment." (29.191)

By inviting people to "love others as they love themselves," Jesus includes both the imperative of compassion toward self and that of compassion toward others. The death of Jesus on the cross was meant to be the last instance of human violence toward the beauty of creation and toward justice-making, compassionate persons. "In his own person Jesus killed the hostility" or the dualism that makes one group of persons chew up another group, Paul writes. He elaborates:

Now in Christ Jesus, you that used to be so far apart from us have been brought very close, by the blood of Christ. For he is the peace between us, and has made the two into one and broken down the barrier which used to keep them apart, actually destroying in his own person the hostility caused by the rules and decrees of the Law. This was to create one single New Man in himself out of the two of them and by restoring peace through the cross, to unite them both in a single Body and reconcile them with God. (Eph. 2:13-17)

While Paul is writing here specifically of the healing that Christ brings to the conflict between Jew and Gentile, the reconciliation of Christ and the spirit of Christ applies to *all* groups, men and women, slave and free, Greek and Jew, and to the cosmos itself, as Paul makes clear in his letters to Galatians and the Romans.

In the introduction to this section we saw Jesus' first public act in Luke's Gospel to be a reading of the prophet Isaiah's proclamation in the synagogue. Here he applies the prophetic vocation to himself, announcing that he would indeed "preach the good news to the poor" because he was anointed by God to do so. Jesus explicitly calls himself a prophet in this instance when consternation was aroused among the people who heard him. "I tell you most solemnly, no prophet is ever accepted in his own country." (Luke 4:24) Jesus is a prophet. As Walter Brueggeman puts it: "Jesus of Nazareth is the fulfillment and quintessence of the prophetic tradition. He brought to public expression the newness given by God. The response to his work and person is amazement. . . . that amazement gave energy, the only kind of energy which gives newness." (5.97) Jesus the prophet arouses others to be prophetic and tells his disciples that they too will be prophetic and will undergo the trials of the prophets. (Matt. 5:11,12) Jesus had to let go of much in order to be prophetic. As Albert Nolan points out, he was not from a disadvantaged class but was himself of the middle class. "He became an outcast *by choice.*" And why did he do so? Compassion is the reason why. "He was moved with compassion for the crowds and he healed their sick. (Matt. 14:14) He was moved with compassion because they were distressed and dejected like sheep without a shepherd. (Matt. 9:36)"[12] Jesus, the compassionate one, was a passionate one as well. The verb used so often in the New Testament for Jesus' compassion means literally, "his bowels turned over." Jesus was in touch with his guts, his feelings, his passion; he had passion-with, that is a compassion with others. When Otto Rank talks about the "new type of personality" that Jesus inaugurated, this is what was new: Jesus calls all persons to be compassionate prophets, transformers of society and of pain and suffering. The spirit of Christ whom Christ promised to send after leaving this life is the Holy Spirit of New Creation and compassion. This spirit cuts through babbling tongues of discord and disharmony to make all peoples sit up and take notice of the goodness of their own creation and of others'. Jesus who is prophet sends the spirit of prophecy on all who will receive it.

In Luke, chapter 4, Jesus says he was anointed "to proclaim the acceptable year of Yahweh." The jubilee year was to be a time for the Jews of political and economic reconciliation, when debts would be erased and "economic life would start over from scratch."[13] According to Deutero-Isaiah, it was a sign of renewal and recreation (chapter 61). But Jesus dares to announce such a jubilee in his very own town—no wonder he was driven out as prophets so often are. A jubilee year is a kind of exodus,[14] so Jesus was a new Moses leading his people away from slavery. Jesus' teaching elsewhere takes up this very same theme of proclaiming a jubilee year. The Lord's Prayer, the Sermon on the Mount, his parables of the merciless servant and the unfaithful steward all point to the same Good News for the oppressed.[15] But it is Good News for all, not for just a private individual. It is about the transformation of society. This insistence on social transformation and on how he and others were to be instruments for compassion and justice actually brought about Jesus' death. The cross was a political event, the result of too much Good News, too much insistence on the human capacity for compassion and justice. The cross, says Yoder, represents "the punishment of a man who threatens society by creating a new kind of community leading a radically new kind of life." Those who follow Christ, trusting in their prophetic vocations as he did in his, will very likely be treated in a similar fashion. "As they persecuted me, they will persecute you." (John 15:21) Followers after Christ not only learn from him but "also share his destiny."[16] The cross is the price one pays for prophecy. But from it too surprises and new birth and new sendings of the spirit can occur.

Jesus Christ, agent of the New Creation, is intimately involved with Eros. He tells people to pray to God in the most intimate of fashions, with the word "Abba," loving parent, as a child communicates with his or her parent. His relationship to the poor is not one of bureaucrat or distanced person but one of touch, of smelling, of dining together, of walking together. Nor were the rich expelled in a dualistic fashion from Jesus' company. His Eros is manifest in his love of life, of people, of nature, of guesting, of hosting. When wine ran low at a wedding feast he did something about it. When the multitude was going hungry he was concerned and he got everyone to share their food. He taught people to let their fears go so that they could truly relate erotically to the blessings of self, others, and existence. He did not counsel force or fear but love of life in all its dimensions. One might say that Jesus came to reveal the Eros of God, the intimacy God shares with creation and especially with the *anawim* of creation. How else could Jesus say that to feed the hungry is to feed the Creator? (Matt. 25) Otto Rank points out that Eros is what made the spirit of Christ so powerful to human history. Ideas, preaching are not enough. "Ideas in themselves are powerless unless they are carried by the life-force of Eros into dynamically powerful ideologies."[7] Jesus' preaching was charged with Eros, he sent people away murmuring, complaining, angry, excited, ecstatic, deeply moved. But after his death it was Paul who would, according to Rank, carry on the Eros of Jesus. "When Paul, inspired by the teaching and experience of Jesus, professed 'the law of love' as an active life-force," then human history was changed. (29.174) What teaching method is more erotic and less abstract than that of parable-telling that we saw Jesus invent in Path III? What is more erotic than the imagery of the vine, promising not only a new people, but a people intimately bearing the divine life in itself as a vine does its sap? (John 15) All the signs that Jesus performs in John's Gospel—that of making wine abundant at the Cana wedding feast, the multiplication of loaves, the raising of Lazarus from the dead, the curing of the blind man, and so on—have to do with increasing Eros in people's lives. Eros implies abundance of life, and that is what Jesus is said to bring. "I come that they may have life and have it in abundance." (John 10.10)

Perhaps Jesus' erotic imagination was nowhere more evident than in his last meal with his disciples, when he insisted that his body and blood be eaten and drunk. Like wisdom in the Hebrew Bible, Jesus prepares a banquet for people, inviting them to eat of his bread and drink of his wine. (Pro. 9:5; Isa. 55:1-3; Sir. 15:3)[17] Jesus did not want to leave the presence of his friends, whether of this lifetime or in the future. He wanted to be-with-them, Emmanuel, God-with-us. And to carry on this memory of earthy and divine presence he left his body and blood to eat and drink. To grasp his action presumes a belief or trust in the visibility of transformation, the transformation of bread and wine into body and blood to eat and drink. He left his gift in the context of memory: "Do this in memory of me," he said. For the Jew memory is a healing, a redemptive and salvific thing. Jewish memory and Jewish history go hand in hand; redemption comes from memory. Jewish scholar Yosef Yerushalmi writes about the Passover meal:

> However dimly perceived, in the end it is nothing less than the Jewish experience and conception of history that are celebrated here. . . . For Passover is preeminently the great historical festival of the Jewish people, and the Haggadah is its book of remembrance and redemption. Here the memory of the nation is annually renewed and replenished, and the collective hope sustained.[18]

Since *zakhor*, the Hebrew word for "remember," means more than just remembering—it means to act—Jesus is also telling us to act in his name, to re-enact the compassion of his life that alone leads to healing and salvation.

A particular work of transformation that Jesus undertook was the task of transforming religion itself. He was not pleased with the way things were going in the religion of his time. He did not approve of the privileges of its leaders and the insensitivity to the poor that certain religious leaders and structures exhibited. One might say he did not like the theologies of his time which were too abstracted, too lacking in erotic care and relationship, too uncritical of injustice, too uncaring toward the dispossessed. In this regard he challenges us to be transformers not merely of social structures but surely of religious ones as well.

This entire book and its journey into creation-centered spirituality also leads to a letting go of certain forms of religion, those based on fall/redemption theologies, structures, and spiritualities. It is about a call to transformation. Religion can and must let go of a dualistic tradition and be transformed into that tradition which is more ancient, more celebrative, more justice-oriented, and more like the tradition Jesus himself lived and preached. Here truly there would happen a New Pentecost, a New Creation, a spiritual awakening that all the world's peoples and all the world's religions might share in. Such a transformation would inspire new ways to read—and translate—the scriptures; new mystics to read and celebrate; new ways to invigorate old doctrines, including those of sin, salvation, and Christ. New ways of seeing spiritual direction, vows, lifestyles, sexuality, economics, work, politics, art, worship, ritual. New ways that are in fact more ancient ways in most instances. The world does not have a lot of leisure time to wait to see this transformation happen. Yet the good news is that it is already happening. It is happening all around us, in and out of church structures, wherever people are responding to the call of the spirit to compassionate living, to simpler lifestyles and the letting go of surplus things. And Jesus, through whom it also happened, is with us still.

Gandhi complained of a "Christianity without Christ." To recover the four paths and the twenty-six themes treated in this book would be to recover a spiritual tradition that Jesus himself lived and would be at home in. It would be a basic step in living the Good News that Jesus lived and died for. It would inaugurate a truly ecumenical era in which global problems might be addressed from the wisdom of global religions and from all four stages of humanity's development. For we all share creation in common. And we all share responsibility for that creation. Therefore, we are all called to re-create. And I can think of no better place to begin this re-creation than with religion itself.

APPENDIX A: TOWARD A FAMILY TREE
OF CREATION-CENTERED SPIRITUALITY

I entitle this section "toward" because this list is by no means full or complete. Much more research needs to proceed, and people listed here, as well as those who are not, are well worth the research of others. Nevertheless, this succinct summary of personages who have lived out or taught the creation-centered tradition demonstrates that there is indeed such a tradition in the West. Beginning with Jesus and extending to the nineteenth century, I have devised a code of stars which indicates that there is a spectrum of fullness in teaching and living out creation-centered spirituality to a greater or lesser degree.

1. The Hebrew Bible. Included as primary data for creation theology would be the work of the Yahwist (J) author, including: Genesis 2:4b-13, 15-16, 21-22, 24-33, 36-50; Exodus 1-14, 16-20, 33-34; Numbers 10-11, 13-14, 16, 20-25, 32; Deuteronomy 31, 34. Also, the Psalms. Wisdom literature including Proverbs, Sirach, Job 28, Esther, Ruth, Ecclesiastes, the Book of Wisdom. The prophets. In the historical books, patriarchs like Abraham, Isaac, Joseph, David were all considered "royal persons."

2. The New Testament. Jesus' parables and especially those of the kingdom/queendom of God as found in all the gospels. The infancy narratives of Matthew and Luke. John 1. A significant amount of Paul including Romans 8; New Creation and cosmic Christ motifs of Colossians, Ephesians, Galatians, Philippians. All references to Christ as wisdom or wisdom in Christ's life. References to prophetic and compassionate ministry of Jesus. In short, the entire Bible, Hebrew Bible and New Testament, ought to be reread with the four paths and twenty-six themes of creation spirituality posing the questions.

3. Jesus Christ.★★★★★

4. St. Irenaeus, Bishop of Lyons (c. 130-200). ★★★½ An important link between East and West, notable for his fight against the Gnostic put-down of matter and for his lavish use of the Hebrew Bible. Stresses Jesus' humanity. He said, "The glory of God is the glory of people fully alive."

307

5. St. Ephraim (306-373). ★★★The basic theologian of the Maronite Church, he was a biblical exegete from Syria. He comments on the scriptures in poetry. He opposed the dualist and anti-semite Marcion.

6. Cassian (c. 360-420). ★★½ From the East, he settled as a monk in Marseilles. He attacked St. Augustine's extreme views on predestination. An important influence on St. Benedict; his two most important books are *The Conferences* and *The Institutes*. He has been called the founder of Semipelagianism and is considered a saint in the Eastern church, though never canonized in the West.

7. St. Benedict (c. 480-550). ★★★The principal architect of Western monasticism, Benedict drew his theology more from Cassian and the East than from Augustine, even though he lived one hundred years after him and in the same territory for a while. He was not ordained, and his theology is steeped in the psalms and wisdom literature.

8. Scotus Erigenus (John the Scot) (810-877). ★★★An Irishman, he taught on the continent at Laon. He could read Greek and was a link with the East. He was the first to translate Pseudo-Denys for the West and tried to reconcile the Neoplatonic idea of emanation with the Christian idea of creation in his greatest work, *On The Division of Nature* or *Periphyseon*. He represents the Celtic love of God in nature and nature in God. He was condemned in 1210 and in 1225.

9. Simeon the New Theologian (949-1022). ★★★The greatest of Byzantine mystical writers, he was called "the brother-loving poor man" and "the Francis of Assisi of the East." Controversial in his day, he was exiled from his monastery in Constantinople when he was abbot.

10. Hildegarde of Bingen (1098-1179). ★★★★An extraordinary renaissance woman, who was a doctor, a pharmacist, a playwright, a poet, a painter, a musician, a mystic, a prophetess attacking church corruption, and an abbess of a dual (male/female) monastery. She is the grandmother of the Rhineland mystics. We possess much of her poetry, music, painting, and writing. She is amazingly ecological in her world view, which is based on a micro/macrocosmic psychology.

11. St. Dominic (1170-1221). ★★★He responded to the cultural crisis of the breakdown of a land and feudal economy and the break-

down of monastic education and religious preaching, by founding a movement to reach the new populations that were swarming into city life and into the new phenomenon of universities.

12.   Francis of Assisi (1181-1225). ★★★★With deep reverence for all of life, a true panentheist, Francis sought to rectify church corruption with a movement of friars who would espouse Lady Poverty. He was strongly influenced by Celtic spirituality and no little bit by Sufism. Unfortunately his earliest hagiographers, Celano and Bonaventure, were not nearly as creation-centered as he, and in their zeal to get him canonized quickly, they introduced dualism and sentimentalism that does not do Francis justice.

13.   St. Clare (1194-1253). ★★½ We do not know a lot about her writings or her spirituality, but since she was Francis's close friend and confidante and as abbess of the first women's Franciscan community, it is difficult to imagine that she would not have shared a basic creation spirituality with Francis.

14.   Mechtild of Magdeburg (1210-1280). ★★★½ A Beguine most of her life, she was an unmarried laywoman who consistently attacked church corruption and was just as consistently driven from town to town for her efforts. She kept a journal/book through her adult life, which she published with the encouragement of her Dominican spiritual directors, entitled *The Flowing Light of the Godhead.* Her images in this book are amazing, and they influenced Meister Eckhart deeply, and most likely Dante as well. She became a third order Dominican and ended her years as a nun at Helfta after the Beguines were condemned and condemned again.

15.   St. Thomas Aquinas (1225-1274). ★★★½ G. K. Chesterton writes that Aquinas "saved us from Spirituality, a dreadful doom," meaning from the dualistic fear of body generated by Augustinian and Neoplatonic spirituality. Aquinas sought a rapprochement with the best science of his day, namely that of Aristotle. This effort at love of creation and study of it was a controversial undertaking, as is indicated by the three condemnations that preceded his canonization in 1323. His was a major effort to move Christianity beyond Augustinian and Neoplatonic dualisms as they had developed in the West. Nowhere was he less successful than in his treatment of women (calling them "misbegotten males" à la Aristotle). Yet, *contra* Augustine, he says women as well as men are made in God's image and likeness.

16. Meister Eckhart (1260-1329). ★★★★The most profound and biblical creation-centered theologian of the West, he was strongly influenced by the Beguines (including Mechtild of Magdeburg); the Celts, who settled all along the Rhine and so influenced Francis; Eastern theology; and above all the creation scriptures of wisdom literature and the prophets. He was condemned following his death, scholars agree unjustly, probably because of his backing of the women's liberation movement (the Beguines) and the peasant movements of his day. A great intellectual as well as a greatly compassionate and involved preacher, he is better known by Buddhists and Sufis and Hindus today than by Christians.

17. Dante (1265-1321). ★★★Poet and philosopher, very much involved in the politics of his day, which led to at least two expulsions from his home town, Florence. His *Divine Comedy*, narrating spiral journeys of spirituality to hell, purgatory, and heaven, ranks as one of the great works of poetry of all time. He was deeply influenced by Aquinas and probably by Mechtild.

18. St. Catherine of Siena (1347-1380) ★★½ A Dominican tertiary who was very active with the sick and poor, she also helped persuade the pope at Avignon to return to Rome. Her letters and her book, *Dialogue*, reveal a well-developed sense of panentheism and of justice along with a certain harshness and antisemitism more characteristic of fall/redemption theology.

19. Geoffrey Chaucer (1343-1400). ★★★½ An English poet and one of the founders of the English language. His *Canterbury Tales* reveal an earthy, sensuous, and spiritual man who is fully capable of criticizing church institutions with the truth but also of praising the "poor parson of a Town" for his compassion. Like Dante, he was a layman.

20. Anonymous Author of *Theologica Germanica* (c. 1340). ★★★ This work is a significant link between Eckhart and Luther, between the Rhineland mystics and early Protestantism. The book is deeply imbued with Eckhartian theology, so much so that Luther, who wrote the preface for the very first printed edition, attributed it to Eckhart's disciple, John Tauler.

21. Julian of Norwich (1342-1415). ★★★½ She was an anchoress attached to St. Julian's church, where she wrote her one book in two versions called *The Sixteen Revelations of Divine Love*. It is a

profoundly creation-centered book, earthy and panentheistic, and very deeply influenced by Meister Eckhart's theology. She is rightly famous for articulating in considerable detail the motherhood of God and even the motherhood of Christ. In spite of her living immediately following the Black Death and during very troubled times, she maintains a hope and joy that are remarkable for their sanity and groundedness. She truly develops a metaphysics of goodness, declaring that "goodness is God."

22. Hans Denck (c. 1495-1527) and Sebastian Franck (c. 1499-1542). ★★½ These radical Protestant reformers develop a word-of-God theology that is based on Dabhar, God's creative energy found in every creature, and not on words. Explicitly hostile to academia's efforts to corral scripture into language courses, they were sensitive to how the illiterate and the poor classes were being excluded from a word-oriented theology. Social critics and reformers, they were indebted to Eckhart's kind of prophetic and creation-centered theology.

23. Nicholas of Cusa (1401-1464). ★★★½ A mathemetician and skilled diplomat, Cusa worked for reconciliation of the Greek church and the Hussites with Rome. A true ecumenist and a brilliant thinker, he was part of the circle of influence around Leonardo da Vinci. He knew Eckhart very well, and though accused of panetheism he successfully defended himself and in fact was a cardinal in the Catholic Church. It has been said that the cosmological theories he presented were the same as those for which Bruno was killed and Galileo was hounded one century later.

24. Erasmus (1469-1536). ★★★ The most renowned scholar of his time, he translated the Greek New Testament into Latin, was a friend of Thomas More and a critic of corruption in the Catholic Church. He remained a Catholic scholar who deeply believed in the power of the intellectual life in the spiritual formation of the Christian.

25. St. Thomas More (1478-1535). ★★★ Lord Chancellor of England who was beheaded by Henry VIII for refusing to support his divorce and to take the oath of supremacy. His home was a center for intellectual life. His best known work was *Utopia*.

26. Teresa of Avila (1515-1591). ★★★ An indefatigable reformer of religious life in the Carmelite Order, she combined deep prayer with busy administrative duties and boldly faced constant political opposition. She was a fine psychologist of the interior life and she

counseled the need for joy, moderation, humanity, and self-knowledge as well as compassion as the test of one's mystical life.

27. St. John of the Cross (1542-1591). ★★★Poet, woodcarver, lover of nature, painter, he has often been misinterpreted in ascetic and fall/redemption categories. In fact, he was not unaware of the creation tradition as Meister Eckhart knew it, and his treatment of the Via Negativa, with themes of the divinization of humanity and the birth of God as child.

28. Giordiano Bruno (1548-1600). ★★★He struggled to relate the new scientific findings of the cosmos to his faith. Early in his career he was pantheistic, but later he altered his views. He believed in what Copernicus was doing and was eventually burned at the stake for his beliefs.

29. Galileo Galilei (1564-1642). ★★★A lay scientist, he invented the hydrostatic balance and discovered the laws of dynamics and the four satellites around Jupiter. His use of a telescope opened up modern astronomy. He was condemned for supporting Copernicus' theory of the universe as opposed to Ptolomy's. Though he was forced to recant under threat of torture and more imprisonment, his work far outlasts that of his inquisitors. He trusted the human mind to explore, invent, criticize, and let go of past images. And he trusted his own.

30. Pierre de Berulle (1575-1629), St. Vincent de Paul (1580-1660), St. Louise de Marillac (1591-1660). Following the Incarnational theology and spirituality Berulle provided, Vincent and Louise dedicated themselves to compassion as action in relieving pain of war victims, galley prisoners, the sick and the poor. Vincent and Louise founded the first congregation of women without enclosure dedicated to caring for the *anawim*.

31. Roger Williams (1604-1683). ★★★A champion of religious tolerance in the New World, he not only befriended the Native Americans but actually learned the language of the Narragansett nation and lived with them when the state of Massachusetts ostracized him because of his views on religious freedom.

32. Angelus Silesius (1624-1677). ★★★A deeply Eckhartian poet, he was a son of a Polish Lutheran nobleman and became a Catholic and a priest. His greatest work is *The Cherubic Wanderer*.

33. George Fox (1624-1677). ★★★½ Founder of the Society of Friends. His spirituality is very akin to Eckhart's in its respect for the divine spark and image in each person and for drawing the hard social consequences of such doctrine. He was a talented organizer and endured with grace the persecution that most prophets undergo. His *Journal* was published after his death.

34. Thomas Traherne (1636-1674). ★★★½ Anglican poet who wrote *Centuries of Meditations*, which is a deeply panentheistic celebration of the glory of nature. This work was not published until 1908, however.

35. John Woolman (1720-1772). ★★★An American Quaker and preacher from New Jersey, he spent his life fighting for black rights and the end of slavery. His best-known work is his *Journal*.

36. Musicians such as: Lassus (Renaissance), Bach, Schubert, Mozart, Beethoven, Mahler, Wagner, Chopin, Bruckner, Ravel, Sibelius, Stravinsky, Dvorak, Schumann, Delius, Shostakovich, Jamacek, Casals, Tippet, Bernstein.

37. Painters such as: da Vinci, Michelangelo, Watteau, Monet, Cézanne, Turner, Renoir, Goya, Matisse, Chagall, Picasso, Miró.

38. Poets such as: Shakespeare, Coleridge, Wordsworth, Holderin, Novalis, Goethe, Blake, Hopkins, Dickinson, Whitman, Rilke, Yeats, D. H. Lawrence, Levertov, Vallejo, Neruda, Rich, Bly.

39. Writers such as: Swift, Dickens, Tolstoy, Dostoyevski, Synge, James, Joyce, Potok, MacDonald, Nin, Chesterton, Kazantzakis.

40. Ecologists such as: Rachel Carson, John Muir, Annie Dillard, René Dubos, Jacques Cousteau, Lewis Thomas, Wendell Berry, Thomas Berry, Loren Eiseley.

41. Other artists such as: Graham (dance), Weston and Curtiss (photography), Rodin (sculpture), Kahn (architecture).

42. Prophets of social change such as: Lucretia Mott, Sojourner Truth, Jane Addams, Elizabeth Cady Stanton, Emma Goldman, Martin Luther King, Jr., Peter Maurin, Dorothy Day, Daniel Berrigan, Mahatma Gandhi, Thoreau, Dom Helda Camera, Rabbi Heschel, Elie Wiesel, John XXIII, Dick Gregory, Dag Hammarskjöld, Jean Vanier, Ernesto Cardenale.

43. Philosophers/Scientists such as: Whitehead, Einstein, Teilhard de Chardin, Buckminster Fuller, Capra, Swimme, Zukav.

44. Theologians such as: Schweitzer, Blondel, Berdyaev, M. D. Chenu, Tresmontant, Marcel, the late Merton, Von Rad, Ruether, Kenik, Vann, Westermann, Stendahl, Roland Murphy, Brueggemann, Haughton, Robert Brown, Motz, Schillebeeckx, Punnikan, Nathan Jones.

45. Feminists such as: Griffin, Spretnak, Daly, Christ, Harrison, Starhawk, Lorde.

46. Psychologists such as: Freud, Jung, Rank, Adler, Horney, Erikson, Maslow, Norman O. Brown, May, Fowler.

47. Liberation Theologians such as: Gutiérrez, Miranda, Sobrino, Friere, Eugenio von Balthazar, Segunder, Nolan, Cornel West.

48. New Age Mystics such as: David Spangler, Jean Houston, Marilyn Ferguson.

49. Non-Christian spiritual traditions such as: Taoist; Kabir (Hindu/ Sufi); Native American; Wikke; African; Zen; Celtic; Hasidic.

Some Reflections on the Family Tree

In examining in this cursory but representative way some of the persons who have lived out a creation-centered spirituality, I realize that some general observations seem in order. It is notable how, in the basic history of Christian theology, those who were creation-centered derived their theology not from the West, but from the East. Consider, for example, how Irenaeus and Cassian were Easterners who moved West; how the entire Celtic tradition got its theology from Eastern theologians; how Eckhart and Nicholas of Cusa also got their theology from the East. It is noteworthy how many women, beginning with Hildegarde, do indeed represent the creation tradition right through to today's feminists. In fact, I do not know of a single woman theologian who could be termed fall/redemption in her theology or spirituality. One wonders whether, if women had been allowed to teach in the churches in the patristic period, creation spirituality might not have been far better known and held much greater influence. Note, too, how with the dechurching of society beginning in the sixteenth century the artists—musicians, writers, poets, painters, etc.—were released to carry on and develop the creation-centered spiritual tradition. With rationalism and the

Enlightenment and industrial society, as education including theological education became more and more exclusively left-brained and patriarchal, creation theology was subsumed almost entirely under fall/redemption ideologies. It was the lay world much more than the clerical world that kept creation spirituality alive, and, more than that, carried it much further and deeper. Beginning with artists in the nineteenth century and extending today to scientists, feminists, New Age mystics, and social prophets, a veritable explosion of creation-centered spiritual energy is and has been occurring. If entire religious bodies such as Christianity could enter into this expanding spiritual energy field, there is no predicting what powers of passion and compassion might become unleashed.

APPENDIX B: FALL/REDEMPTION AND CREATION-CENTERED SPIRITUALITIES COMPARED AT A GLANCE

Fall/Redemption	Creation-Centered
Key Spokespersons: Augustine; Thomas à Kempis; Bossuet; Cotton Mather; Tanquerry	Key Spokespersons: Yahwist author; wisdom writers; prophets;Jesus;Paul;Irenaeus; Benedict; Hildegarde; Francis; Aquinas; Mechtild; Eckhart; Julian; Cusa; Teilhard; Chenu; feminists; liberation theologians; artists; musicians; poets (See Appendix A)
Faith is "thinking with assent" (Augustine)	Faith is trust
Patriarchal	Feminist
Ascetic	Aesthetic
Mortification of body	Discipline toward birthing
Control of passions	Ecstasy, Eros, celebration of passion
Passion is a curse	Passion is a blessing
God as Father	God as Mother, God as Child, as well as Father
Suffering is wages for sin	Suffering is birth pangs of universe
Death is wages for sin	Death is a natural event, a prelude to recycling and rebirth
Holiness is quest for perfection	Holiness is cosmic hospitality
Return to past to a state of perfection and innocence	Imperfection is integral to all nature
Keep soul clean	Make soul wet so that it grows,

	expands, and stays green (Hildegarde, Eckhart)
Begins with sin	Begins with Dabhar, God's creative energy
Emphasizes original sin	Emphasizes original blessing
Introspective in its psychology	Cosmic (microcosm/macrocosm) in its psychology
Emphasizes introvert meditation	Emphasizes extrovert meditation, i.e., art as meditation
Miracle is outside intervention contravening the law of nature	Basic miracle is the wonder of existence, isness, creation
Egological	Ecological, cosmic
Sciences of nature are unimportant	Science, by teaching us about nature, teaches us about the Creator
Dualistic (either/or)	Dialectical (both/and)
Suspicious of body and violent in its body/soul imagery; "soul makes war with the body" (Augustine)	Welcoming of body and gentle in its body/soul imagery; "soul loves the body" (Eckhart)
Humility is to "despise yourself" (Tanquerry)	Humility is to befriend one's earthiness (humus)
In control	Letting go—ecstasy, breakthrough
Pessimistic	Hopeful
Climbing Jacob's ladder	Dancing Sara's circle
Elitist	For the many
Particular	Universalist
No cosmic Christ	Cosmic Christ
Emphasis on Jesus as Son of God but not on Jesus as prophet	Emphasis on Jesus as prophet, as artist, parable-teller, and Son of God who calls others to their divinity

317

Original Blessing

Personal salvation	Salvation and healing of the *people* of God and the cosmos
Build up church	Build up Kingdom/Queendom
Kingdom = church	Kingdom = cosmos, creation
Human as sinner	Human as royal person who can choose to create or destroy
Struggle to clean one's conscience	Struggle to make justice of injustice and to balance the cosmos
Time is toward past (lost perfection) or future (heaven): unrealized eschatology	Time is now and making the future (heaven) begin to happen now: realized eschatology
Spiritual journey follows three paths of purgation, illumination, union (Plotinus)	Spiritual journey follows four paths of Via Positiva, Via Negativa, Via Creativa, Via Transformativa
Mysticism = mortify the senses	Mysticism = let go of today's ideologies
Repent!	Transform and be transformed!
Eternal life is after death	Eternal life is now
All pleasure should be moderate (Tanquerry)	Enjoy divine ecstasy in creation's pleasures
Contemplation is goal of spirituality	Compassion, justice, and celebration are goals of spirituality
A spirituality of the powerful	A spirituality of the powerless, the *anawim*
Emphasizes the cross	Considers the cross as significant for the Via Negativa, but also emphasizes the Resurrection, the coming of the spirit and creation, co-creation

Tends toward christolotry and docetism with an under-developed theology of the Creator and the Holy Spirit	Trinitarian in full sense of celebrating a Creator God, a prophetic Son of God, and the Holy Spirit of divine trans-formation
Emphasizes obedience	Emphasizes creativity (obedience to the image of God in one)
Tends to abstractions	Sensual
Righteousness	Justice
Duty	Beauty
Guilt and redemption	Thanks and praise
Purity from world	Hospitality to all of being
Apolitical, i.e., supportive of status quo	Prophetic, i.e., critical of status quo and its ideologies
Soul is in the body to guard it	Body is in the soul to enlarge the soul
Nothingness as psychological experience	Nothingness as metaphysical experience
Humanity is sinful	Humanity is divine and capable of demonic and sinful choices
Faith is in intellect	Faith is in imagination
Suspicious of the artist	Welcomes the artist since all are called to be co-creators with God
Theistic	Panentheistic

APPENDIX C: AN ANNOTATED BIBLIOGRAPHY IN CREATION-CENTERED SPIRITUALITY

I have limited myself to forty-six books in this brief bibliography. Other books may be found in the footnote references, in the bibliographies of the books mentioned here, and in pursuing the Family Tree personages and movements.

1. Edward A. Armstrong, *Saint Francis: Nature Mystic*. University of California Press, 1973. This book demonstrates definitively the immense role that the creation-centered Celtic tradition played in Francis's spiritual movement.

2. Thomas Berry, *Riverdale Papers*, vols. 1-8. Riverdale Press, c. 1974-1983. The author, who calls himself a "geologian," critiques religion and culture from an ecological/spiritual perspective.

3. Wendell Berry, *The Unsettling of America: Culture and Agriculture*. Avon Books, 1977. A powerful and beautifully sensual and spiritual reflection on the land and how we cherish or destroy it. The author is a small farmer who is also a poet.

4. Robert McAfee Brown, *Theology in a New Key*. The Westminster Press, 1978. A balanced, lucid, even at times humorous presentation of liberation theologies and their meaning.

5. Walter Brueggemann, *The Prophetic Imagination*. Fortress Press, 1978. A modestly sized but exciting tour de force by a reliable scholar of the Hebrew Bible about what the prophetic vocation is and how it is linked to art and imagination. See also the same author's *The Land* and *In Man We Trust*.

6. Robert Bly, *The Kabir Book*. Beacon Press, 1977. These beautiful mystic poems from India express images and lessons of the creation tradition as found in the East but that transcend all cultures.

7. Robert Bly, *News from the Universe*. Sierra Club Books, 1980. This volume constitutes a veritable anthology of creation-centered poems.

8. Robert Bly, translator, *Selected Poems of Rainer Maria Rilke*. Harper & Row, 1981. Rilke is a thoroughly creation-centered

poet whose work on embracing darkness and on naming the Via Negativa is unparalleled—"I have faith in nights," he declares.

9. Fritjof Capra, *The Tao of Physics*. Shambhala, 1975. While this may not prove to be the longest-lasting or the finest of the works on Einsteinian and post-Einsteinian physics and mysticism, it is among the very first written by a physicist who makes these essential connections. The author knows only Eastern spirituality, unfortunately, and nothing of the Western creation mystics such as Eckhart or Hildegarde.

10. Carol P. Christ, *Diving Deep and Surfacing*. Beacon Press, 1980. The author/editor gathers together women writers' views on the quest and vision of women's spirituality and offers an exciting summary of key themes found in women's journeys— themes that parallel those of creation-centered spirituality.

11. Anne Douglas, *The Feminization of American Culture*. Knopf, 1977. This book examines the rise of sentimentalism in modern religion and culture (especially the mass media) with the advent of industrialization in the nineteenth century—and is a veritable digest of what creation-centered spirituality is not— i.e., it is not "sentimental," which the author defines as "rancid political consciousness," or "political consciousness turned inwards."

12. Brendan Doyle, *Meditations with Julian of Norwich*. Bear & Company, 1983. Julian of Norwich was steeped in Eckhart's creation-centered spirituality and was an innovator and theologian in her own right who developed a veritable metaphysics of goodness. She deserves the nondualistic translation and format for prayer and artistic response to her lively mystical images which this book provides.

13. Matthew Fox, *On Becoming a Musical, Mystical Bear: Spirituality American Style*. Paulist Press, 1976. This book deals in a critical fashion with the meaning of prayer in both its psychological (mystical) sense and its social (prophetic) sense, bringing together social action and mystical prayer as forming the basic ground for a radical response to life.

14. Matthew Fox, *Whee! We, wee All the Way Home: A Guide to a Sensual, Prophetic Spirituality*. Bear & Company, 1980. This book offers a practical guide to developing disciplines of ecstasy, symbolic consciousness, and struggle for social justice which

mark a prophetic spirituality that is always nondualistic and therefore sensual.

15. Matthew Fox, *A Spirituality Named Compassion.* Winston Press, 1979. This book explores in depth the most important category in creation-centered spirituality, that of compassion, by examining its biblical, sexual, psychological, artistic, scientific, political, economic, and symbolic meanings.

16. Matthew Fox, editor, *Western Spirituality: Historical Roots, Ecumenical Routes.* Bear & Company, 1980. This book brings together sixteen scholars who write on topics of biblical and historical creation spirituality ranging from creation spirituality in the Hebrew Bible to Celtic, Eckhart, Rozensweig, Aquinas, Berdyaev, Hasidism, etc.

17. Matthew Fox, *Breakthrough: Meister Eckhart's Creation Spirituality in New Translation.* Doubleday and Doubleday Image, 1982. This book reproduces for the first time from the critical Latin and German sources thirty-six of Eckhart's sermons, with a commentary following each and a major introduction which demonstrate his grounding in biblical and creation spirituality.

18. Matthew Fox, *Meditations with Meister Eckhart.* Bear & Company, 1983. A presentation of Eckhart's spirituality in his own words, arranged by the four paths and in a format suited for prayer, ritual, artistic, and mystical response.

19. Matthew Fox and Brian Swimme, *Manifesto for a Global Civilization,* Bear & Company, 1982. For the first time in three centuries, a theologian and a physicist team up to compose a work heralding a new paradigm emerging from letting go of Newton in science and Augustine in religion.

20. Susan Griffin, *Woman and Nature: The Roaring Inside Her.* Harper Colophon, 1978. A recovery of a language that can truly be called spiritual based on the experience women have had in a basically dualistic and fall/redemption patriarchal society—"matter," "body," "transformation," "earth," "night," "union" become holy words once again.

21. Herbert Haag, *Is Original Sin in the Scripture?* Sheed & Ward, 1969. The president of the Catholic Bible Association of Germany explains why original sin is not in the Bible and why it deserves to play a lesser role in Western theology than it has.

22. Raghavan Iyer, *The Moral and Political Thought of Mahatma Gandhi*. Oxford University Press, 1978. Probably the finest presentation of the thinking of Gandhi, who struggled with bringing creation-centered spirituality back to a Hinduism that was rendered passive by an excessive ideology of personal salvation. Gandhi said that the person who does not know that religion and politics go together does not know what religion is.

23. Jung Young Lee, *The Theology of Change: A Christian Concept of God in an Eastern Perspective*. Orbis Books, 1979. In attempting an Asian interpretation of Christianity, the author calls for a veritable redoing of Christianity along creation-centered themes.

24. Barry Holstun Lopez, *Of Wolves and Men*. Charles Scribner's Sons, 1978. A beautiful book that lays bare the Western soul's fear of the animal in itself and therefore the projection of repressed violence onto an animal that in fact knows much about play, about cooperation, about spirit and interdependence. A must for anyone who believes, as I do, that animals make deep spiritual directors.

25. Thomas Merton, *Conjectures of a Guilty Bystander*. Doubleday Image, 1968. This, one of Merton's last and most mature works, reveals the fruit of his conversion from being a romantic monk of the fifties to being a prophetic Christian in the sixties, a conversion which came about on reading Zen and Eckhart in 1960 and which underlies his growth from fall/redemption theology to creation-centered theology.

26. José Miranda, *Marx and the Bible*. Orbis Books, 1974. Latin American scriptural exegete Miranda draws out the profound implications for a theology of liberation in reunderstanding how love and justice cannot be separated in biblical spirituality.

27. Albert Nolan, *Jesus Before Christianity*. Orbis Books, 1978. Third World theologian Nolan (from South Africa) paints a picture of Jesus' person and message as found in the gospel stories and his parables. In doing so, he makes Jesus live again, and his message comes alive with passion and compassion, announcing a creation-centered and prophetic spirituality.

28. Otto Rank, *Art and Artist*. Agathon Press, 1975. A difficult-to-read but brilliant book on the psychology of the artist and

therefore on the psychology of every person as image of God. See especially chapters XII-XIV.

29. Otto Rank, *Beyond Psychology*. Dover Publications, 1958. A brilliant and evocative book in which Rank relates why he believes psychology must yield to mysticism and creativity if the West is to regain its soul and the cosmos. Written on his deathbed in 1939, the book contains among other gems a chapter on feminist versus patriarchal psychology.

30. Adrienne Rich, *The Dream of a Common Language*. Norton, 1978. In the fullest tradition of the Jewish prophets, Rich presents a feminist journey which names in unforgettable images all four paths of joy, darkness, birthing, and transformation. An indispensable book for entering into the creation-centered spiritual tradition. See also her *Selected Poems*.

31. M. C. Richards, *Centering*. Wesleyan University Press, 1964. This book, written by a literature professor-turned-potter, is a veritable bible of art as meditation or extrovert meditation. It is itself a process book written in a spiraling and nonlinear pattern, in much the same way as a pot spirals on the potter's wheel as it grows to fullness.

32. Rosemary Ruether, *New Woman, New Earth*. Seabury, 1975. This is both a critique of patriarchal religion and psychological ideologies, and a vision of how feminism would transform culture. See also her *Women of Spirit* (as editor); *Liberation Theology; The Radical Kingdom; Faith and Fratricide*.

33. Jonathan Schell, *The Fate of the Earth*. Knopf, 1982. Perhaps the finest and most moving meditation on the meaning of the nuclear arms race and nuclear war for creation and for humanity as part of creation.

34. Edward Schillebeeckx, *Jesus*. Seabury, 1979. This "experiment in Christology" lays forth the creation-centered person and message of Jesus. See also his *Christ;* and *Interim Report*, chapters 6 and 7.

35. E. F. Schumacher, *Small Is Beautiful*. Harper & Row, 1973. Economist Schumacher offers a vision of a world where work is understood as personal creativity and land and human creativity are respected to the point of being included in economic world views which he feels suffer from the myopia of abstract figures and giant, impersonal, growth-oriented ideologies.

36. Jon Sobrino, *Christology at the Crossroads*. Orbis, 1978. Latin American theologian Sobrino reconsiders Christ from the perspective of victims of Western oppression. Chapter six offers a particularly illuminating critique of the "magical conception of redemption" and the mystification of the cross in the predominant fall/redemption Christologies of the West.

37. Charlene Spretnak, editor, *The Politics of Women's Spirituality*. Doubleday Image, 1982. A rich collection of essays on women's religions, the goddess spiritualities, and what they mean to today's issues of social and personal transformation.

38. Starhawk, *Dreaming the Dark: Magic, Sex and Politics*. Beacon Press, 1982. Offers a vision of how the ancient goddess religion can imbue today's consciousness in healing the dualism between spirituality and politics. Includes rituals for personal and group discipline to celebrate such holism. See also her *Spiral Dance*.

39. Krister Stendahl, *Paul Among Jews and Gentiles*. Fortress Press, 1976. A brilliant and indispensable guide to rereading scripture with creation-centered glasses. His essay "Paul and the Introspective Conscience of the West" is a classic statement of how the West has, under the introspective conscience of Augustine, been misreading Paul and the scriptures in general for centuries.

40. Pierre Teilhard de Chardin, *Human Energy*. Harcourt Brace Jovanovich, 1969. One of Teilhard's last and most mature works, calling for a vision of social transformation according to "the spirit of the earth," the one universal spirit of all humankind.

41. Frederick Turner, *Beyond Geography: The Western Spirit Against the Wilderness*. Viking Press, 1980. A look at American history beginning with Columbus from the perspective of the Native Americans. The author correctly understands his contribution as an "essay in spiritual history," for he lays bare the sadistic impulses behind the fall/redemption ideologies that drove so many whites to genocide against the "savage" and the wilderness he represents. An indispensable book for experiencing the price paid by victims of fall/redemption theology over the centuries.

42. Gabrielle Uhlein, *Meditations with Hildegarde of Bingen*. Bear & Company, 1983. Hildegarde of Bingen, a renaissance woman and a truly ecological thinker of micro/macrocosmic psychology,

is the grandmother of the Rhineland movement of prophetic mysticism. This is the first time her words have ever been published in English, and the book draws from several of her eleven works, presenting her words in a format appropriate for prayer, ritual, and artistic response.

43. Gerhard Von Rad, *Wisdom in Israel*. Abingdon Press, 1974. A basic work in the theology so basic to creation-centered spirituality, that of wisdom literature.

44. Claus Westermann, *Blessing in the Bible and the Life of the Church*. Fortress, 1978. A basic work in that almost-forgotten theological theme of Israel, the theology of blessing. See also his *Creation* and *Creation versus Chaos*.

45. Alfred North Whitehead, *Science and the Modern World*. Macmillan, 1927. Philosopher-scientist Whitehead explores the implications of twentieth-century physics for the coming together of science and religion and the healing of the bitter breach between the two that happened in the past few centuries.

46. Susan Woodruff, *Meditations with Mechtild of Magdeburg*. Bear & Company, 1982. This represents the only version of Mechtild's work currently in print for English readers. It is arranged according to the four paths and in a prayerful format. Mechtild speaks of the play of prophetic struggle with deep and fresh creation-centered images that inspired both Meister Eckhart and Dante in their naming of the spiritual journey.

NOTES

INTRODUCTION

1. Alfred North Whitehead, *Science and the Modern World* (New York: 1927), pp. 269f.
2. Michael Polanyi, *Personal Knowledge* (Chicago: 1962), p. 141. Noam Chomsky has called this the "greatest book on the philosophy of science ever written."
3. Thomas Berry, "Our Children: Their Future," *the little magazine*, Bear & Company, Vol. 1, Number 10, p. 8.
4. Jonathan Schell, *The Fate of the Earth* (New York: 1982), pp. 9,7, 154.
5. The study was undertaken by Employment Research Associates of Lansing, Michigan, and was issued in October, 1982. See "Jobs 'Lost' When Pentagon Buys," in the *Chicago Sun Times*, October 25, 1982, p. 22.
6. Printed in *Pax Christi/England Newsletter*, n.d.
7. For example, see Matthew Fox and Brian Swimme, *Manifesto for a Global Civilization* (Santa Fe: 1982). Dr. Swimme is a physicist who teaches at the Institute in Culture and Creation Spirituality at Holy Names College, Oakland.
8. I am indebted to poet Lee Pieper, currently a student at ICCS, Mundelein College, for this word.
9. Pierre Teilhard de Chardin, *Human Energy* (New York: 1969), p. 32.
10. See Jung Young Lee, *The Theology of Change: A Christian Concept of God in an Eastern Perspective* (Maryknoll, NY: 1979).
11. See Starhawk, *The Spiral Dance: A Rebirth of the Ancient Religion of the Great Goddess* (New York: 1979), and *Dreaming the Dark* (Boston: 1982).
12. See Matthew Fox, *Breakthrough: Meister Eckhart's Creation Spirituality in New Translation* (Garden City, NY: 1980).
13. Thomas Merton, *Zen and the Birds of Appetite* (New York: 1968), p. 81. An excellent job of redeeming the creation-centered

lineage of the Carmelite tradition is being done by Camille Campbell. See Camille Anne Campbell, O. Carm., "Creation-Centered Spirituality," *Spiritual Life* (Fall, 1981), pp. 131-142; and "Creation-Centered Carmelites: Teresa and John of the Cross," *Spiritual Life* (Spring, 1982), pp. 15-25.

14. Edmund Colledge and James Walsh, *Julian of Norwich: Showings* (New York: 1978), pp. 183f. In three volumes of collaboration on Julian of Norwich, the authors never mention Meister Eckhart's name once. The ignorance of the single most important influence on Julian of Norwich, this male carrier of the feminist spiritual tradition, might explain the numerous dualistic mistranslations in their otherwise useful work. It is also telling how Julian's passage on how going to the bathroom is holy (see Theme Three above) was simply edited out by all fall/redemption translators in certain nineteenth- and twentieth-century editions of her work.

15. Johann Metz, *Faith in History and Society* (London, 1980), p. 111.

16. Susan Griffin, *Women and Nature* (New York, 1978), p. 46.

17. Cf. Carol P. Christ, *Diving Deep and Surfacing: Women Writers on Spiritual Quest*, (Boston: 1980), pp. 68f.

18. Otto Rank, *Beyond Psychology* (New York: 1958), p. 189.

19. Frederick Turner, *Beyond Geography: The Western Spirit Against the Wilderness* (New York: 1980), pp. 68f.

20. Edward Schillebeeckx, *Christ* (New York: 1980), p. 530.

21. Krister Stendahl, *Paul Among Jews and Gentiles* (Philadelphia: 1978), pp. 16f.

22. Leo Scheffczyk, *Creation and Providence* (New York: 1970), pp. 121, 103.

23. Claus Westermann, *Blessing in the Bible and the Life of the Church* (Philadelphia: 1978), chapter one.

24. Jolande Jacobi, ed., *C. G. Jung: Psychological Reflections, A New Anthology of His Writings* (New York: 1978), p. 304.

25. *The Small Catechism of Dr. Martin Luther* (Philadelphia: n.d.), pp. 7-9.

26. Each of these books is available at Bear & Company, Santa Fe, New Mexico.

THEME #1

1. Sebastian Franck, *Chronicle of World History.* Cited in Steven E. Ozment, *Mysticism and Dissent* (New Haven: 1973), p. 148. Cf. Hans Hut's doctrine of "the gospel of all creatures."

2. In John Malcolm Brinnin, ed., *A Casebook on Dylan Thomas* (New York: 1965), p. 3.

3. Thomas Berry, "Our Children: Their Future," *the little magazine*, Bear & Company, Vol. 1, Number 10, p. 8.

4. Cited in Linnie Marsh Wolfe, *John Muir: Son of the Wilderness* (New York: 1951), p. 123.

5. Thomas Berry, *art. cit.*, p. 10.

6. Richard Wilhelm, trans., *The Secret of the Golden Flower* (New York: 1962), p. 11.

7. "In wisdom literature as a whole it is rather wisdom that is spoken of as creative. Cf. Prov. 8:22." Alexander Jones, ed., *The Jerusalem Bible* (New York: 1966), p. 1095, note h. See also Sir. 42:15, called "one of the earliest appearances of the doctrine of the Creative Word." Cf. Sir. 43:26; Gen. 1; Ps. 33:6; Wisd. 9:1f.; John 1:1f.

8. Leonard Bernstein and Stephen Schwartz, *Mass* (New York: Columbia Records, 1971), p. 11.

THEME # 2:

1. Robert Bridges and W. H. Gardner, eds., *Poems of Gerard Manley Hopkins* (New York: 1948), p. 74.

2. Elie Wiesel, *Messengers of God* (New York: 1976), pp. 29f.

3. Annie Dillard, *Pilgrim at Tinker Creek* (New York: 1975), p. 9.

4. Pablo Casals, *Joys and Sorrows* (New York: 1970), p. 295.

5. John Muir, *My First Summer in the Sierra* (Boston: 1979), p. 61.

6. Walter Brueggemann, *Tradition for Crisis* (Richmond: 1968), p. 69.

7. Timothy Ware, *The Orthodox Church* (Middlesex, England, 1963), p. 229.

8. For a fine article on Irenaeus's creation-centered theology, see Conrad Simonson, "Irenaeus and the Future of Man," in George Devine, ed., *A World More Human A Church More Christian* (New York: 1973), pp. 53-68.

9. 43:102. Cf. Peter de Rosa on how Augustine was the first person to translate the Greek as "in whome" and how the Greek fathers themselves "never took it to be that." Peter de Rosa, *Christ and Original Sin* (Milwaukee: 1967), p. 100.

10. 22:181. See Theme Eighteen for more on dualism as original sin and its healing in the creation spirituality tradition.

11. William Eckhardt, *Compassion: Toward a Science of Value* (Oakville, Ontario: 1973), pp. 4f.: "Compassion is a function of faith in human nature, while compulsion is a function of lack of faith in human nature (the belief that man is basically evil)."

12. Ashley Montagu, *Growing Young* (New York: 1981), pp. 120f.

13. Paul Ricoeur, *The Symbolism of Evil* (Boston: 1964), p. 239.

14. Adolphe Tanquerry, *The Spiritual Life: A Treatise on Ascetical and Mystical Theology* (Westminster, Md.: 1930), p. 101.

15. Jacques-Yves Cousteau, *The Whale: Mighty Monarch of the Sea* (Garden City, NY: 1972), pp. 215f.

THEME # 3

1. Roland E. Murphy, *Wisdom Literature* (Grand Rapids, Michigan: 1981), p. 104.

2. Starhawk, *The Spiral Dance: A Rebirth of the Ancient Religion of the Great Goddess* (New York: 1979), p. 65.

3. John M. Rich, *Chief Seattle's Unanswered Challenge* (Seattle: 1947), p. 40.

4. Pierre Teilhard de Chardin, *The Divine Milieu* (New York: 1968), p. 69.

5. "At the Wedding March," in Robert Bridges, ed., *Poems of Gerard Manley Hopkins* (New York: 1938), p. 47.

6. Adolphe Tanquerry, *The Spiritual Life: A Treatise on Ascetical and Mystical Theology* (Westminster, Md.: 1930), p. 232.

7. Edna Hong, *Clues to the Kingdom* (Minneapolis: 1968), p. 44.

8. Erik Erikson, *Gandhi's Truth* (New York: 1969), p. 198.

9. Helena Curtis, author of a textbook on biology used by millions of college students every year, writes: "The wisdom of nature is a sentimental notion." Helena Curtis, *Biology* (New York: 1979), p. 12.

10. C. G. Jung, *Psychological Types* in Bollingen Series (Princeton: 1974) #415, pp. 244f.

11. Gerhard Von Rad, *Genesis* (Philadelphia: 1972), p. 278.

12. Claude Tresmontant, *A Study of Hebrew Thought* (New York: 1960), p. 103.

13. Marvin H. Pope, *Song of Songs* (Garden City, NY: 1977), p. 326. I am indebted to the fine study done by my colleague, Mary Anne Hoope, BVM, "The Church as Vineyard: A Creation-Centered Ecclesiology," (Chicago: unpublished, 1982) for many insights regarding the sensual and spiritual in biblical vine imagery.

14. See M. D. Chenu, "Body and Body Politic in the Creation Spirituality of Thomas Aquinas," in *Western Spirituality*, Matthew Fox, ed., (Santa Fe: 1981), pp. 193-214.

15. For the diversity of images of soul found in the mystics see Matthew Fox, "Searching for the Authentically Human: Images of Soul in Meister Eckhart and Teresa of Avila," in Francis A. Eigo, ed., *Dimensions of Contemporary Spirituality* (Villanova, PA: 1982), pp. 1-40.

THEME # 4

1. "Position Paper of the Native American Project of the Theology in the Americas," (Detroit II Conference, July/August, 1980), p. 2.

2. Pierre Teilhard de Chardin, *The Divine Milieu* (New York: 1968), p. 38.

3. Andrew Weil, *The Natural Mind* (Boston: 1972), p. 179.

4. Jacques-Yves Cousteau *et. al., The Cousteau Almanac* (Garden City, NY: 1981), pp. 734f.

5. John the Scot, *Periphyseon: On the Division of Nature* (Indianapolis: 1976), p. 137.

6. Thomas Berry, "Our Children: Their Future," *the little magazine*, Bear & Company, Vol. 1, Number 10, p. 8.

7. Cited in Linnie Marsh Wolfe, *John Muir: Son of the Wilderness* (New York: 1951), p. 123.

8. M. D. Chenu, *Nature, Man and Society in the Twelfth Century* (Chicago: 1957), p. 6.

9. Cited in John Lobell, *Between Silence and Light: Spirit in the Architecture of Louis I. Kahn* (Boulder: 1979), p. 18.

11. Paul Ricoeur, *The Symbolism of Evil* (Boston: 1969), pp. 12f.

12. Richard Wilhelm, trans., *The Secret of the Golden Flower* (New York: 1962), p. 11.

13. Thomas Berry, *art. cit.*, p. 11.

14. G. K. Chesterton, *Saint Thomas Aquinas, The Dumb Ox* (Garden City, NY: 1956), p. 165.

15. Gabriel Marcel, *The Decline of Wisdom* (New York: 1955), p. 42.

16. Starhawk, *The Spiral Dance: A Rebirth of the Ancient Religion of the Great Goddess* (New York: 1979), pp. 77f.

17. Eugene La Verdiere, *Luke* (Wilmington, DE: 1980), p. 12.

18. A statement by Bartolomé de Las Casas, cited in Frederick Turner, *Beyond Geography: The Western Spirit Again in the Wilderness* (New York: 1980), p. 150.

19. Leo Scheffczyk, *Creation and Providence* (New York: 1970), p. 100.

20. R. A. Markus, "St. Augustine," in *The Encyclopedia of Philosophy*, Vol. I (New York: 1967), p. 204.

21. See Introduction, note 2, above.

22. Titus Szabo, "L'Extase chez les théologiens du XIIIe siècle," *Dictionnaire de Spiritualité*, vol. IV, col. 2130.

23. Cousteau, *op. cit.*, pp. xviif.

24. Nicholas of Cusa, *De pace fidei* i. fol. 862f. Cited in Ernst Cassirer, *The Individual and the Cosmos in Renaissance Philosophy* (Philadelphia: 1979), p. 29.

25. Position paper of the "Native American Project," *ed. cit.*, p. 4.

26. Roland E. Murphy, *Wisdom Literature* (Grand Rapids, MI: 1981), p. 11.

27. F. S. Perls, *Gestalt Therapy Verbatim* (New York: 1971), p. 34.

28. Robert Henri, *The Art Spirit* (New York: 1960), p. 144.

THEME # 5

1. Robert Henri, *The Art Spirit* (New York: 1960), p. 47.

2. Walter Brueggemann, "The Trusted Creature," *Catholic Biblical Quarterly*, Vol. XXXI (1969), p. 488.

3. Alfred North Whitehead, *Process and Reality* (New York: 1978), p. 83.

4. Roland E. Murphy, "Wisdom Theses," in *Wisdom and Knowledge*, II, (n.d.), p. 190.

5. Brueggemann, *art. cit.*, p. 484, n. #2.

6. *Ibid.*, pp. 486f., 489.

7. *Ibid.*, pp. 492, 491, 495.

8. Tresmontant, *A Study of Hebrew Thought*, (New York: 1960), p. 26.

9. St. Irenaeus, *Adverses haereses*, IV, xxxvii, 7.

10. *Ibid.*, xxxix.

11. William Eckhardt, *Compassion: Toward a Science of Value* (Oakville, Ontario: 1973), pp. 4f.

THEME # 6

1. Cited in David Blum, *Casals and the Art of Interpretation* (Berkeley: 1980), p. 208.

2. John of the Cross, "The Spiritual Canticle," 13. In Kieran Kavanaugh, *The Collected Works of St. John of the Cross* (Washington, D.C.: 1973), p. 714.

3. Edmund Colledge and James Walsh, *Julian of Norwich: Showings* (New York: 1978), chapter six (long text).

4. Lecture by Dr. Ron Miller at ICCS, Mundelein College, Chicago, January 18, 1982.

THEME # 7

1. Martin Luther King, Jr., *Why We Can't Wait* (New York: 1964), p. 30.

2. Pablo Casals, *Joys and Sorrows*, (New York: 1970), p. 295.

3. Bernard W. Anderson, *Creation vs. Chaos* (New York: 1967), p. 177.

4. Roland E. Murphy, *Wisdom Literature* (Grand Rapids, MI: 1981), p. 61.

5. See Ps. 9:7-10. I am deeply indebted to Professor Helen Kenik's work on the royal person. See 16:27-75.

6. Louis Hartman and J. T. Nelis, "Kingdom of God," in *Encyclopedic Dictionary of the Bible*, Louis Hartman, ed. (New York: 1963), col. 1272.

7. Lecture by Professor Krister Stendahl to Lutheran Pastors of Iowa in July, 1981.

THEME # 8

1. Martin Luther King, Jr., *Why We Can't Wait* (New York: 1964), p. 86.

2. Herbert Marcuse, *Eros and Civilization* (New York: 1962), pp. 211f.

THEME # 9

1. George A. Panichas, *The Simone Weil Reader* (New York: 1977), p. 114.

2. John Lobell, *Between Silence and Light: Spirit in the Architecture of Louis I. Kahn* (Boulder: 1979), p. 64.

3. Erik Erikson, *Gandhi's Truth* (New York: 1969), p. 399.

4. Cited in David Steindl-Rast, "A Deep Bow: Gratitude as the Root of a Common Religious Language" (Mount Saviour Monastery: n.d.), p. 1. Rev. Shimano is a Japanese Zen master.

5. Adolphe Tanquerry, *The Spiritual Life: A Treatise on Ascetical and Mystical Theology* (Westminster, Md.: 1930), p. 177.

6. Cited in Roy Fairchild, *Finding Hope Again: A Pastor's Guide to Counseling Depressed Persons* (New York: 1980), p. 34.

7. Adrienne Rich, "Stepping Backward," in *Poems: Selected and New* (New York: 1975), p. 9.

8. W. F. Albright, *Matthew* (Garden City, NY: 1971), p. 72.

9. See Matthew Fox, *A Spirituality Named Compassion* (Minneapolis: 1979), chapter one.

10. Hans Jonas, *The Gnostic Religion* (Boston: 1963), p. 310.

11. Alexander Jones, ed., *The Jerusalem Bible* (New York: 1966), p. 805, note c.

12. See Ps. 98, 104, 145, 147-49; Daniel 3:51-90, for example.

THEME # 10

1. St. Irenaeus, *Proof of the Apostolic Preaching* (New York: 1952), p. 51.
2. Edward Schillebeeckx, *Interim Report on the Books Jesus and Christ* (New York: 1981), p. 128.
3. Eugene La Verdiere, *Luke* (Wilmington, DE: 1980), p. 38.
4. Edward Schillebeeckx, *Christ* (New York: 1980), p. 526.
5. Eloi Leclerc, *The Canticle of Creatures: Symbols of Union*, Chicago: 1977), p. 211.
6. St. Irenaeus, *op. cit.*, pp. 30f.
7. Gustaf Wingren, *Man and the Incarnation* (Philadelphia: 1975), p. 126. Wingren comments, "Irenaeus holds Creation and the Incarnation together." (p. 84)
8. Norman O. Brown, *Life Against Death* (Middletown, CT: 1972), p. 307.
9. Alexander Jones, ed., *The Jerusalem Bible*, (New York: 1966), p. 782.
10. Cf. Jon Sobrino, *Christology at the Crossroads* (Maryknoll, NY: 1978), chapter six.
11. William Blake, "Jerusalem," pl. 7,1. 65. Cited in Norman O. Brown, *Love's Body* (New York: 1968), p. 212.

PATH II: INTRODUCTION

1. C. G. Jung, "Foreword to Suzuki's 'Introduction to Zen Buddhism'" in Bollingen Series XI (Princeton: 1975), #893-895, pp. 547f.
2. Cf., for example, Bengt Hoffman, *The Theologica Germanica of Martin Luther* (New York: 1980), who fails in his commentaries to understand panentheism at all. Still, I wish to commend the author for this and his other work, *Luther and the Mystics*, for beginning the process of awakening Protestants to their own mystical sources in the Rhineland tradition. I hope this present study of mine deepens that process.

THEME # 11

1. Cited in Alan W. Watts, *The Way of Zen* (New York: 1957), p. 136.

2. Thomas Merton, *"Emblems of a Season of Fury,"* The Collected *Poems of Thomas Merton* (New York: 1977), p. 353.

3. Thomas Merton, "The Strange Islands," in *ibid.*, p. 280.

4. Thomas Aquinas, *Summa contra gentiles,* I. v.

5. "East Coker," III, in T. S. Eliot, *The Complete Poems and Plays* (New York: 1952), p. 126.

6. © Lee Pieper, 1983.

7. Teresa of Avila, *"The Seventh Dwelling Place,"* in *The Interior Castle,* chapter three, #11.

8. James Legge, trans. Cited in Thomas Merton, *The Way of Chuang Tzu* (New York: 1965), p. 152.

9. Starhawk, *The Spiral Journey: A Rebirth of the Ancient Religion of the Great Goddess* (New York: 1979), p. 19.

10. C. G. Jung, "Commentary," in Richard Wilhelm, trans., *The Secret of the Golden Flower* (New York: 1962), p. 93.

11. John the Scot, *Periphyseon: On the Division of Nature* (Indianapolis: 1976), p. 358.

THEME # 12

1. Wolfgang Hildesheimer, *Mozart* (New York: 1982), p. 55.

2. Simone Weil, *Notebooks.* Cited in Susan Griffin, *Woman and Nature: The Roaring Inside Her* (New York: 1978), p. 219

3. Dorothy Day, *Meditations* (New York: 1970), p. 8.

4. Cited in *The Other Side,* January, 1982, p. 60.

5. See Arthur J. Deikman, "Deautomatization and the Mystic Experience," in Charles T. Tart, ed., *Altered States of Consciousness* (Garden City, NY: 1972), pp. 25–46.

6. Translation by Denise Levertov in Denise Levertov, *Light Up the Cave* (New York: 1981), pp. 98f.

7. Adolphe Tanquerry, *The Spiritual Life: A Treatise on Ascetical and Mystical Philosophy* (Westminster, Md: 1930), p. 346.

THEME # 13

1. John of the Cross, "The Ascent of Mount Carmel," Book I, in Kieran Kavanaugh, *The Collected Works of St. John of the Cross* (Washington, D.C.: 1973), pp. 103f.

2. *The Complete Works of D. H. Lawrence* (New York: 1971), p. 728.

3. Martin Luther King, Jr., *Why We Can't Wait* (New York: 1964), p. 115.

4. Erik Erikson, *Gandhi's Truth* (New York: 1969), p. 186.

5. *Ibid.*, pp. 398, 400.

6. Irving Kolodin, "Comments on Beethoven's 'Pastoral' Symphony" conducted by Reiner, Chicago Symphony (New York: RCA Corporation, 1963).

7. Comments by Raghavan Iyer in *The Moral and Political Thought of Mahatma Gandhi* (New York: 1978), p. 46.

THEME # 14

1. Cited in Erik Erikson, *Gandhi's Truth* (New York: 1969), p. 306.

2. I am grateful for these reflections to Carol Slater, a student at ICCS, Mundelein College, Chicago, December, 1982.

3. Fernando Belo, *A Materialist Reading of the Gospel of Mark* (Maryknoll, NY: 1981), p. 162.

4. Chaim Potok, *My Name is Asher Lev* (New York: 1972), p. 150.

5. For more information on the Synoptics' seeing Jesus' journey as parallel to that of the suffering servant in Isaiah 53, see: Matt. 8:16f.; 20:2; Luke 22:37; Mark 15:28f.; 9:12f.; 10:45; 14:24.

6. 34. 421. I am indebted to the research of ICCS student Brendan Doyle for this section on the transfiguration in Mark's Gospel.

PATH III: THEME # 15

1. Thomas Berry, "Perspectives on Creativity: Openess to a Free Future," in Francis A. Eigo, ed., *Whither Creativity, Freedom, Suffering?: Humanity, Cosmos, God* (Villanova, PA: 1980), pp. 13f.

2. Gregory Baum, *Religion and Alienation* (New York: 1975), p. 244.

3. Dorothy Day, *The Long Loneliness: An Autobiography* (New York: 1952), p. 255.

4. Claude Tresmontant, *A Study of Hebrew Thought* (New York: 1960), p. 151.

5. Cited in Steven E. Ozment, *Mysticism and Dissent* (New Haven: 1973), p. 127.

6. Berry, *art. cit.*, p. 3.
7. See Matthew Fox, *A Spirituality Named Compassion, op. cit.*, pp. 117-126.
8. Pablo Casals, *Joys and Sorrows* (New York: 1970), pp. 24f.
9. Day, *op. cit.*, p. 255.
10. Alfred North Whitehead, *Adventures of Ideas* (New York: 1967), p. 271.

THEME # 16

1. Cited in José A. Arguelles, *The Transformative Vision* (Berkeley: 1975), p. 165.
2. Adrienne Rich, *Of Woman Born* (New York: 1976), p. 29.
3. Claudio Naranjo and Robert Ornstein, *On the Psychology of Meditation* (New York: 1971), p. 199.
4. Starhawk, *The Spiral Dance: A Rebirth of the Ancient Religion of the Great Goddess* (New York: 1979), pp. 22f.
5. Kenjo Miyazawa, "Life as Art," (unpublished translation from his thoughts of 1926 done in 1962), p. 2.
6. Rollo May, *The Courage to Create* (New York: 1975), p. 12.
7. Nicolas Berdyaev, *The Meaning of the Creative Act* (New York: 1952), p. 322.
8. Thomas Berry, "Our Children: Their Future," *the little magazine*, Bear & Company, vol. 1, number 10, p. 9.
9. William Blake, "The Laocoon," in Geoffrey Keynes, *Complete Writings* (London: 1969), p. 775.
10. Hildegarde of Bingen, *Scivias* (Brussels: 1978), pp. 5f.
11. Erik Erikson, *Gandhi's Truth* (New York: 1969), p. 260.
12. Berry, *art. cit.*, p. 9.
13. See, for example, Betty Edwards, *Drawing on the Right Side of the Brain* (Los Angeles: 1979); or Mike Samuels and Nancy Samuels, *Seeing with the Mind's Eye* (New York: 1975).
14. C. G. Jung, "Commentary," in Richard Wilhelm, trans., *The Secret of the Golden Flower* (New York: 1962), p. 94.
15. Knud Martner, ed., *Selected Letters of Gustave Mahler* (New York: 1979), p. 242. Italics his.

16. Gabriel Marcel, *The Existential Background of Human Dignity* (Cambridge, Mass.: 1963), p. 126.

17. Thomas Merton, in Thomas P. McDonnell, ed., *A Thomas Merton Reader* (New York: 1962), p. 426.

THEME #17

1. See Ranier Maria Rilke, *Letters to a Young Poet*, letter #3.

2. Pablo Casals, *Joy and Sorrow* (New York: 1970), p. 76.

3. Arturo Paoli, *Meditations on Saint Luke* (Maryknoll, NY: 1977), p. 6.

4. Kenji Miyazawa, "Life as Art" (unpublished translations from his thoughts of 1926 done in 1962), p. 1.

5. *Ibid.*, p. 2.

6. Casals, *op. cit.*, p. 76.

THEME # 18

1. Ann Belford Ulanov, *The Feminine in Jungian Psychology and in Christian Theology* (Evanston: 1971), p. 191.

2. Karl Rahner and Herbert Vorgrimler, *Theological Dictionary* (New York: 1965), p. 468.

3. Ernest Newman, *Musical Studies* (New York: 1969), p. 15.

4. Kenji Miyazawa, "Life as Art" (unpublished translation from his thoughts of 1926 done in 1962), p. 1.

5. Personal conversation, spring, 1979.

6. Clement of Alexandria, *The Pedagogue*, III, 1; PG, vol. 8, col. #556C.

7. Alfred North Whitehead, *Adventures of Ideas* (New York: 1967), pp. 265-67.

8. Susan Griffin, *Woman and Nature: The Roaring Inside Her* (New York: 1976), pp. 54, 95, 96, 106, 152.

9. Beverly Wildung Harrison, "The Power of Anger in the Work of Love: Christian Ethics for Women and Other Strangers," in *Union Seminary Quarterly Review*, XXXVI (1981), p. 47.

10. Cited in Ernest Cassirer, *The Individual and the Cosmos in Renaissance Philosophy* (Philadelphia: 1979), p. 45.

11. *Ibid.*, p. 44.
12. Whitehead, *op. cit.*, p. 257.
13. *Ibid.*, p. 286.
14. Edward Schillebeeckx, *Christ* (New York: 1980), p. 525.
15. Andrew Porter, "Notes to Beethoven Mass in C Major, OP. 86," (Hollywood: Capitol Records, 1959).

THEME # 19

1. Adrienne Rich, *Of Woman Born*, (New York: 1976), p. 101.
2. C. G. Jung, "Psychology and Literature," in Brewster Ghiselin, ed., *The Creative Process* (New York: 1952), p. 222.
3. Abraham Heschel, *The Insecurity of Freedom* (New York: 1972), p. 125.
4. I am indebted to Dr. Sandra Schneiders, IHM, for her insight in this matter in a lecture at ICCS, Mundelein College, winter, 1981.
5. See Norman O. Brown, *Life Against Death* (Middletown, Conn.: 1972), pp. 66f.

THEME # 20

1. Denise Levertov, *The Poet in the World* (New York: 1973), p. 53.
2. Karen Horney, *New Ways in Psychoanalysis* (New York: 1966), p. 250.
3. Erich Fromm, *The Sane Society* (New York: 1955), p. 301.
4. Ernest Becker, *Denial of Death* (New York: 1973), p. 173.
5. Paul Tillich, *The Shaking of the Foundations* (New York: 1948), p. 137.
6. Norman O. Brown, *Life Against Death* (Middletown, Conn.: 1972), p. 312.
7. Dorothy Day, *The Long Loneliness: An Autobiography* (New York: 1952), p. 153.
8. Thomas Merton, "The Theology of Creativity," in *The Sacred Land*. Brother Patrick Hart, ed., *The Literary Essays of Thomas Merton* (New York: 1981), p. 360.
9. Evelyn Underhill, *Practical Mysticism* (New York: 1915), p. 27.

10. Adrienne Rich, *Of Woman Born* (New York: 1976), pp. 64f.

11. *Ibid.*, p. 168.

12. *Ibid.*, pp. 170f.

13. See Matthew Fox, *A Spirituality Named Compassion* (Minneapolis: 1979), chapter four, "Creativity and Compassion."

14. Rich, *op. cit.*, p. 246.

15. Thomas Aquinas, XI *De Malo*, 3 and 4.

16. Ernest Cassirer, *op. cit.*, p. 68.

17. Becker, *op. cit.*, pp. 84f.

18. John Reumann, "Creatio, Continua et Nova (Creation, Continuing and New)," in Vilmas Vajta, ed., *The Gospel as History* (Philadelphia: 1975), p. 103.

19. Day, *op. cit.*, pp. 151, 153.

20. Erik Erikson, *Gandhi's Truth* (New York: 1970), p. 111.

21. *Ibid.*, pp. 402f.

22. *Ibid.*, p. 260.

23. Brother David Steindl-Rast, OSB, in a lecture at ICCS, Mundelein College, February, 1983.

24. Henry Miller, *Tropic of Cancer* (New York: 1961), p. 253.

PATH IV: THEME # 21

1. Erik Erikson, *Gandhi's Truth* (New York: 1970), p. 410.

2. Norman O. Brown, *Life Against Death* (Middletown, Conn.: 1972), p. 64.

3. Cited in Adam Margoshes, "Friedrich Wilhelm Joseph Von Schelling," in *The Encyclopedia of Philosophy*, vol. VII (New York: 1967), p. 308.

4. *On the Trinity*, XII, 14:22. In Vernon J. Bourke, ed., *The Essential Augustine* (Indianapolis: 1978), p. 37.

5. Such a dualistic pitting of contemplation against action and action against wisdom is not necessary, however. See Matthew Fox, "Redeeming the Word 'Contemplation,' " *the little magazine*, Bear & Company, vol. 1, number 2, pp. 2-5.

6. E. Polster and M. Polster, *Gestalt Therapy Integrated* (New York: 1974), p. 25.

7. Thomas Berry, "Perspectives on Creativity: Openness to a Free Future," in Frances A. Eigo, ed., *Whither Creativity, Freedom, Suffering?: Humanity, Cosmos, God* (Villanova, PA: 1980), pp. 11f.

8. *Ibid.*, p. 6.

9. Cited in Erikson, *op. cit.*, p. 306.

10. Bruce Vawter and J. T. Nelis, "Creation," *Encyclopedic Dictionary of the Bible*, Louis Hartman, ed. (New York: 1963), col. 443.

THEME # 22

1. Abraham Joshua Heschel, *God in Search of Man* (New York: 1955), p. 255.

2. Cited in Erik Erikson, *Gandhi's Truth* (New York: 1970), p. 383.

3. Martin Luther King, Jr., *Strive Toward Freedom* (New York: 1958), p. 72.

4. Abraham Joshua Heschel, *The Prophets* (New York: 1962), p. 202.

5. *Ibid.*, p. 205.

6. Walter Brueggemann, lecture at ICCS, Mundelein College, Chicago, January, 1983.

7. Erikson, *op. cit.*, p. 183.

8. "Karla Hammond: An Interview with Audre Lourde," *The American Poetry Review* (March/April, 1980), p. 19.

9. Claudio Naranjo and Robert Ornstein, *On the Psychology of Meditation* (New York: 1971), p. 74.

10. Alexander Jones, ed., *The Jerusalem Bible* (New York: 1966), p. 935, note e.

THEME # 23

1. Gustavo Gutiérrez, in *The Witness*, April, 1977, p. 5. See Robert McAfee Brown, *The Unsettling of America: Culture and Agriculture* (New York: 1977), pp. 70-72.

2. "Position Paper of the Native American Project of the Theology in the Americas," (Detroit II Conference, July/August, 1980), p. 2.

3. Paulo Freire, *Pedagogy of the Oppressed* (New York: 1966), p. 55.

4. Cited in Mary Ward, *The Impossible Dreams* (Maryknoll, NY: 1980), p. 13.

5. Dorothy Day, *The Long Loneliness: An Autobiography* (New York: 1952), p. 124.

6. Nathan Jones, lecture on black spirituality at ICCS, Mundelein College, Chicago, winter, 1980.

7. Caroll Quigley, *The Evolution of Civilizations* (New York: 1961), pp. 218f.

8. "Position Paper of the Native American Project," *art. cit.*, p. 3.

9. Cited in Starhawk, *Dreaming the Dark: Magic, Sex and Politics* (Boston: 1982), p. 217.

10. See Matthew Fox, "The Spiritual Journey of the Homosexual and Just About Everyone Else," in Robert Nugent, ed., *A Challenge to Love—Gay and Lesbian Couples in the Church* (New York: 1983), pp. 157-204.

11. Jon Sobrino, "The Witness of the Church in Latin America," in Sergio Torres and John Eagleson, eds., *The Challenge of Basic Christian Communities* (Maryknoll, NY: 1981), pp. 164f.

12. John Berger, *Pig Earth* (New York: 1979), p. 12.

13. Nathan Jones, *Sharing the Old, Old Story: Educational Ministry in the Black Community* (Winona, MN: 1982), p. 31.

14. Cornel West, *Prophesy Deliverance!: An Afro-American Revolutionary Christianity* (Philadelphia: 1982), pp. 17, 16.

15. "Message to the Black Church and Community," (Atlanta: National Conference of the Black Theology Project, 1977), p. 2.

16. James H. Cone, *Black Theology and Black Power* (New York: 1969), p. 101.

17. Clarence Rivers, *Soulful Worship* (Washington, D.C.: 1974), p. 14.

18. James H. Cone, "Sanctification, Liberation and Black Worship," *Theology Today* (1978), p. 140.

19. See Mary Aileen Schmiel, "The Finest Music in the World: Exploring Celtic Spiritual Legacies," in Matthew Fox, ed., *Western Spirituality: Historical Roots, Ecumenical Routes* (Santa Fe: 1980), pp. 164-92. See also Book 1 in Appendix C. For information on the colonial oppression of Ireland, I am indebted to Marvin A. Anderson, "On the Great Starvation in Ireland, 1845-1849" (Toronto: unpublished, 1983).

20. Pierre Delooz, "The Social Function of the Canonization of Saints," *Concilium*, vol. 129, pp. 14f.

21. *Ibid.*, pp. 19f.

THEME # 24

1. Elie Wiesel, *Messengers of God* (New York: 1976), p. 57.

2. Adrienne Rich, "Stepping Backward," in *Poems Selected and New* (New York: 1975), p. 8.

3. Thomas Merton, "Marxism and Monastic Perspectives," in John Moffitt, ed., *A New Charter for Monasticism* (Notre Dame: 1970), p. 80.

4. Lewis Thomas, *The Lives of a Cell* (New York: 1975), p. 147.

5. Audre Lorde, "Uses of the Erotic: The Erotic as Power," in Laura Lederer, ed., *Take Back the Night: Women on Pornography* (New York: 1980), p. 297.

6. *The Oxford English Dictionary*, Vol. II (Oxford, England: 1933), p. 714.

7. Bernhard W. Anderson, *Out of the Depths* (Philadelphia: 1974), p. 69.

8. See note 5 above.

9. Ann Belford Ulanov, *The Feminine in Jungian Psychology and in Christian Theology* (Evanston: 1971), p. 155.

10. Lorde, *art. cit.*, p. 300; Ulanov, *op. cit.*, p. 191.

11. Ashley Montagu, *Growing Young* (New York: 1981), p. 195.

12. See 17.288.

13. See Thomas Berry, "Foreword," in Gabrielle Uhlein, *Meditations with Hildegarde of Bingen* (Santa Fe, 1983).

14. Montagu, *op. cit.*, pp. 119f.

15. Letter of April 29, 1834. Cited in Thomas Brown, *The Aesthetics of Robert Schumann* (New York: 1963), p. 167.

THEME # 25

1. © Lee Carroll Pieper, 1983.

2. Harry James Cargas, *In Conversation with Elie Wiesel* (New York: 1976), p. 3.

3. Jean Vanier, *Followers of Jesus* (New York: 1976), p. 7.
4. Thomas Berry, "Contemplation and World Order," in *Riverdale Papers*, V (Riverdale, NY: n.d.), p. 2.
5. *Autobiography of St. Teresa of Avila* (Garden City, NY: 1960), p. 122.
6. Audre Lorde, "Uses of the Erotic: The Erotic as Power," in Laura Lederer, ed., *Take Back the Night: Women on Pornography* (New York: 1980), p. 300.
7. Abraham Joshua Heshel, *The Prophets* (New York: 1962), p. 204.
8. *Ibid.*, p. 209.
9. Erik Erikson, *Gandhi's Truth* (New York: 1970), pp. 133, 100.

THEME #26

1. See Marie Augusta Neal, *A Socio-Theology of Letting Go* (New York: 1977).
2. Dorothy Day, *On Pilgrimage: The Sixties* (New York: 1972), pp. 206f.
3. Mohandas K. Gandhi, *An Autobiography* (Boston: 1968), p. 504.
4. Thomas Merton, *Conjectures of a Guilty Bystander* (Garden City, NY: 1968), p. 165.
5. Robert Bridges and W. H. Gardner, eds., *Poems of Gerard Manley Hopkins* (New York: 1948), p. 95.
6. John Howard Yoder, *The Politics of Jesus* (Grand Rapids, Mich.: 1980), pp. 62f.
7. Bernhard W. Anderson, "Exodus Typology in Second Isaiah," in Bernhard W. Anderson, *Israel's Prophetic Heritage* (New York: 1962), pp. 184. See Isaiah 40:21-31; 42:9; 44:24-28; 45:8-13; 48:7.
8. Martin Luther King, Jr., *Why We Can't Wait* (New York: 1964), p. 67.
9. Cited in Yoder, *op. cit.*, p. 225.
10. Raymond E. Brown, *The Birth of the Messiah* (Garden City, NY: 1977), p. 314.
11. *Ibid.*
12. See Albert Nolan, *Jesus Before Christianity* (Maryknoll, NY: 1978), p. 27; and Matthew Fox, ed., *Western Spirituality: Historical Roots, Ecumenical Routes* (Santa Fe: 1980), chapter one.

13. Yoder, *op. cit.*, p. 38.

14. See *Ibid.*, note 17.

15. *Ibid.*, p. 74.

16. *Ibid.*, pp. 63, 128.

17. See Raymond E. Brown, *The Gospel According to John* (Garden City, NY: 1966), p. 107.

18. Josef Hayim Yerushalmi, *Haggadah and History*. Cited in Harold Bloom, "Memory and Its Discontents," *New York Review of Books*, February 17, 1983, p. 23.

INDEX

A

Abraham (Abram), 45
Acedia, 203, 234-235, 254
Adam, 48, 51, 84-85, 123
Adler, Alfred, 110
Africans, 272-273
Alcoholics Anonymous, 263
Amazon, 268
America, 65, 141-142, 168, 176, 184, 191, 211, 232, 238
Anawim, 11, 16, 98, 100, 248-249, 264, 267-268, 270-271, 275-276, 303
Anderson, B., 97
Angelus Silesius, 152, 280
Anselm, St., 242
Anthropomorphic, 40, 46, 116, 134
Apophatic, 130, 175
Appalachia, 274, 290
Argüelles, José, 188, 203
Aristotle, 76, 268-269
Art as Meditation, 183, 192, 194, 252
Asceticism 60, 129, 159, 176, 206-207
Asians, 272
Atari, 160, 227, 234
Auden, W.H., 43, 55, 287-288
Augsburg College, 289
Augustine, St., 11, 16, 21-24, 26, 28, 48-51, 54, 63, 75-76, 83, 111, 155-156, 202, 213, 217, 251, 267-269, 271, 279, 298-299
Auschwitz, 10, 231, 247

B

Barghusen, Marilla, 197
Barth, Karl, 217

Barth, Markus, 298
Baudelaire, 38, 227
Baum, Gregory, 178
Beauty, 236
Becker, Ernest, 106, 229, 236
Beethoven, 154, 219
Belo, Gernando, 169
Benedict, St., 275
Benedictines, 16, 20, 217
Berdyaev, Nicholas, 59, 76, 189
Berger, John, 273
Bergman, Ingmar, 191
Bernstein, Leonard, 39
Berry, Thomas, 12-13, 35, 65, 68, 72, 178, 180, 189, 192, 252-253, 279, 283, 287
Berry, Wendell, 58, 65
Birmingham, 298
Black Theology Project, 274
Blake, William, 123, 188-189, 191, 243
Blessing in the Bible and the Life of the Church (Westermann), 44
Bonaventure, St., 76, 275
Bossuet, Cardinal, 11
Bourdaloue, 155
Brazil, 10, 268
Bronx, 290
Brown, Norman O., 121, 163, 227, 229, 250
Brown, Raymond, 300
Brueggemann, Walter, 45, 81, 83-84, 203, 257, 260-261, 263, 294, 301
Bruno, Giordano, 10, 248
Buddhist, 12, 16, 49, 153, 215

349

351

ACKNOWLEDGMENTS

Acknowledgment is gratefully given to the following publishers: W.W. Norton & Co. for permission to cite from Erik Erikson's *Gandhi's Truth* copyright © 1969 by Erik Erikson and from Adrienne Rich's *The Dream of a Common Language* copyright © 1978 by Adrienne Rich and *Poems: Selected and New* copyright © 1975 by Adrienne Rich; Viking Penguin, Inc. for permission to cite from Frederick Turner's *Beyond Geography* copyright © 1980 by Frederick Turner, and from D.H. Lawrence's *The Complete Poems of D.H. Lawrence,* Vivian de Sola Pinto and Warren Roberts, eds., copyright © 1964, 1971 by Angelo Ravagli and C.M. Weekley, executors of the estate of Frieda Lawrence Ravagli; Charles Scribner's Sons for permission to cite from Barry Holstun Lopez's *Of Wolves and Men* copyright © 1978 by Barry Holstun Lopez; Harcourt Brace Jovanovich, Inc. for permission to cite from T.S. Eliot's "East Coker," III in *The Complete Poems and Plays* copyright © 1952 by Harcourt, Brace and Company; Sierra Club Books for permission to cite from Novalis's "When Geometric Diagrams..." and from Juan Ramón Jiménez's "Oceans," both translated by Robert Bly in *News of the Universe,* translation copyright © 1980 by Robert Bly; Bantam Books, Inc. for permission to cite from Annie Dillard's *Pilgrim at Tinker Creek* copyright © 1974 by Annie Dillard; New Directions Publishing Corp. for permission to cite from Thomas Merton's "Emblems of a Season of Fury" and "The Strange Islands" in *The Collected Poems of Thomas Merton* copyright © 1962, 1968 by the Abbey of Gethsemani, Inc.; from Denise Levertov's *Light Up The Cave* copyright © 1981 by Denise Levertov; and from *Poems of Dylan Thomas,* copyright © 1939 by New Directions; Harper & Row, Publishers, Inc. for permission to cite from *Selected Poems of Rainer Maria Rilke* translated by Robert Bly, copyright © 1981 by Robert Bly; Beacon Press for permission to cite from poems #1, 8, and 19 from *The Kabir Book* by Robert Bly, copyright © 1977 by the Seventies Press; Oxford University Press for permission to cite from *The Moral and Political Thought of Mahatma Gandhi,* copyright © 1973, 1978, 1983 by Raghavan Iyer; Pantheon Books, Inc. for permission to cite from Alan W. Watt's *The Way of Zen,* copyright © 1957 by Pantheon Books, Inc., a division of Random House, Inc.; Orbis Books for permission to cite from Albert Nolan's *Jesus Before Christianity* copyright © 1976 by Albert Nolan; Houghton Mifflin Company for permission to cite from John Muir's *My First Summer in the Sierra* copyright © 1911 by John Muir, copyright © 1916 by Houghton Mifflin Company, copyright renewed 1939 by Wanda Muir Hanna; Villanova University Press for permission to cite from *Whither Creativity, Freedom, Suffering?: Humanity, Cosmos, God,* Francis A. Eigo, ed., copyright © 1980 by Villanova University Press; Augsburg Publishing House for permission to cite from Edna Hong's *Clues to the Kingdom,* copyright © 1968 by Augsburg Publishing House; Institute of Carmelite Studies for permission to cite from Kieran Kavanaugh's *The Collected Works of St. John of the Cross* copyright © 1979 by ICS Publications; and from G. Schirmer, Inc. for permission to cite from Leonard Bernstein and Stephen Schwartz's *Mass* copyright © 1971 by Leonard Bernstein and Stephen Schwartz; international copyright secured used by permission from G. Schirmer, Inc., New York.

ABOUT THE AUTHOR

Matthew Fox holds masters degrees in philosophy and theology and a doctorate in spirituality, received summa cum laude, from the Institut Catholique de Paris. He did postdoctoral studies with Johannes Metz at the University of Münster and is a member of the Dominican Order.

He is currently director of the Institute in Culture and Creation Spirituality (ICCS) at Holy Names College in Oakland, California, which he founded in Chicago in 1978. He is a prominently featured lecturer at universities, religious and cultural conferences, and educational workshops in the United States, Canada, Australia, New Zealand, and England where he has delivered more than 800 addresses. He is the author and/or editor of twelve books on spirituality and culture.

Matthew Fox's programs at ICCS include certificate, sabbatical, and masters degrees in Spirituality and Culture and two new tracks in Geo-Justice (creation spirituality and planetary peace-making) and Spiritual Psychology. His institute also has produced video tapes on *Original Blessing* and related subjects, which include other members of the ICCS faculty. For information on programs and video tapes, write: Friends of Creation Spirituality, PO Box 19216, Oakland, CA 94619.